BEFORE THE SUN
Meeting Rudi

BY JOHN MANN

PORTAL PRESS
Lummi Island, WA

First Edition Copyright © by John Mann 2014
All rights reserved
divineandrogyny.com

No part of this book may be used or reproduced in any manner whatsoever without written permission except for brief passages in connection to a review.

Cover photo courtesy Dean Gitter

Cover & book design by Robert Sink: **webworksnyc.com**
RUDI: The Teachings of Swami Rudrananda DVD: **rudimovie.org**

Mann, John, 1928 -
Before The Sun: Meeting Rudi / by John Mann — 1st ed
    p. cm.
ISBN: 978-1495397196
1. Mann, John — Autobiography.
2. Author, American — Autobiography — Contemporary
3. United States, India, Nepal, Tibet — Rudi, Swami Rudrananda, Albert Rudolph, inner work, learning student-teacher relationship.

Before The Sun: Meeting Rudi by John Mann, © 2014 eBook—1st edition

PHOTO CREDITS:

Our gratitude to all of you who shared the many archival pictures included in this book: Bruce Joel Rubin, David Rudolph, Dean Gitter, M. D. Suvarna, Robert Sink, Rudi Movie Project, Stephanie JT Russell and Wm. Terrell Hasker.

Special appreciation is extended to our compatriot and friend, the late Barry Kaplan, who was asked by Rudi to document his growth as a teacher. The many hundreds of photos that Barry captured are one of the major legacies that we have of Rudi. The teaching pictures continue to transmit Rudi's energy to this day.

DEDICATION

*To Rudi's students
whoever they are
and whatever that have become...*

*I am the sun
and you are the moon...*

— Rudi

Contents

Dedication	iii
Introduction	ix
Prelude	xi
Meeting Rudi	19
The Elephant God	31
Rudi's World	35
Early Developments	49
The First House	65
The Possibility Of Teaching	77
Raising The Serpent Power	87
A House In The Country	91
The Contract	101
Journeys To The East	107
PHOTOS: The Early Years	123
The Summer Place	127
A Chinese Banquet	135
In The Slums	135
Close Relationships	141
Teaching Six Chimpanzees	155
Working With Indian Saints	171
PHOTOS: India	189
The Martial Arts	195
A Search For Manhood	203
Becoming A Little Teacher	209
Sacrifice	213
Attempted Murder	221
The Nature Of Kundalini Yoga	225
Death And Rebirth	239
Two Moves	253
Swami Rudrananda	267
Big Indian	273
The Invitation	281

Preparation	287
Swami Muktananda Comes	307
PHOTOS: Big Indian	315
New York City	321
The West Coast	327
End Of The Affairs	337
Astral Flight	343
The Price Of Teaching	353
Experience and Fulfillment	363
Acceleration	371
The Ganesh Festival	393
Nepalese Interlude	409
Meeting Above The Ganges	413
Aftermath	425
Security In The Future	433
Rudi's Work	439
The End Of The Meeting	447
Return To India	455
Afterword	465
PHOTOS: Rudi	471
A New Life	477
Rudi's Work	489
40 Years Later	489
Appendix A	491
Appendix B	507
Appendix C	517
Other Books By John Mann	521

INTRODUCTION

When ***Rudi 14 Years With My Teacher*** was first published in 1987, it was not generally known that a number of versions of the manuscript had preceded it.

In order for the book to be published at all, the views of many people needed to be taken into account. In the process about one-third of the manuscript was eliminated.

What follows is the restored version which I had approved somewhere along the line of the varied history of the manuscript itself. It represents my experience as Rudi's student and friend, taken as an indirect approach to the description of Rudi himself and what it was like to be in his presence.

As I have read through the manuscript, in order to proofread the digitized version, I have occasionally been moved to add to or alter its content. It is not surprising that I should be moved to make these additions since approximately thirty years have elapsed since it was first completed. I have also been led to the conclusion that it might be of general interest to summarize what has occurred in my own life in the forty years since Rudi's death that in any way bears testimony to Rudi's continuous influence on me and indirectly on those whom I may have influenced.

Having got to that point I was led to the further conclusion that it might be relevant to briefly summarize my own earlier life up until the point that I met Rudi to help the reader understand the filter of my own personality through which this manuscript emerged. All errors of time and place are mine. At the age of 84 my memories blend and the details slowly fade, but Rudi's influence and impact is as real today as when I last spoke to him on the day of his death.

John Mann

x

PRELUDE

This is the history of my meeting with Rudi and all that subsequently transpired. It is inevitable that the description of these events should be influenced by my own personality. For this reason I am going to briefly describe some of the relevant moments in my own development, subsequent to my fateful meeting with him. If that is not of interest to you, then skip to Chapter One. But since we are potentially going to spend some time in each other's company, I hope you will find the Prelude of some relevance.

When I was in the 9th grade I was given the assignment to write my autobiography. I began with the following memorable few sentences:

Countless billions of years ago there was a nebulous mass of gases. It was not anything very strange as there were millions of other nebulae. The great universe was filled with them. But this nebula was destined for an important and freakish happening which could not only affect but cause LIFE.

I was then about 12. I was basically shy, though somehow I was elected to be Vice-President of my 9th grade class. I didn't even know that it had occurred until the President was absent for a meeting and I was told to take over for him. I had been elected while I was home sick.

I was generally more of an observer than participant. But in Junior High I came up with the quixotic idea that each male student should go out with each female student once. It seemed like a good idea at the time, but there were no takers. I decided to practice what I preached and asked out a girl who I was pretty sure would accept the invitation.

What I remember most vividly was that we went to the World's Fair via the subway. On the way home when I got to my stop, I got up, thanked her, and got off leaving her to go the rest of the way alone. Not a promising beginning for someone interested in the universal

Prelude

sharing of relationships.

A year later I ran for President of the Student Council. I nearly won when I gave a dramatic announcement in Assembly about helping the World War II effort. Instead of a strictly verbal statement, I suddenly dropped to my knees and announced that we were about to be strafed by enemy aircraft. Needless to say, I gained everyone's attention. But I did not win the election, which was probably just as well for all concerned.

At that time I wrote a column for the school newspaper entitled *You Are There*. Instead of reporting on school topics such as a basketball game in terms of who did what to whom, I would start out:

> **You are sitting in the stands waiting for the game to begin. Around you everyone is talking to everyone else in a rising tide of excitement.**

My orientation was to place the reader in the midst of the action, somewhat similar to the orientation of this book.

In a similar vein when I asked a girl to a dance and got turned down because she was going steady with someone else, the whole encounter got written down word for word as part of an English assignment, which, as fate would have it, I had to read aloud to the whole class. It wasn't hard for my classmates to figure out who the lucky girl was from her amazed embarrassment as she listened to me share what had been a private encounter.

Next I became interested in acting. The major production of the year was Peer Gynt. I tried out for Peer, but didn't get the part. I later was grateful because the role entailed memorizing an enormous number of lines.

But I did get another part. I was cast as the Button Molder, a Scandinavian version of Death. This was the role that Lawrence Olivier played in a London Production. If it was good enough for him, it was good enough for me.

My acting career continued when I went on to Harvard. There were two acting societies. The more desirable was the Hasty Pudding Club. When they held auditions for *Waiting for Lefty* by Clifford Odets I decided to try out. I don't know what possessed me. I had almost no experience and was unknown to them.

On the fateful day that I auditioned, the Director barely looked up from the script, handed me a page and said, "Read".

I cleared my throat and started. After 30 seconds, the phone rang. I was relieved because I knew that I was not doing well. If I didn't come up with an inspiration, I was through.

In desperation, I started counting internally "one, two, three….." When the Director got off the phone and waved for me to continue, I kept the count going. I stopped counting when I finished the page and looked up for the first time. The Director was regarding me with a slightly stunned expression. I got the part. It was a feature role. I appeared at the end of the play where I delivered a monologue for 15 minutes building up to the climactic moment when I inspired the assembled members of a labor union to go out on strike.

The Boston Globe gave me a favorable review. That was the climax and conclusion of my theatrical career, but not the conclusion of my fascination with drama.

I was taking a course on the unlikely subject of Altruism that had a remarkably wide-ranging reading list. Among these books was a volume entitled *Psychodrama: Vol. 1* by J. L. Moreno. I took it off the library shelf and casually started reading.

After the first few paragraphs the library faded and I was in a new world in which the psychological, sociological, psychiatric, aesthetic, creative and cosmic realms were woven together in a seamless garment that only a genius could have envisioned. Like any great work of art, it must be experienced to be fully appreciated; it cannot adequately be described. Moreno was a psychiatrist trained in Vienna whose career overlapped that of Freud. While his interests were extremely wide ranging, his focus was on healing.

In his early days he created a Theater of Spontaneity in which scenes based on current events were enacted in the form of a Living Newspaper. From this work he gradually realized that the actors could experience therapeutic benefit from playing certain kinds of roles. From this insight Psychodrama evolved as a new form of spontaneous therapeutic and creative expression.

At the beginning of the Psychodramatic session the Leader or Director talks with different members of the audience. From this conversation a topic of general interest and concern gradually emerges. A volunteer from the audience (the protagonist) is then selected to act as the focus of the drama that is about to unfold. The content is drawn directly from the life of the protagonist. Other roles are taken by audience members or specially trained assistants who improvise as needed.

At the end of the drama the audience shares its reactions to what has occurred resulting in a general catharsis.

From this format the further developments of Group Psychotherapy, Sociometry and Role Playing evolved and spread throughout Western society.

As I sat in the library reading his book I naturally assumed that Dr. Moreno lived in Vienna, since that was where his book was published. But I later discovered to my astonishment that he was working in New York City.

As part of my senior class work I did an undergraduate thesis on "the effect of simple rhythmic patterns on human emotions." I wrote to a number of authorities (including Dr. Moreno) to ask what they knew about the subject. To my surprise most of them replied in a friendly manner. To my further surprise Dr. Moreno invited me to see him on my next trip to New York.

That meeting, when it occurred a few weeks later, reminds me now of my later meeting with Rudi in that both figures were larger than life. But after that meeting my daily routine went on much as before, though my fascination with Psychodrama remained.

During this time I was struck by emotional lightning in the form of a fateful love affair. It began in a large horseshoe shaped auditorium in which the Boston Symphony was performing. As I looked across the way, I saw the most beautiful girl I had ever beheld.

I said to myself, "If I ever see her again I will somehow meet her." That was the beginning of a heart-rending experience that had the positive effect of my starting to write poetry; the following is an example:

A blind man said,

Help me across the street.

I am only half alive.

I am only

Only half

Half Only

Without you.

My life plan at that point was to go to Medical School and become a psychiatrist. I was accepted at Yale and the following fall started the demanding life of a first year medical student.

All went well for several months. Somehow during that time I found time to read *The Fourth Way* by P. D. Ouspensky. Many years before I had come on his book *Tertium Organum* which immediately impressed me as a work of genius. Thus I was particularly struck by the appearance of *The Fourth Way* which was the first account in print of the teachings of G. Gurdjieff, his principle spiritual master.

But though I found the book absorbing, my demanding life went on as before. One day as I was sitting in the medical library diligently studying an anatomy illustration, I paused to rest my eyes. And then an inner voice that was not my own said,

"What are you doing here?"

That was all, but I realized as soon as I heard it that nothing would be the same. It was as if I was being shown that there was a pilot light inside my soul that was in danger of being extinguished if I didn't devote myself to its care.

It took another month to temporarily withdraw from classwork and get a job in a laboratory maintaining rats that were being used for experiments.

My parents were understandably disturbed by this turn of events, and at their urging I began to see a series of psychiatrists to no particular effect. But when Dr. Moreno finally agreed to treat me as a psychodrama patient, I was delighted since that was what I wanted in the first place.

As with many highly creative people, Dr. Moreno was easily bored. After a few sessions he lost interest in me as a patient and started to include me as a helper in his public psychodrama sessions. He was sufficiently impressed with me to allow me to take over as Director for one of the sessions that he was scheduled to conduct. I was thoroughly pleased with this development since I never thought that I needed psychotherapy. What I needed was to save the light of my soul from being extinguished.

I worked with Moreno for five years in what proved to be the height of my therapeutic experience.

During this time I learned that, just as Moreno had moved from Vienna to New York City, Ouspensky's work had moved from England to New Jersey. In an unlikely series of coincidences I discovered that a series of lectures were about to be given in Manhattan on the esoteric work that Ouspensky had received from Gurdjieff.

I attended and was invited to visit his country retreat center in Mendham, New Jersey, to which I faithfully returned each weekend for the next five years. That was the beginning of my serious spiritual work.

Both Ouspensky and Gurdjieff died a few months before I had made contact with their active work. At first I thought there was no point in pursuing it if they were gone. However I soon discovered with a little humility that there was more than enough to keep me busy for the foreseeable future.

Part of this work consisted of a series of highly conscious physical movements. One day the teacher of that work took me aside and said,

"Mr. Mann, I have the feeling that there is only a thin invisible membrane separating you from a real breakthrough."

Unfortunately the membrane proved remarkably resistant. I did not break through it for more than a decade, while I was working with Rudi, long after I had left the Ouspensky work.

During this time I completed an MA in Clinical Psychology, a PhD in Social Psychology, got married, and started a family. I worked as an Intern for the Russell Sage Foundation and ultimately became an Assistant Professor in the Sociology Department at New York University.

From the outside I appeared to be living a relatively fulfilling and successful existence. I even went to Hollywood to make a pilot film for a psychodramatic TV series.

One of the recurrent themes of my life was a fascination with modern architecture. It ultimately led to contact with Frank Lloyd Wright who designed the third from the last project of his universal career for my wife and me.

During discussions about the cost of construction, Wright unexpectedly died. I remember wandering the streets of Greenwich Village in a daze. What would happen now?

As I walked by a bookstore a title caught my eye: *Concerning Subud*. It was not so much the title as the author, J. G. Bennett, that attracted my attention. I knew him as a respected teacher of Ouspensky's work.

But what was Subud? I went in and bought the book. Bennett began by acknowledging that he was not able to describe Subud as well as he might have wished. But he felt that it was important to present something about it for the interested reader, even if what he had written was imperfect.

I brought the book home and started to read. As I sat there I had the sense that I could begin the process just by allowing it to occur spontaneously. I seemed to be right. Something definitely began to occur.

After a time I began to get concerned that the process was getting too strong and might just take over my life. I decided to write to Bennett who had a large center in England and ask his advice.

I sent off an air letter and was totally amazed when two days later there was a reply from Mr. Bennett's secretary telling me that Mr. Bennett was currently in New York City preparing for the arrival of Pak Subuh, the Founder of Subud, who was on his first world tour. The letter told me how to contact Bennett and suggested that I do so as soon as possible.

A day later I was in his presence. He advised me to be initiated into the Subud experience as soon as possible, which turned out to be within the hour.

This brings me to the end of the Prelude. There are many other events in my life that might be included in this history, but this is not fundamentally my story. What I have written is enough, perhaps more than enough, to give you a taste of my character.

The time has now come to tell you how I met Rudi and came before the sun.

Chapter One

MEETING RUDI

I was seated on a hard bench in a large room. I had just gone through a spiritual exercise in a system of inner work called *Subud*. (This work was developed in Indonesia by its founder, Pak Subuh, and is based on complete surrender to a spiritual force that has a deep cleansing action on the individual who opens to it.) A woman was sitting next to me, facing in the opposite direction. She was talking with someone whom I could not see without turning around. I paid no particular attention because I was feeling quietly detached. When the woman mentioned a reasonable Eastern art dealer in Greenwich Village, I began to listen more closely as I was interested in oriental painting. Then the conversation ended. The other person left.

The woman and I continued to occupy the same bench, two slightly awkward strangers who would shortly move apart. Though it was unlike me to do it, I turned to her and said,

"I couldn't help overhearing your conversation."

She looked around at me, slightly surprised, "Yes?"

"Do you think the dealer you mentioned might have any Chinese landscapes?"

"I'm not sure. Here is his address." She reached into her purse and took out a simple business card. When I was alone I looked at the card. It said: *Rudi Oriental Arts*.

A few days later I decided to visit Rudi's shop. It was in West Greenwich Village on Seventh Avenue. I found the right block, then almost walked by the store because it hardly existed. The biggest part was the window which contained a bronze reclining Buddha, six or seven feet long. The store itself went off like a distorted pie section, cut at an acute angle about ten to twelve feet in depth. It was crammed with art, and within this space was Rudi himself. He was physically large. His hair was short. His eyes were gentle and very bright, and he was dressed in old corduroy pants and a worn pullover sweater. He didn't fit my image of an antique dealer, he looked more like a happy Sumo wrestler whose most striking quality was that he was more aware of his surroundings than he ought to be.

"A woman in Subud gave me your card," I began. "She said you were very reasonable."

"I am in Subud myself," said Rudi. "Pak Subuh is my teacher."

I ignored his statement and got right to the point.

"Do you have any monochrome Chinese landscapes?" I asked.

"No," he said.

And with that I was ready to leave. It had been a pointless trip.

"Just look around," Rudi suggested, interrupting my immediate disappointment. "Maybe you will see something you like."

It was an ordinary thing for a storekeeper to say, but if he had not said it I would have walked out and never come back. On such a slender thread the future turns.

I looked in the semi-gloom with halfhearted interest. After a time, I came on two circular plaques painted in gold. They were owls done in a Chinese style, each about a foot in diameter.

"How much are these?" I asked.

"Sixty-five dollars for the pair," said Rudi.

"They're interesting," I said mostly to be agreeable, "but I wasn't thinking of anything like that. What are they?"

"They're wood carvings from the outer doors of a Chinese temple."

"Oh," I said, with mild enthusiasm.

"I'll hold them for a few days if you like," he said, moving them under his small desk.

"All right," I said politely, "thank you."

I prepared to leave. As I walked through the door I had the sudden feeling that both he and the store might vanish behind me without a trace, but I shrugged it off as ridiculous.

A few days later I returned to buy the owls. I was somewhat puzzled by my own actions since I didn't like them that much. Rudi didn't seem surprised. He wrapped them up in a brown paper bag. I wrote him a check and left. That was all. Then as I walked out the door and onto the street, I was abruptly seized by the feeling that I should ask him to visit me. I struggled with the impulse and then gave in.

Rudi looked at me quizzically as I reentered the store.

"I just came back to ask if you would like to come to supper next week."

Rudi in his store

"Sure," he said, "I would be happy to come."

We arranged a date. And then I left, feeling more at ease though bemused by my impulsiveness.

The intervening days were full. I was getting ready to move from an apartment in the city to a house in the country. My place was in a mess the night Rudi came. Boxes and crates were everywhere, but disorder didn't bother him.

After he had settled down, we ate and he began to talk.

"When I last saw my teacher, Pak Subuh, he told me to sell my business and move to New Zealand."

"Are you going to?" I asked casually.

"Yes," he said. "I am leaving with a few people who are close to me."

"Such as whom?" I asked.

He described them as mostly young unsettled kids, hanging

around the fringes of Greenwich Village. As he spoke I had the very clear thought, "The last thing on earth I would ever do is move to New Zealand with such a bunch of characters."

"How do you like the temple owls?" Rudi asked, interrupting my thoughts.

"They're fine," I said. I didn't really know how I felt about them, but it no longer mattered. "Have you been in your store long?" I asked.

"A few years," said Rudi, sipping his coffee. "You probably think it's a small place, but it still seems big to me. In the beginning, I didn't have a store at all, just a room in which to live. I bought a few things with the little money I had. The rest I found by getting up at five in the morning and going through the neighborhood garbage cans for anything that could be fixed — a toaster, lamps, pieces of antique metal. When I sold them, I used the money to buy more art. It was a major undertaking to open the store. When you start from nothing, a little seems tremendous."

I found it difficult to visualize Rudi as having nothing. He seemed surrounded by an atmosphere of riches.

Since he had stopped talking, I brought up the subject of Subud.

"It's strange that I never saw you in any of the classes," I said. "I have been going for several months."

"You didn't see me because I haven't been there very much lately." He paused in recollection and then said, "I helped to start Subud in New York. It was better then. We were a small dedicated group. Now it is getting too big. Whenever something starts to get packaged for mass consumption it is already dying."

"I wouldn't know," I said. "It's all very new for me. I don't really care about the politics. I just want to use the sessions to get into a better state."

Rudi smiled. "You're right. But for me, it is harder. I am a little too visible. I gave a talk a few weeks ago, and before I was done, half the people were sobbing. They thought it was wonderful, but it only made the Subud leaders envious. And when that happens, relations begin to get complicated. But good things still occur.

"Just a few nights ago, some of the founding members met in my apartment. We decided to have a session. One of them had brought along his girlfriend, who wasn't particularly interested in what we were doing. But as the force started to work, she got caught up in the whole experience. And then the room was filled with a blinding light.

At first I thought something had happened to the electricity. I looked at the light bulbs, but they were the same. Then I glanced around the room and saw that the light was pouring out of this girl. Her soul had opened up like a great flower. I don't know if it meant much to her, but it certainly was wonderful for me."

"What did you do before you were in Subud?" I asked, not knowing how to respond to what Rudi had just said.

"I studied for four months with the Shankaracharya of Puri, and I was in the Gurdjieff work for five years."

I was shocked. I had been in the Gurdjieff work myself.

"When were you there?" I asked.

"I left about two years ago. Why does that seem to surprise you?"

"I was there for about five years. I used to go out to their farm estate in New Jersey every weekend."

"I guess that's why I never saw you," said Rudi. "I refused to do farm work. I've done enough physical work in my life. I went to one of their groups in the city. What did you do on the farm?"

"I worked with Dr. Borden on roofing. He was quite a taskmaster."

Rudi shook his head and smiled. "I used to go to him in the city for foot treatments."

At ten-thirty, he got up to go.

"I'll walk you to the subway," I said.

We put on our coats and left, talking of nothing in particular. In a few minutes we reached the bottom of the long escalator that runs from the street to the elevated subway station at 125th Street and Seventh Avenue. Rudi said a friendly goodbye and stepped onto the escalator. I watched him slowly being carried upward and away from me. Suddenly I felt that no matter how hard I worked for the rest of my life, I would never catch up to him. This did not bother me. Even at that moment I knew it was my greatest protection.

Rudi's store was less than a mile from my office. I was, at the time, an Assistant Professor at New York University. I began to stop in regularly to look at the art and talk with him. If it was a warm day we would sit outdoors on folding wooden chairs near the ceaseless Seventh Avenue traffic. His idea of warmth was about ten degrees lower than mine, so I looked forward to moving into the store where there was a

Meeting Rudi

small gas heater, but only room for about two people. If a customer came I took a walk.

I can hardly remember what we said. Often he was silent. I watched and waited; for what, I didn't know at the time.

When he had visited my apartment, Rudi had mentioned his students. Shortly, they appeared. They were a pretty ragged looking crew, young kids looking for hope with varying degrees of desperation.

Since I was physically present I couldn't help seeing what he was doing, though in another sense, there was nothing to see. All that happened was that he would sit opposite one of his students and stare intently at him for perhaps five to ten minutes. No words were spoken.

I was intrigued. I felt like an anthropologist who had stumbled on a new and unreported phenomenon, however I did not seriously consider the possibility of working with Rudi myself. I felt above the level of his students whom I looked at with interest and the detached superiority of the observer. Rudi said nothing, allowing me to watch and occasionally talking to me about their backgrounds. The most interesting and promising of them was a young jazz drummer named Roy Burns who lived around the corner from the store.

"I watched him walk by every day for a whole year," Rudi said, "knowing he would by my first real student. All that time he didn't once look in the window. One day something caught his eye. He came in. We started talking. Before he left we had begun to work together."

"How could you wait all that time?" I asked, surprised by such patience.

"I knew that it was necessary. He had to make the first move. But the most remarkable thing was that Roy could have been so oblivious of my existence since he is very psychic."

"In what way is he psychic?" I asked, mostly out of morbid curiosity. My whole attitude toward such abilities was quite negative at the time.

"He can find answers to my questions. I can get my own answers if I need them, but it takes a lot of effort. Roy is lighter inside than I am. He can go where the answer is and bring it back."

"I don't know what you are talking about," I said, feeling vaguely uncomfortable.

"The whole problem with getting an answer to any question," said Rudi, ignoring my reaction, "is to ask the right person. That is where a lot of people make a big mistake. They think that just because a psychic is in contact with some spirit that the answer which he gives is necessarily correct. In everyday life, they wouldn't be so gullible. You have to be able to go to the right place. Otherwise, you may end up with some minor official who will pretend to know and give you a stupid answer with complete confidence."

"But how can you know where to go?" I asked, more out of curiosity than any conviction about the reality of the discussion.

"You ask to be sent to the place in the universe where the answer exists. Then you surrender and open to whatever happens. It is very helpful for me to have Roy check things out. Anyone who relies solely on their own judgment is a fool. It may serve for a time, and then at the crucial moment it will fail. Everyone's work needs to be checked out by another. That is what a teacher is for."

As I spent time in the store, I got to know Roy better. He was very easygoing, as interested in being a jazz drummer as in developing his psychic and spiritual abilities. Rudi advised him on both, telling him how to work to absorb the inner qualities of his idol, the jazz drummer Buddy Rich.

"When you are with him," said Rudi, "you have to be completely open. Approach him as if he were your guru, with love and devotion. He will feel it even if he doesn't understand what is happening. He will have to open to you in return."

"But what if I don't really like him," said Roy.

"Look," said Rudi, gesturing excitedly with his hands. "You want something from him. It is up to you to consciously create the conditions that will help you get it. What I am telling you is fundamental. You are dealing with a man who represents a remarkable quality in a particular area. He is not going to give anything away. You almost have to steal it when he isn't looking. And he will be looking, unless he feels you love him."

"But how do I find out how he plays certain things that seem physically impossible?"

"It is partly technique and partly his inner state," said Rudi.

"He is able to do it because he knows that he can, like someone running a four-minute mile. What you need to do is allow him to work through you by temporarily assuming his psychic identity."

"But how can I do that?" asked Roy.

"I have already given you the first step. Open to him unconditionally. When you can really do that, irrespective of how he reacts, I'll give you the next step."

I listened to them talk with interest and skepticism. It was real to them. I did not have to pass judgment.

Roy was struggling at the time, but he was able to support his small family. The other students were less fortunate. Most of them were on the borderline economically, and some of them were deeply troubled emotionally. But it didn't matter to Rudi. He took them as they came.

"I don't choose my students so much as I attract them by the level of my being. They appear and choose me. I open to the possibility that they represent and do everything I can to fulfill it. I would rather attract people who didn't have problems, who were clean and even glamorous. But I accept whoever comes and do everything I can to raise their level.

One day after Rudi had been working with one of his students, we were left alone. A few minutes passed in silence. I felt a growing sense of anticipation.

Suddenly he broke the silence. "John, would you like me to work with you?"

Left on my own, a year might have gone by before I said anything. Perhaps I would never have taken the initiative. However he made it easy for me, and without giving the matter much thought, I said, "Sure."

We sat in his tiny store and I looked at him. I had no idea of what to expect, though I had watched the process numerous times. At one moment I saw his familiar, round, friendly face in front of me. Then abruptly his expression changed. I felt power flowing into me. It lasted for several minutes. Then he looked away.

It was the essence of simplicity— pure vitality given from one human being to another. And yet I immediately had the conviction that what I had experienced was available nowhere else in the world. I also suspected with increasing intensity during the following weeks that this experience — invisible, silent, and almost casual — was the most important single thing that had ever happened to me.

Rudi himself assumed that there were other people working as he did. As he traveled over the earth, buying art and pursuing his spiritual development, he always expected to find them. He never did.

During the next month I continued working with him whenever there was an opportunity and he was willing. Each time I was drawn a little further in a direction I could only dimly sense, and nevertheless knew to be real. Other students saw lights and observed various figures appear and disappear when Rudi worked. I saw nothing and it was not necessary. I could feel the force. We did not talk about it. There was nothing to say. With each passing week I increasingly came to feel that my one opportunity for inner growth lay in working with Rudi. It is hard for me to explain why I felt this way, just as it is difficult for anyone to explain why they have fallen in love. I was not in love; I had walked through a door and in front of me was a path. I had been looking for such a path for a relatively long time. Fifteen years before I had started reading mystical literature. I had written a paper on various forms of yoga in college at a time when most people had never heard of yoga. I had been actively involved in various forms of spiritual work since the age of twenty-one.

My main conclusion as a result of all this effort was that I was virtually unreachable. As long as this was my fundamental condition, I realized that there was no hope. In Rudi's work I had found something that could reach me. I was honest enough to realize the truth of my situation, desperate enough to appreciate the opportunity that was presenting itself to me. Nothing else seemed important.

When I came to this conclusion I was faced with an immediate problem. Rudi was moving to New Zealand in the late spring. It was not what he particularly wanted to do, however Pak Subuh, his spiritual teacher, had told him to go and he had agreed. I found myself also deciding to go, regardless of the practical implications. I was married and had two children. I had just bought a home in the country. My work at New York University obviously required my presence there. But I was not going to let anything hold me back.

I told Rudi what I was feeling late one afternoon during the waning of winter.

"When you first came to my apartment and talked about going to New Zealand," I started hesitantly, "my immediate reaction was that it would absolutely be the last thing I would ever want to do." I paused as Rudi smiled.

"I know," he said. "I understand."

"But now it's changed. I feel that you are the one chance I am going to have. If you move to New Zealand, I want to go too."

Rudi smiled again and said, "I'll have to work on it. Come back tomorrow; I'll let you know then."

I was puzzled that he couldn't give me an immediate answer, but at least he was taking my request seriously.

Meeting Rudi

The next day I was waiting for him when he came to open the store. In the interval, I had gotten pretty nervous. "Well?" I said, as soon as he had unlocked the door and walked inside.

"I worked on your question," he said. "The answer is, 'Yes. You should come, if I go.'"

Since he was going, that seemed an unnecessary qualification. But on the basis of his answer I returned home to break the news to my unsuspecting wife. I got right to the point.

"I am going to New Zealand with Rudi. You can come or stay here, whichever you want."

"What about your work? How long are you going for?" she asked with dawning disbelief.

"Permanently, I guess."

"Do you really mean it?" she said, in the vain hope that I didn't.

"Of course I mean it," I said.

"Then I guess we'll come, though it sounds really crazy to me."

I began to collect travel folders and books on New Zealand. I spent hours looking at pictures of the beautiful scenery— the glaciers and waterfalls, the high alpine fields with grazing sheep, the natural Polynesian beauty of the native Maoris, the totally foreign setting with the familiarity of English language and culture. It all excited my imagination. But at the same time it didn't really matter. I realized we would be in a world of our own that I couldn't visualize beforehand. Rudi never so much as opened a travel folder; it didn't interest him. He was going because he had been told to go.

As winter turned to spring, I arranged a leave of absence from the college that could be extended for two years if necessary. I looked into the process of immigration, updated my passport, got a lung x-ray, and gathered together all my money.

Rudi liquidated his business. He owned more art than I had realized. A number of his larger pieces, too big to fit in the store, were on loan. In the end he sold much of his stock at a loss so that he would be free to leave.

By early summer he was ready. He set out on a trip to disband the network of people in India and elsewhere in the East that he had organized to locate, buy, and ship art goods for him. On the way back he intended to stop in New Zealand, look over the country, and possibly purchase a sheep farm.

I settled down to my normal routine and waited for his return in a state of suspended animation. Two weeks after his departure I was surprised to find an overseas airmail letter in my mailbox. It was the first and last letter I ever received from Rudi. He had written from India. I opened it, puzzled, but interested in what he might have to say. Probably he was just sharing the impressions of his trip.

"Dear John, I hope you won't be angry, but I have changed my plans. I am not going to New Zealand. I'll be home shortly and explain every-thing. Love, Rudi."

My only reaction was one of great relief. I had never wanted to go anywhere.

A week later, Rudi returned and quickly reestablished his business. He found a larger store on the same block and bought back most of his old goods at a loss. Then, as he had time, he told me what had occurred in India to change his life.

Chapter Two

THE ELEPHANT GOD

"As I traveled through the East," Rudi began one day as we sat outside his new store on two folding wooden chairs, "I contacted the people connected with my business. It was hard to tell them I was disbanding everything I had built up. Most of them were really upset. But I did what I had to do.

"In the course of my travels, I also met a number of people connected with Subud. Some of the things I heard from them disturbed me. They said that Pak Subuh was buying vast tracts of land for himself in Indonesia with money obtained from Subud centers around the world. They told me stories about the dirty politics that had occurred in various centers in India. All of this shook me but I took it as a test of my sincerity and carried on. Pak Subud was my teacher. It was not for me to question his actions.

"When most of my work was done I went to stay with my friend, Beebee. He's a multimillionaire whose hobby is saint-hunting. When he hears about a new saint he goes to pay his respects, leaves some money, and then begins to spread the word.

"When I got to his house, the first thing he said to me was," I just found a new saint, Bhagavan Nityananda. He is only about two and a half hours from Bombay. Do you want to meet him?" Never knowing what I might find, I said, 'Sure', though my mind was on my own affairs.

"The next morning without really thinking about it I found myself in Beebee's car on a road that grew steadily worse until it ended in Ganeshpuri, a town carved out of the jungle by the man we were going to meet. We left the car and walked toward a doorway in a plain-looking building that admitted us into a large room where the saint held audience. The first impression was overwhelming. There were people crowded in every corner in a state of religious hysteria. In the front of the room sat a large dark man in a semi-trance. I was completely repelled. What was I, a sophisticated Westerner, doing in

The Elephant God

Bhagavan Nityananda

this weird scene? How could this utterly strange person have anything important to give me? He did not even seem to be physically aware of his surroundings. For one long moment, I was filled with the impulse to turn around and walk away. But I have learned not to trust my instinctive reactions.

"Instead, Beebee and I watched for a time as people approached to receive the saint's blessing or to ask him a question. A few minutes passed.

"Then, to my dismay, I found that we were being led to the front of the room. Beebee was well-known here. Perhaps he had recently made a generous donation. Before I could say anything I found myself being presented to the holy man who seemed completely indifferent to my presence. I was asked if I had a question. There was only one thing that occurred to me, so I said,

"'I am planning to move to New Zealand shortly. Is this the right thing for me to do?' I was not sure why I asked since I already knew the answer.

"The saint's response was unbelievable. 'You are completely out of your mind,' he said. 'Any decision that you make must be wrong. Go home!'

"I was deeply shocked. With one stroke he had cut through my whole life. I left the room in a daze.

"On the way back to Bombay, Beebee asked me, 'Well, what did you think of Bhagavan Nityananda?' Before I could answer, he went on, 'He is considered to be an incarnation of the elephant God, Ganesh.'

"'Who is Ganesh?' I asked, partly to cover my own shocked condition.

"'He is the God who is propitiated at the beginning of any new undertaking,' said Beebee.

"As the day passed, I felt the growing conviction that I had heard the truth. Since I am not one to hesitate I wrote to you and a few other people the next day. Then I did what I could to pull the pieces of my business back together to the relief of everyone concerned. A week later I was on the plane. And here I am talking to you," Rudi concluded, raising his arms to take in the surrounding scene of West Greenwich Village which had been transformed into India while he talked.

※ ※ ※

Rudi's meeting with Nityananda was a major event in his spiritual development. But this was far from evident at the time. When he went back to India a few months later on one of his regular business trips he hoped to visit Nityananda again, but he was relatively casual about it.

On his return from the trip he was very subdued.

"I don't know quite what I expected," he said, "but I was totally unprepared to find that Nityananda had taken Samadhi."

"What do you mean?" I asked.

"When a great saint dies he enters into Samadhi. It is a conscious act. His body dies but his soul force remains. It is hard to understand unless you visit his shrine. The pure essence of the man is there, ringing in the atmosphere and saturating the walls. All I had to do was open and breathe it in.

"As I sat by his tomb absorbing what had happened, I realized that I had been in a state of shock ever since I met him. The power that poured out of him had completely paralyzed my psychic system. It was more than I could bear. It has taken all this time for me to begin to digest it.

"He is not dead in any spiritual sense. That is the important thing to understand. The essence of a holy man is the level of the energy working in him. The higher the energy, the nearer he is to God. It is this energy that remains after his body disappears.

"If I were to die you might be upset because of our personal relationship. But if the energy that you find in me were still available, it really wouldn't matter. You could continue on. If you ever go to India you will understand what I mean. There are many sacred places where you can feel a special sense of presence. They are either in a location where higher forces are naturally focused, or they have been produced by the work done by holy men in the past that has magnetized the location.

"The first time I was in Ganeshpuri I met a man who was acting as Nityananda's lieutenant, Swami Muktananda. I usually get along better with the second in command than the leader. We seemed to understand each other, though he spoke no English. Nityananda made no effort to appoint a successor. It was not his way. He was totally uninterested in any kind of organization. Consequently after his death things were rather chaotic. In time the situation will either fall apart or one of the older students may emerge to fill the vacuum. I have a feeling that it might be Muktananda. I made a special effort to be open to him when we met again, not that I completely trust him. But I don't wish to eliminate any future possibilities."

Chapter Three

RUDI'S WORLD

Slowly the familiar pattern of Rudi's life returned. He sat all day in his new store. People came through the doorway seeking art, friendship and spiritual guidance. He gave to each generally more than they expected.

A Zen monk recently from Japan entered the store, attracted by a Japanese Buddha in the window. He had no money but he stayed to talk. Rudi offered him tea, and they became friends. Every few months the monk would reappear. Slowly his fortunes improved, and he was able to buy some small Buddhist statues.

On one notable day he bargained endlessly for a fine bronze Buddha. Finally Rudi became slightly exasperated and said, "Well you tell me what you want to pay."

The monk replied instantly: "Nothing."

Slowly it dawned on Rudi that he had just been tricked.

He could have argued about it, but he didn't choose to do so. He wrapped up the statue, which certainly cost him several hundred dollars, and gave it to the monk who left in triumph. Many years later the monk was to tell the story in great good humor as an example of the day he got the better of Rudi. But what he never knew was that from that time on Rudi automatically doubled his prices whenever the monk appeared. He may have won the battle but Rudi won the war.

The store was Rudi's world. People entered on his terms or they stayed away. In the course of time such famous artists as Ben Shawn came to buy and talk. Rudi was willing to listen, but he didn't hesitate to ask celebrities or their representatives to leave if they started to use the setting as a showcase for their egotism.

One day a harried woman rushed in and breathlessly asked,
"Do you have a Krishna?"
"Yes," said Rudi.
"Would you bring it to the Maestro so that he could see it?"

Rudi was friendly, but not terribly helpful.

"You don't understand," said the woman, "Leopold Stokowski isn't going to come here!"

"Well," said Rudi, "that makes two of us. If he wants to see the piece this is where he is going to have to come."

I enjoyed Rudi's total independence when it wasn't directed at me, but he didn't manifest it for my approval. He simply wanted a certain standard of equality to be established in his world. That wasn't much to ask, since as far as I could see, he was superior to those with whom he dealt, whether they were famous or not.

The new store was six times larger than the old one, but very shortly it was no less crowded. In the back, at the end of a dark hall, was a small bathroom. It was not much but the previous store had only had a sink.

Rudi sat behind a small desk where he could survey the passing scene through the front window and keep an eye on the entranceway. At times his mother, Rae, helped out. She had very definite ideas about Rudi's life, his business, and his friends. Rudi either ignored her or yelled at her in a way she seemed to expect. It was surprising for me to see him lose his temper, but at least it made him more human and that made me more comfortable. Rae and I got along fine; she approved of me.

✳ ✳ ✳

One day a strange-looking young man flung open the front door and slammed it closed behind him. Rudi seemed to know him and motioned him to a chair.

The man glared at Rudi, refusing to sit. Rudi shrugged. The man sat. His first words were,

"I am on my way to Bellevue."

"That's good," said Rudi. "How have you been?"

"I am going crazy. You look like a Buddha sitting there."

"That's what a lot of people tell me," Rudi responded smiling, though I didn't see what there was to smile about. I blended into the shadows and hoped that the man wouldn't get violent.

"What are you smiling about," he demanded suddenly.

"It's nice to see you," said Rudi quietly.

"I must really be going crazy," the man said. "I see light coming out of your head."

Rudi said nothing. Then they made small talk until a customer walked in. Rudi excused himself and the man looked at the customer as if he wished him dead. Suddenly after a minute, he threw over his chair and stalked out without a word. I was relieved to see him go. Rudi's comment was,

"I am his last stop before he checks in at Bellevue. He is sane enough to know when he is going crazy. If he would come here when he gets out instead of when he is going in, maybe I could help him. But either way, I like to see him once in awhile."

"Why?" I asked. I was still shaking inside.

"When you are with a person like that, you have to be totally aware. He senses every breath you take. If my attention wavers a moment, he knows it. Crazy people are a hundred times more sensitive than normal ones. I wouldn't like him for a steady diet, but he forces me to function at a higher level while he is here, and for that I am grateful.

"But what really fascinated me was that I could see the force that was driving him crazy, slowly wrapping itself around his head. When it gets all around he will become psychotic. I hope he is in the hospital by then."

* * *

The next time I entered the store Rudi greeted me with,

"You just missed an Indian saint."

It was hard for me to believe. What would an Indian saint be doing in Greenwich Village?

"All day long as I was sitting here I felt this unusual energy," said Rudi. "I didn't know what it was, but it was very strong and pure. It didn't seem to belong to the environment.

"And then an hour ago in walks a swami accompanied by two of his followers. He couldn't speak any English, but we got along fine. He seemed more surprised about my existence than I was about his. But then, I knew he was coming. You can still feel his presence in the atmosphere."

It did seem as if a silvery light filled the air. Rudi looked wonderful. We sat together quietly bathing in the afterglow.

Then Rudi started to work with me and the rest was forgotten.

As the day ended, Rudi invited me to supper at his apartment. I gratefully accepted, knowing that he was an excellent cook and I was curious to see where he lived. His apartment was quite small, essentially a bedroom and a living room, both filled with art. He had recently received a small shipment that was partially unpacked. The contents were spread out on a table, mostly jewelry and small statues. I watched as he picked Indian necklaces made of semi-precious stones from the pile, and held them up to a lamp made from a Japanese bronze vessel. He seemed completely at ease and yet totally strange, a character from the *Arabian Nights* surrounded by his treasures. As I watched him, a cold chill spread through me. I had never known anyone like him. He almost shouldn't exist, and yet he was more real than I was.

He looked up and broke the spell by saying,

"How about potato pancakes with sour cream for supper? They're one of my specialties."

I smiled in agreement.

While he prepared supper I looked around the apartment. It contained his greatest treasures, in particular a statue which he called Alfred. It was displayed in a glass cube that prevented it from being touched. I had never seen anything remotely like it.

"How did you learn its name?" I asked, as we sipped coffee after the last of the pancakes were gone.

"He told me."

"Who told you?"

"Alfred. I sat with him. After a while I began to understand who he was. I nodded as if I understood. I didn't question what Rudi said. I had grown to realize that in many areas I was in no position to judge him. He had never lied to me in any way that I could detect. If he said he had talked to the statue, I tended to accept it.

"I discovered Alfred a few years ago. Are you interested in the story?" Rudi asked, smiling at me because he knew I couldn't resist.

Without waiting for my reply, he started.

"I had gone to England. I love England, particularly the people. They are supposed to be reserved, but it isn't true. You just have to know how to approach them. There is one very rich little old lady whom I really love. One day I picked her up and tossed her in the air. She thought it was the most wonderful thing that ever happened to her. Of course if someone else had tried it she might have called the police.

"Anyway, one of my friends told me about a great collection of large Buddhist statues located on an old estate. It sounded too good to be true, but I went to take a look. There were five greater-than-life-size bronzes. The reclining Buddha in my window was one of them. Another stood fourteen feet high.

"My first thought when I saw them was, 'I'll never be able to afford them.' But I was wrong. The family had no feeling for the statues. They had been brought back from the East by an eccentric uncle. All that they wanted was some quick money. I made a ridiculous offer and they accepted.

"I couldn't get over my good fortune. It cost every cent that I had, but it was certainly worth it.

"Of course there was one catch. There was no way to get them out of the house. The existing road could not support their weight. A stone path had to be built from the house to the highway. I hired some masons and tried to keep calm as they set to work.

"In the midst of all this excitement I began to have a deep inner sense that I should return to New York immediately. It was hard to accept the possibility that anything other than personal disaster should make me return. Everything seemed to require my presence in England. But logic had nothing to do with it.

"I made the best arrangement I could for the packing and shipping of the statues and took the first plane back. Almost immediately on my return I heard of a Tibetan collection that was for sale. Tibetan art is my first love. A great psychic once told me I would have the greatest collection of Tibetan art in the Western world. I couldn't resist going to take a look. It was beyond belief. I had no money, but they wanted almost no money. I bought a number of pieces, among them this statue which I now call Alfred. And then I proceeded to forget all about it.

"Six weeks went by. I was absorbed in raising money to pay for the shipment coming from England. When a crate containing the Tibetan statues arrived, I was almost surprised. I eagerly opened it up, but when I got to Alfred I was very disappointed. He was just a dead piece of tin. I put him on the floor in a convenient corner and went about my business.

"Three days later, when I entered the store, I received the shock of my life. There was Alfred on the floor where I had left him, surrounded by a great blue light, completely alive and very angry. He told me that he was offended by the way he had been handled. If he wasn't treated with greater respect he would leave.

"From that day I placed Alfred in an honored position. I had the glass case built for him. I don't know his real name. I call him Alfred to make him more familiar, like a friendly uncle. Actually, he represents a very high, very strange quality that I find extremely frightening when I get close to it. In the course of sitting with him I came to understand that he is the god of Astral Flight. I never have seen any picture of him or read of him in a book. But I am sure that is his nature. He is my holiest possession."

"Do you ever work with him?"

"No, I am not developed enough to work with him. I just let him work with me when I am asleep."

✻ ✻ ✻

During this period, Rudi had about ten students, including the woman who had first given me his card, Edith Montlack. She was one of Rudi's closest friends. Edith was an artist and an amateur psychic. She had painted a remarkable portrait of Rudi dressed in a lama's robes.

One day, when there was a lull in the conversation, I asked her about our chance meeting.

"I rarely talk to strangers," I said. "I don't know why I talked to you."

"It was just as unusual for me," Edith replied. "I have never given Rudi's name to anyone I didn't know very well, before or since."

All of Rudi's students were kids, with the exception of Edith and myself. I was about thirty-two at the time and Edith looked like a typical middle-aged suburban housewife. Rudi listened to Edith and respected her advice. He spent at least two evenings a week in her company, along with her nephew and her husband David.

Rudi's other particular friend at the time was an ex-actor, Reynolds Osborne. Reynolds also had psychic abilities, but as with so many psychics he had difficulty in using them for his own development. One day before he had met Rudi, he felt particularly depressed. He went into a trance during which he asked for help to bring meaning to his life. He received a message to go to a certain place on a certain day where he would meet a spiritually-gifted person who would grow into a great teacher. He followed the instructions and met Rudi. Reynolds and Edith both appreciated Rudi's potential. Reynolds seemed to use the reflected light of Rudi's energy to maintain his own existence, but shared some of my own inner ambivalence as to how far to go in becoming part of the group that Rudi was forming around him. He valued his own special relation as confidant and sometime advisor.

Occasionally it got a little out of hand, as Rudi related to me one day when we were going to visit Reynolds for supper.

"Last December Reynolds told me how to look into the future. He encouraged me to try it out on New Year's Eve. I have never been curious about the future except as a guide to my work in the present. But I figured, 'What harm could it do?' Boy was I wrong!

Painting By Edith Montlack, C. 1965

"On New Year's Eve I got off by myself for a few minutes and did what he had told me."

"What happened?" I asked, with skeptical curiosity. "Did it work?"

"Yes, it worked, but it nearly drove me out of my mind. Without any warning I started to experience everything I would have to go through in the next nine months. It was unbearable! I can pay for one day at a time, but to feel the accumulated pain, boredom, and frustration of all those days simultaneously was awful. After that experience I decided to let the future take care of itself."

Nevertheless, Rudi was a natural psychic. I watched him casually tell people what they were thinking, announce who was calling him when the telephone started ringing, and analyze a person's character at a glance. I very quickly came to take it for granted. My whole attitude puzzled me when I thought about it. As a social scientist I should have been impressed and excited to see such evidence of paranormal ability on a daily basis. But it seemed entirely natural that Rudi should know these things. It would somehow have been much stranger if he had not.

My own role at that time was almost totally passive. I sat and waited, slowly absorbing the energy that flowed and overflowed from Rudi's being. He tolerated my presence endlessly and fate cooperated with me.

* * *

One evening, a student at New York University asked my advice about a project being developed at St. Vincent's Hospital. Shortly thereafter I was invited to talk with the Director of Social Services at the hospital. She had just submitted an evaluation proposal to the Office of Vocational Rehabilitation. She wanted me to act as the Research Director. I agreed, not only because the project seemed interesting, but mainly because by remarkable coincidence the hospital was directly across from Rudi's shop.

In due course the project was funded, and for the next three years I had a professional reason for being in the immediate neighborhood of the store where I consequently spent several hours a day.

In spite of all this exposure, if I had been asked at the time about the nature of Rudi's work I could hardly have given a coherent reply. I knew it was real and that it constituted a trail through the maze of my own wilderness that I was slowly following. That was enough.

In any case, he refused to give it a name.

"What difference does it make what it's called?" he said. "If I give it a name you will think you understand it. As soon as people can name things and get them organized, life is already departing from them."

It was clear that when he worked he generated and transmitted a higher energy. This could be felt by the student with whom he was working, who afterwards looked healthier and generally felt more radiant. At the same time Rudi said that he took into himself psychic poison given off by the student.

"Why would anyone consciously want to take poison from anyone else?" I asked him one day. It seemed crazy to me.

"How else can it be?" he said. "If something of a higher nature comes into you, something must come out to make room for it. What comes out of you is poison. What goes into you is nourishment.

"I am very strong inside. In some ways I am a mutant. I have more energy than I know what to do with. It drives me crazy. I need to find ways to use it. So I give it to my students, and take their problems and tensions into myself. My psychic mechanism is able to break most of it down into a form which I can digest and use for my own growth. What I can't digest, I drop."

"But I still don't know what is really happening," I said.

"Did you need to know what was happening in order to come with me to New Zealand?"

"No."

"Then stop worrying about it. Take what is given. Absorb it deeply within you. The rest will take care of itself in a natural way.

Rudi's health was generally excellent. He suffered a lot from the pressures of his inner work and the changes in his chemistry which it induced, but he almost never had ordinary illnesses. Thus it was unusual for him to complain about severe pains in his abdomen. Edith was concerned. She insisted that he see a doctor who in turn put him in a hospital for observation.

I heard nothing further until he emerged a week later, slightly sobered but full of energy.

"I used to spend a lot of time in hospitals when I was a kid," he said. "I had endless operations on my feet and on my head. So I really hate the places. But against my better judgment I let Edith talk me into going into this one. I didn't actually think there was anything wrong with me except that I felt terrible. But I am used to that.

"The doctor decided that my liver was severely swollen and decided to take a biopsy. Fortunately he didn't tell me what was coming. When he suddenly stabbed me in the stomach I was completely unprepared. It hurt like hell, though all he did was take a small tissue sample from my liver. He was right about one thing. My liver was very swollen.

"I decided to make the best of the situation. I kidded with nurses who were also Sisters because it was a Catholic hospital, and got lots of rest. By the time the biopsy results were in my liver had reduced itself to normal size. Needless to say the results were negative.

"When I thought about it I realized what was wrong. The liver is traditionally the organ which stores up negative psychic tensions. I must have taken in more poisons than I could drop. My liver suffered the consequences. Once I understood the problem I got better all by myself.

"The nurses were really sweet. This one sister in particular tried to convert me to Jesus. I ended up converting her. Maybe she will come to class.

"But the whole thing should never have occurred. I won't let it happen again."

"How can you prevent it?" I asked. I was glad to see he took the problem seriously.

"I have an exercise for dropping psychic tension that I developed out of my own need when I was younger. It is very simple. You take a breath into your heart, then you ask from within that center for help to surrender negative psychic tensions. You hold your hands open and down at your sides, and the poison just begins to flow out, like taking the skin off a cup of cocoa. It sounds very simple, and it really works. Remind me and I'll give the exercise to everyone in the next class...."

✳ ✳ ✳

Spending so much time in the store I could not ignore the art. My original interest had been solely in Chinese landscape paintings. When I met Rudi I didn't know there was such a thing as Tibetan art. Then as I observed that this was what he valued most, I began to become interested in it.

One day in a quiet moment I picked out a Tibetan thangka which I decided to buy. I knew absolutely nothing about the figure represented in the painting, but something about his expression touched me. Rudi himself seemed surprised at my choice.

"What do you like about the painting, John?"

"That's hard to say. Maybe it's the mysterious smile of the central figure."

"It's a very mystical painting," Rudi said as he rolled it up for me. Years later I discovered that the figure was Padmasambava, the magician saint who founded Tibetan Buddhism. That was my first purchase of Tibetan art.

Even at that time it was rare and relatively expensive. And yet whenever a shipment arrived, I bought whatever Tibetan pieces were available after Rudi had removed those he was keeping for himself. I had a sum of money saved toward the construction of a modern house. This gradually began to be funneled into Eastern art. I had never conceived that I might be a collector of such art, thinking that it would be too expensive for me to afford. However, Rudi's prices were reasonable, and I met him at a time when I had money. Once started, the buying process continued on its own momentum. When the money ran dry Rudi extended credit without interest. As long as it got paid back eventually, he didn't care how long it took.

Rudi loved to discover art, buy it, and unpack it. He was relatively uninterested in selling it. He would just as soon have given it away to people who shared his love for it. But being in the store gave him the opportunity to sit quietly, do his own inner work, and at the same time relate to a large number of people who were constantly passing through the doorway of his miniature world.

Courtesy John Mann

One day a man walked in and removed some wrapped objects that he wanted to sell from a small paper bag. I caught a glimpse of them. They were golden Tibetan and Siamese statues. I withdrew until the bargaining was over. To my surprise, Rudi let them go by.

When the man left, I asked,

"Were they too expensive?"

"No," he said. "They were too cheap."

"I don't understand. I never saw you turn down a bargain. I would have been happy to buy them."

"You don't get the picture, John. He started cheap, and when I hesitated he immediately cut the price in half. They must have been stolen. It is very dangerous to buy something from an unknown person who walks in off the street. If you end up with stolen goods you can lose your money and also ruin your reputation. It just isn't worth taking the chance, no matter how tempting it might look."

While I was thinking that over, a station wagon pulled up unexpectedly and the driver called out,

"Hey, Rudi! We have only three plants left. Take them off my hands. I'll give them all to you for five dollars."

Rudi knew the man. He bought the plants, put two in the window, and sold one to me. I still have it.

* * *

The most exciting and difficult time in Rudi's business was during the arrival of a shipment. When it had cleared customs and was about to be delivered to a nearby warehouse, Rudi closed the store or got someone to take care of it. He recruited all available help, including friends, students and customers to go around the corner and unpack the crates. It was a collectors' Christmas. Before the arrival of the shipment Rudi would often have black and white pictures of the merchandise, but until it came you couldn't be sure what it would really be like. It might be much bigger or smaller than you expected. And you couldn't guess the colors from the photograph.

The scene at the warehouse was a wild mixture of types and motivations. The professional warehouse men were entertained and dismayed by the rest of us. They took charge of unloading the crates from the truck, aided in breaking the metal bands, and prying open the carefully-nailed crates. Then we got into the act with hammers, crowbars and screwdrivers. Each opened crate revealed a new treasure. I was constantly torn between stopping to look at each object and getting on with the job. Rudi was everywhere, telling people what to do, yelling at them for doing the wrong thing, calling someone over to look at a particular piece that had just been removed from its packing.

Somehow in the midst of all this confusion, the shipment emerged and was lined up along the wall of the warehouse. Then it was taken to the store a little bit at a time on a small four-wheel dolly with one of us pulling and the other pushing. We moved along a bumpy side street and then onto Seventh Avenue, halfway down the block against the traffic to Rudi's store.

After five hours of such activity the shipment was in place, and we were all exhausted. However that was not the end of it. Once in the store, the inspection of the art began in earnest. Collectors would suddenly materialize out of the woodwork, somehow sensing the arrival of the art like mice smelling cheese. All of them were haunted by the fact that someone else might snatch up a desired object before they discovered it. I was no different, except that I felt so dazed by that time that I hardly knew what I was doing. After an hour or so Rudi closed the store and I went home to collapse.

Contact with a large amount of Eastern art is a shocking experience, not only because of all the impressions involved, but primarily because of the energy contained in the art itself. During the shipping process this energy accumulates. When it is unpacked the energy is released. Handling hundreds of objects produces an overpowering effect.

"I always loved Eastern art but I had only forty dollars when I started the store," Rudi once told me. "I was out of work at the time. I had been offered a good job at a factory but I would have had to perform the same operation all day long. I was horrified because I was convinced that it would drive me insane. And I didn't have too far to go at that point in my life. In desperation I walked for miles down Seventh Avenue. As I passed this block, I heard a voice whisper to me, *This is your store.* I looked around and saw an empty hole in the wall. I wanted to walk away but the voice kept repeating, *This is your store. This is your store.* I trusted the voice because the thought of the factory terrified me. I hunted down the landlord and we came to an agreement.

"I bought a few prints and a vase with the little money I had. I supported myself by washing dishes in the nightclub down the street.

"When I had made about four hundred dollars, someone offered me two Japanese figures that cost just that amount. I didn't see how I could spend it all on those two figures. But they were very beautiful, so I decided to buy them. I have never regretted it.

"So many things that were once easily available became priced out of the market a few years later. Five years ago a Chola Bronze was a hundred dollars. Today the same piece goes for thousands. Way back at the beginning when I had nothing, a man offered me half a million dollars to go into partnership with him. I give him credit for sensing my potential, but I reluctantly refused. I would not sell myself in that way. The road I was following might take longer, but I was free and doing what I loved."

Chapter Four

EARLY DEVELOPMENTS

Rudi always worked with his students one at a time in between waiting on customers at the store. Sometimes he taught outside on the sidewalk, sitting on a folding wooden chair with the student directly in front of him. Occasionally a stranger would stop dead in his tracks to observe the remarkable scene presented by Rudi and the student as they stared at each other. At such a moment he might stop teaching to gaze intently at the stranger and ask,

"Is there something you want?"

That was usually enough to break the spell. Understandably most of the teaching was done in the store. This created other difficulties. For the most part, the students didn't mind waiting until Rudi was free. I certainly didn't. I waited hours if necessary. The problem was with the customers. Even though Rudi stopped teaching when they appeared, they often could sense that something had been happening that they couldn't understand. It was like opening a familiar doorway and finding a waterfall. Some people took one quick look inside and fled. Others stayed, and were distinctly ill at ease.

Thus it was not a total surprise when Rudi announced, "Next Thursday night I will hold a group class in my apartment." I was not really pleased with this development, though I was curious as to what he might have in mind. Without recognizing it, I had unconsciously built up a pattern of expectation about how the work was done. As far as I was concerned it involved a transmission of a higher force between Rudi and a single individual. I didn't see how it could be as intense if he worked with ten to fifteen people simultaneously.

Rudi's apartment was quite small. The living room was about 12 x 14 feet, furnished only with a small sofa and a lot of art. When the day came every available chair was moved into the living room. Rudi sat on the sofa facing the rest of us. He started to work. We all looked at him, even though he could only look at one of us at a time. The familiar silence that rang with energy descended.

The class continued for about thirty minutes. I tried to absorb his vitality but my heart wasn't in it. How could working in a group compare with working individually? I felt cheated, but I kept my mouth shut.

When the class ended we quietly dispersed. As I walked along the street to my parked car, I became more certain that it was all a big mistake. Hardly anything had happened for me.

The next afternoon when I saw Rudi, I decided to express myself.

"I know that I'm in no position to judge what you're trying to do," I said, "but I felt that last night was a letdown."

"How do you mean?" he asked in a resigned manner.

"I didn't feel anything much happening. It just wasn't as strong as working with you alone."

"That's what Edith said," he replied. "She felt that you were touched in only a very limited area."

"I guess so," I said. "I can see it might be easier for you to work with all of us together, but it isn't the same for us."

"Actually, it was a wonderful class for most people," said Rudi. "But the thing that really gets me, John, is that here I sit hardly able to move, feeling like someone kicked me in the balls because of the effort I put into giving that class, and what happens? You have to pick this moment to tell me that as far as you were concerned, it was nothing."

"I'm sorry," I said. "I should have kept my mouth shut."

"That's the way it always is. You never say anything. But the moment I am down you decide to unburden yourself. Do me a favor. Go away and leave me to my misery. But don't worry. You will get used to the group."

I retired from the store feeling ashamed, but unconvinced.

But Rudi was right. As time passed, the class began to seem totally natural. I could hardly remember it being any other way...

One of Rudi's earliest Indian friends was a Hindu gentleman named Mr. Rahman. I occasionally saw him when he stopped in the store, but just as a passing stranger. Consequently I was not particularly disturbed when Rudi told me that he had died. I knew that he had served as a useful friend and important contact for Rudi in the earlier years before I had known him, but that period had little reality for me.

Rudi's work had not dealt with death previously. We were all therefore surprised when he announced:

"There will be a special class for Mr. Rahman this weekend at Edith's house in White Plains."

On that Sunday, seven of us assembled for the purpose. The day was spent in quiet conversation and a growing sense of anticipation. Finally, in the early evening, we met in the living room, all equally uncertain about what to do, except Rudi.

"Just sit anywhere," he said. "I want to talk for a few minutes." We settled down around the room in chairs, on the sofa, seated cross-legged on the floor.

"Try to become quiet inside as I talk," he said. "There is nothing to think about. We are simply going to perform an exercise for the dead. Very few people are prepared to meet their own physical death. They become frightened and uncertain. They need the comfort, encouragement, and the energy of the living to help them through the transition which they are undergoing.

"Usually, they get just the opposite. Instead of quiet love, they find hysteria, anguish, and a desperate effort by the living to hold on to them just when they should be freed.

"None of us were so intensely attached to Mr. Rahman that our emotions about his death should present any problem to him. I was closest to him, so I will be in the center of a circle which the rest of you should form around me. When you have settled down, ask from deep inside yourself, as if a voice were speaking from the center of your chest,

'Please help me to open and surrender.'

"Repeat this several times until you feel something deeply responding within you. Then try to connect with Mr. Rahman. See him as you remember him. Be quiet and feel peaceful inside. Ask to be able to give him whatever he needs. Wish him well on his journey. But, more than anything else, surrender. Then surrender more deeply, and then more deeply. Let the experience carry you. No effort is necessary on your part, other than what I have said. Is that clear?"

No one said anything. After a pause, Rudi moved to the center of the room. We formed a rough circle around him. He lay down on the floor. We sat facing him and closed our eyes.

"Help me to surrender," I said to myself.

The silence deepened.

"I want to be able to give Mr. Rahman whatever he needs," I repeated silently.

I waited, trying not to think about what was happening. Did I believe in it? Was it a fantasy? I tried to go deeper.

"Help me to let go of everything."

With each wave of surrender, the sense of the situation deepened. Images of Mr. Rahman flickered before me. I paid little attention to them.

I began to relax and cease to care whether anything happened. The room had taken on the quality of a spiritual class, a dynamic ringing quiet. But this was not an ordinary class. No energy was being transmitted directly from Rudi to others.

The atmosphere settled and grew deeper. It held me quietly and firmly. There was a merging of individuals in their surrender to the unknown which they shared.

I lost all sense of time. But after about what I later discovered was fifteen minutes, Rudi slowly sat up, indicating in this way that the session was over. During the next hour we were all subdued. But after that the atmosphere gradually returned to normal.

I was still very unclear about the experience, so I asked Rudi about it at the first opportunity.

"You know I never see anything," I said, "so something may have happened and I would never know."

"Something happened," said Rudi.

"I could sense a change in the atmosphere," I said, "but it is very easy to imagine such things."

"Actually," said Rudi, "Mr. Rahman was shocked out of his mind to find a group of Westerners helping him out of this world. Indians don't really believe that anyone knows about spiritual things but them. It was almost funny to watch his expression. But it was also wonderful. I am very happy to have been able to do it for him."

"It's strange," I said, "listening to you talk about what I couldn't experience. I don't doubt what you say, but it makes me feel I somehow missed the whole thing."

"No, John. Of all the people in the circle, you were the closest to Mr. Rahman and gave the most."

A few days later, in the midst of a conversation about the next art shipment, Rudi said,

"I am still in contact with Mr. Rahman. He is doing quite well."

I never knew how to respond to such statements, so I said nothing, which seemed to be what Rudi expected. At least he went right on.

"There is a period of transition after physical death during which the living can be of great help to the dead if they know what to do. That is why I am making the effort to maintain my contact with Mr. Rahman, regardless of what else is going on."

"Is that what you have been doing the last few days?"

"Yes," he said. "It is no different than holding someone in your memory. You probably thought I had completely dismissed the whole event from my awareness."

"Yes," I said. "I really had."

"It's not that Mr. Rahman was my greatest friend or anything like that, but he played an important part in my life. He was my first real contact with Indian culture. I interested him. He felt that I was an uncut Western gem that he could help to form. He used to invite me to his house occasionally. The first time I thought it was for dinner. But when I got there I discovered I was the main course. I was supposed to perform psychic feats. I really resented being tested like that, particularly since it was totally unexpected. But that's the Indian style. At each step of the way you have to prove yourself by passing some test that they create for the occasion.

"So there I was expecting dinner and trying to adjust to the atmosphere created by a group of Indians, most of whom I was meeting for the first time, when suddenly he handed me a totally nondescript spherical brass object and asked me to identify it. About the only thing I could tell physically was that it was man-made and looked old. There was nothing else to go on.

"I wanted to throw it at him, but I realized that it was important that I find the answer if I could."

Rudi paused as he remembered the experience. I knew better than to ask him how he went about identifying such an object. He wasn't going to tell me unless he wanted to, and he generally discouraged talking about psychic techniques.

"So," he said, starting up as if he hadn't paused, "I did the only thing I could, I connected with the energy that came from the object and compared it to the energies of various cultures with which I was familiar. At first I thought that it looked like a Chinese animal, but I put the visual impression completely out of my mind. It could only

Early Developments

The Shankaracharya of Puri & entourage

interfere. I concentrated on the vibrations in the object and tried to sense the man who had made it.

"The energy didn't seem Eastern. Neither did it seem Middle Eastern or Western European. There was a quality of sharpness associated with it that was too pointed to be English. But the vibration was too internal to be French. I could associate the sharpness with German, but not the quality of pointedness.

"I finally announced that I thought it was Austrian. They were all quite impressed. I had given them the right answer, but I was still angry.

"The next time I was invited, I thought it would be different. The only difference was in the nature of the test. Every time I came to visit I was made to perform. But somehow during the process, I was accepted. That is, my potential was accepted, and Mr. Rahman and I became friends. He eventually opened some doors for me in India and, of course, was responsible for my meeting with the Shankaracharya of Puri. For that alone I will always be in his debt."

Again Rudi was silent. I waited, hoping he would continue. I was fascinated with this glimpse of his earlier life.

"It happened totally without preparation," he said suddenly.

I wasn't quite sure what he was talking about, but I kept my mouth shut, hoping it would become clear. I didn't want to interrupt the flow of his recollection.

"I went to Mr. Rahman's for Sunday dinner," he said. "His friends were a little preoccupied. He did not ask me to perform any psychic feats that day, but after the meal, he casually suggested taking a ride to the airport, explaining,

"'I have a friend stopping over for a few hours whom I would like to see.'"

"When we got there the terminal was filled with the familiar crowd. But there was one unusual feature. Several small groups of people were holding garlands. Perhaps someone was coming from Hawaii.

"Finally, after what seemed like a very long time, the plane carrying Mr. Rahman's friend arrived. I didn't know what to expect.

"A very old man walked slowly off the plane, but I could barely see him. A brilliant white and gold light surrounded him and extended beyond his body a foot in every direction. I almost immediately went into shock, as I felt love for this man filling my being. He was like my grandfather. I had been waiting to meet him all my life.

"Mr. Rahman, seeing my condition, whispered to me,

"'That is the Shankaracharya of Puri [1]. He is like the Hindu Pope. I will introduce you to him.'"

"The old saint was quickly surrounded by a crowd of people. I stood on the outskirts for a few minutes while the others milled around and received his blessing. Then I suddenly became aware that he was very tired and needed to go to the toilet. I worked my way closer and whispered,

"'Holiness, do you wish to wash your face?'"

"He looked at me with gratitude, and a great radiance filled me. I helped him to the men's room and stood guard until he was finished. But he was still exhausted, so I managed to find him a bed. I sat with him while he slept, willing to guard him with my life. When he awoke I offered to go with him to California where he was headed at the time. But he told me he was going to return to New York in five weeks for an extended stay. I could serve him then, if I wished. I spent the intervening time preparing myself by surrendering everything in my life that might stand in the way. The Shankaracharya was my first real spiritual teacher. Without Mr. Rahman, I would never have met him.

---

[1] His Holiness Jagadguru Shankaracharya Sri Bharati Krishna Tirtha, ecclesiastical head of the Govardhana Monastery in Puri, the apostolic successor of Shankara who founded the Vedantic order in the ninth century, lived from 1880 to 1960. His visit to the United States in 1958 was the first time any leader of his order had ever ventured to the West. He was known as a saint, a scholar of vast learning, a brilliant mathematician, and a gifted speaker to world peace and the unity of all religions.

"That is why as I go about my daily life I keep a thin line of awareness with Mr. Rahman to help him out of this world. But that won't be necessary much longer."

I waited to see if Rudi was going to say anything else. I was still getting used to the idea of his continued contact with a dead man. But he had nothing more to say. He got up and started to move some statues around the store. It was too late for me to ask any questions.

✳ ✳ ✳

As long as I can remember, there were always people coming and going, with Rudi as an island in the stream of their lives. They would stop to spend an hour, an evening, and move on to return in a week or a month. Some were expected and planned for in advance. But others simply walked through the door of the store to make a purchase and be caught in the energy that Rudi wore around him like a psychic garment.

One day a thin intense-looking man appeared and began to ask about various Indian gods. I retired to the hallway next to the bathroom until he had gone.

When I reemerged, Rudi said,

"That was really something. This man walks in from the street and asks me, 'Which are the main Hindu gods?' I tell him and then he says, 'I'll take one of each.' He is coming back for them this evening."

He reappeared several hours later on a motorcycle to pick up the statues. Thus did Wayne Marcus enter the scene. He was a slightly wild stock broker who valued his freedom. Wayne was fascinated by Rudi, who in turn enjoyed his directness and intensity. He lived only a few blocks from the store and often detoured on his way home. He loved to roar out of the Seventh Avenue traffic on his motorcycle and screech to a stop in front of the store.

During the next few months, he bought more art and talked about becoming one of Rudi's students. Occasionally he gave Rudi a ride on the back of his motorcycle. It helped to break up the long day Rudi spent sitting in the store. I watched with mixed emotions as the two of them disappeared into the endless impersonal traffic that flowed down Seventh Avenue. I relaxed only when they reappeared from the opposite direction and Wayne brought the motorcycle to a sudden halt next to the sidewalk where I stood.

* * *

About that time, Rudi heard of a large Tibetan statue that was buried in the storage attic of the Newark Museum. One of his friends, Eleanor Olsen, was the curator of the Tibetan collection of the Museum. With her cooperation, we made a trip to Newark to see the statue.

The Museum was interesting, the sculpture gardens lovely, their Tibetan collection beautifully displayed. We waited patiently as we were given the full tour. Finally Rudi asked, "What is the history of this piece we are going to see, Eleanor?"

"It belonged to a Russian count," she said. "When he died, we were asked to hold it until his estate was settled."

"Who owns it now?"

"I'm not exactly sure. It has been sitting in the Museum for about ten years. Are you interested in it?"

"How can I tell until I see it?" Rudi said, though it was hard for me to imagine a Tibetan sculpture in which he would not have been interested, particularly if it were large.

When we got to the Museum, Eleanor led us up to the attic storage area. It looked like the living room of a deserted estate. Everything was covered over with sheets. Anything might have been under them — pianos, Greek statues, or old dishwashers. Eleanor wove her way through the confusion to an object that appeared to be the size of a knight on a horse. Nothing could have ever prepared me for the wild macabre vision of Tibetan mythology that greeted our eyes as she carefully removed its covering.

"This is a statue of a Lhamo," she needlessly explained. Rudi knew what it was. A wild, life-size feminine figure in flames riding, side-saddle on a mule, surrounded by sacred symbols and attendant animals.

I took one look and thought, "I would go crazy if I lived around that for any length of time."

I sensed that Rudi was shocked by the size and power of the statue. But he only made some noncommittal comment and when we returned downstairs asked Eleanor to look into the ownership so that he might make an offer if he decided to do so.

On the way back to Manhattan, I asked him, "Are you interested in the piece?"

"I think I have a customer," he said. "Wayne is crazy enough to buy something like that."

That was all I heard about it for a while. Negotiations proceeded, but nothing surfaced for about six weeks. Then one day Rudi announced, "I am buying the Lhamo. Do you want to come along when I pick it up from the Museum?"

"I wouldn't miss it," I said. "Are you going over with a truck?"

"No. We'll just take a van."

"Is it going to fit?"

"Don't worry," said Rudi. "It will fit."

A few days later a small group of us departed for Newark. Rudi was very excited. A real coup was in the offing. He didn't say exactly what he was going to pay, but it was obviously very little. The executors didn't understand the value of the piece or know what to do with it. The Newark Museum had never cared to make an offer on the treasure they were storing. Rudi's only fear was that they might change their mind at the last minute.

As we drove into the back entrance of the Museum, he said very intensely, "Everyone do exactly what I tell you. Don't act excited. Don't say anything. We just want to get in and get out as fast as we can."

We entered the Museum quietly, but with the air of bank robbers in a French thriller. Eleanor offered tea. We politely declined.

"I have some customers coming to the store. I have to get back," Rudi said.

Eleanor had been partially briefed, so she didn't delay us. We proceeded directly to the statue which had been brought down from the attic. Rudi looked at it very casually to check that all the major parts were there.

"Okay," he said to us. "Let's go."

We carried the smaller and larger pieces to the freight entrance. The main figure was moved onto the elevator. The museum people prepared to take it down to the basement. They were used to moving things very slowly, a piece at a time.

"No, no, no," said Rudi, stopping the elevator by standing in the doorway. "We will load it all at once."

The Museum people were slightly shocked. But Rudi didn't want them to have too much time to stand around and think about what they were losing.

We squeezed all the parts of the statue onto the elevator and then crowded in ourselves.

"All right," said Rudi to the elevator man, "take her down!"

As we descended, the shaken museum people slowly disappeared from sight. They looked as if they were unsure whether to feel dismayed or relieved. We quickly moved our prize onto the loading ramp where the van was waiting. I didn't see how it could ever possibly fit, but Rudi was confident. We arranged the larger sections and then wedged the smaller ones in-between. Somehow there was still room for us and the more delicate symbolic ornaments, which we carried on our laps.

"We can take our time now," Rudi told me. "Drive very slowly."

We pulled away from the Museum feeling a great sense of relief. Rudi was obviously elated.

"There isn't another piece like this in the world. I'll never understand how the Tibetans could have allowed it to leave the country. Maybe that is why the Chinese conquered them. The Lhamo was the protectress of the Dalai Lama, and I'll certainly never understand how the Museum could have had it all that time and shown absolutely no appreciation of it. It's worth at least fifty to a hundred times what I paid for it."

"What are you going to do if Wayne doesn't like it?" I asked.

"Who cares? I'll keep it myself."

That is what happened. Wayne liked it, but thought it would be too much to live with. Rudi was not upset. It became one of the great pieces in his Tibetan collection.

* * *

A few days later, during a quiet period at the store, I said to Rudi,

"It is a pleasure just to sit here with you without a million different things going on simultaneously."

"Appreciate it while you can," he said.

"Haven't you always been surrounded by people?" I asked.

"I used to be before I opened the store. But when I started my business I had to change my pattern. I knew lots of creative and artistic people. I loved to go to their parties, but it wasn't what I needed. I wanted to grow so I sat in the store from ten in the morning until ten at night, as if it were an egg and I were a hen waiting for it to hatch, except I was the egg and it was the hen. I used to watch couples walking along the street, going to the corner movies or out for the evening.

I would sit here with tears streaming down my face, feeling totally alone, but it didn't matter. I understood the necessity and that made it possible for me to do it."

A customer came in. Rudi got up to wait on him. I drifted toward the back of the store and idly began to unroll some paintings I had not seen before. I came upon a Tibetan thangka that fascinated me, though I could not exactly say why. Rudi quietly walked up behind me and interrupted my thought.

"You don't like that one do you, John?"

"It's really unusual."

"It certainly is. I had put it aside to take it home."

"Can I buy it?" I asked uncertainly.

"I was going to keep it," said Rudi, in case I hadn't understood him the first time.

I waited. I would do whatever he wanted. After a short time he shrugged his shoulders.

"All right you can have it. But appreciate what you have. It is a picture of this work."

I didn't ask him what he meant, and he didn't explain further. All he said was, "You can listen to this picture. It radiates music."

I looked at it intensely for a minute and it did seem to sing. I suddenly felt very happy.

Rudi walked over to his desk and motioned me over to a chair, indicating he would work with me. We sat toward the back of the store, out of the immediate sight of any customers who might wander in unexpectedly.

The familiar but always unknown process of energy transfer began. I submerged myself in it with a sense of necessity and dedication. The flow strengthened, and I felt partially anesthetized. It continued for perhaps ten minutes. Then Rudi said,

"How do you feel, John?" It was unusual for him to ask.

"I feel okay, why?"

"Because you are about to have a breakthrough," he said.

"I don't feel very different," I said.

"It'll probably hit you in a minute. I'm going to step outside for some air." And he left.

I sat there afraid to do the wrong thing, uncertain if there was anything to be afraid of.

The silence deepened. The force working within me began to

strengthen and swell. I felt unaccountably sad. Then, like sound heard first in the distance, a great wave began to break through me. I started to sob, more out of gratitude that something was actually happening than any sorrow. I felt carried out of myself. I could not say where I was. I could hear singing around me. It sounded like a chorus by Bach or Handel, yet not one I had ever heard.

After a few minutes, I uncertainly walked outside feeling purged and renewed. Rudi was standing under the awning of the nightclub in which he had at one time washed dishes. He looked at me and smiled, but said nothing.

"How did you know that it was going to happen?" I asked after a pause.

"Does it really matter?"

"No, I guess not,"

"But what does matter," he said, "is that if you had followed your own inclination you would have walked out here with me after we worked, and the whole experience might never have taken place. You don't have enough sensitivity to your inner condition to know what's good for you."

I stood there feeling stupid and grateful.

Rudi smiled and looked around the Greenwich Village scene. But he did not seem to be seeing the little stores, or hearing the screeching brakes, or smelling the polluted air of New York City. I waited patiently until he started to speak.

"When you work," he said, "it is like surfing on the waves of cosmic energy as they move through the universe. These waves uphold creation. They are the freshest energy that exists. When you contact them it is like drinking rain water before it hits the earth.

"I ride these waves as they break through the atmosphere, absorbing, absorbing, absorbing. It is the most wonderful thing in the world. Sometimes during a long afternoon, the energy changes abruptly. I don't know why or how, but it is immediately obvious. Occasionally I phone up an astrologer friend of mine and ask him, what happened at 4:10 this afternoon?"

"He calls me back in a few minutes to say, 'How did you know that Venus and Jupiter were in alignment at just that time?'

"I doubt that he would believe me if I told him that it would be an effort on my part not to know."

"The waves change continually. Every day is different. Sometimes every hour is different. There are some astrological events that occur only once in several hundred years. The energy at such a time is unique. If you don't happen to be working, then you miss the chance to absorb it. You will have to wait hundreds of years for the same opportunity to recur. And that particular quality of energy may be necessary to fill a vital gap in your own development. That is one reason why it is necessary, once you undertake this work, to do it faithfully every day for the rest of your life.

※ ※ ※

The next time I saw Rudi he looked very strange, as if he had been through a remarkable ordeal.

He didn't seem to want to talk about it, so I left him alone. Finally, with a sigh he began.

"I was riding in the car with Edith last Sunday, feeling very peculiar, which isn't so unusual for me. I happened to look down at my hands and I got the shock of my life. They weren't my hands. They were much larger and longer. I don't mind admitting I was frightened. I had no idea what was happening to me. But I haven't worked all my life just to throw away such experiences because I'm scared.

"I immediately surrendered everything. I could feel the energy of another being entering me, obliterating my personality, but leaving me a central core of awareness that could observe what was happening.

"I looked down at my hands again, and I suddenly understood. They were Nityananda's hands. He was coming into me. My whole mind rejected the possibility. So I surrendered my mind.

"For the last three days, as I have gone about my normal routine, Nityananda has been moving in and out of me continually.

"My whole internal chemistry is in an uproar. But by now I am getting used to it. It is absolutely remarkable what a person can accept after a few days. By next week I probably won't be able to remember a time when he wasn't part of me. But right now I feel that every bone, muscle and nerve cell in my body has been altered. I can never return to what I was before."

Before The Sun

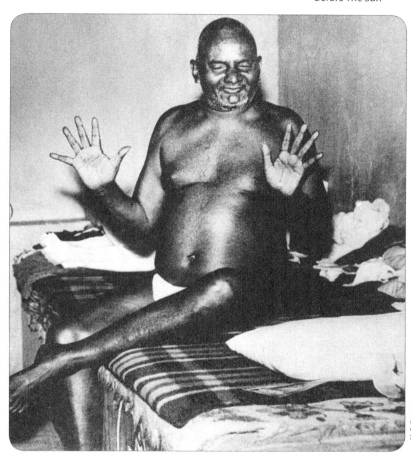

Bhagavan Nityananda

Chapter Five

THE FIRST HOUSE

Every year or two Rudi moved. But it was a big decision, even for him, to shift from renting an apartment to buying a house. He decided to do it because he needed more space for storing his art and a more substantial setting for his spiritual work. He looked for many months at an endless variety of buildings. And just when I had finally concluded that he would never buy anything, he abruptly announced:

"I have found a house. No one else wants to touch it because it used to be a funeral home. There is a large room downstairs that was used for services, and the bathroom adjoining the master bedroom was used to wash down the corpses. But the price is right and I like the symbolism. It is the nature of spiritual work to resurrect the dead."

The house was relatively small, but the work involved in renovating it exceeded all expectations. The simplest task turned into a nightmare. Painting the ceiling, for example, seemed easy until chunks of plaster began to fall out for no apparent reason. Rudi insisted that his bathtub be washed down twelve times to get rid of the smell of the cleaning fluid that had been used to wash the corpses. Anyone who stopped by to see how things were going was shortly involved in the work. Rudi was there with us, working harder than anyone else, while also arranging for meals, giving orders and buying the supplies.

※ ※ ※

Though the house was used primarily as a setting for spiritual work, he did not ask for payment of any kind.

"I work with other people because it helps me to grow," he said.

"Why should they pay me for that? Besides, I want to be free of the situation; accepting money would limit my freedom."

His attitude was directly at variance with the Hindu tradition from which he drew his basic sustenance. A holy man in India expects to be supported by his students. Rudi financed himself and a number of others as well. Many years were to pass before he asked for money, and then only because the magnitude of his work had exceeded his own immediate ability to support it.

None of this seemed strange to us at the time. We realized only in retrospect that it was almost unique.

※ ※ ※

One day during a brief lull at the store, Rudi, while shuffling some papers on his desk said, "Would you mind witnessing my will, John?"

I was slightly dumbfounded. I could not conceive of Rudi ever dying.

"Wayne is going to be the other witness," he continued. "He should be here in a few minutes."

"If you want me to," I said reluctantly.

"It's very simple," said Rudi. "I am leaving everything to my mother."

I was tempted to say something; Rudi's mother was not in good health. Only his prompt action had saved her life several times in the past. At the same time he was in his prime. Why should he leave everything to her? But I kept my mouth shut. It was none of my business.

Wayne appeared and we both signed. Then the document was returned to its legal envelope and disappeared into Rudi's desk. A moment later it was all forgotten. Occasionally I wondered whether Rudi's mother knew of the will and what she thought about it. But I did not ask. I figured it was his way of giving her a sense of financial security.

※ ※ ※

Rudi generated strong emotional reactions in the people around him. It was therefore remarkable that there was relatively little jealousy among them. It was also fortunate because there was constant shifting between people and situations as Rudi himself grew, and the quality of his being attracted some and repelled others.

"When someone becomes close to you," I said one day, "it doesn't seem to bother me."

"Ordinarily it would," replied Rudi. "People get most upset when someone with whom they are involved forms a new relationship."

Before The Sun

Rudi & mother Rae in his store

"So why don't I feel that way?" I asked.

"Because when I meet a new person it in no way threatens our connection. Most people cannot stretch themselves to encompass new situations without letting go of the old. I don't permit that to happen inside myself. If someone leaves, I can't stop them. But as long

as they remain and preserve a certain vitality in their effort, I work to stay open to them.

"But there is another side to the situation," continued Rudi. "There is nothing you or anyone else could do if I decided to cut the connection between us. The student is at the mercy of the teacher in that respect. A true teacher is a servant, not so much to the student, but to the force that comes through him. When he works, his personality is suspended. It is the higher force that directs his actions. If that is not entirely the case, the student is partially at the mercy of the ego of the teacher. There is nothing he can do but go along with the situation in order to get what he wants — the higher force. If he can't find this kind of humility inside himself, he is out of luck. It may not seem just, but if you want something that someone else has to give, you play the game according to his rules.

"I make it very, very easy for people. The only thing they have to do is put up with the impact of the changes in my internal chemistry produced by my own growth. There isn't much I can do to shield them from that. But otherwise I expect almost nothing. Probably I make it too easy for my students. If people don't pay enormously for what they get, they don't value it. It's unfortunate."

"But why should it be that way?" I asked.

"If they felt more worthy," said Rudi, "they would take it in a quiet and grateful way, understanding that there was nothing they could really give in return. That is the simple truth. No matter how long you continue to know me, John, and it will probably be for a long time, there will never be anything you can do for me that I really need. All you can do is receive the nourishment from me that you require, assimilate it inwardly, and use it well. That is all I ask of anyone, but how many can accept something that simple?

"You have to study in the East to appreciate what I am offering. Most people think of holy men and saints as quietly smiling, highly moral individuals freely giving their help and blessings. It isn't true. The saints I have met were a strange group of characters. Sainthood has to do with level of being, not personality. A saint can be a son of a bitch. There is nothing you can do about it if he is, except surrender or leave. You look doubtful, John."

"It's just so different than I thought."

"I'm a good human being because I want to be that way," said Rudi. "But if I wasn't, what could you do about it? If I was mean and sarcastic, would you leave?"

"No."

"If I lied to you, would you leave?"

"No."

"Why not?"

"Because it wouldn't matter. I would still need what you have to give."

"Most people wouldn't be able to look at it that way," said Rudi. "But it's true. You wouldn't have any choice. That's what I face in India. I constantly have to prove myself, and at the same time accept what they put on me. The Indians don't believe that an American could be spiritual. If you're not born an Indian, you've had it as far as they're concerned.

"But even if I were an Indian, I would still have to accept whatever the guru did. He makes the rules. If he expects to be loved, you have to love him. If he wants to be served, you have to serve him. Sometimes it is easy, sometimes not, but either way you have to find it in yourself to do what is required or you can't possibly get anything from him. And he can make it very difficult."

"I've never had any particular desire to visit the East," I said.

"It would be a waste of time if you did. You haven't got the background or the capacity to get anything from the saints you might meet. And don't think that they would tell you what to do. They wouldn't. I make it very easy in comparison. Not only do I give energy away, but I teach people how to take it. I have never known anyone who taught students how to tap them. None of you really understand how simple I am making it for you."

"It doesn't seem simple to me," I said.

"There is a difference between difficult and impossible. To work in the East is more or less impossible. To work with me is difficult, just because growth is hard. It isn't really natural to grow. Everything in the universe is against it. The whole pattern of one's existence is based on equilibrium. Anything that threatens the balance creates a complex counter-reaction, inside and out. Every significant move a person makes is tested by how he handles the reaction it produces. It must be that way. First you have to find something. Then you have to be able to hold onto it.

"And the worst of it is that the relatively few people who seek for a path are often destroyed by the schools and teachers they approach.

If you survive an esoteric school that is a major test in itself."

"You survived the Gurdjieff work all right," I said, thinking of the school in which we both had studied many years before.

"They tried to kill me," said Rudi. "They might have succeeded if they weren't so sure that I would die anyway."

"How do you mean, 'kill you?'"

"They told me that I would die when I reached thirty-one. Can you imagine telling anyone a thing like that? Most people would have been scared shitless by such a prediction, and died just to be agreeable. It was a hard thing for me to fight because there was truth to what they said. There was a break in my life line during my thirty-first year. If I had denied it, I would still have been vulnerable. I had a vision of how I would die and it didn't fit their image. So I decided that what they said was death, would be death and rebirth. And so it was. You met me a few months after the rebirth had occurred."

I felt a cold chill, and couldn't speak for a few moments. Then I said, "How could they tell you such a thing?"

"I was a threat," said Rudi. "I stood out too much. In class I was the only person who would ever ask questions. No one could shut me up. Experiences they described as difficult to attain seemed to happen to me effortlessly. When they tried to withhold something from me, I just reached inside them and took it. It was my need that helped me to tap the nourishment within them even when it was hidden by a ten-foot stone wall or sunken a hundred fathoms deep. I found it because I had to find it. They didn't want to give it to me.

"But that is the way most schools are. They unconsciously attempt to fit the student to the method. If the student doesn't fit, they cut him to size. If you live through such treatment you get stronger. If not, you hobble away. Most people don't survive. You were lucky that you were so deeply buried at the time that they didn't know how to get to you."

"That's a hell of a thing to say."

"But it's true, John. And you know it's true, or you wouldn't be so patient now. It may not flatter your ego, but the only hope anyone has is to accept his condition and begin to want to change it.

"You decided to give up the world when you were five years old. Now you are retracing your steps. That's one reason it takes so long. You have to get back to what you left behind, and then begin again.

"A person pays a terrible price for his fantasies about himself. It takes a great deal of energy to sustain them. And even worse, it deprives him of the one motivation for change that he needs to get through the inevitable difficulties he must encounter."

"It doesn't seem fair," I said, "that people who are searching should be subjected to such treatment."

"Who said anything about fair? It is the way things are. They have always been this way. The earth is perfect. It's performing a certain function in the universe that has nothing to do with what we want or how we imagine things should be. Fairy tales are nearer the truth. There is always a search for some inaccessible treasure, with endless obstacles and temptations lying in wait. The Hero may succeed, but it is never easy. And in life you never know who the Hero is, until after the story is over.

"Everything I give I have either dug out of myself or stolen from someone else. No one ever gave me anything, except the Shankaracharya of Puri." Rudi paused and seemed to go backwards in time. His eyes grew softer as he continued. "He was an old, old man when he came to America. I was with him for three months, and all that time almost no one asked him a real question. Slowly it dawned on me that there was no reason for him to come to America except for me. If he hadn't come, I would have gone out of my mind. I couldn't control the energy in me and I was choking on the waste products that my inner work was creating.

"Whenever the need is great enough, it draws a response. My need drew him, even though I didn't know he existed until I saw him get off the plane with a great shining halo around his head.

"I remember once he asked me what I wanted in life. I said, 'to work and to suffer.'

"'No, no,' he said, 'that is wrong. You should wish to work and be happy.'

"'Unfortunately you have twenty more years of hell to go through, but at the end of that time you will begin to experience a flowering of overwhelming happiness and love.'

"'How did I get into this situation?', I asked him."

"You were conceived by two parents who hated each other. Your soul was pure, but immediately on conception it was surrounded by a hard core of bitterness and misunderstanding that expressed your parents' relationship. That is the hell you have to work out of in order to find your way to the light. It is not your own nature that surrounds you, but the conditions of your birth."

"Then I asked him a remarkable question. I said, 'When I have completed my work, why should I continue doing it?'

"There I was, a kid in torment, asking about a time twenty years in the future.

"His answer, which I certainly didn't understand at the time was, 'you work to keep the wheel turning.'

"In the long hours that we spent together, I would beg him again and again to tell me about my future and how it would unfold just to give me the courage to live through the pain. I was like a child pleading to hear his favorite bedtime story.

"And so he would tell me of the happiness waiting for me at the end of the twenty years of torment. At this point I still have ten years to go."

"That's hard for me to believe," I said. "You seem much happier to me than most people."

"I probably am, but you really don't know what my inner work costs me. I'm glad you don't have to know. You couldn't stand it. I have a tremendous capacity for absorbing pain. When I was in college they gave a test to measure frustration tolerance. I went off the top of the scale. They couldn't devise anything frustrating enough to get me to quit.

"I have been going through pain all my life. I was even dropped on my head the day I was born. Don't laugh. It's true. That's how my life in this world began. Then I had something wrong with my feet that required endless operations. It became a way of life. As a young kid I would walk into the hospital by myself to check in for the next round of surgery."

"I don't know how to react," I said.

"There is nothing to say. Fortunately it is in the past. When I was almost ten and a half, I had three different operations on my nose to correct a problem of mucus congestion that was poisoning my system. Then someone hit me in the face. I went back to the clinic. I had to go by myself because my mother was always out working to keep the family going.

"The doctor was very sympathetic, but he couldn't avoid telling me the truth. I needed at least three more operations. I knew what the operations would be like. They were horrible, a form of medieval torture using a hammer and chisel to break the bone and pliers to reset it.

"I walked across a huge empty field near the hospital and felt unable to face what was to come. I decided to throw myself under a subway. I wasn't being dramatic. It seemed like the sensible thing to do at the time. But suddenly in my desperation, I began to feel a strange energy. I looked up into the sky and saw a vast beam of light shining down. Then I heard a great voice that said,

> **You are going through this horrible suffering because I love you. You are paying now for something which will bring you and many other people peace and happiness in the future.**

"As a child of ten I couldn't really understand what was happening. But it gave me the capacity to go on and that was what I needed."

I couldn't respond. Rudi looked at me for a moment and then said, "I don't expect you to say anything. I'm not looking for sympathy.

The First House

All those experiences were necessary to help me get used to pain. The greatest obstacle for most people is their inner inertia and fear of pain, which is really the same thing. Fear is the door to the prison in which people live. It keeps them where they are unless it is directly confronted.

* * *

"When I was in the ROTC in college they sent me over the side of a liberty ship to repaint it. I was very scared of heights. Within the first minute I had dropped the brush and the paint into the ocean. In the next minute I fell off the scaffold myself, but I wasn't scared. The only thing that worried me was what to do about the lost materials. We had been so poor when I was a child that the fear of losing anything was bred into me. My own life seemed a relatively unimportant thing in comparison to a paintbrush. It was this peculiar reaction that enabled me to survive the situation, and even go back to work after they had fished me out.

"An astrologer once told me that I would be in an airplane crash at sea from which I would be rescued. I thought about it and decided it didn't make much sense to go crazy every time I took a plane across the ocean. I did what I could. I began swimming regularly at the YMCA to be ready in case it happened. And then I forgot about the whole thing and put my energy into more productive channels."

* * *

"Man is an animal. He seeks pleasure and avoids pain. But he has the power to reach for greater fulfillment. The taste of that possibility can enable him to act like a salmon fighting his way up the rushing stream until he reaches the source.

"Most people who think that they are seeking for inner fulfillment are either looking for an experience in which to bask, or a system to follow blindly. It can't be that way. A system is needed and experiences should come, but growth is its own reward. What starts as a needed discipline turns into a mindless tyranny. What is felt as the flowering of an inner experience turns into a spiritual hedonism that retreats when resistance is met. There are natural departure points where a person can leave. But fundamentally, if you want to fulfill your potential, there is no end of working. It is for the rest of your life."

So Rudi spoke to me on different occasions until it seemed as if I had always been there in the store listening, watching, and waiting. But it was not so. There had been many years of searching before I met him. When I was fifteen, I underwent my first inner experience. I began to hear an inner dialogue between myself and a presence that I sensed as utterly alien. This other being told me that I was condemned to live alone in a haunted house for a long period of time. As the dialogue proceeded I had the chilling realization that the alien being was my real self, and that the familiar person to whom it was talking to was an artificial creation.

During the next fifteen years I led an outwardly normal life. But nothing that occurred, except for a love affair, ever really touched the inner isolation to which I was condemned without knowing why. It took several years after I met Rudi for anything to change.

In spite of the drama of some of the events which I have described, I was still fundamentally buried throughout this period. When I sat in the store it was as a shadowy and silent presence. It did not greatly matter since Rudi talked enough to fill in any vacuum that existed. He understood my condition and tolerated it, knowing that nothing but effort and patience would gradually lead to a change.

One day we were standing outside on the street. The weather was cool, and the sky cloudless. Then the phone rang, and Rudi reentered the store. I had been feeling strange, but that was not unusual when spending time around Rudi. Whenever something was occurring within him, it inevitably affected those around him, leaving them dizzy and disoriented.

"As I waited for his return I found myself unaccountably remembering that alien dialogue half a lifetime before. I thought how prophetic the words had been. And then, like the gentle flicker of wind caused by a passing bird, I realized that the spell had been lifted. The door to the haunted house was unlocked. I was free to emerge.

It was not a moment of high drama, but I knew it was real. When Rudi returned from his phone call I was feeling very light and happy. I did not say anything. There was no need.

Chapter Six
THE POSSIBILITY OF TEACHING

Several months before my own thirty-third birthday, I spoke to Rudi about my own prospects in the work he was developing.

"Do I have any chance of becoming a teacher?" I asked hesitantly.

"Is that what you really want, John?" said Rudi, looking up from a mystery he was reading.

"I think so," I said.

"That isn't good enough. You have to be absolutely sure. Teaching is opening a door to the unknown. If you don't like what comes through, you might want to quit. It doesn't matter too much what a student does, except to himself. But a teacher is the connection between his students and a higher force. If he quits or falters, all his students are affected. You have to have the capacity to persist, regardless of what happens, if you want to teach. Otherwise it's better to forget about it."

"I would like to say I am absolutely sure," I said, "but it wouldn't be true and you wouldn't believe it. However if I were sure, would it be possible? That's my question."

"Yes!" he said.

"Any buts?"

"Many!"

"What should I do about it?" I asked.

"You have to find a place inside yourself that is sincere and then ask from there to become a teacher. But if you ask, you must be willing to pay the price. You cannot determine the price beforehand and you generally cannot know what you are going to receive. But unless you are prepared to pay, don't bother asking. It's the only way to approach such a situation."

"What specifically should I ask for?"

"Say to yourself, 'I wish to become a teacher. I am willing to do whatever is necessary.' Beyond that, you can only surrender everything, including the wish, and wait for some inner response. If you

The Possibility Of Teaching

want to try it, ask on your thirty-third birthday. That is traditionally a significant date in one's inner development. Let me know what happens." Rudi went back to his mystery.

Several months later when my birthday came, I was at home in the country. During the afternoon, a great thunderstorm struck. I went up to the second floor of our refinished garage where I could be alone. There was a large picture window that looked out over a vast apple orchard. I sat down and quietly started to work. I was scared. I still wasn't sure if I was sincere, but waiting wasn't going to help me decide. I watched the trees shudder in the wind. The lightning blazed and the thunder reverberated through the skies.

The power of the storm quieted me. I was not going to turn back.

"If it is possible for me ever to become a teacher," I said inside myself, "I want it to happen. I am willing to pay whatever is required."

I surrendered everything. The storm seemed to fill the void. Beyond that nothing happened, but perhaps nothing was supposed to happen. I asked again with more intensity.

"I want to become a teacher if it is right for me to do so. I am willing to pay whatever price is necessary." I surrendered again. This time, there seemed to be a mildly affirmative inner response.

I repeated the sequence a third time. The answer seemed clearer. It was positive, I could become a teacher. But I honestly didn't know if the whole thing wasn't some form of self-suggestion.

The next day I was in New York and I spoke to Rudi about it.

"I did as you said."

"And?"

"It seemed to take."

"Good!"

"Don't you have anything else to say?

"No."

"Okay," I said, relieved that my experience hadn't been passed off as a fantasy.

The next thing I knew, Rudi had told Roy, who greeted me with,

"Hey, that's great about teaching!"

"I'm not sure I believe it yet," I said.

"You'll get used to the idea," said Roy.

On the spur of the moment I invited him to visit me in the country on the following weekend. He accepted enthusiastically.

***

The next day when I came to the store, Rudi was busy maneuvering a huge standing figure through the doorway. It was a multi-headed Kwan Yin.

He had just removed the air conditioning unit above the doorway to make added room for the figure as it was carried slowly toward the back by four movers.

"Isn't it going to go through the ceiling?" I asked. "It looks huge."

"Don't worry," said Rudi, "It will fit. And if worse comes to worse, I can always drill a hole in the ceiling."

Fifteen minutes later the statue was slowly raised into place. There was four inches to spare.

"Wait a minute," said Rudi, grabbing the ladder from behind the door. "I have to put back the little heads that go on top." As with many tantric figures there were multiple heads fitting into each other. Rudi had taken them off to protect them during the moving process. When he finished replacing all twelve of them there was a half-inch between the statue and the ceiling.

"See," he said, smiling broadly, "It fits."

A half-hour later as we sat drinking coffee, I said to him,

"I have $1000. What's the best thing I could buy?"

"The standing Chinese Buddha," he replied without a moment's hesitation. "It is the most spiritual piece I have in the store, and just by good fortune it costs exactly $1000.

"I don't know whether you're joking or not," I said, "but I'll take it."

"It's a wonderful piece," said Rudi. "You can work with it."

"I don't quite understand."

"It's very simple," said Rudi, "You sit in front of the statue, look into its eyes, and then work with it as you do with me. You can connect with any spiritual art in this way, or you can use a photograph of a saint as a point of contact. It is like looking at a picture of someone you love. The picture itself arouses the emotions you feel toward them. There is nothing magical about it. The difference is that you are doing it consciously to contact a higher energy which naturally flows in the saint or the art work. Once the contact is made, you just have to open to it and absorb it in your own system. I have been doing it for years. Why don't you try it now?"

I sat in front of the Buddha. To my surprise as soon as I began to relax, it started to look back at me. I had to remind myself that it was made of wood.

"Don't worry about what you experience," said Rudi. "It is your energy bringing it to life. It's like priming a pump. Once it starts going, it can serve you."

✳ ✳ ✳

On the following Sunday when Roy visited me in the country, he brought a bottle of champagne to celebrate my imminent teacher-hood. But first we meditated with the Chinese wooden Buddha for twenty minutes. When we finished, Roy said,

"I began to hear a bell tolling. People started assembling. It must have been the Chinese temple where the statue originally was placed."

I was not so fortunate as to have a vision, but Roy's presence helped me enter more deeply into the sense of the statue and feel it as a living presence.

A half-hour later Roy brought out the champagne and removed the cork with a gentle explosion. He poured two glasses, raised his in toast to me, and said,

"To your future as a teacher."

I didn't say anything, just sipped the champagne and felt grateful. After half a minute, I asked Roy, "What about you?"

"I don't know," he said. A few days ago I was trying to get an answer for Rudi about a question that was bothering him, and I heard these two beings — angels, I think, who were talking about me.

"One said, 'Will he make it?'

"The other said, 'Oh, he can get out here all right, but he'll fall back to the earth. That's probably what he wants anyway.'"

"Is that true?" I asked.

"It's what happened," said Roy. "I don't know whether it's true. I hope not."

We sipped the champagne in silence. I thought about Roy's toast. It seemed to make it official. And yet I had almost no concept of what teaching involved, how soon it might begin, or even why I was interested in doing it other than the challenge it presented and the opportunity for growth it might bring.

Whatever turns the conversation took, my mind was on the toast. It could be the beginning of a new life.

"I'm really happy you're here," I said to Roy.

"I'm glad to be here," Roy said, raising his glass again to the future.

It seemed very imminent as he did that. But I did not start to teach for another six years. And Roy was long gone by then.

※ ※ ※

A few days later Rudi unexpectedly said to me,

"I would like to work with you in a different way."

I didn't know what he had in mind, but I said "Sure." How could I refuse?

Shortly thereafter the opportunity came. We were on the first floor of Rudi's house surrounded by a partially unpacked shipment. No one was there.

"I want you to take off everything but your shorts," he said, "Don't be concerned about it. If you grow tense the whole experience will be wasted."

I did as he asked, and tried to relax. He also undressed to the same extent.

"Now come and sit on my lap facing me. I am going to work with you very directly. Try and absorb it as you usually do, but also take in energy through your whole body as if it were a great sponge."

I sat as he asked. It was slightly awkward at first. We were both heavy. His eyes were perhaps six inches from mine, boring through me. I could feel great heat coming from him. It was intimate but not sexual.

After ten minutes Rudi closed his eyes and released me. I got off his lap and got dressed.

"It must have worked," he said. "My whole spine hurts." I didn't know how I felt. I was still slightly in shock. "In a few minutes," said Rudi, "you should begin to feel great." In a few minutes, I did. My whole body began to radiate.

"What we did was a much more intense way to transfer energy. But I rarely do it. People brought up in this culture could misunderstand too easily. I knew you would accept it, because you have enough faith in me to try anything I suggest."

"That's true," I said. "I might be uneasy, but I would try it because everything you have done with me in the past has always worked."

※ ※ ※

The Possibility Of Teaching

In the next few months Rudi slowly clarified the basic outline of his teaching. He did not present it all at once, but continued to develop the details for many years. His basic conception was that there existed a psychic digestive system within the human organism. Its function was to directly transform internal and external energies into nourishment for higher human and spiritual functions which were usually dormant due to lack of proper nourishment. This conception was not in itself unknown. It existed in varied forms of yoga philosophy. But the specifics were quite different, and his approach as a teacher was unique.

"The third eye," said Rudi "is the mouth of the psychic digestive system. From there, the energy comes straight down the center line of the body, into the throat and the heart center, which is in the middle of the chest. Once you can identify this experience of energy flow in yourself, you consciously work to circulate the force, drawing it all the way down to the sex organs, and from there backward to the base of the spine. Then it rises upward through the spinal cord and ultimately emerges in the top and back of the head. That is the complete circuit of the psychic digestive system.

"It really is very simple. But few people ever experience it as a completed cycle because the various centers and their connections are not open. They generally do not open except under the influence of strong emotion or special circumstances. And then they quickly close again. Unlike the physical digestive system, which works almost totally by instinct, the psychic system works only through conscious effort.

"What I have given you is the simplest description of what is involved. A person develops by transforming the level of the energies that are working within him. Every situation we have ever had is potential food.

"When the psychic system begins to open we can digest these situations more fully, and begin to work backwards on the junk accumulated in our unconscious. It is all fuel. We burn what can be burned and eliminate the rest.

"Religious belief has nothing to do with it. The psychic digestive system is not the possession of Hindus, Buddhists, Christians, or Jews. Anyone can verify its existence through his own experience, if he is willing to do the work involved over long enough periods.

"Under every system that I know, the student is basically on his own. He is taught how to breathe, what to focus the mind upon, how to surrender. But he must do the work. There is, in fact, no way to avoid the responsibility of doing one's own work.

"But I make it much easier by giving a higher energy directly to you. The first or second time that I open to a new student, a spiritual energy flows from both of us and meets in the middle. I see it manifested as a Tibetan *yab-yum* figure where the man and woman come together in a complete embrace. There is nothing sexual about it. The meeting occurs in another dimension, and it symbolizes the beginning of a real relationship between us. Once this connection is established, you have only to absorb the energy that comes from me like water from a faucet. This is much easier than having to extract energy out of the atmosphere through your own efforts.

"There is a wonderful little Chinese book called *The Secret of the Golden Flower*. In it they speak of 'circulating the light' and 'reversing the flow'. If you read the book you will see that they are describing essentially what I have said, but from the book alone you would never understand it. 'Circulating the light' is digesting energy by bringing it through the psychic centers. 'Reversing the flow' describes the direction. Instead of the energy rising up and going out to other people as is usually the case, it is drawn down and back. Behind these poetic Chinese phrases lies a very practical understanding of inner development.

"When a person begins to work, it is something like renovating an abandoned house. Each section of the heating, electrical, and plumbing systems must be tested, repaired, or replaced if not working correctly. In a material sense this requires the services of a skilled technician who can diagnose the situation and make the correct adjustments.

"For most people the psychic system is weak and perhaps clogged through lack of use. If something has degenerated or broken, the individual is generally out of luck. The ordinary teacher cannot begin to handle this difficulty because it requires psychic surgery."

Rudi didn't talk about it often, but he could manipulate the psychic system, as a doctor might work on the arteries, muscles and organs of the body. He aligned parts, replaced worn-out mechanisms, and opened up clogged passageways. If a new part was needed, he had to create it and then graft it into the individual. Over the years I was one of the main recipients of such surgical efforts. Evidently I required them. Also, they were successful, which justified the effort as far as

Rudi was concerned.

When he performed a psychic operation, it cost him a great deal internally. He was usually exhausted and often in pain afterwards. But he did not mind if the result was good.

Each step involved in the opening of the psychic system, whether produced naturally or through direct intervention, was crucial since it constituted a link in a chain of connections. But clearly the turning point in the process was the awakening of the Kundalini force at the base of the spine. Much has been written about this force — fanciful, misguided, and completely misleading. It has been described as everything from the basic creative force in the universe, to an evil influence that feeds illusions and imagination. Equally fanciful are the means utilized to awaken Kundalini. Rudi characteristically approached this highly charged step in a very practical manner.

"The highest force that normally exists in the human mechanism lies asleep in a psychic center at the base of the spine. The only natural way to release this force is to give this center the nourishment it requires. Then it begins to open and the force is free to rise. Unfortunately this nourishment does not normally exist in the human mechanism. It can, however, be created by transmuting sexual energy. The purpose of everything we do in the preliminary phases of this work is to make such a transformation possible. By absorbing the cosmic force in the atmosphere and bringing it down through the various centers, the original energy is progressively altered. When it reaches the sex center a chemical reaction occurs. More accurately, it is an alchemical reaction. The base metal of natural sex energy is changed into the gold of transmuted sex energy. This refined product is the natural stimulus for releasing the Kundalini force.

"This is why the suppression of sex or the denial of its relation to inner work successfully castrates anyone's possibility for growth. It is true that sex, in the ordinary sense, leads nowhere except to its own satisfaction and possibly children, which is all that nature intended. Sexual relations resulting in the birth of a child is the nearest that most people get to being creative and, as such, is their bid for immortality. Generally it backfires as the children seek their own independence and refuse to fulfill the dreams of their parents. But from our viewpoint the crucial aspect of sexuality is that a small amount can be transformed and fed into the base of the spine. Gradually this arouses the serpent force held there in an enchanted sleep, and it rises up a passageway in the center of the spine. Until this begins to happen, everything is preparation. When this process is activated, inner growth becomes a possibility."

For six years the possible arousal of Kundalini was something I had to take on faith. When I was particularly open and relaxed, I could feel something stirring at the base of my spine. But there was nothing I could describe as a living flow. During all that time I waited patiently, but when the Kundalini was finally aroused it was not an anticlimax.

Chapter Seven

RAISING THE SERPENT POWER

Two months later I was teaching a seminar in group relations when suddenly the lights went out. I opened the door. The surrounding rooms were also dark. Since we were in a recently renovated building, I assumed the trouble was with the wiring.

I continued lecturing somewhat hesitantly, and then prematurely dismissed the class.

The elevator wasn't working, so we stumbled our way down the stairs. When we got outside I received a major surprise. There were no lights anywhere, and night was falling. People wandered along the street in a slightly disoriented manner. In snatches of conversation that I overheard, it became evident that all of lower New York was without electricity. I did not have a car, and the subway and electric trains were not running which meant that I couldn't get home. I looked at my wristwatch. It was 6:30. I set out across town to see if Rudi was still in his store. He usually stayed open until 7:00. Cars began to slowly cruise the streets, their lights the sole source of illumination. A slightly tense holiday spirit prevailed. People streamed out of their apartments and began to walk along the sidewalks, uncertain about the effects of the coming darkness. I walked also, enjoying the situation and not feeling terribly involved in it.

When I reached the store the door was locked. Rudi was gone. There was little reason for him to stay open without lights. But suddenly I felt very, very lonely. What was I going to do? My parents lived ten miles away. I couldn't think of anywhere else to go.

I started over toward Hudson Street to see if Rudi had gone home. I walked quickly and with increasing insecurity. From a distance I could see that his house was dark. That was to be expected; there was no electricity. I pushed the bell. There was no answer but maybe it wasn't working. I knocked. Nothing happened. I knocked louder. Nothing. I banged for twenty seconds. A neighbor looked out the window. I stopped knocking and moved away. Maybe he was at the store now. But it didn't seem likely. He could be anywhere.

Meanwhile a bright moon had risen, casting a friendly but slightly haunted glow on the streams of people moving on the sidewalk and in the street. Where was Rudi when I needed him? It was almost as if he had never existed.

As I wandered along I overheard people saying that the blackout extended over most of the East Coast which only added to my sense of disorientation.

When I got back to the store it was still locked. I continued walking uptown, having no destination.

Suddenly a hand reached out of the gloom and grabbed my arm. I began to tense.

"John," a familiar voice said. It was Rudi. I had walked right past him. He had found me.

"Let's go to the house," he said.

I followed along, feeling a growing sense of relief. It was almost 8:00 by then, the time Rudi regularly met with students. I asked half seriously, "Are you going to have a class tonight?"

"Why not?"

"I may be the only one there."

"It doesn't matter. There is something I wanted to do with you anyway. This would be a good time."

"What?" I asked.

"It's better that you don't know in advance," he said.

We walked silently the rest of the way to the house. It took Rudi a minute or two to get the front door unlocked in the dark. We groped up the stairs, found some candles, and in a moment filled the living room with dim flickering light. It was slightly after 8:00 when someone began banging on the door. I couldn't believe it. People were showing up for class. I asked Rudi,

"Will you still do whatever you were talking about, even if other people are here?"

"Don't worry," said Rudi. "If the entire East Coast is blacked out, the least I can do is to see if I can light you up."

I answered the door. Two people were waiting outside. We waited another ten minutes but no one else came. Finally Rudi said,

"I am going to give a special class tonight for John. The rest of you can act as witnesses."

He motioned for me to sit directly in front of him on the floor. Then he said quietly,

"Kundalini rises gradually if it awakens at all. It is also possible to activate it directly. That is what I am going to do tonight."

When I heard that I was thankful that he hadn't told me anything beforehand.

"You have worked for a long time, John, and been extremely patient," Rudi continued. "I feel very right about doing this for you."

I sat still, trying to relax.

"Begin," said Rudi, "by asking from deep in your heart to be able to open to whatever is about to happen to you. Remember all the efforts you have made in the past, and ask to receive the result now. Then let go of everything. There is nothing else for you to do but work in the usual way. Absorb the force in the atmosphere. If I should touch you, absorb the force in my hands. Otherwise let me do the work."

Rudi looked at me. The candlelight was reflected in his eyes. I could sense that he was making an effort, but I had no idea what he was doing. I concentrated on following his instructions. I kept asking inside and then surrendered. Nothing seemed to be happening, but I didn't dare stop long enough to judge.

I felt like I was crossing a woven suspension bridge across an abyss. I could only walk forward and keep my eyes on the further edge.

Five minutes passed. Rudi paused and said,

"The opening in your spine is much smaller than I expected. It is hard for the Kundalini to emerge."

He got up and appeared to look through me for a moment. Then he touched the base of my spine. His hands exerted pressure. It was painful. The pressure built. He stepped away. I sat there trying to surrender. Then without warning my back began to arch, and I went into a spasm. I was frightened, but tried not to interfere. The next spasm carried me onto the floor. I lay there racked by the force that had been released within me. I lost track of time and my surroundings.

When the physical impact began to recede, I slowly and hesitantly sat up. The room and the candlelight came back into focus. Rudi was sitting in front of me smiling happily.

"You just had your first real spiritual experience," he said. "How did you like it?"

"I don't know yet. It felt more like getting raped than anything else."

"That's the way it usually feels," said Rudi. "Go inside and rest for a few minutes. Give the energy a chance to settle."

I went into the bedroom and was happy to collapse. As I lay there the immediate impact began to pass, and I felt for the first time that a warm current was flowing in my spine. It felt wonderful. There was no mistaking the experience. After a few minutes Rudi called to me from the other room.

"You can come back now."

I reluctantly got up. He must have been talking to the other people. They looked at me as if I were some kind of wonderful freak. They wanted to ask me questions, but restrained themselves. Rudi looked at me proudly but with a slightly pained smile.

"You must feel great, because I feel terrible," he said. "For a while there I didn't know if you were going to make it."

"Suppose I hadn't?" I asked.

"You did. Why speculate? I never lose a patient," said Rudi.

I sat quietly for a minute, feeling the force rising in waves up my spine.

"I've never seen you look better," he said.

"I've never felt better."

"I'm glad that it worked, John. I don't know anyone who could raise Kundalini directly."

"Is that really true?" I asked.

"Sure, it's true. In the East, the Kundalini starts to flow only because of the student's effort over time and the fact that it is already released in the teacher. But to reach inside and start it going through is psychic surgery. I've never seen it done or ever heard of it."

"I don't know what to say."

"There's nothing to say. Appreciate that it has happened and use it well. That's all I ask. Now, if you don't mind, I'm going to collapse for the night. I don't feel so good. Make yourself at home. I'll see you in the morning."

The other students said goodnight. I was left alone in the darkness that covered the East Coast. There was no heat or electric lights; subways were stalled and elevators had stopped between floors. But within me a current of fire was flowing and a light that I had never seen before had been released.

Chapter Eight

A HOUSE IN THE COUNTRY

Before I met Rudi, my hobby and my mania had been modern architecture. Every Sunday I loved to look at the real estate section of the New York Times. Occasionally I went house-hunting in spite of the fact that I had no reason to move anywhere.

One Sunday my eyes caught on an ad that had to be a mistake:

Three stone houses on eight acres and a lake. Beautifully landscaped grounds near Peekskill, reduced $20,000. Price $55,000.

The next day when I saw Rudi there was a lull in the conversation. Knowing that he was interested in real estate, I said to him,

"I saw this really ridiculous ad in the paper yesterday."

"What was it?" he asked.

"I don't remember exactly, but the idea was three stone houses on eight acres, with a lake, for $55,000 in upper Westchester. Maybe they left off a zero."

Rudi didn't say anything immediately. I looked at him, expecting some sort of response. He closed his eyes for a few seconds. Then he said in a very quiet voice,

"I would look into it."

"You've got to be kidding."

"All right. Don't look into it."

I wasn't sure whether he was putting me on or not. He didn't look like it. I decided it was worth a short trip to find out.

The next morning my wife and I drove over to see the house. I didn't even know why she had agreed to come along since she certainly didn't want to move anywhere. It was the middle of winter. It had snowed recently. I had phoned ahead so that the real estate agent expected us.

We drove out to the house in the agent's car. I had never been in the Northwestern part of Westchester. I was amazed at its beauty. After a short time we came to a long stone wall. This was the border of the property we had come to see. We turned onto a steep driveway to the main house. For the next fifteen minutes I was in a state of progressive shock. The house was large, but not too large for our needs. It was finished in imitation stone, but it looked fine. Then further back there was another house, finished in real stone and concrete. And down by the lake was a small, all-stone house. Snow covered everything. At one point the real estate agent, who asked us to call him Jerry, cleared the snow away with his foot to show the stone work underneath.

"There are flagstone paths from here to the lake, and all over the property," he said.

I didn't believe him. I figured there was one flagstone under the snow which he had just uncovered. He didn't seem to care whether we believed him or not, which was odd for a real estate agent.

The grounds were beautiful, even in winter. There was a small orchard, a lily pond, and (so the agent claimed) an underground sprinkling system. We returned to the real estate office. Jerry mumbled something in farewell and walked inside. My wife and I sat there, mute. After a minute or two I said,

"I think it is absolutely incredible. We will never get a chance like this again. I want to go in and leave a deposit."

"If that is what you feel is right," she said. She was too overwhelmed by what she had seen to protest.

The agent was honestly surprised when I reappeared in his office. He thought we had left.

"I want to leave a binder," I said. "Is a few hundred all right?" "Sure!" he said with no particular enthusiasm. I wrote out a check and he gave me a receipt. I said goodbye, and got back in the car.

The ride home was very quiet. Neither of us was quite sure what had happened. The last thing we had in mind that morning was to buy anything, especially a house. We already had a house. On the other hand, there was always a bright side — we had nothing to lose but the several hundred dollars in the binder, and I could always stop the check.

※ ※ ※

In my next visit to the store I carried on excitedly to Rudi, "I've seen it but I still don't believe it. Even though the main house is finished in imitation stone, all the rest of the ad was true. In fact, it was better than I could have expected. The house is part of a community so there are neighbors for the kids. How did you know?"

"Maybe it was a guess," said Rudi, smiling.

"You never told me to go and look at anything before."

"Do you want to dissect the goose that laid the golden egg?"

"Forget that I asked," I said.

In my subsequent talks with Jerry, the real estate agent, I discovered that the house had originally been offered for $100,000. After a time, the rich owner had reluctantly reduced the price to $75,000. Many people came to look, but no firm deals were made. The owner went to Florida for the winter. Then Jerry, who was nothing if not daring, decided to reduce the price to $55,000. He neglected to tell the owner of his decision, but proceeded to put the ad in the paper where we had seen it. After I had given him the binder he had gotten on the phone and explained what had happened to the owner who was not a man used to having his decisions made for him by others. At first he flatly refused to have anything to do with the deal. But Jerry, who had said almost nothing to us, was extremely persuasive with him.

He pointed out that the house had been on the market a long time, and that he didn't really need the money. The owner weakened slightly, agreeing to see me when he returned from his vacation. I consulted with Rudi on proper strategy.

"The man is a millionaire," said Rudi, "and probably a ruthless bastard in business. But he also has an image of himself as a country gentleman. Appeal to that. Don't argue with him about anything or you're finished. Be friendly, cultured, treat him like your favorite uncle. Act as if it never entered your mind for an instant that he could conceivably back out."

"You really think I should lie like that," I said.

"No. Not if you don't want the house. But if you care, you better be convincing. Really brainwash yourself until you believe it.

"When I know that I am going to see a fine collection I work myself into a condition of complete indifference. By the time I see the collection it looks like so much garbage to me. Inwardly the owner senses that my attitude is, 'How much do you want for all this shit?' and he reacts accordingly. Later, after the sale is concluded I can afford to go wild with appreciation."

"It doesn't sound very spiritual to me," I said.

"If someone has what you need," said Rudi, "there are really no

Courtesy David Rudolph

limits. You do whatever is necessary to produce the kind of response you want. It's fair. He is doing the same thing to you. That's what business is all about. It is what life is all about.

"The only reason that you have a chance of getting this house is because of the owner's illusions about himself. I don't know the man. But if his image of himself is radically different from reality, you appeal to the image and he has to go along with you or sacrifice his fantasy, which most people are reluctant to do.

"When I am in the East, if a saint wants me to love him, I love him. If he wants me to crawl along the ground, I crawl, I have no ego. I have to fight inside myself before I do these things. But I always come to the same conclusion. I cannot afford the price of my ego when it interferes with my growth. These men have something of a higher nature that I need. They set the conditions, I accept them. You must also."

"I do, I'm not proud," I said.

"That's true. If you were proud it would be impossible for me to work with you. A person has to understand his own situation in order to do what is necessary to change it. Otherwise he will never have enough motivation. Life is about understanding what is needed, and providing it to the best of one's ability.

"From your point of view, this man must be your benign uncle who has come to you with a great gift. Just keep it that way. If he turns into a business man, you have had it."

* * *

My first meeting with the owner was subdued. He intended to dispose of the whole matter as quickly as possible, so I avoided any direct conversation about the house. I talked about his trip to Florida, the weather, his family, my family. Finally, I said,

"It has really been wonderful talking with you," and got up to go.

He didn't know quite what to make of it all. He called me back.

"I was quite disturbed," he said, "when Jerry called me in Florida to say that a binder had been accepted at $55,000. I never had authorized such a thing."

I tried to look slightly bored.

"I understand from what you were saying about your situation," he continued, "that you probably couldn't afford any more than that, but you can understand my position."

I said nothing, still ready to leave after our friendly conversation. I didn't have the vaguest idea what his position was or would be, but I forced myself to think long quiet thoughts and kept repeating inwardly, "You are a wonderful old man, very generous and understanding."

"Well," he concluded, since I didn't answer, "I'll talk the situation over with Jerry and he will be in touch with you."

I left quietly and reported my progress to headquarters on the next day.

"Very good," Rudi said. "You certainly gave him something to think about. You'll probably get the house. But it won't be easy."

While I was waiting for further developments, I discovered that Jerry had a dubious business reputation. This did not add to my sense of security. I mentioned it to Rudi.

"If he were more honest," said Rudi, "he would never have lowered the price without authorization. You should be grateful to him."

"But he might screw me at any time if he figured it was worth his while," I said.

"That's true. You can't bank on his principles. But it isn't so much a question of his honesty as whether you can work with him. I have to deal with some downright crooks in my business. Personally, I am extremely honest. But I know that some of them lie, cheat and bribe. That is the way they function. They know that I know what they are. I know that they know what I am. Because I understand and accept them, they respect me. But I don't turn my back on them. And I get burned every once in a while.

"Life is hard, John. It is hard for everyone. We are in this world to learn and grow and eventually get beyond it all to something better. Nobody is here as a reward. Everyone you will ever meet is here because they didn't make it last time. No one has a right to be proud. There is only one thing that is worthy of admiration, a man working to break down his resistance and overcome his own past. By the time you get this house, you will appreciate it because you will have earned it."

"Would you like to take a look at it?" I asked. "I am going up this Sunday."

"All right," said Rudi. "I'm curious, though strictly speaking, it isn't necessary."

He paused and then abruptly changed the subject and said,

"Let's go to the neighborhood diner and have a sandwich."

"Sure," I said. I was always ready to eat.

We started across the street. A Greenwich Village derelict stumbled in front of us. I must have made a disgusted face, because Rudi stopped in the middle of traffic and said,

"You have the wrong attitude, John. That might be Shiva in disguise."

Cars started honking, so we moved on. But I was vaguely stunned.

✷ ✷ ✷

The next Sunday I took Rudi to the house. I didn't have the keys, but we walked around the grounds. The snow had melted. What the agent had said was true. There were beautiful flagstone walks everywhere.

"I am slowly learning the history of the place," I said to Rudi as he pushed through some leaves with his shoes. "The original owner was a millionaire who made his money profiteering in World War II. He had four gardeners. The lawn used to win prizes. He planted hundreds of flowers and shrubs. When they stopped blooming he tore them up and planted more. It must have been really beautiful, but that has all been let go. One old deaf man takes care of the whole place now."

"It's great," said Rudi looking all around. "I love it. It will be worth a lot of money, though that isn't what matters. But you can certainly sell off some building lots!" He busily proceeded to dispose of the property before I owned it.

"I can't wait to visit you," he finally concluded.

"I'm glad you're so confident," I said.

We kidded around and finally left to look for some place to have lunch. The only thing we could find was a little diner near the railroad station. It helped to bring us back to earth. I put Rudi on the train and drove back to Rockland County where I still lived.

For the next few months the deal teetered on the brink of dissolution. But the longer it went on, the better the chances of eventual success seemed to become. Eventually the owner, who was still reluctant to sell the house, agreed to contribute $5,000 toward the purchase price of any other house I might find. I could hardly refuse to look.

Several months passed with mounting frustration. There was nothing on the market that looked as good as what I had already discovered. Then one day, sitting in the real estate office which had become my home away from home, I overheard Jerry talking about an estate in which he apparently owned an interest.

"What are you talking about?" I asked.

"Nothing you could handle," he said.

"Tell me anyway."

"It*s a complicated deal. There's an estate about two hours from New York. It's in Connecticut and goes halfway around a lake. We are trying to work out a deal to sell off part of it and buy the rest. But the zoning in the area is very strict."

"I'd like to see it," I said.

"If you have the time I'm going over there this afternoon," he said shrugging.

We departed an hour later. I kept pumping him for information. The more I heard, the more excited I got. The plumbing fixtures were gold and silver. There was a cedar closet bigger than a bedroom. The basement could be turned into a skating rink.

We finally arrived, driving in through the stone gateway up to a beautiful solid stone building that overlooked a private lake. It was vast. The furnishings had been completely removed, but the structure was in perfect condition. There were about 145 acres around the house. Complete privacy was assured. There was even an elevator from the first to the second floor.

I wandered around in a daze, trying to take in all that I saw. I didn't seriously look at it as anything I might own, but just enjoyed the experience of breathing the pine-scented air, looking across the lake at the estate on the other side, wandering through the woods and looking at two other houses on the property that were also both beautifully constructed. Then I began to think about the prices that Jerry had mentioned while driving over in his car. I wasn't in the best state to think clearly, so I didn't take my calculations very seriously. But still, it didn't seem impossible.

"If I bought the whole property, sold the smaller house for $65,000, which the owners said they could do," I thought to myself, "and sold off 100 acres at $4,000 an acre (which they also thought they could do), I could take the main house off their hands for $75,000 and maybe five acres to go with it. My God, I could do it!"

I kept my mouth shut, but my mind was racing. From a pipe dream designed to fill in an afternoon, I was suddenly confronted with a vast possibility.

Later we stopped at a diner to have coffee. I made for the nearest phone and called Rudi.

"Guess where I am?" I said to him, in a slightly hysterical condition.

"In the country?"

"In Connecticut."

"Why are you calling?"

"I have just seen something really amazing. I'll spare you the details until I see you. But the basic thing is that I have stumbled on a great estate which I might be able to get at a price I could afford. Of course, there are a lot of unknowns but..."

"Tell me about it," he said.

"It's a beautiful huge stone building about an hour and three quarters from New York. There are no furnishings any more, but the place is in perfect condition."

I continued on for another minute or two. When I stopped, there was only silence. Finally I asked,

"Don't you have any reaction?"

"What's the question?"

"Should I look into it further?"

A short pause.

"No! Forget about it!"

"But why?" I was taken back.

"Because you can't afford something like that."

"With the right mortgage, I think I could swing it."

"I am not talking primarily about money," said Rudi. "Psychologically you aren't strong enough to support a building of that magnitude. It would bleed you dry."

"I really don't understand," I said. "I don't know whether all the details could be worked out, but it seems to me an incredible opportunity."

"It happens to fit one of your dreams. It is only an incredible opportunity to commit psychic suicide," Rudi said.

"How can you be so sure? You haven't even seen a picture of the place."

"I can see it through your eyes."

"I admit," I said, "that I am not in the most rational condition at the moment. But I can't believe that it isn't worth talking over tomorrow, when I feel more relaxed and you have had a chance to think about it."

"There is nothing to think about, John. You asked me, so I am telling you. Don't believe me if you don't want to. I am not volunteering a reaction. I am answering your question."

"But I don't understand what you are saying."

"I'll try to explain. Psychically you have to be able to fill and bring life to wherever you live. This place is too vast for you at this time. It would continually drain your energy just to fill the space. If it were going to be occupied by twenty people, it would be different. But that isn't going to happen. It would take you at least two and a half hours to commute. I have been in that area, I know what it's like. It would eat up your money, your time, and worst of all — your energy. If you want to sacrifice your life for a dream, go ahead."

I didn't say anything for a moment. Then I took a big swallow and said, "All right. I get the message. It's forgotten."

"Good," said Rudi. "I'll talk to you tomorrow in the store..."

Eventually after further searching, I reluctantly came to the conclusion that the original house was the best alternative. The owner was unhappy, but he knew that I had really looked, so he agreed to sell. In the end, nine months passed between leaving the binder and taking possession. It was a long time to be pregnant with a house.

Chapter Nine
THE CONTRACT

I stopped at the store when I turned thirty-seven because Rudi usually gave students a special class on their birthday. This time he invited me to lunch.

"Do you feel like some fish?" he asked.

"Sure," I said. Anything would have been fine.

We left the store and proceeded down Greenwich Avenue. Rudi made New York City seem like a small town. On every block he stopped to talk with someone he knew. If there was no one on the street, he wandered into neighborhood stores.

Finally we arrived, were seated, and ordered. When the fish came I got right down to business because I knew Rudi would want to get back to the store, however he didn't eat much.

After a few minutes I noticed that the atmosphere was unusual. I stopped eating and immediately felt dizzy and slightly nauseous. Rudi had grown quite withdrawn.

"Is something happening?" I finally asked.

"Just be quiet and surrender inside," he said in a strange voice.

Gradually the intensity that surrounded us diminished.

"What happened?" I ventured again.

"You were being programmed for your next year."

"I don't understand."

"On a person's birthday, the pattern of their next year is projected. It is like a computer program. Unless you are sensitive to the process it will go right by, and you will never know the difference. It can only settle in you if you open to it."

"Did it take?" I asked, still slightly bewildered.

"Yes. I was here to make sure it did. Why do you think I invited you to lunch?"

"I thought it was a treat."

"Not to me. I couldn't touch my food," he said.

"But nobody knows anything about the possibility."

"Like many things, you have to be told first. Now you know. Next year you may have to open on your own."

"How should I go about it?"

"For the moment, just stay quiet and absorb what has happened. But when the time comes next year, you have to be very sensitive to your inner condition. At the slightest unusual sign, drop everything and open for all you're worth. It's like being prepared for a knock on the door. If you are waiting, it is easy to hear it. But you have to answer quickly or the visitor may be gone."

Rudi paid the check and we silently returned to the store.

* * *

Later that afternoon Rudi suddenly said, to my total surprise, "I definitely feel that you can write."

"That makes one of us," I replied. "I don't mind writing professional papers, but I do it just to get ahead at college."

"I'm not talking about that," said Rudi.

"But you never seem interested in what people write," I said. "I've never seen you read anything but mystery stories. Why do you want to push me into something you don't believe in yourself?"

"The one thing has nothing to do with the other," said Rudi. "If you have the potential, you should develop it. There may not be any immediate reason for it now. Maybe ten years from now you will need it. But if you don't want me to talk about it I'll save my breath."

"Just give me time," I said. "I never react well to new ideas. The idea of writing just doesn't fit my own self-image."

"That's the best thing about it," Rudi said.

"But what do you actually have in mind?" I asked.

"You should write a book."

"About what?" I was completely at sea.

"What do you know most about?"

"Psychology... Social Psychology."

"That's a popular subject," said Rudi. "You ought to be able to develop something."

"But who is going to publish it? I've never written a book. I don't want to compose an exercise in futility. There is too much work involved."

"I have an idea."

"About the amount of work?"

"No. About how to get it published. I have a friend who is a science editor."

"He may be your friend, but he's not going to give a contract to an unknown writer."

"That's true," said Rudi. "But trust me. I'll figure something out. The main thing is, are you willing to do the work?"

"I guess so," I said. "What's your plan?"

"You think of the book. I'll take care of the plan," said Rudi, ending the discussion.

I didn't know how seriously to take the whole conversation, but I decided that a book could be written about various frontier areas in psychology. I had already met Harold, the editor Rudi had mentioned. He was an interesting, but demanding, character. Rudi felt that he had a touch of genius. I really couldn't judge. When I was around he seemed primarily concerned with the misdeeds of his landlord with whom he carried on a chronic cold war.

The next time I saw Rudi he seemed pleased with himself. "Harold is coming over to the house for supper tonight," he said. "Can you make it?"

"Sure. How am I supposed to act?"

"Do you have a book in mind?"

"Sort of. Why?"

"Because if you don't, I won't bring up the subject."

"Don't you think it would help if I knew what you are going to do?"

"No!"

"All right," I said, accepting the inevitable.

That night Harold appeared at the house and we all had a relaxed meal. During a pause in the conversation, Rudi said innocently,

"Harold, I'd like your advice on something."

"Sure, what?" He was feeling good after dinner.

"John has an idea for a book. It sounds pretty interesting to me, but I'm not a professional. Would you mind giving him your opinion?"

"All right," said Harold. "Do you have anything on paper?"

I shuddered inwardly and said, "Not with me. But the basic idea is very simple. Many people are interested in psychology, but the latest developments are hidden away in professional journals. I would like to write a book called "Frontiers of Psychology", or something like that, to summarize these developments in understandable language for the layman."

"Give me a few examples," said Harold.

"Things like studies of creativity, the implications of space medicine, behavior change, computer applications. There must be at least twelve to fifteen such topics of that nature I could cover."

Harold thought for half a minute. Then he said, "It might be interesting. It depends on how you handle it. I can't really say without a detailed outline. Did you say you had one at home?"

"Not really. Just some notes."

"It might be worth developing," he said.

Then the conversation moved onto other things, including Harold's continuing battle with his landlord. After a few minutes, I noticed Rudi was giving me the high sign to disappear. I departed, thinking that the whole affair had been mildly pointless.

The next day I discovered that at least one concrete result had emerged from the evening. Harold was moving into the currently unoccupied third floor of Rudi's house.

"What about the book?" I asked, more out of morbid curiosity than genuine interest.

"There should be more chance to talk about it with him living in the house," Rudi said.

"But how do you feel about that?" I persisted. "I know that he's your friend, but being his landlord is something else. He could be a pretty difficult tenant."

"You're right," said Rudi. "He already is. On the first night, he complained about cracks in the ceiling, garbage collection, and the noise in my apartment."

A few weeks later, I happened to see Harold at the store. He was very friendly.

"Have you done any more with the book?" he asked.

"I've been compiling some notes," I said, lying.

"Why don't you prepare a brief outline and send it to me. Then we can make an appointment to talk it over in my office."

I nodded my head affirmatively; I was too surprised to say anything.

The setting for the meeting in Harold's office was very different from any in which we had met before. The space was small, the pace hectic. Rudi had briefed me beforehand. "Do whatever he asks, even if you don't see the point."

Harold outlined some questions that he wanted answered. I agreed to send the answers in writing. A few weeks later, we arranged a lunch at which final details were to be clarified. Somehow or other, the project was materializing.

We met in a pleasant French restaurant. During the appetizer, we discussed Rudi's latest shipment and other matters irrelevant to the book.

During the main course, I asked, "Did you get my letter?"

"Yes. Let's talk about it later," said Harold with a slight frown.

I ate my way through the steak. Then came the salad. I bided my time. Finally dessert. I ventured again, "About my letter!"

Harold looked at me with disapproval.

"Not yet," he said.

There didn't seem to be very much time left, but it was his show. I shrugged my shoulders and tried to enjoy the food. When he asked if I'd like an after-dinner cordial, I agreed, just to keep the meeting going.

When the drinks came, he smiled and said, "Now let us talk about your contract. Would $1,000 on signing and $1,000 on delivery of a finished manuscript be satisfactory?"

"That would be fine. But can I ask you one thing?"

"Sure," said Harold, folding his napkin and preparing to leave.

"Why couldn't you have said that a half hour ago? I've been going crazy."

"That's just not the way we do things in publishing. No business until the last course."

"Next time I'll know," I said, downing my drink.

I reported my success to Rudi. He was pleased, but not particularly surprised.

"Just make it a good book," he said.

"'I'll try."

"Do more than try!"

"You act as if it were costing you."

"It is costing me, John. Harold and I made a deal. When he moved into the house, it was on condition that he gives you a contract."

"Are you kidding?"

"No, I'm not kidding. He's a wonderful man, very brilliant. But he certainly can be a difficult tenant."

"I don't quite get it," I said. "Why did you do it?"

"I knew that he wanted to move in. It was the best way to get you the contract. Otherwise, he wouldn't have bothered with you."

"I'm amazed!" I said.

"Are you? Well, don't be. Just write a good book so I don't regret doing it."

"I can't believe that you would do such a thing for me."

"What's so surprising about it, John? Every time I teach, I am giving my life's blood. This is a much more external thing; I want you to have a chance to develop your abilities."

"I'm grateful," I said, "even though I'm not crazy to write the book."

"Just drum up some enthusiasm and get on with it," Rudi said ending the discussion.

That was the first of ten books I was to write in the next decade. [1]

---

[1] See the last chapter "Other Books by John Mann"

Chapter Ten

JOURNEYS TO THE EAST

Rudi made two to three trips to the East each year for spiritual and practical purposes. Their practical aspect was a tireless treasure hunt throughout the Orient. His spiritual quest took him to India.

Rudi never left until he felt thoroughly prepared. Six weeks before the trip he began to accelerate the intensity of his inner effort. He worked late into the night strengthening the force within him, breaking down whatever resistances existed, raising himself to a pitch of inner preparation as an athlete might train for an Olympic event.

A few days before a trip I said to him, "You look like a wrestler about to go into the ring."

"That is exactly what I am," he said, "a spiritual wrestler, struggling with powers that try to stop me."

"I would hate to be in your way," I said.

"There is nothing I wouldn't do when it comes to my spiritual growth. That is the source of my strength. Everything else comes with time. But without that resolve there is no cement to hold it all together.

"Nothing has ever happened for me quickly. You look at me and think I am completely beyond your own experience. But I have been working inwardly since the age of six.

"When I was young I was completely innocent. I was open to everyone unless they tried to attack me. I lived in a very tough neighborhood in Brooklyn. I remember one day a gang cornered me on the steps of my house. They were going to beat me up. I didn't know what to do. Suddenly I had an inspiration. I pulled down my pants and peed on them. They were utterly flabbergasted. By the time they recovered I was gone. Another time, when one of my brothers was tormenting me, I decided to refuse to accept it. He was much bigger than I was and five years older, but that didn't stop me. In the middle of the night I took a baseball bat and hit him with it. When he woke up screaming I told him, 'if you don't stop picking on me, the next time

I will kill you.' There was no more trouble after that. I just wouldn't allow for the possibility inside myself, so it couldn't occur.

"But most of the time I loved everyone and was perfectly happy just to be alive, even though we were very poor.

"One day I was playing in the park when two strange figures came out of a tree and approached me. I was too naive to be afraid when they told me that they represented the Heads of the Yellow and Red Hat sects of Tibetan Buddhism, and that they were going to place within me all of their energy and spiritual understanding. I accepted it like an exotic Christmas present. Some large jars appeared next to them and they put them into me in a space between my belly button and my bowels. They said that when I reached the age of thirty-one the jars would begin to open and gradually reveal their contents through my own inner efforts, starting a process of assimilation that would continue for the rest of my life. That was the beginning of my spiritual work.

Rudi (then Albert) growing up in Brooklyn

"The first time I went to India, many people referred to my Tibetan aspect. One psychic said that he saw strange books and broken pieces of pottery inside me.

"When I was eleven years old, I began to have a recurring dream. It must have happened almost a hundred times. In the dream I was quite old, maybe seventy or eighty, but I looked wonderful. I was standing on a great box about four stories high, dressed in a white gown. I raised my arms to the sky and noticed I was surrounded by thousands of people with beautiful faces. I took a great breath and slowly began to rise into the air. When I got about a thousand feet up, great flames began to spurt from my lower body. I sped upwards faster and faster until suddenly I exploded into dust which spread out across the sky and became a rainbow. It was this vision that enabled me to survive the predictions of my death at thirty-one made by the Gurdjieff people.

"But the experience that had the greatest effect on me occurred when I was eleven and a half. During that period my body and spirit began to separate, I would wake up in the middle of the night and be able to look down at myself asleep in bed. I assumed it happened to everyone.

"Then one day I felt very strange. I had a headache and felt a little nauseous. This kind of discomfort was often a symptom of a coming spiritual experience. My chemistry was preparing itself. That night I awoke to find myself detached from my body, as usual, but when I looked down to see my sleeping self, there was nothing there. I wasn't afraid because I didn't know how strange that was. I just tried to relate to my physical self even though I couldn't see it. At that point I entered another dimension. I saw vast stone doors that were incredibly magnificent. I sensed, rather than saw, a great mountain disappearing in the clouds. And then I realized that it was not a mountain, but a foot and part of a leg.

"A great booming voice, which I instinctively felt belonged to God, began to lecture me. It said,

> ***Everyone who has ever grown spiritually and begun to teach stopped growing. They sold out because they thought they were there to serve the world and not me. They got caught up by their position and their external duties. Promise me that no matter what happens, you will never stop working!***

"I promised innocently, like the small child I was. I did not understand what was being asked until many years later.

"After I had committed myself, the voice continued,

> ***You will have everything you want except that you can never have a permanent relation with another human being. By staying free, you can serve others and serve me. If you do this you will have everything, but you will not be attached to it. Every experience will become nourishment for your own growth.***

"And that is what happened. As I have grown, the fiery stream inside me that consumes everything it touches has grown too."

"It is a great gift," I said.

"It is a great something," said Rudi. "It drove me crazy for years. There is nothing as nice as a pure fountain forever flowing, but nothing as repulsive as a polluted one. For years I was a polluted fountain. It's hard for you to believe because you didn't know me then. But it was true. I had no choice but to destroy the flow or work to purify it.

"The energy drove me wild. Sometimes I had to walk the streets all night just to wear myself out. When I wasn't walking the streets I used to go to all-night parties. I knew lots of theater people. They found me very entertaining. But I was going crazy inside.

"For a time before you met me I was living with a friend who worked with me in the antique business. One night I was awakened by the sound of my own voice screaming. I could not remember anything about my dream, but I was frightened by my state. My friend had naturally been woken up also. I asked him, 'Has this happened before?'

"'It has happened,' he said, 'about once a week for the last six months.'

"That was one of the most shocking statements I had ever heard.

"After that it got much worse. I began to have terrible headaches and started to hemorrhage from my nose and ears.

"During that period I briefly lived with a murderer."

"Are you serious?" I asked.

"He had killed a man and was perfectly capable of killing another. But I wasn't worried and didn't care. The energy took care of everything. The worst he could do was put me out of my misery, and I always knew that I wasn't meant to have such an easy way out.

"The energy made me work, and the work dug up more garbage which had to be dumped. I fell behind in the garbage removal. I was choking on the results of my own efforts and didn't know it. The more congested my system became the harder I worked, and the more garbage I produced.

"At the time I had an image of a great train that would pull inside me every morning. At night it would pull away carrying nothing but garbage in every car. This went on day after day for years.

"I might have died in the end. But I met the Shankaracharya and he saved my life.

"I always felt warm in his presence. But one day as I walked through the doorway to his room, I began to burn. It was extremely painful. I couldn't understand what was happening. I had to force myself through the doorway inch by inch. The only thing that made me do it was my faith in him. I couldn't believe that anything associated with his presence could really hurt me. When I was finally in the room, my whole body caught fire. That is the only way I can describe it. This process went on for two years and destroyed all the garbage. You were lucky you didn't know me then."

"I doubt it," I said.

"I wouldn't have been of much help to you. I was like a crazed idiot dancing on the flames. Anyway, the best proof is that even though we were both in the Gurdjieff work at the time, we never met."

I couldn't say anything to that.

※ ※ ※

Rudi left on his trips as quietly as possible. One or two people would drive him to the airport and would pick him up when he returned. He never wanted a fuss. He was concentrating on the inner level he had attained and wanted to stabilize it. I rarely saw him on the day of his departure. But once when I did, he looked like a totally different person: vast and invincible.

Invariably, before he left it would rain. It always rained at significant times in his life. Only once in all his trips did the sun refuse to be dimmed. Rudi recalled it on his return.

"I was riding out to the plane with Edith and David. We were talking about trivial things. But inwardly I felt some concern. There had been no rain. Was that a bad sign? Should the trip be postponed? I didn't think so. I am not superstitious, but I certainly watch for signs. I tried to surrender the whole thing, but it remained in the back of my mind. As we neared the airport, I made a casual remark to Edith.

"'It seems like this is a first,' I said.

"'Yes,' she said. 'No rain!'

"And at that moment we drove through a great puddle which completely spattered the windshield. David had to use the wipers. We all laughed. I felt better. But since it hadn't rained in days, where did the puddle come from?"

Rudi always went to the Far East during the winter if he could possibly arrange it. I used to kid him about getting away to the tropics as the snow fell in New York. As usual, he turned the situation around on me.

"I double my growing season," he explained. "The natural cycle is to die in the winter and be reborn in the spring. By going to the tropics in the winter I have two seasons for rebirth.

Rudi usually returned from his trips exhausted. But he was also burning inside with the impressions and energies he had absorbed in the Far East. I always tried to see him as soon as possible, to get the full impact of his experience.

On his first trip to India, he had known no one. Every contact was yet to be established. He went with money for the ticket and a small additional amount for buying art. From that meager and lonely beginning, he had assembled, disbanded and reassembled a network of dealers, collectors, and shippers who worked the year around to prepare for his coming. I heard about these people only indirectly. They remained exotic strangers made familiar only through Rudi's colorful recollections of his latest dealings with them. I never met them unless they came to America.

The man who could have most easily made the trip, Beebee, the multimillionaire who had introduced Rudi to Nityananda, came only once. We visited him in his room at the Waldorf Astoria. When we entered he was watching cartoons on television. While we were there, he continued watching. As we left he was still absorbed. That is my memory of the fabulously wealthy Indian aristocrat. I think he was laughing at Donald Duck as we closed the door.

✶ ✶ ✶

Everything that happened to Rudi while he was away came to me in bits and pieces through his own words. Most of it was told shortly after his return as we sat in the store or stood on the sidewalk, but additional nuggets would surface at unexpected moments. Sometimes the pattern would only emerge much later.

For example, a year after Nityananda's death Rudi took Swami Muktananda as his teacher. It seemed a natural transition, though the rationale was not entirely clear. It was only during the following decade that the reasons for this decision slowly became evident.

Rudi's relations to Muktananda were always mixed, but his approach was very practical.

"Swami Muktananda is always after me to learn Hindi because he doesn't know English. But I put him off. It would only be a distraction for me to know everything he says. Let other people get absorbed in his words. I go for the essence of the man.

"But otherwise, he can demand whatever he wants," Rudi said. "There is nothing I can do about it but to give what he wants or leave. What does it matter? If he expects devotion, I have to provide it."

"How do you create a feeling you don't have without his sensing it?" I asked.

"There is only one possible way," said Rudi. "It has to be real. I work on myself until I get into a condition that makes it real before I enter his ashram. If I don't feel it, I wait. If you had to do the same thing before stepping through the door of this store I wouldn't see much of you. Maybe I should start a new policy."

I said nothing, trusting that he was kidding. Rudi smiled and went on.

"I work myself into a condition where I feel he is the key to everything I want, the embodiment of God in human form, my spiritual father. It is more of a test than anything else. Swami Muktananda probably doesn't really care what anyone thinks of him.

"Then there is the other side of it. Each time I go to the East I get slaughtered. In a way, it is one of the reasons I go. It helps me grow stronger. But I am human. Before I go I try to figure out how to protect myself. Nothing I ever think of works for more than a day. It's childish on my part to try to outwit him. In any case, that is the way he teaches. He creates difficult and painful situations that I have to transcend."

"It sounds more like a military school than an ashram," I said.

"It's all a question of what you want," said Rudi. "For most people who go there, it is a place to follow their dreams. They simply exist in the environment. They never open themselves to a depth where the energy of Swami Muktananda, or whoever the guru may be, can affect them profoundly. They go to be part of the atmosphere, and have the illusion that they are pursuing a spiritual life. Most gurus don't care. A person can sit around half a lifetime and no one will say anything to them, as long as they do the required work and don't cause trouble. They don't have to grow.

"Personally, I think that whole attitude stinks. It encourages fantasy and weakens the atmosphere. But in India they aren't interested in creating the best conditions. They are much more creative about placing obstacles in your way than in removing them. That is how they teach. You must wait and wait, overcome and overcome. If you survive the treatment you grow very strong. For the most part people settle for some comfortable level and only struggle to remain there.

"I will never forget the time I visited a very famous woman saint. I had been waiting for about an hour for her appearance. Finally the door opened and she entered. At the same moment, the musicians who had been idly tuning up began to perform. Shortly thereafter temple dancers began a sacred dance. It was enchanting until it struck me that everyone was listening to the music and watching the dance. No one was paying any attention to the saint. It had obviously been planned that way. Once I understood the situation I completely ignored the show and concentrated on her, opening to receive the inner energy of her being. But I doubt if anyone else in the room was even aware of her presence. Maybe they would get around to it when the music stopped. I wondered about that.

"When the music did stop she quietly arose and excused herself. The opportunity to receive her energy had passed. They had probably all missed it with only a momentary sense of regret.

"I am used to being tested in this way, but I would never do it to any of you. It isn't necessary. Life provides enough tests. The teacher doesn't have to create new ones. But I never had any choice in my own studies in the East. I am not complaining. It forced me to cultivate various psychic abilities that I might have otherwise ignored. But I still hate it.

"They never really teach you anything in India. You almost have to steal it. Last week in class I gave a new kind of breathing to increase the flow of Kundalini in the spine. I'll tell you how I got that. I was sitting with Swami Muktananda, and I noticed that he made a strange snorting sound. No one else noticed it. If they had, they might have thought he had a cold. My assumption was that he does nothing by accident. He didn't have a cold. There must have been a conscious reason for that noise, so I imitated it. I had no idea what to expect. I tried it a few times as quietly as I could and found out what it could do. I didn't say anything. I didn't even ask him about it. He used it for himself, but because I was awake I reached out and made it part of my own work. How many of you would be capable of such a simple thing? How many of the people who surround him would do it unless he specifically told them what to do?

"Of course, it's different when you come halfway around the earth. I would not accept the possibility of returning empty-handed. That's

Before The Sun

Rudi in India, c. 1968

my underlying attitude. It is part of the inner conditioning that I go through. My preparation causes him to prepare also. He doesn't admit it in words, but I can feel it happening at a distance.

"Most saints that I know have worked tremendously hard. By the time that I meet them, they have stabilized a level that is acceptable to them and idealized by their students. They stay there unless forced to change, or unless they are willing to force themselves. The major change that usually occurs is an expansion of their work on the physical level. Their time becomes more in demand. This can prove useful if the teacher makes a greater effort so there is more of his being to go around, or it may simply dilute what is available.

"Occasionally however, the teacher attracts a great student. When this happens, it may force them both to work beyond themselves. This may be done in a partly competitive spirit, or more ideally as an expression of their mutual devotion to God. But the dynamics of the situation contain tremendous potential for growth if the teacher accepts the challenge and the student refuses to be limited. Often in such situations the teacher consciously or unconsciously seeks to weaken the student so that he is easier to control. If that doesn't work, they may come into open conflict and the student is forced to leave. Either way it is a terrible waste.

"You have to respect the essential quality of a teacher if you are going to open to him. Otherwise it is a foolhardy act. Most people find it so difficult to open to anything that they feel it is an achievement when it happens. Unfortunately, we open most easily to people and situations that are bad for us. You cannot trust your instincts at such a time. I don't trust mine. When I go to a party and look around the room, I am inevitably attracted to someone who, sooner or later (usually sooner), proves himself to be the worst possible person for me to know. Either he brings out a quality in me that I am struggling to overcome, or he offers nothing but the illusion of enchantment.

"If that is what happens to me, and I am a fairly shrewd judge of character, what chance do other people have? We are usually drawn by death in human form. It is the most powerful attraction that exists for most people. If you offer life, almost no one will take it, once they realize that the responsibility to preserve it goes along with the gift. You don't have to take care of death. It takes care of you.

"When I am with Swami Muktananda it is a struggle between two spiritual heavyweights. It is a battle of energies. I assume that what he is doing is for my own good. I don't know what he assumes. It doesn't matter because the results are good for me. Through this process I have gradually come to realize that he is a great magician."

"What do you mean?" I asked, slightly horrified.

"He uses his will to change the world. He's an illusionist."

"Is that what you want?"

Swami Muktananda in the Big Indian meditation hall

"No. It's the last thing I want," said Rudi. "But the great spiritual beings are gone in India. There was a final generation of giant God-men. They all died within a few years of each other. Bhagavan Nityananda was one of them. And who is left to take their place? Either kind, devoted swamis who lack the power and grandeur of the men who taught them, or great magicians. A nice little old man can't do much for me. A great magician can make me strong. I have to grow to contend with him. He has to keep growing to be ready for me. We both need each other.

"And then Muktananda is the partial inheritor of Nityananda's spiritual force. His ashram is in the town Nityananda created. There is a psychic connection between them which I can experience and use, and also have my own contact with Nityananda.

"In most ashrams in the East, the guru doesn't pass on his power and position until death intervenes. As he leaves the earth, the energy with which he has worked is freed to be used by others. One may have to wait half a lifetime for this opportunity to occur. Then, and only then, the man he has designated, or the man who arises to fill the vacuum left by his passing, can receive the inner mantle of the teacher.

"I don't believe in doing it that way. There is no reason that death has to be the source of the gift. I intend to pass on my own capacities during my lifetime. I am glad to do it, and in this way free myself to go on to other levels of development.

"The major teachers I have known died shortly after I met them. It was wonderful for me. It gave me a great opportunity for absorbing what was released at their death. The initial contact was enough to create the possibility. It happened with the Shankaracharya.

"The three months I spent with him were enough. On my next trip to India I was within fifty miles of Puri, but I didn't visit him. It didn't seem necessary. Later I heard that he had died. But I didn't feel bad. The inner contact was still there. He is a living force to me. The same thing is happening in relation to Nityananda.

"But you must be able to assimilate their inner content when it is available. Then their essential quality is inside you, and can continue to attract the energy they leave behind. That sounds rather obvious, but you can't assume that people will understand it.

"When I stopped at the Divine Light Mission at Rishikish on my last trip, they took me to the room where the late Swami Shivananda used to live. He was one of the great saints of Nityananda's generation. The whole ashram was recovering from his death six months before. The whole place looked deserted and run down. It was depressing until I walked into his room. He was still there! His force was shining and ringing. Nobody seemed to notice it. I asked to stay in the room for a few minutes. They left me alone, and I worked deeply to absorb this marvelous energy. I emerged in ten minutes filled with radiance and overflowing with joy. They were still sad. It was ridiculous! The essence of their teacher was with them, but they could not open to accept the possibility. For them he was dead. For me he is alive!"

"Is it going to stay that way?" I asked.

"Who can say? I expect that in time his presence will fade. Why should he stay there with the vastness of the universe to inhabit? No one of a higher order will stay connected with a particular location for long if their presence is not utilized.

"It's a different story with Swami Nityananda. Partly through Swami Muktananda's presence on the scene, a beautiful marble temple is being built to house Nityananda's remains. It is becoming a spiritual place of pilgrimage. As long as seekers and holy men go there with an open heart looking for nourishment, there is no reason that the energy should not remain and even grow stronger. But there is nothing inevitable about it. The only thing one can assume about higher energy is that it will disappear quickly unless it is consciously appreciated.

One reason it takes so long to grow inwardly is that no matter what energy level you contact, it won't do any good unless you can absorb it deeply before it evaporates. It is like rain in the desert — wonderful, unexpected, rare, and almost before you know it, gone. A little into the earth, most of it back to the sky. It is almost totally useless except for highly specialized organisms such as cacti, which absorb and hold all of it that they can.

"The ordinary person is full of leaks. Every tension is a leak. Every strongly held belief is a leak. Every relation into which we pour energy is a leak. What makes the situation more difficult is that the first thing we lose through these leaks is the higher energy, because it is the most volatile. We are not used to working with anything so refined. It is almost inevitable that the first few times, perhaps the first hundred times, that we make the necessary effort to accumulate a little of this rare energy within us, we lose it almost immediately. It is only based on the frustration and futility of such an experience that we begin to see the need for plugging our leaks and allowing nothing to rob us of this rare element which can only be gathered consciously from a source that has it to give.

"Timing is crucial. When you have received a gift of inner spiritual force, you must remain open and quiet for about half an hour to allow it to penetrate more deeply into your system. Anything that disturbs you will impede or abort the process. It is vital to take this extra time or all your efforts, whatever they may have been, will be partially or totally in vain.

"Growth is gradual and basically natural. The life a person has attracted around him when he starts to work is the best possible life for him. It contains all the elements which represent him in an external form. If he casts it away, how will he ever understand why he attracted it in the first place? The way to change is to absorb what surrounds you, digest it, and grow beyond it. Then some of it will naturally and inevitably fall away, like the lower leaves of a plant. Everything is connected. You cannot change one part without producing unintended consequences.

"That is the problem with breathing exercises in Pranayama Yoga. Breathing is very important. You cannot absorb *prana* from the air without the right kind of breathing. But at the same time many of those exercises place an arbitrary scheme on the normal pattern of breath. It doesn't make too much difference unless one takes these methods seriously. But if they are done with sufficient intensity, they begin to take over and the body loses its understanding of how to breathe. This in turn sets off reactions in the nervous system that were unintended. and may be harmful. This doesn't occur from normal breathing itself or a relatively gentle conscious extension of its basic pattern.

"Your body understands the need for breath. But instinctively it absorbs only a small part of the energy in the air. We can increase the amount through our own conscious desire. We have to breathe from a place within us that wants to be nourished. And that is much simpler than it sounds. If you walk along the seashore or in a pine forest, what is the natural thing to do? You take a slow, deep breath and savor the odors of nature as you absorb them. That is the beginning of conscious breathing. Then if you take in something you value and enjoy, such as fine wine, what is the next natural thing to do? You hold it on your pallet and let the sensation spread through you. In the same way, after you have breathed in slowly and with awareness, you hold your breath and allow the energy you have received to expand in your system.

"Finally in the last phase, when you breathe out, you can let go of all kinds of tensions — physical, emotional, and psychic. But if you slowly absorb energy when you breath in, allow it to go deeper while you hold it inside you. Consciously allow tensions to flow from you when you breath out. Each completed breath is a unit of work. And when the energy absorbed by this type of breathing is fed into the psychic digestive system, it vitalizes the whole transformation process.

"The problem with more arbitrary breathing exercises is that we have insufficient understanding of the inner functioning of the person using them, and consequently cannot anticipate all of the effects which they may produce.

"A teacher has his own experience to guide him, and he accumulates the experiences of his students who are passing the same way he has already traveled. But each individual is somewhat different. Inner growth is not like following a recipe. It is more of a treasure hunt, the clues to which are all buried in the present. Or rather, they lie in eternity and flash through the present when we least expect them. They are usually lost as fast as they appear because the person doesn't see them.

"Time is not an iron band or a straight line going from the past into the future. It is elastic and can disappear altogether as one's consciousness varies.

"You have been sitting in the store with me all day. Does it seem long or short to you?"

"Sometimes very short," I said. "At other times like weeks. But right now it seems as if I have been here forever. I feel as if I were a deep-sea fish swimming to the surface of the ocean. When I break through into the sunlight, my whole perspective changes. All the earlier time seems confused and meaningless. It is only now that anything seems real."

"It is, John. The hardest thing to imagine is a level of consciousness that we have not attained. No matter how vivid our fantasy, the next level is always the one we cannot imagine. It is the same with most of the problems we have. The one solution we never think of, no matter how obvious, is the right one. We really can't resolve most of our problems because all our thoughts occur in a certain context which we take for granted.

"There are two directions we can pursue in resolving any situation. We can attempt to think it through, or we can try to go to a place where the powers of understanding are greater. That is why I have to go halfway around the earth to pursue my own development. In India these powers still exist, though they are dying out. And the irony of the situation is that when one contacts them, it's on a different dimension. They aren't on the earth at all."

Before The Sun

PHOTOS: THE EARLY YEARS

Brother David and Albert Rudolph, age 1

Photos: The Early Years

Albert and sister-in-law, 1955

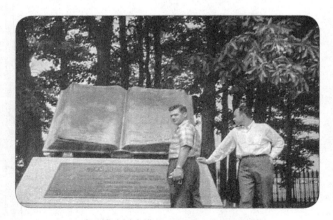

David Rudolph & Albert visiting Gettysburg, 1957

Before The Sun

Thanksgiving with family

Photos: The Early Years

Albert, making a toast at David's wedding

David's marriage vows

Chapter Eleven

THE SUMMER PLACE

As the scope of his work grew, Rudi decided to buy a house in the country. He started to explore the areas surrounding New York, but nothing materialized.

Then one day he returned from his search full of enthusiasm.

"I saw this marvelous place in a pine forest, completely isolated. It was built by a modern sculptor who just died. The whole ground floor is one great room built on solid rock. I think it was an old stone quarry. The cement walls were poured right on the stone."

"Where is it located?" I asked.

"Near Woodstock. This would be a perfect place for me to also have a country store."

"Why do they want to sell it?"

"His widow doesn't want to live there all alone."

"How large is it?"

"The main house is big and there is another house and out-buildings. There is plenty of room. We'll all go out to see it pretty soon."

A few weeks later I set out for the house, guided only by a vague set of directions that Rudi had provided.

The first part was easy enough. *Go to Woodstock.* From there on it became increasingly obscure. *Turn left at a deserted gas station; follow the road until it shifts from asphalt to dirt; look on the right for a track going through an open field into the forest.* It was the latter that was particularly puzzling. There are a lot of tracks going through open fields when you start to look for them.

I saw one that appealed to me because it didn't look too treacherous. I made my way slowly over the bumpy field and into the woods where the semblance of a road was restored. I drove for another half-mile with growing insecurity until I saw several familiar cars parked in a small clearing. I had made it! So had everyone else, which was amazing, given the ambiguity of the directions.

Rudi was eagerly waiting to take us on a guided tour of the forest and the house. The woods were great. The house was rather crude for my taste, but no one was asking what I thought, so I relaxed.

It was late spring. The air was warm and the country blooming. Rudi was ready to move in immediately. But there were, as always, a number of legal issues to resolve. The widow, Sara, took a deposit and agreed to let Rudi have occupancy in three weeks whether or not the sale was completed by then. That was unusual but Rudi assured her that anything we did over the summer would only improve the value of the place, which was true. Most owners would not have wanted the responsibility of so many people who were not invited guests coming and going. But Sara was lonely and appreciated the company.

As with every move that Rudi made the result was always the same— WORK! Every weekend we came up and painted, cleaned, repaired, and removed accumulated junk. We paused only for classes.

Though it wasn't immediately obvious the productivity of our efforts greatly depended on Rudi's presence. He didn't do too much of the work himself, but supervised the entire process and kept it moving.

* * *

One day, he went away for four hours. I watched with helpless fascination as things began to decay. People who had been working quietly began to drift off. Others who usually had their own ideas about what to do, which they kept to themselves in Rudi's presence, began ordering other people around. Little was accomplished. Most of that was sloppy and incorrect. The wall that was supposed to be orange was painted blue. Machinery that should have been protected by a drop cloth got spattered with paint.

Rudi returned, took stock of the situation, and in ten minutes had everything straightened out. But I never forgot the implication of what I had watched. Remove Rudi from the situation and decay set in almost immediately. He understood what he was dealing with, and knew how to keep otherwise stupid or difficult people moving along the right lines.

A few days later during a pause in the work Rudi gestured with his hand for me to join him. He was sitting on a partially decayed log. At first he was quiet.

"I could hardly believe what was happening while you were

gone the other day," I said, to fill the silence. "Everything began to disintegrate."

"I know," said Rudi. "But no one else noticed the difference."

"How could they not see it?" I said.

"Just ask them. You'll find out they thought it was fine. The fact that everything we are trying to build was being undone escaped them. You saw it because you know something about working from the years you spent in the Gurdjieff system. But you were probably happy that I was away, too."

"Sure," I said. "It was much more relaxing."

"At least you're honest. I don't enjoy having to yell at people and push them in a direction that's good for them. It isn't my nature. If it were up to me, I would be lying on the beach at Fire Island. I need a place in the country like a hole in the head."

"Why are we here then?" I asked,

"Because," said Rudi, "we are interested in growing, not vegetating. You can't just do what you want. Growth always occurs against resistance. The seed breaks out of its husk. It would rather stay a seed.

"It's just as hard for me as it is for you to take a step and experience the inner changes it produces. It's harder for me because I am much more aware of my condition. You are still partially anesthetized. But don't worry, I can feel for you and keep you moving in the right direction. But who is going to do that for me? I have to be sensitive to myself or I'm in trouble,

"I don't mean to sound down on you, John. Actually everyone else is worse. Edith is my friend, but she really has no burning desire to change her life. She is fascinated by my potential, but that is not the same thing. And even she, for no apparent reason, sometimes slaps me on the head just when I am in a very delicate condition. It really drives me crazy. She mumbles something about killing an insect, but that doesn't justify the action. I know why she does it. She is threatened by my growth. It is her way of interfering with my development. But understanding the situation doesn't make it any easier for me to take. Roy has a wonderful potential for spiritual development, but I have no illusions. He is just as likely to drop the whole thing in the pursuit of his career. There is really no one to whom I can give in depth because no one wants it enough to make the effort. If I could just cast it away like a farmer scatters seeds, I would. But it isn't possible. Unless the other person has worked very hard, and for a certain time, there is no place in him for it to go. The ground isn't prepared. And even if it were, the person wouldn't have the discipline and responsibility to care for the seedlings when they sprout. They would die, and it would all be for nothing."

"Why are you telling me all this?" I asked.

"Because, John, with all your inner deadness you are the only one who might have a chance to receive some of what I have to give."

I was silent, trying to absorb what he had said. It was flattering, but also sobering. The amount of work that might be required gave me pause. I was already working hard enough as far as I was concerned.

I didn't know if I was supposed to respond. I didn't know how I wanted to respond. Was Rudi just expressing a mood of discouragement with his students, or was something deeper surfacing at an unexpected moment, an opportunity which I must grasp or lose for a long time to come.

"Do you want me to say something?" I asked.

"If you have something to say," said Rudi, looking off into the distance.

"I am persistent," I said, "but that is not enough."

"It isn't really anything," said Rudi. "It just gives you a certain opportunity,"

He stirred restlessly. I felt compelled to say more. "Are you talking because of a passing mood or not?"

"What do you think?" he asked.

"I think you're not."

"You're right. Just because I seem very involved with certain people doesn't mean I lack objectivity when I need it. I see them for what they are."

"I know, I know," I said. "It's just hard for me to accept the possibility that I might be the only one to whom you could give more."

"I'm not flattering you. Who else is there? You show me. It is really up to you, John. If you can work harder — much, much harder — then I can fulfill my promise. If not, there is nothing to say."

We parted in silence. I went back to painting. Rudi walked off into the woods. I do not look back on that day with pride. I know that Rudi spoke the truth. I know that I did not take advantage of the offer which he made. Perhaps I was incapable of making the effort at the time. There are many explanations, and some of them are true. But there is no way to eliminate the ache of lost opportunity.

※ ※ ※

As the summer wore on, Rudi complained of sleeping difficulties. He felt drained instead of refreshed after a night's rest. He was more puzzled than alarmed. Finally, he decided to investigate.

A few days later, looking tired but content, Rudi said to me, "I found out what was happening. I had to stay up most of the night to do it, but now I know."

"What was it?" I asked.

"It's Sara. She's been absorbing my energy while I was sleeping. Probably she doesn't even know what she's doing, but the effect is the same. Something in her is very hungry. And this hidden aspect is awake at night and feeds on my force."

"But why doesn't she just join the work?" I asked.

"Maybe she will, but this is mostly an unconscious thing in her. Her personality does not want to work. But asleep I am like a defenseless T-bone steak. How can she resist?"

"Are you going to talk to her?"

"No. Now that I understand I can defend myself, so there is no need to tell her."

After that Rudi began to sleep through the nights undisturbed. I never knew precisely what he did to protect himself, but it obviously worked.

✹ ✹ ✹

Each passing weekend we poured in time, materials, and energy. The house was cleaned up, painted, and minor repairs were made. There was little opportunity for relaxation beyond an occasional Saturday night movie or swimming in a nearby river once or twice. Water was a scarce commodity in the Catskills, and the river shrank as the summer progressed.

On the few times we went swimming the cold water covered only about half our bodies. Rudi relaxed, but that only seemed to increase the intensity of the energy in him. We splashed and laughed, but it was hard to be casual next to an atomic pile.

As the season drew to a close we went up to Woodstock for a final weekend. The work we had done was immediately obvious — cleared land, cut brush and painted houses. It was satisfying to view the results of our efforts, particularly when there was no immediate prospect for having to do more. I took one last walk in the pine woods. Rudi was off somewhere talking with Sara. Evidently there were still a few legal matters to be settled.

The woods were always my favorite part of the property. They were completely private, whispering, and primeval. I said goodbye to them quietly, and then returned to look for the others.

We departed as we had come three months before, through the

Rudi soaking in a Catskill Mountain stream

woods, across the bumpy field and onto the main road. The summer disappeared behind us in our wake.

※ ※ ※

Three weeks later when I entered the store Rudi said with a sigh, "It's hard to believe, but it didn't go through."
"What didn't go through?"
"The house in Woodstock. The title was defective. I can't get title insurance."
"Are you going to buy it anyway?" I asked.

"No!"
"But all that work!"
"So what!"
"If it doesn't bother you, it doesn't bother me," I said.
"It served its purpose," said Rudi. "I would have been happy to have the house. I am happy not to have it. Maybe next year I can go to Fire Island and lie on the beach."
"Are you going to look for another country place soon?" I asked.
"Not just yet. There really is no need. That is one of the things the summer taught me."
Rudi did not look again for seven years.

Chapter Twelve

A CHINESE BANQUET IN THE SLUMS

I don't remember the first time I went to Chinatown with Rudi, but it was always an event. Sometimes it was planned in advance, but usually it was a party. It grew as the day progressed from a casual impulse on Rudi's part to include a number of people who happened to appear during the day, and who were free for dinner. By 8:30 we descended on his latest favorite Chinese restaurant which usually specialized in good food and simple decor.

When we walked through the door the owner would come running, crying out "Mr. Rudi, Mr. Rudi!" in happy but broken English. As soon as we were seated they entered into a furious conversation about the dinner order. We never were sure what was coming until it arrived. But we sat, often crushed together, drinking tea and growing ravenous. It was festive and intense, but never entirely casual. At any moment the tide could turn as Rudi skewered someone with a few words such as, "You're making yourself crazy with all that tension in your head!"

When the food came it was a torrent of delight. The dishes tumbled over one another and the food disappeared at an astonishing rate. The main conversation came down to one sentence, "The food is great!" Rudi ordered more. We consumed everything in front of us in an orgy of flavors.

The main impression one had at the time was the deliciousness of the food and the relaxed comradeship of the people. But in retrospect it was the hidden intensity of energy exuding from Rudi that charged everything it touched with enthusiasm and love, and made the moment come alive. He almost always paid on these occasions. It was his pleasure. Occasionally, I returned to these restaurants without him. It was never the same. The waiters were bored. The food was indifferent. It tasted like yesterday's leftovers.

But all of these experiences, wonderful as they were, paled in

A Chinese Banquet In The Slums

comparison to the incredible evening when I attended Irving's Chinese banquet in the slums.

Sitting in the store, I eventually met everyone there was to meet. This included Irving, the crazy electrician, whose principal devotion was to painting and cooking. His electrical work was excellent, but eccentric. He required two qualities in his customers— infinite patience and absolute acceptance of anything he did. If either of these principles were violated he would pack up his tools and leave without warning. The wiring would remain as it was for an indefinite period until he decided that the offending customer had learned his lesson. Even Rudi, who went out of his way to be friendly and tactful, was subjected to the same treatment.

One day when the electrical work was done, Irving offered to make Rudi a sign for the store. Rudi agreed. Irving built himself a scaffold and proceeded to write large Japanese letters across the front of the store above the window. He claimed that it said, "Rudi Oriental Arts", but Rudi wasn't so sure. It might have said anything, including, "Irving G., expert electrical work". But Rudi figured that not too many of his customers could read Japanese, so it didn't really matter. In any case the sign certainly attracted attention, especially at night, when it was lit up with spotlights that Irving had insisted on installing.

Finally, one great day, Rudi said to me, "How would you like to go to Irving's for dinner? He's an incredible Chinese cook."

"I'd love to come," I said, never one to pass up a good meal.

"Okay. It'll be this Saturday."

"Should I bring anything?"

"Just your appetite. And remember to keep your mouth shut. If you must say something, just tell him the food is wonderful, which will be the truth. Otherwise, silence."

"That'll be easy for me," I said.

On Saturday a small, select group descended on Irving's slum apartment in lower Manhattan. From the outside it was completely nondescript, but once through the front door the house was filled with delicious and exotic odors.

"He's been cooking all day," his wife said. "Don't interrupt him!"

Rudi called through the doorway of the kitchen.

"Hi, Irving. We're here."

"Don't interrupt me," Irving yelled. "I'm in the final stages. It'll be ready in an hour. You all like Kirsch, don't you?" He didn't wait for a reply, but submerged himself in his cooking.

Before The Sun

Rudi's Fourth Ave store

An hour passed slowly. We sat and talked. We looked at some of Irving's paintings that were hanging on the walls.

"Come over here, John," Rudi said. "This is a remarkable work of art."

It was a small painting of an airplane in a silver and gold sky. I had never seen anything that gave the shimmering airy effect of space in quite that way. The airplane was suspended in another reality.

"He spent nine months painting this little picture," Rudi said. "That's why he does electrical work. There are very few modern artists who would devote that much time to anything. It doesn't pay. But this was worth the investment. It is a great picture."

Irving appeared in the doorway to announce, "Five minutes!"

His wife proudly said, "Rudi was just saying he thinks your picture is marvelous."

"I like it too," said Irving. "Do you want to buy it?"

"How much?" said Rudi.

"How about $2,500?"

"I'll think about it seriously," said Rudi, not wanting the meal to disappear before our eyes.

"In that case," said Irving, "prepare yourselves. The first course will be right in."

We sat down expectantly.

"I have eaten Chinese food in the finest restaurants all over the world," said Rudi, "but I have never had anything as good as Irving's. He is a master Chinese chef."

Irving appeared on cue, carrying two dishes. We were all dizzy with starvation, and high on the spicy odors that had settled permanently in his apartment.

After my first taste I felt as though I had never eaten before. All the ingredients had been carefully selected from the endless little markets of the lower East Side. The most familiar food took on an unknown, unsuspected taste as it passed through the alchemy of Irving's kitchen. I had no difficulty keeping my mouth shut. I was too busy chewing.

Irving continued to cook as we ate. An hour passed before he got to eat anything himself. But he didn't care. Cooking fulfilled his hunger.

After the first few dishes it became evident why Irving had asked whether we liked kirsch. It's a relatively tasteless, but extremely potent, form of alcohol. He had used it very liberally. The first thing I noticed was that I was getting numb. I attributed it to the unknown spices in the food, and continued on to greater delights. After a few minutes Rudi peered at me searchingly. "How do you feel?" he asked. I must have looked on the verge of a stroke.

"Strange. Very strange," I managed to get out.

"I forgot to tell you. Irving uses lots of alcohol in his cooking. If you feel paralyzed, don't worry. It's natural."

"I'm glad to hear it," I said. "Anyway, it's too good to stop. As long as someone can put me in a taxi."

Irving thought we were kidding. The alcohol had only a mild effect on him.

I was beginning to sink slowly into a semi-coma when Rudi said, "Wait until you taste dessert. Irving is famous for his desserts."

"Does it have kirsch in it?" I mumbled.

"No," said Irving, "it has liquor."

Anything that could reach me through my alcoholic haze had to be good. The dessert was ambrosia. That was the last thing I remember clearly.

※ ※ ※

A few days later Irving reappeared at the store to finish some wiring that he had abandoned three months before.

"I'm going to California next week," he announced.

"For how long?" asked Rudi?

"Permanently."

"Just like that?"

"I've been thinking about it for awhile. Do you want me to make you another sign before I go?"

"No, there's no room."

"We could paint it on the window."

"That's a great idea," said Rudi. When you get back from California we'll talk about it..."

Irving left the city on schedule. I never saw him again. Shortly after his departure the picture of the airplane in the sky appeared on Rudi's wall.

"Did you pay $2,500 for it?" I asked.

Rudi looked at me as if that was a stupid question. I had the feeling he hadn't paid anything. Or, perhaps he had paid the full price to make Irving's trip possible.

Chapter Thirteen

CLOSE RELATIONSHIPS

Though Rudi was once engaged in his earlier days, he had never married. In a nostalgic moment he recalled the situation.

"The girl was nice. The problem was her family. I was a simple idiot in those days, and didn't realize what they were like until my mother got seriously ill. She was in the hospital for three weeks. During all that time not one member of the girl's family came to visit her. They didn't even send flowers. Slowly I got the picture. They just didn't care. I still loved the girl, or thought I did, but if her family was that unconcerned about my mother they certainly wouldn't care about me. I wanted nothing to do with them. I'm not sure the girl ever really understood why I broke the engagement. She didn't see the connection."

"Do you think you'll ever get married?" I asked.

"No. It's too late. My students are my children. A teacher is primarily a parent. He helps to complete what the physical parents have failed to accomplish, to produce balanced individuals who have the possibility for spiritual development. Students come as semi-wild animals. They have to be housebroken before anything else is possible."

"But what does this have to do with your getting married?" I persisted.

"I am becoming complete in myself," said Rudi. "The male and the female inside me are producing a balanced growth. I certainly don't want any physical children."

"Why not? You seem to love children."

That was startlingly true. Most of the children in the neighborhood treated him as a beloved uncle. They insisted on dragging their parents into the store. Their parents might pretend that they were interested in buying some art, but it was obvious that the children were behind the visit. They would sit on Rudi's lap, search for candy that he had hidden, talk about school, or look at the Buddhas in the store. Rudi would often give them a little piece of Indian stone or

Middle Eastern metal to help them start collections of ancient objects. The parents were very grateful. The visit usually ended riotously with Rudi chasing the kids down the street, catching them, throwing them in the air, and then blowing on their bellies to their delighted screams.

"No matter how far I go," said Rudi, "I'll always drop what I am doing to play with a child. It may shock some people to see me do it. But I don't care. A child is ripe and free. I absorb something of their natural quality and drop off a great deal of the tension that is accumulating in me. It doesn't go into the child. He is too innocent to attract it."

"Why don't you want to have children of your own?" I repeated.

"When I am around any kid for longer than half an hour, he begins to drive me crazy," said Rudi. "But the basic reason that I don't want children is that they are a psychic tie to the level of the earth."

I thought about that for a minute and then asked,

"Why didn't you ever say that before?"

"What good would it have done? When we met you already had children."

"So now what do I do?"

"Just what you're doing, try to act like a father. You have to be concerned about your own children. They are part of your lifeline. If they get into serious difficulty or turn against you, it will cripple your own chance for spiritual growth.

"And it is the same in relation to your parents. A person cannot deny his roots without cutting himself off from his own development. It doesn't matter what you think or feel. You cannot abandon inner contact with your own heritage without paying a terrible price. I know you don't really believe it. That's why I have to watch you so carefully. If you could feel the emotional reality of what I am saying you would be much safer."

I couldn't say anything. Rudi wasn't looking for a response. What he was saying was probably true. My own basic sense of myself was that I was almost totally invisible, connected to people and situations only in a very tenuous manner.

"Your detachment from almost everything is the only reason I can work with you," he continued. "In other respects, you are almost impossible. You don't really care about anyone or anything, except perhaps me. And you don't feel that much, even for me. You are in limbo. Not as much as you used to be, but you're still there. Under ordinary circumstances, you would spend the rest of your life like

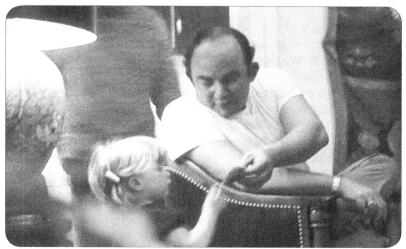

that. The truth is, John, you were never meant to have a life. But that same quality is your greatest blessing. You don't really care, so you can surrender and change without great resistance. You don't have much motivation, but you don't have much attachment either."

"How am I supposed to react to what you are saying," I asked.

"Just open and surrender, I am not asking for your opinion, I wouldn't say anything if I didn't sense that something in you was ready to listen, A person can walk in the dark for a long time, but there comes a moment when conscious understanding is essential so that he can begin to take responsibility for his own direction."

"So you never had any children," I said, partially to shift the subject away from myself.

"I might have one running around Hong Kong, that's what the girl claims. There's no way to be sure, it was many years ago."

I never asked Rudi whether that would tie him to the earth. But I was sure that if there were an escape clause he would find it.

I had talked about Rudi occasionally with my parents, but they had never met him. They were mildly suspicious of his mystical aspects but could see the good results of my own work with him, so they suspended their judgment. But I was still surprised when Rudi told me,

"Your mother called and invited me to supper next week."

"Are you going?"

"Sure, I'd like to see where you came from."

"Fine," I said, "We can go together."

On the appointed day we entered the apartment building where my parents lived, and took the automatic elevator to the eleventh floor. As the door opened, a man was waiting to enter. For an awkward moment he stepped back so that we could leave the elevator.

A little while later when we were munching on hors d'oeuvres in my parents' apartment, my mother, who was a psychologist, said,

"You just missed running into one of my patients."

"I saw him," said Rudi. "He was the man with scars on his face."

My mother paled slightly.

"He used to have scars several years ago, but they were removed by surgery."

"They were not removed psychically," said Rudi.

"I know," said my mother, "he has been quite disturbed. But the situation is turning around."

Then she made the mistake of asking, "Do you think he can be cured?"

"No," said Rudi. "I think he is going to commit suicide in a few months."

After that statement a slight chill fell on the gathering.

After we had left the apartment, I asked Rudi,

"How could you see the scars like that?"

"I didn't have time to think about it. I glanced at him for only a moment and saw everything. There are many ways to perceive any situation. While we were at your parents I put myself inside you at one point to be able to see them through your eyes. It was quite informative.

"Sometimes I can be talking with one person and watching another with eyes in the back of my head. It's not so remarkable. You just have to know how to do it and then be willing to make the necessary effort.

"But the main thing I want to impress upon you, John, is that your parents are good people. And even if they weren't, you would have to open to them for the sake of your own growth. All it takes is a little conscious effort on your part and it will repay you greatly. They will inwardly give you their blessing. And that is very important."

I forgot the whole conversation until several months later when my mother said to me in a subdued voice,

"Rudi was right. The patient quit therapy soon after that night, and I just heard that he committed suicide last week. How did Rudi know?"

All I could say was, "Why don't you phone him up and ask him?"

* * *

Throughout his life Rudi always needed to have someone with whom he was particularly close. Such a relationship helped to neutralize the pain of his own inner work. Edith and Reynolds fulfilled this role when I first met him, but only to a limited degree. As the nature of his work changed and more people were attracted, Reynolds began to fade into the background. Rudi didn't want this to happen, but there was nothing he could do to prevent it. It was produced by the magnitude of his own growth. Reynolds had to face the possibility of losing the particular position which he had held with Rudi, and becoming one of a larger group. This he was not prepared to do.

His place was taken by a young man named Bill who eventually moved into the house with Rudi. Bill was studying modern dance. Rudi encouraged his efforts because it meant so much to him, though he doubted that dancing would ever enable Bill to make a living.

The climax of Bill's efforts came during a dance festival in Connecticut. Rudi, Edith, David and I went up to see him perform. Rudi was right at home in the environment. He knew a number of people in the dance and theater world, both as customers and from his earlier days when he stayed up all night at their parties. But what was most remarkable was not the dancing or the people, but Rudi's inner state at the time. When we met for breakfast the morning after our arrival, he looked totally different from the night before. It was as if he hadn't slept at all, and at the same time as if he had slept for a week. There was a sense of peace about him, like a hidden pool in a forest. He seemed only partially aware of his surroundings.

After a time he began to talk.

"I am very deeply happy today." There was a pause. We waited. Rudi seemed to have forgotten that he had said anything.

"I don't really have anything to say," he continued. "But I feel like a great flower has opened inside me."

We all sat there conscious of the noises around us and sensing the atmosphere of Rudi's happiness.

"I am glad that you all are here," he continued, "though in another sense it doesn't matter where I am."

He paused again.

"Happiness is not conditional. It is a state of being. The outer situation always changes and happiness usually goes with it. But a state of being has consistency. You can live and move within it and everything you do is cast within its light. If you all suddenly vanished, nothing would change. If someone began to yell, if an old and dear friend unexpectedly walked through the door, none of it would make any real difference."

Again, there was a period of silence. I did not think about what Rudi said, but tried to sense the condition within him from which it came.

"I go through a great deal of physical pain as I work," he continued quietly. "Nothing comes easily for me. It is always a fresh birth and a great deal of emotional turmoil that disturbs existing relationships. Inevitably it is just those who are closest to me who leave because they cannot change when I change. That is a terribly wrenching experience for me. I don't want them to leave.

"I am not saying these things because I am feeling them strongly now. Just the opposite. I feel how little they all matter. I am seeing how necessary they are for my own evolution.

"They say in India, 'a human being is a seed. You plant him in the earth and he sprouts. But a teacher is a scorched seed. You plant him in the earth and nothing happens.'"

"I would have thought it was the opposite," I said, puzzled.

"No. You don't understand. A human being is constantly creating more karma for himself, constantly being involved in new situations. You put a seed in the earth and something sprouts. There is no end to it. But a teacher is someone who has been through life and is no longer attached to it. He has been scorched by his experience and no longer sprouts. It is then, and only then, that spiritual force can exert a gentle but continuous influence. Otherwise it begins to work and is disrupted or destroyed by the first new experience that the individual attracts.

"It always seems like a great sacrifice at the time when something precious is taken away. But it is only giving up an ultimate bondage in order to receive the beginning of freedom. That is what I feel so deeply this morning. I am saying these words because they in no way disturb my inner condition. I feel a great happiness and sense of security in my own direction which I want to share with all of you."

We ate breakfast quietly, bathed in the atmosphere of joyful acceptance that surrounded him.

* * *

The next time I saw Rudi at the store, my eye was immediately caught by a beautiful multi-armed life-sized Japanese Kwan Yin.

"How many $1000's is that going for?" I asked.

"Oh, it's not so much, John," Rudi said smiling at me. "Actually the piece was an incredible bargain. I have a friend who is in the import business. He doesn't particularly deal in oriental art. But for some reason I had the impulse yesterday to visit him. When I got there he was unpacking a shipment. I asked him whether he had anything that would interest me. He wasn't sure, so I poked around until I came on the statue. It was as you see it, except the arms were all scattered around the packing case. The Japanese make their statues in pieces. It's easier that way.

Courtesy John Mann

"I called him over and said, 'This is a nice statue. It's too bad the arms are all broken off. It won't be worth much.'

"He looked at me very seriously and said, 'Well, is it worth anything to you?'

"I named a ridiculously low figure which he was happy to take. Consequently, John, the price is right if you are interested."

I was! I left the store that day with twenty-two arms and one torso.

* * *

Shortly thereafter, a rough Irish kid named Joe appeared on the scene. He became Edith's friend and part of the inner circle. Rudi was interested in him because he had an incredible physical energy that was almost totally undisciplined.

This was remarkably demonstrated when the next art shipment

was unpacked. Ordinarily those of us who were helping waited quietly at the warehouse for the shipment to arrive. Then we continued to wait while the truck was maneuvered into the warehouse and the crates were carried from the truck to the floor. Then with hammers, crowbars and chisels, we went to work, breaking metal bands and prying the crates apart, usually with great care so that they could be used again.

With Joe it was a very different story. While waiting for the shipment, he stalked up and down the sidewalk like a caged tiger. When the truck finally appeared down the street, he jumped aboard in one great leap and started to work as the men backed the truck into the entranceway. The first time it happened I paid no particular attention. I knew Joe was eager. But then Rudi pointed at the truck and said,

"Look at Joe. He's opening the crates with his bare hands!"

I stared, but could hardly believe what I saw. Joe was breaking the metal bands and pulling the crates apart without as much as a screwdriver. He was having a marvelous time.

Rudi watched with amusement and let him destroy a crate before he intervened.

"We want to save the shipping crates. Take it easy, Joe."

Joe slackened his pace slightly. It was practically the only time I ever heard Rudi tell anyone that they were working too hard.

"I used to be something like that when I was his age," he said later in the store. "I worked like an ox for sixteen hours a day. I had two full-time jobs working in the garment district. They saved the heavy crates for me. Some of the boxes and racks I shoved around weighed a ton. It probably would have killed most people, but I really needed to do it, not only for the money, but to break down my own inner chemistry."

"You never speak very much about that period," I said.

"I talk about it sometimes. But it's nothing I particularly want to remember. It was a very brutal existence. Most people complain about the Army. For me, it was heaven in comparison.

"My early life was very difficult. My father walked out on the family when I was a little kid. He was a psychopath. You could not depend on him in any way. My mother, who is a pretty tough cookie in her own right, had to support me and my two brothers all by herself. At one point she danced in the Follies!"

"Are you serious?"

"Ask her. She'll be happy to tell you about it. Her relatives would have helped her, but she was too proud to accept it. And she never wanted to get married again, though it would have made things easier for her and for us. She was always under a great deal of tension — a woman alone with three little boys. She used to yell at me a lot. Today I can understand why, but at the time I felt innocent. I had to learn to defend myself. Those days still affect my relation with her. That's why we still fight when we are together. It is part of the pattern from the past.

"When I was a little kid, nothing that I did was ever right in her eyes. She made me feel totally worthless. That was hard to accept at the time, but it is beginning to pay off now. No matter how many wonderful things happen to me or what incredible predictions are made about my future, I still hear my mother telling me that I am no good, and it helps me to keep a sense of balance.

"It will take a long time for all those feelings from the past to drop away. But since they are there, I try to use them consciously. When I argue with my mother, I release a great deal of tension that .builds up in other situations. This prevents me from exploding against people who couldn't take it. My mother is tough. It doesn't hurt her. If I didn't argue with her, she would think I didn't care about her. She can't help trying to fight what I am doing, either in my inner work or in my business. Psychically, we are very close. Whatever happens to me affects her, whether she likes it or not. When I am inwardly disturbed, so is she. I have a reason for going through these inner storms. But she has no reason. She isn't doing our work. It is inflicted on her because she is my mother. I have to remember that even when she is driving me crazy.

"That is one reason I like to buy her gifts, to make up for what my inner growth puts her through. She loves expensive jewelry. It gives her a sense of security. I'm sure if I bought her a million dollars' worth it wouldn't be enough, but I enjoy seeing how happy a new ring or earrings makes her. She is like a kid in a toy shop. Only the toys are pretty expensive.

"She used to have her own little antique store before you knew me. She sold $5 and $10 items. It's almost impossible for her to adjust to the way I do things — buying in bulk, selling cheap, and having a rapid turnover. It goes against her whole experience. And besides, she has an irrational fear of poverty, which nothing in the present can reduce. She has financial security at this point. Probably she will be rich in a few years, but it won't really make any difference. Something in her will

Close Relationships

still be living as if she didn't know where her next meal was coming from."

"If you have difficulty together," I asked, "why do you have her working with you in the store?"

"It's good for her, and she frees me to do other things when she isn't driving me crazy. That is part of the reason. The other part is that I am trying to build her up. That may be difficult for you to understand. You never build anyone up that's close to you. Your whole idea is to escape from them. But my mother is, in a way, my limitation. I don't really have a father. There isn't much I can do about my brothers, except help them out if they need it. But if my mother grows, it increases my potential enormously. It is a very conscious decision on my part to have her with me. There are days when I ask myself over and over, 'Why do I have her here? She is driving me wild.' But then I remember. It's an investment in the future, hers and mine. She will grow stronger and even sweeter in time."

"I don't have any trouble with her," I said.

"Why should you? She isn't your mother and, as far as she is concerned, you're a good customer and my friend."

Courtesy David Rudolph

Rudi's Brothers & Mother: (L to R) Rudi, David, Rae, & Albert

※ ※ ※

Rudi was never physically ill, though he went through endless physiological turmoil produced by the effects of his own growth. But he did have a hereditary disposition to gout. When his system became excessively overburdened, sometimes he had an attack. The pain was severe, but he kept on with his normal routine.

On one of those occasions a friend offered to cure him. She was by no means a professional healer, but Rudi had faith in her ability. I happened to be in the store when she came. She was a rather voluptuous woman, more given to attracting glances than curing ailments, but there was more to her than met the eye.

She arranged his foot comfortably on her lap and then gently began to caress it with her hands. It probably felt good, but I didn't think it could do much for gout. At the end of twenty minutes she asked Rudi,

"How is it feeling?"

"Much better," he said with relief. "That really helped."

"It should have," she said. "Look at my hands." She held them up. They had turned into tight, withered claws. It was horrible.

"I hope you know how to drop all that poison," I said.

"I would be in real trouble if I didn't." She disappeared into the back room for an extended period. When she emerged her hands were normal.

I was impressed. Rudi was grateful. It was rare that someone was in a position to help him.

※ ※ ※

Rudi was extraordinarily loyal once he had made a commitment to anyone. This occasionally made him appear naive when the other person failed to fulfill their part of the relationship. But he wasn't really concerned how the other person acted. That was their responsibility.

"Once I have begun a relationship," he said, "I am willing to do 70%, 80% or even 90% of the work to keep things in balance. It's not that I'm doing someone else a big favor. It is my way of being responsible. Just because I choose to ignore another person's limitations doesn't mean that I don't see them. And if I ever decide that a friend has ceased to value me, I can react very quickly and permanently."

"I am sure you can," I said, "I hope it never happens to me."

"I hope it never does either, John. But if it should, it wouldn't matter how long we had known each other or what you had been through. It only takes a second to cut the connection."

※ ※ ※

A few days later, Rudi was driving in the city with Edith when she said casually,

"It is really quite a strain to come in from Westchester to see you every Tuesday and Thursday."

Rudi didn't reply. The conversation continued. Edith was perhaps only half serious, but also half honest. The car stopped for a red light. Rudi said,

"Excuse me," opened the door and got out. Then he walked to the nearest taxi and went home.

"That's the end of our relationship," Rudi said as he told me of the incident the next day.

"For five years I have faithfully seen her two and three times a week. There were lots of other things I could have done with my time. I know many interesting people. But I valued my relationship with her. I didn't always feel like going to see her, but I always went. If Edith didn't know my potential it would be forgivable. But she, more than anyone else understands what I can become. If she doesn't deeply wish to see me, then there is no basis for the relationship."

"If she calls what will you say?" I asked.

"There is nothing to say. I am not being temperamental. It is really wrong for me to spend time with people who don't truly appreciate me. The force working through me requires respect. I know this may be hard for you to understand. You really think I am blind to other people's faults, overflowing with love and willing to forgive anything. I can certainly love and forgive. But once the glass cracks, it cannot be repaired. Edith told the truth last night. She didn't expect me to take her so seriously or she would have kept her mouth shut."

"She must really be in shock," I said.

"First she has to realize what has happened. Then the shock will follow," Rudi concluded.

※ ※ ※

During the next several years a number of the early people drifted away. Roy Burns spent more and more time on the road, doing jazz concerts, and finally moved to the Midwest. Rudi was not unduly disturbed. It was, in fact, what he expected. But it was hard for me to understand why someone with Roy's gifts would want to leave.

"It's simple," said Rudi. "He's more interested in being a drummer than growing spiritually. The irony is that if he stayed with me his drumming would also improve. But even if he believed that, he would go. As far as he is concerned he has had enough spiritual work for this life. Besides, the work has changed and I have changed. He doesn't want to make the effort that would be necessary to keep up with it."

"But it's such a waste," I said. "He was your first real student."

"Yes, well, all Roy knows is that he wants to be a great jazz drummer," said Rudi. "You don't have any such interest, so it is hard for you to understand. If you left this work, what would you do?"

"Nothing much. Drift."

"That's why you are in no immediate danger. It's not a social thing with you, and you're not attracted to anything else. Some day that may change. If it does, you'll have to make a choice."

"What choice is there?"

"None, actually. But how many people realize that. I accept what Roy is doing, just as I waited for a year for him to walk into the store. It's part of the pattern. If you can't see it, the result comes as an unexpected shock. But if you look at the person objectively you cannot be very surprised when they finally do what is inevitable.

"It hurts me to see him go, but I wish him well and will try to keep the door open if he should return. But that is almost impossible. I have seen lots of people try. It has nothing to do with my attitude. The doorway simply disappears. When someone comes back they attempt to connect with what they knew. But that is precisely what is gone. Their only chance is to completely drop everything from the past and begin again. It is ten times easier for a new person to start than for an old one to return."

In parallel with Roy's departure, Rudi's close friend, Bill, became more and more involved with his own artistic and personal life. When a professional opportunity appeared he decided to leave. This was difficult for Rudi to accept even though supporting the relationship required real effort on his part. When Bill departed Rudi decided to live alone. It was not easy. It went against his nature, but he felt that his own growth required a period of enforced loneliness, just as it had when he first opened the store.

Chapter Fourteen

TEACHING SIX CHIMPANZEES

"The amount of effort it requires to teach is unbelievable," said Rudi as we sat outside the store one cloudy day. "If there were any other way for me to grow, I would take it. But there isn't. In fact, if all my students disappeared, I would line up six chimpanzees and work with them. I don't know if it would help them any, but it would sure be good for me."

Two early students, George and Charlie, were examples of the ends to which Rudi was prepared to go in fulfilling the role of teacher.

George had been in the Gurdjieff work, and had emerged charred and drained. Charlie had not been in any work. He was a pleasant, detached character. Both were at loose ends. Rudi suggested that they prepare themselves for some business or profession. He recommended chiropractic school. Neither of them had any money. Unknown to me, Rudi paid for their schooling.

Charlie got through the first year and then flunked out. Shortly thereafter, he drifted away.

George was more persistent. He eventually completed school and obtained his license. But he was constantly getting involved in personal situations from which Rudi periodically had to save him.

"You have to understand your position, George," he would say on such occasions. "It is fine to wish to help someone whom you care for, but you can't afford it now. You don't have the energy or the detachment. It doesn't do them any good, except that they temporarily feel better. And it does you harm because they suck you dry."

"I can't see where trying to help another human being can be bad," said George.

"If your children were hungry and you gambled away your weekly paycheck, would that be right? Even if you gave it away to a beggar in need? Your first responsibility is to your own. And that is you. If and when you get stronger the day will come when you can share from your own abundance, not from your weakness. That will be good for others and for you. But if you keep up what you are doing now, you will never grow because you are giving away the energy which I am giving you. That is not what I am giving it to you for. If you continue to act so irresponsibly I am just going to kick you out."

George looked crestfallen, but held his peace.

"I appreciate your motives," Rudi continued. "But what you are doing is a cheap substitute for the effort required to grow. I know you are lonely and want some situations in which to be involved. But you have to be more objective. You are not a normal person. You are recuperating from years of emotional malnutrition and tension. Save your vitality for yourself, or you will never get well."

It was hard for me to understand at the time why Rudi was willing to invest so much money in George and Charlie. Neither one of them seemed to have exceptional potential, or even to represent a good gamble. One day while they were both in school, I said to Rudi,

"Don't take this wrong, but why are you putting Charlie and George through school?"

"Sometimes I wonder myself," said Rudi, smiling.

"Somebody has to do something. They need to be able to support themselves if they are ever to have any kind of life."

"But why you?"

"Who else is there? It's my money, I enjoy spending it this way. Much as I love art I would rather invest in people than anything else. Maybe it will all come to nothing. But I can afford the money, and this way I won't be haunted with the question of whether I might have turned their situation around if I had been willing to help."

"But what teacher gives his own money to his students?" I asked.

"None," he said, "They hate me in India because I do things like this. It is always the students who support the teacher. I don't want that. It would limit me. I want to be responsible for my own material existence and not depend on anyone who is dependent on me.

"But it's partly a question of tradition. In the East, particularly in India, it would be unseemly for a holy man to support himself. He's expected to devote his life to sacred matters. But if you are paid for teaching spiritually, it exerts a subtle influence. The students have an image of the guru and his teaching. The teacher is supported, in part, to help to fulfill that fantasy. But inevitably there comes a moment when the teacher must destroy the dream. He may not do it, or delay doing it, if his livelihood depends on the good will of his students. It is better that the issue should never arise.

"In any case money has no value unless it is used. The saddest spectacle in the world is an insecure millionaire who hordes his fortune. It serves nothing, except to allay his own fears. I would rather give than hold back. Fortunately I can afford to do it. But when I have to hold back I can do that too, sometimes for a very long time."

"It won't bother you then if the money you are investing in Charlie and George comes to nothing?" I asked.

"I almost have to assume it will come to nothing in order to be able to give it. I don't want them to be beholden to me for the rest of their lives. It's a gift. If they choose to receive it they can do with it as they wish. It's the only way to give. Otherwise it would drive me crazy and weaken them. If I truly thought they had no chance I wouldn't give it. But there is a chance, and who am I to judge? I have a certain sense of the future. I can detect a possible turning point in a person's life. But I cannot foretell just who will come through and to what extent any more than a farmer can tell the fate of an individual seed when he sows the field. It doesn't matter! You use the best seed that is available, do what is necessary, and then wait to see which sprouts. It is the harvest that counts.

"Not that I don't have my own preferences among the seeds. But usually what I wish for doesn't happen anyway, or if it does, not in the way I had foreseen. I can't help wishing, but I know that I have to surrender the wish when the seeds germinate. I can't afford to mourn very long for those that remain buried under the earth.

* * *

Another early student was Paul. He stood out from the crowd because of his relatively fastidious taste in clothes. One day I appeared in the store as he was leaving.

"I am going to try an experiment," said Rudi, after Paul had shut the door and I had sat down in my favorite folding wooden chair.

"I am going to work with him at a distance. I want to find out if I can speed up the growth process that way."

"What do you mean?" I was puzzled.

"I will work on him without his being here," said Rudi.

"Does he know what you are doing?"

"No. If he knew, he would only start to imagine things."

I wanted to ask Rudi why he picked Paul, who didn't seem a particularly dedicated student, but I knew it was really none of my business. The use of his energy was Rudi's responsibility, not mine. As long as I received what I needed, there was nothing for me to say. Nevertheless, after a pause I did venture to ask,

"What do you expect to achieve?"

"Probably nothing. But it's worth a little waste of energy to find out. It might turn out to be more effective working indirectly with Paul than in class. His defenses won't have as great a chance to mobilize."

Three days later I returned. Paul wasn't present, but he had been there earlier in the day. I was curious.

"How did it go?" I asked.

Rudi shrugged his shoulders.

"Is that all you're going to say?" I persisted.

"It worked."

"In what way?"

"He burned for two days."

"You don't seem very pleased about it."

"If he had been in the store and I had worked with him directly, he would have burned too."

"What did you expect?" I asked.

"I wasn't sure," said Rudi. "Now I know. It wasn't worth the effort."

"So you won't do it again?"

"Not in a hurry. It might be necessary in an emergency to see someone through a crisis, but under ordinary conditions there is no reason for it. Growth is always gradual. Feeding should be gradual too. It takes a lot of strength to be able to absorb a concentrated dose of energy. That is basically why I take four to six weeks to prepare internally before I go to India. When I am there I absorb tremendously. Some of it is in the atmosphere. Most of it I get from contact with saints. The preparation that I require is to make room inside myself to receive what they have to give.

"Most people go tilt when they are subjected to strong higher forces. They lose consciousness or go into shock. If that doesn't happen their capacity to absorb is quickly exceeded, and the excess flows over and is lost. There is no point to it. The psychic system is no different than any muscular system. It develops its strength through gradual and consistent use. There is nothing passive about it. You have to stretch, surrender, and if necessary, break through endless resistances which you uncover only as you get to them. Hatha yoga is helpful on the physical level and represents, in a visible sense, what you must do on the psychic level in order to grow. But nobody is really willing to make that effort."

"It doesn't sound so difficult," I said.

"It isn't," said Rudi. "It is like deciding to hold your breath for one second longer each day until you get to three minutes. It is simple enough, once you get into the habit. But everyone is very quick to feel that they have done enough. It's not that human beings aren't capable of remarkable efforts, but mostly they do it for unreal or insane reasons. A person will devote himself to revenge, to competition, to achieving his version of security or fame. He can accomplish incredible feats of endurance in wartime. But the last thing anyone is willing to struggle for is their own inner development. They are satisfied with what they are unless it is really terrible. Even then, they often tolerate it. Only when other people also find it terrible do they begin to react. If we could put the same energy and intensity in our inner work that a child puts into getting a candy from an adult, there would be no problem. But the unfortunate truth is that perhaps only two percent of a person wants to grow. The rest doesn't care or else actively opposes it."

"Those aren't very good odds," I said, feeling vaguely uneasy.

"No, but every other alternative is worse, though nobody wants to believe it. That is why people are so easily led astray. They get interested in their own development, like they get interested in anything else that catches their fancy. They move in that direction until they hit their first major source of resistance. Then they pause. Next they begin to move sideways, still thinking they are going forward. Then they begin to look for reasons why they should stop. They are not getting results. The methods are wrong. The teacher is imperfect. Then they move away into something else or back to their old life which, if imperfect, is at least familiar.

"There is only one antidote when this begins to happen. A person has to have made the same mistake so often that he begins to realize inwardly that it must stop. That is the function of life, to learn that one fact. Then when the ship begins to flounder, the individual understands from his past experience that there is no alternative but to stay with the ship, make necessary repairs, and continue on the assigned course.

"Nothing else matters. The inner direction is either the central fact of one's existence or a person is a conditioned robot governed by society or his own compulsions. And knowing the truth of what I am saying makes no difference. You know lots of things from your work with the Gurdjieff people and your own reading of mystical literature. What real good did any of it ever do you?"

"It helped me to understand my predicament," I said.

"And what good did that do?"

"It gave me motivation."

"Maybe a little," said Rudi. "But I doubt that you had to read in a book that you were in a bad way in order to know it. Just living your life with a minimum of awareness would tell you that hundreds of times a day."

"How about Paul?" I said, returning to the original topic and shifting Rudi's attention away from myself.

"How about him?" said Rudi. "He'll do what he wants, like he always has."

A year or so later, Paul drifted away.

✸ ✸ ✸

During all this time I continued my work at the college. I taught my classes, had office hours, and then departed, leaving it all behind. But as I was in the graduate school, there was no escape from serving on an occasional doctoral oral examination. At such times I was forced to marvel and shudder at the lives of my colleagues. I did not think myself better, but I could never get used to the importance they attached to minute distinctions of analysis, and the way they masked their egos in displays of rationality.

One day I came directly from an oral examination to the store.

"I'm still shaking inwardly," I said after I settled down.

"Academic people are very frightened of the world," said Rudi.

"I guess that's it. They attach such importance to minutiae. But I can't say it's nothing to them. So I don't say anything."

"I'm glad you have learned to keep your mouth shut," said Rudi. "College is a game for grownup children. If you play it well, you get a reward. But all life is like that. Only college people hardly ever touch real life inside their insulated walls.

"Intelligence is a wonderful thing, John, but there is nothing cheaper. It is a futile ability unless one also knows how things work. A man of power buys and sells people who can think. The average intellectual is helpless removed from his environment, whereas he should be like a cat, landing on all fours wherever he is thrown. But the one thing you must never do with any of your colleagues is to threaten their security unless you are prepared to replace it with something better. They will never forgive you, and it is an irresponsible act."

"I don't. I haven't," I said.

"I know, but you might get brave some time and decide to tell them all what you think of them," said Rudi.

"I don't think anything that bad. Most of them are nice as individuals. And besides, there is nothing better for me to do right now than teach!"

"It is a good place for you," said Rudi. "It is near my store. It is relatively easy. It has prestige, and you are invisible. If you weren't studying with me it might be different. Another kind of work that was more demanding might be useful. But this way you make the money you need to support your family and still have 90% of your energy to plow back into your own growth. You are very fortunate in that respect. But in another sense you require that kind of situation in order for growth to be possible at all. I hope you realize that."

"I guess so, but doesn't everybody?"

"Not at all. I've told you how I used to work at two full-time jobs. It wasn't just for the money. I had to break down my internal chemistry that way. If I had had one easy job it would have been terrible for me. But you need a gradual approach. If it couldn't be that way, it wouldn't work for you. At the same time, your greatest obstacle is that your life is too easy. It has always been too easy. You have never had to struggle for anything. But don't worry. I know that is only externally. Inside, it is very difficult. That is why

Rudi in college

I accept the outside.

"When I was in college," continued Rudi in one of his startling shifts of emphasis, "I studied engineering."

"You've got to be kidding," I said. Rudi disliked and avoided anything connected with too much rationality.

"I didn't say I was a natural, but I did the work."

"Why?" I was really puzzled.

"Just because it was unnatural for me. I figured if I could do that, I could do anything. I hadn't even been to high school. But I wanted to go to college so much that I convinced the admissions officer to take a chance on me. I'm sure he must have been amazed by his own actions, but there was nothing in me that would accept any other possibility. "

"How did you do?" I asked, amazed at this latest bit of information.

"I wasn't at the top of my class. But I passed all right. That was when I learned to cook."

"I don't see the connection."

"I had to support myself. I got a job as a short-order cook. I didn't know anything about it, but I sure learned how in a hurry."

"I'm glad you didn't become an engineer," I said, still feeling a little breathless from all this information.

"I don't think I could have stood it. But, in a way, what I am doing now is psychic engineering. It is the same thing on a different level. And you should realize that there is more than one type of such engineering. What I have done on you in the past involves a direct intervention through touch and energy transfer from my system to yours.

But there is another more important type that has no physical aspect.

"The last time I stopped in Japan I was feeling rather strange. It was at the end of my trip and I had absorbed all I could take. But when I was falling asleep I smelled something like chloroform. It was so real that I got up to look around, but there was no obvious source. So I returned to bed. During the night I was bothered by clicking sounds in the air, but I was very tired and always went back to sleep.

"Sometime in the early morning, I awoke in a detached state. My body was beneath me. It was in an operating theater. There were some strange beings working on my head. The clicks I had heard were the sounds of the instruments. If I hadn't been through such experiences before I might have panicked. But once I got the picture I even managed to go back to sleep. The next morning I had a terrible headache. And the next night they went back to work on me. You look shocked."

"How do such things come about?"

"You earn them. It is not so much what you do that is important. It is the capacity to work enough to get to the point where the force finally begins to work on you. When it takes over then things begin to happen. That is when you have to surrender everything and have faith.

"When I was in college," Rudi continued, shifting backwards in time, "I stayed for the summer with a very rich family in Oregon. It was wonderful. I loved them. They loved me. They wanted to adopt me. But I couldn't stay. It would have undermined my whole development. In the end I had to force myself to return to an uncertain, brutal existence. I did it for the sake of my own growth."

"It seems a little extreme to me," I said.

"John. You don't know what I am being prepared for. I can't afford to take the easy way out. It will catch up with me later when I really need the strength. At this point it may not be necessary. But I am not just living for today. I am living for what may be required ten years from today.

"Many people in spiritual work live a rarefied existence. They eat only certain food, see only certain people. I do just the opposite. I train myself to be able to eat anything, relate to anyone.

"The whole conception of a holy man as being too spiritual to touch is unreal. The Shankaracharya of Puri was an old and delicate man when I met him. He was one of the highest dignitaries in the Hindu religion. He fit my stereotype of a saintly man — refined, dignified and holy.

"Then one night I accompanied him on an overnight train trip. He had a berth. I slept sitting up in the next car. At about 5:30 in the morning I was horrified to hear what sounded like a water buffalo in the area where his holiness was sleeping. I jumped up to silence the offender, but was puzzled to find no source for the noise. Then I realized with a shock that what I had heard was the Shankaracharya stretching as he woke up. He was totally uninhibited. I never looked on him as unapproachable again. He might be holy, but he was very real."

※ ※ ※

On the following day I happened to ask Rudi a question about psychic engineering that had arisen in my mind from our talk of the day before.

"I don't know what you are talking about," he said to my surprise.

I wasn't sure whether to believe him, so I asked the question again.

"I no longer remember anything about it," he said, sensing my uncertainty. "When we were talking yesterday, it filled my attention. As soon as we finished I dropped the whole thing."

"How could you do that? Do you suppress your thoughts?"

"No. I let them go. They are like water drops over the waterfall."

"That is a lovely image," I said.

"You think it is poetic because of the difference in our states. Understand it is literally true. It gives me tremendous room for expansion. I am not haunted by the past."

"I should think that would be extremely disorienting."

"If you are in a state of surrender," said Rudi, "you are not concerned with being oriented. As long as you think you should know where you are and what you are doing, then you need to be oriented. I don't care where I am. I don't know what will happen next. When I am in this state, my own words are more of a surprise to me than yours. I listen to myself as if I were hearing someone else speaking."

"But you always know the price of every item in the store," I said, trying to pin him down.

"I need to know. But I don't learn it by heart. I absorb it. The object and its price are part of me. I know the cost like I know how many fingers I have. It is there. I just look inside."

"Why can't I do that?" I asked.

"Because you can't surrender your thoughts for more than a few seconds at a time. You feel the need to be oriented. It would frighten you to cease to remember. It takes great inner strength and a very firm sense of reality to let go of thinking.

"One of my favorite Hindu sayings is, *The mind is the slayer of the soul.* You can't understand the depth of those words until your mind surrenders in the midst of action. Then you realize that nothing is lost except a screen which dims and distorts your perception of reality. You don't have to think about anything to perceive the world. You don't have to think about anything to sense the inner state of another human being. You don't have to think to have a spiritual experience. Thinking is designed to steal reality from us. It is tremendously overvalued in this society. But don't misunderstand. The mind can be a useful instrument. It can help to keep things moving in a direction we consciously desire. It performs simple calculations. But it does not create. It cannot really choose. For that, we have much subtler mechanisms.

"How many people do you know who think themselves out of their personal problems? Usually they think themselves more deeply into them. Thought is a tool, not a solution. Scientists do not follow the scientific method. Read some autobiographies. Hunch and intuition play an enormous role, which is usually ignored in the official accounts of scientific discoveries. A hack uses his mind. A really talented man uses intuition. Later, of course, he subjects his conclusions to a common sense process of testing.

"Over the years I have developed an intuitive inner computer that feeds me answers. I don't really understand how it works, but the results are usually excellent. I don't mind applying the answers to myself, but when I am told something inwardly that concerns someone else, I have some bad moments before I force myself to act on it.

"A few weeks ago a fellow I know came into the store with one of the strangest looking girls you could imagine. She looked and acted like she had been raised by wolves in the forest. In order to get the full picture you have to know this fellow. He is a rather delicate, rich, spoiled man who is not particularly interested in women. It was one of the most bizarre combinations I had ever seen.

"In the midst of talking with him I heard this inner voice saying to me, 'They should get married.' I was horrified. She could eat him alive before breakfast. But the message came through loud and clear.

"I didn't have enough faith to act on it immediately. Anyway, no one was asking me for my opinion. They had met only a short time before.

But two weeks later he was back wanting to know what I thought of her. I couldn't very well ignore the question, so I said, half-jokingly, 'Why? Are you thinking of marrying her?'

"'It's kind of sudden,' he said, 'but I might be. Do you think it would be a good idea?'

"'As a matter of fact,' I said, 'I think you should.'

"He looked at me vaguely shocked, but didn't ask me why I thought so, which was lucky because I don't know what I would have said."

"What's going to happen now?" I asked.

"I have fulfilled my part of the story," said Rudi. "He needed to know what I thought. I had been told what to think. If it turns out to be a horrible abortion I will know the next time not to believe that voice. But I have heard it many times in the past and it is almost always right.

"When I was a kid, I used to do palm reading and fortune telling. I was very good. Nobody taught me how. I hadn't read any books. But I knew. The capacity was born in me, and the challenge of the situation brought it out."

"You keep that side of you will hidden," I said.

"I didn't want to be a freak, so I stopped displaying psychic gifts. Sometimes I will look at a person's palm to get a quick impression or to clarify a particular point. I occasionally go to astrologers and psychics. I use them to get a fix on the future. I take what three or four of them say and see how their predictions overlap. It helps me get a sense of perspective. But it is so easy to use a gift as a substitute for growth. I didn't want to be a psychic. I wanted to be a human being. I let the one go for the other. Now I hardly need anything like that. I feel my way directly into a person to find out what is there. And also it is written on the forehead if you know how to read it."

"What are you talking about?" I asked.

"Exactly what I said. As you grow, different signs and symbols appear on the forehead."

"Are you talking about using psychic vision?" I asked.

"Some of it is psychic. Some of it is physical that anyone could see. You may notice that I glance in the mirror when I go to the bathroom. I'm not admiring my beautiful profile. I'm checking my forehead."

"That's kind of hard for me to accept."

"That's what I mean by thoughts being the enemy. You have ideas on the subject. Your ideas don't agree with what I am saying. You begin to feel threatened and tense. It's absurd. There is nothing to

Before The Sun

Courtesy Barry Kaplan

think about. It is either true or not. Look and see. Don't think about it!"

"I'm looking. I don't see anything. What am I supposed to see?"

"If a little man popped out and said 'hello' in Tibetan you wouldn't see anything. Come over here!" He went over to the mirror and examined his reflection.

"Here," he said, outlining an area with his finger. "Can you see the circle inside the cube?"

"Aren't those just lines on your forehead?" I asked obstinately.

"How many circles have you seen on anyone's head lately?"

"I don't know. I haven't looked."

"Well, next time you see me, look again. The circle will probably be gone," said Rudi.

"But how can you expect me to accept such a thing?" I persisted.

"If it's true, you will have to accept it. The hardest thing to understand is that the laws on different levels of experience are not the same. On the strictly physical level we have some idea of how the body functions and the interrelation between the various vital systems. But the psychic system is on another level. We have very little understanding of how it acts. If this were a scene in a science fiction story or part of a dream, you wouldn't be surprised if symbols appeared on someone's forehead. Perhaps approaching it that way will make it easier for you. But however you look at it, eventually you will have to look for yourself. And then you will begin to see."

"Does everybody have these symbols?"

"No. Hardly anybody. But you can read a lot from the shape of someone's head. It is the simplest guide to the extent of their development, if you know what to look for."

"It's hard for me to accept that," I muttered doubtfully.

"I can sympathize with your reaction," he said. "I live my life among statues and paintings of Eastern gods and saints. I am saturated with them. As you must have noticed, they have some pretty strange features — bumps on the head, halos, snakes coming out of the back of their neck, little men on the forehead, rods going through their brains. There are endless variations, all having one thing in common. No ordinary person ever looks like that. I assumed, as you would, that these features were strictly stylistic and symbolic. It couldn't be further from the truth. They are literal representations of experiences that occur at a specific stage of growth. I have had this demonstrated in my own work hundreds of times, but it still comes as a surprise to me. You don't have to believe it. It isn't a question of faith. The experiences spring on you when you least expect them.

"It's hard for me to talk to you about these things because you don't see manifestations in class. But by now you must have some confidence that they occur."

"Yes," I said. "The first time I really believed it was when I walked into the warehouse the other day to help you with a shipment. I could feel a strange sense of pressure right in the center of my forehead. You took one look at me and said, 'Well, John, I see that you're really learning how to take my energy.'

"And when I asked, 'Why?' you said,

"'Because there is a clear white light coming out of the center of your forehead.' And then you touched my head exactly where the pressure was. I couldn't doubt that."

Rudi smiled and said, "Last night when I was teaching the class, the force suddenly became very strong and I levitated. I was several inches off the ground. You couldn't see it, but Alan saw it. I thought his eyes were going to fall out of his head. It is all part of an unknown world. You haven't even touched the outer surface."

"That's great, after more than seven years of work," I said.

"You have the rest of your life. The longer it takes, the better it will be in the end."

Chapter Fifteen
WORKING WITH INDIAN SAINTS

"I don't talk about it much," said Rudi as he dusted off some statues on his desk, "but they make it very difficult for me at Swami Muktananda's ashram. Hardly anyone accepts me. I am generally either ignored or being tested. I don't feel sorry for myself. I am not going all that way just to be loved. But it is still hard. I get along best with the children in the town. When they see me coming, they drop whatever they are doing and start to jump up and down. We roll down the hills together, I chase them around, throw them up in the air and blow on their bellies. It isn't just a way for me to let off steam. I desperately need the sense of love that I get from them. Otherwise the whole situation gets too grim. It's like climbing rock cliffs eighteen hours a day.

Rudi in India

"I have one friend, Mr. Japatti. He looks like an Indian Alfred E. Neuman, but he is a wonderful psychic. If it weren't for his sense of my future I would find it pretty difficult to keep going. He works for me out of love. The rest of the people leave me alone because of their fear and prejudice.

"In the end, it doesn't really matter. I come to receive what I need for my growth or to be examined on what I have attained. And then I leave. I don't stay an hour longer than I have to. Often Swami urges me to stay for a few days more. I have to plan my retreat without offending him. It's a question of very careful timing.

"When I first arrive we are both totally involved in the encounter. Any mention of leaving, on my part, would cause him to insist that I stay for at least three weeks. So I keep my peace and wait. I know that nothing ever interests him for more than a few days. I bide my time until the fourth day. Then I say casually, 'I must be leaving the day after tomorrow, because I have heard of a collection I should see.' He expresses great regret, and he allows it to happen. I promise to stay for an extended period the next time. He makes a few remarks about my business activities and my spiritual life interfering with each other. But I counter by asking, 'Do you think that I should give up my business?' He would rather have me successful than permanently around him. He accepts the inevitable.

"On the final day we go through an elaborate farewell with expression of regret and love on my part. He responds accordingly, but I can see that he has already lost interest, and is just as happy that I am going."

"Doesn't he really care about you?" I asked.

"That isn't the point. You can only go so far in any direction at a given time. Once that has happened, why drag it out? It is always better to leave too soon than outstay your welcome. That way your next visit will be anticipated."

✳ ✳ ✳

"Nityananda is as real to me as Muktananda," said Rudi on another day. "One is alive, the other physically dead. It makes no difference. In many ways Nityananda is easier to deal with. Swami Muktananda can make me wait for days in agony before he does anything about it. He may have someone say something against me just to see how I will react, or he might even use magic against me to see if I can overcome it. But understand one thing, John. I complain about him when I am in New York. That is my privilege. But God help anyone else who ever does that in my presence. He is my teacher. If you respect me, you

Before The Sun

Rudi in the presence of Swami Muktananda in India

must also respect him. Do you understand that?"

"I have never said anything against him, have I?"

"That isn't the point. In accepting me you must accept him. Otherwise, you would have to assume that while I am fine for you, I don't know what is right for me. It can't be. If I don't understand myself, how can I understand you? Swami Muktananda can be very difficult. He doesn't really care about other people. It is part of his detachment, and also a lack of heart. But I am learning and growing through my contact with him. I need the challenge which he presents. It would be more pleasant for me if he was sweeter, but I would not grow as fast. If you or anyone else were to go to him at this point you would get nothing because he is too difficult to understand. He would distract you with some little trick, ignore you, or perhaps cast a spell of some kind on you which you wouldn't even suspect."

"Who would want to go near a man like that?" I said.

"You don't have to," said Rudi. "I do it for you. But even I don't take any chances. When I leave the ashram and return to Bombay, I go to a place where there are all kinds of fortune tellers and magicians to get their help in removing any spell that might have been put on me. I know that sounds strange to you, but why should I be a schmuck? Swami Muktananda likes to drop me on my head just to hear my cries of pain. I don't care what he does as long as I grow. If he wants to enchant me to test whether I am conscious enough to realize what has happened and strong enough to get out of it, I accept his right to do it. But don't look so sick, I'm not going to do anything like that to you."

"Could you if you wanted to?" I asked uneasily. I had never looked at Rudi in that light before.

"I could find out how to do it in a hurry if I needed to. But all life is a magic spell. Why add to the weight of it? I don't want to use my own will against other people. How can they grow that way? I have never made anyone go through tests which I have devised. That has been done so often to me that I hate it. Life is difficult enough.

"If Nityananda had lived he might be as hard for me to get along with as Muktananda. When Nityananda didn't like someone's inner state he was liable to pick up a stick and start to beat them. When he was younger he used to live in a tree. If anyone came near he threw stones at them. He had renounced the world and didn't want to be disturbed. But if children came, he threw flower petals.

"Since he died I don't have to contend with his personality, for which I am grateful. The cosmic part of him is still there. I see him, talk to him, and have the same basic experience as I would have if he were alive. I can't really expect you to believe that, but I'm not talking to make you believe anything."

"So why are you talking?"

"It is necessary," Rudi said. "It helps me get perspective on my own experiences. It is one thing to go through them alone. It is another to listen to myself as I tell someone else about them. Then I begin to understand what I couldn't see at the time, and also sense whether it feels real to me as I recall it. I have many reasons.

✳ ✳ ✳

"The first time I went back to Ganeshpuri after Nityananda had died, I was still numb from the experience of meeting him a few months before. It was too soon for me to feel any sense of personal loss. I didn't honestly think he was that important to me. But when I entered the room that held his remains I immediately realized that the presence of the man was there just as real as before. There could be no doubt about it."

"Would I feel it if I went there?" I asked.

"Yes. You would feel it in the same way that you feel my presence. You might not know exactly where it came from, but you would experience it like the force that works when I give a class.

"Nityananda didn't teach people through giving them his energy. He worked and worked to transform the energy he drew into himself. Because of the magnitude of his effort there was a continual overflow. In that way he enriched the atmosphere and permanently polarized the area around him so that it continued to attract higher force. There is really no loss involved in his death if you understand how to relate to the energy that remains."

"How do you relate to it?" I asked.

"I am a special case. I have had to learn to open to all kinds of forces under terribly difficult circumstances. If necessary I can enter inside almost anyone and drink their vitality. That may sound like becoming a vampire, but I am not interested in anything like that. I don't know about black magic. I never even studied hypnotism. I see no reason for it. The problem is to wake people up, not to put them under a spell.

"I generally don't tap people if they are on a lower level than me.

Bagavan Nityananda

But there are exceptions. When I go to the theatre or the circus, I drink in all the raw emotion that is being given out. No one else wants it. I can get a tremendous amount of energy that way. But I wouldn't recommend that you try it. Your inner system has to be strong to handle such crude force and break it down into a form you can use. Eventually you will be able to do it, and then you will begin to see that every situation in life either involves something that you feed on for conscious reasons or something from which you can draw. The rest is unconscious slavery.

"There is only one irreplaceable commodity in the world — energy. How you use it is what you must answer for when you are ultimately judged. Successful people apply energy toward a practical goal, and eventually achieve their objective. The rest of humanity gets along as best it can and is bled dry in the process. It achieves no particular distinction but avoids unnecessary anxiety. The rarest individual is someone who has an overriding objective, but who simultaneously can surrender to a will beyond his own. This is precisely what is required in spiritual work, dedication and surrender to a higher power.

"Nothing is really valuable in itself. Everything is an obstacle, a mirage of meaning that we read into it. But to the man who is moving in a direction, each situation is either an aid or a distraction. If it is neither, it may be a luxury, a nice thing to have if he can afford it. For someone without a basic objective there is no morality. There are only the standardized laws of society that he learns through social conditioning.

"Morals are learned like anything else. They serve to keep life orderly. They are not necessarily useful for growth. Even religious precepts cannot be automatically applied. On the whole they may be useful, but they cannot be universal. So much of Christian morality, for example, is designed for persons who have already achieved a higher level of being. Very few Christians have either the heart or the awareness to follow Christianity. It is not that they are weak. They simply cannot do it for the same reason that a dog cannot speak. For most people to follow Christianity is to invite personal disaster. They would not survive in a brutal world.

"People often think I am a simple-minded schmuck, giving away things to others who don't deserve them. I enjoy doing it. From a worldly viewpoint some of it is foolish. But for me, it is good. I enjoy sharing as a way of opening to others and reducing some of the suffering and physical pain that I go through.

"The sun shines. It doesn't spend its time determining how worthy each person is to receive its light. In the same way, Nityananda never worried about how his soul force would be used. It poured out of him. If no one used it at all it would still have overflowed as long as he opened, circulated, and surrendered to God.

I have had many encounters with Nityananda when I've been in Ganeshpuri. I never know what to expect. I may see his figure pointing to the hot springs near his tomb. He wants me to bath and purify myself. I take off my clothes and sink into the wonderful warm sparkling waters. After a few minutes he motions again. I am to follow him. I emerge, get dressed and go where he has indicated. It may be his Samadhi temple where his body is enshrined, or the room where he slept and held audience. And there, with or without words, he works with me. He is as real to me at those times as you are now. But you have to understand one thing. This isn't everyone's experience. He can work with me and through me because I am willing to open myself to him. Otherwise nothing would happen."

"Would he work with me if I were there?" I asked.

"He is already working with you, but you are too insensitive to know it."

"What good is it then?"

"Only a limited good. But you are looking at the whole thing in the wrong way. It isn't a question of whether you would have my experiences. Why should you? But it is crucial that you are nourished by Nityananda's energy. That is already occurring. Through my inner contact with him, his energy reaches you. This is the significance of the lines of work which are emphasized in all spiritual teaching. When you open to a teacher you open to everyone with whom he is connected. He is simply the last link in a chain extending backward in time. It is a lack of concept and scope that prevents people from opening to what is in front of them and using that as a doorway into eternity."

"I never thought of it like that," I said.

"That is your limitation," said Rudi. "What I have told you can, if you use it properly, give you a direct contact with Nityananda and the line of teachers that he represents. Even without understanding the possibility you still have the contact. His energy is one of the main currents that flows through me when I work. You have been receiving it all this time without understanding what it is."

"Is it really the same as if I met him while he was alive?"

"Not exactly. When I work, all the energies that I can attract flow together in a great stream. There may be five or ten small streams combining for this flow. They may come from various cultures and different historical periods. This work is not originally Indian or Tibetan. It was developed in Atlantis. But once the streams merge it's impossible to separate them for analysis, any more than you can isolate the ingredients of bread once it has been baked. But there are times when Nityananda manifests particularly strongly. If you could see psychically at that moment you would see his presence in me, or rather you would see me disappear and him appear. But don't worry about that, John. Psychic sight can be a great distraction. Anything you see is only the manifestation of higher energy hitting a lower level. Its only significance is how much of it you can absorb and use for your own growth.

"In my last trip to Ganeshpuri I saw and felt the whole experience I had at the age of six with the two Tibetan monks repeat itself. I experienced them releasing energy and knowledge which they had put into me so many years ago. If I thought too much about the reality of it all I would probably drive myself crazy, and I know that in the end everything comes down to work. And the more you work, the more you become aware of your own nothingness. That is the antidote.

"A teacher is really a servant, something many teachers would rather forget. In some Buddhist scripture it says, *The Buddha is a shit stick*. It can't be put more graphically than that. Just because a higher force flows in a genuine teacher does not mean he is to be worshipped. His function is to serve the student's potential. Most teachers demand a great deal of respect, which is correct, if it is the cosmic force that is respected. But it too easily shifts into honoring the personality of the teacher. It requires a willingness on the teacher's part to surrender the subtle advantages of his role for the relationship to remain mutually productive.

"No situation, no matter how satisfactory, is an end in itself. It is all material for surrender. You build to give away. Otherwise what starts as a creation ends as a prison which you have constructed for yourself.

"There can be nothing permanent if you wish to grow. Anything you hold onto will in the end turn out to be precisely what you have to surrender. It is not cruelty on anyone else's part. It is an inevitable aspect of growth."

"That sounds reasonable," I said, "but I don't see where it applies to me particularly."

"You are a somewhat different case," said Rudi. "You don't care enough about anything to make it worth sacrificing. What do you have except the art you bought from me that would be a sacrifice for you?"

"The problem is the other way around," I said.

"Exactly. With you, it is a question of growing strong enough to attract a real situation that you would want to hold. Then you will have something to sacrifice."

"I would rather not know about it in advance," I said.

"Don't worry about it," said Rudi. "You will forget the whole thing by tomorrow. But in the years to come you can think back to what I said today when the situation finally arises for you.

"And by the way," said Rudi, suddenly shifting the subject again, "do you need any incense? I just got a shipment. It always arrives just when I am running out or when I'm going through a difficult period and need direct contact with India."

"You get the best incense I have ever been able to find," I said.

"That's because it is completely fresh. They airmail it to me from the factory," said Rudi.

I helped myself to one package of each scent. Rudi never charged his students for the incense. Occasionally he charged a customer, though he was reluctant to sell it to anyone not working with him.

There was another pause. Then Rudi said,

"Would you go to the deli around the corner and get me two franks with mustard and sauerkraut and a dill pickle on the side?"

"Sure!" I said, happy for the diversion.

Rudi didn't offer to buy, which was unusual. But I was glad to pay. There was little enough I could do for him.

Leaving the store was always a shock. I never knew how deeply I had been affected by its atmosphere until I was out of it. Rudi's power anesthetized me. As that receded, the underlying impact became more evident. I could feel the energy I had absorbed glowing within me.

I walked along the street breathing deeply and feeling wonderful. I ordered the franks and returned carrying a warm bag filled with delicious-smelling food.

Rudi undid the foil surrounding each frankfurter and ate them quickly.

"Most people eat slowly and breathe quickly. I breathe slowly and eat quickly," he said.

There was a contented silence. Then Rudi asked innocently, "Isn't there anything you would particularly like to have, John?"

I hesitated. "I'm afraid to make a wish. I'm never sure of the implications."

"Very wise," he said. "Nevertheless you can always add, 'don't give it to me unless it will help me grow.'"

"I suppose," I said. There was nothing casual about the conversation. I knew I was being given an opportunity.

"What should I wish for?" I asked.

"That's up to you," he said.

I had the sense that there was more involved in buying the frankfurters than fulfilling his request. They were a gift that had to be given so that he could offer something in return.

Rudi seemed to enjoy the situation.

"Just sitting here, John, isn't going to get you anywhere if you don't know what you want."

"I hate to be asked what I want," I said. "They did that once to me in the Gurdjieff work when I went to live on their farm. The first night three of the advanced students sat me down and asked me why I was there. It really irritated me. All I could say was, 'If I truly knew what I wanted, I wouldn't be here!' I thought that was a really good answer. But it didn't impress them much. I knew what they wanted to hear, but I had many different feelings, some of them directly opposed to each other. So if I gave them the right answer, it would have been a partial lie."

"I understand all that," said Rudi. "But I don't care what you say, or whether you say anything. It's an invitation, not a command."

"That doesn't make it any easier," I said.

"Then sweat a little," said Rudi. He got up from his chair and moved outside. I continued to sit in the store. There was no use following him outside. He wasn't going to be any help.

I continued to sit. I felt a sense of waste and anxiety. I was afraid that someone would come along and distract Rudi before I had a chance to act.

I looked out the door. He was talking to someone from the neighborhood. He saw me looking at him and waved casually. That didn't make me feel any better.

After five long minutes he came back in the store.

"Well!" he said.

"I don't know," I said.

"That's not good enough, John."

"You don't have to tell me. I feel like an idiot."

"There isn't a child who walks past the store who doesn't know what he wants," Rudi said, "It's still not too late."

"But I don't know what to ask for."

"It isn't that."

"What is it, then?" I asked with mounting frustration.

"Do you really want to know?"

"Yes!" I said.

"You could think of at least ten different things to ask for," said Rudi. "You don't ask because you don't want the responsibility which goes along with the fulfillment of the wish. That is my gift to you, the truth. You can sit here with me for years until I go away or finally throw you out. You will grow. But only to a certain point. Other people come and go. They don't persist. Your longevity is a virtue, but not if it is mindless. A couple of years have passed since you first asked if you might ever become a teacher. That is the real symbol of responsibility. You don't ask me about that any more. You sit and wait."

"I felt you would tell me if I was ready."

"You can't wait for me. You have to make a move in yourself. It's true that right now there is no particular need for anyone else to teach. Nor are you ready. But you don't really care. You are just as happy to let it drag and leave it all in my hands."

"What can I do to change?" I asked.

"You can begin to ask from deep inside your heart center."

"But for what?"

"To want to accept responsibility for your own growth. To mature. If you don't want it, I can't inflict it on you."

"And all this from two lousy frankfurters with mustard and sauerkraut," I said.

"Do you want me to leave you alone?" Rudi persisted.

"No. I don't want that. Don't pay any attention to me. I'm glad you put me on the spot," I said.

"I'm not doing it because I enjoy it. It's easier for me to let things go. But I can't afford it. In India they say,

God is patient. He can wait many lifetimes. But the guru is impatient. He wants the student enlightened in this very life.

"You are my limitation. If I let you hang on indefinitely, it will slow me down. So I am warning you. Passive working and waiting is not enough. There is a natural period for everything. You need a long time to grow. I accept that. But a long time is not forever. If the day comes that you run out of time before taking the next major step, I won't hesitate to throw you out. It may not seem just when it happens. And it could come with as little warning as today. But everyone gets many chances. They just don't happen to know when the last one is coming up. They kid themselves into thinking that new opportunities will always develop. They only learn the truth when it is too late.

"Every year there is a new crop of students. Others from previous years leave. You may not have noticed, but the ones who come are generally of better quality than the ones who go. We are working with a refining energy. It attracts students at a higher level. This makes it more and more difficult for those who started earlier. There is nothing I can do about it. There is nothing I would want to do about it."

"You are succeeding in scaring me," I said.

"It's about time. What is the good of all of the effort and time you have put in, John, if it doesn't lead you somewhere in the end? I don't want you to be a sacrifice to the ascending level of the work. You have to dig deeper to find a place inside yourself that hates your inertia and stupidity."

"I know all that," I said. "You don't have to convince me."

"But it doesn't do you any real good to know it!"

"No. Not really. But why not?"

"Because there is only one little place in you where the truth is kept. It has to spread all through you like ink in a blotter. It has to keep you up nights and haunt the ease of your life. Stop living off your relation with me. What would you do if I disappeared?"

"I don't know."

"You better think about it. There isn't that much keeping me here. I stay in New York because it is the most difficult place on earth to work. I grow very strong overcoming the tension of the city. Buried far under the ground is a great dragon that lives on the negative energy released by the millions of people. It sucks them dry. This is what I must transcend in order to grow. When I get to the point that I don't require that kind of resistance I will leave. Nothing will keep me. I am not going to sacrifice my own existence to your inadequacy. I pay a hundred times more than you do for what is received. I have the right to choose what is done with it and ultimately where I go when I work my way out of this situation. It won't happen tomorrow or even five years from now. But I am absolutely certain it will happen. And maybe it will be tomorrow."

"I wouldn't blame you for leaving if you could," I said.

"That's all very well," said Rudi. "But what would you do then? I know what's going to happen to me. I know the basic outline of the rest of my life. I even know how I am going to die."

"How?" I couldn't help asking.

"I'm going to explode and burn alive. But that isn't the point. Stop living in my drama. Face the fact that you don't really expect a life of your own, John. That is your basic problem. I have told you before, you really weren't meant to have one. But you will, if you keep working. If you start really working. You don't know the meaning of the word yet, even after all these years."

"I don't understand," I said. My feelings were hurt.

"You don't know the meaning of work. You don't want to know, so you don't know. The last time I went to India, I started to get ready way in advance. Immediately before I left I stayed up the whole night, just to be sure I was prepared. Hour after hour I surrendered every thought and tension that might stand in the way, building the flow of energy within me until it turned from a quiet stream into a vast river. You didn't know it. I didn't talk about it. Even when I felt I was ready, I didn't stop. I over-prepared.

"The moment I got off the plane in India and started for Ganeshpuri I began to burn. It went on continuously. But Swami Muktananda ignored me. I was making a great effort but he said nothing, gave me no sign of recognition. I went on and on for three endless days like some crazed traveler in the desert. I didn't dare stop. On the fourth day I decided that something must happen to break the torment. I would grab hold of Swami Muktananda physically if I had to, until he released me from the terrible tension of my state. That didn't prove necessary.

"After several hours of waiting, he gestured for me to approach. He put his hand on my head. It was a small action, but it was enough to trigger the tremendous charge I had built up within me. The next thing I knew I was on the floor, being shaken by great electric currents. Then there were flashing lights. People were taking pictures. I got very angry. What was I, some sideshow exhibit? I wanted to get up and smash their cameras. But I caught myself. 'Stupid', I said to myself. 'Is this what you have worked for? What difference does it make what they do? Let go!' In the background I heard Swami Muktananda commenting on what I was going through as if I was a scientific phenomenon.

Swami Muktananda and Rudi in India

I didn't go for that very much either. Then I surrendered — him, the people in the ashram, my own life.

"After about an hour the intensity of the experience began to subside, and I discovered that I was back in my room. They must have carried me there. I felt that I had done as much as humanly possible. I started to relax. And then a great voice spoke to me. I will never forget what it said as long as I live."

He paused, lost in recollection.

"What did it say?" I finally asked.

"It said,

This is how you should always be working.

"I didn't know whether to laugh or to cry. I turned over and fell asleep. When I woke up the next morning the voice was still there. It said,

Now you can begin to understand what it means to work.

"Believe me, John, I didn't want to hear that voice. It meant only endless effort. For what? For whom? Hadn't I done enough? Certainly I had already worked harder than anyone I had ever met. But the voice just laughed at me and said,

This is your reward for the effort you have made.

"There is very little competition for such rewards. No one wants the burden. I don't want it either, but I can accept it as necessary. Many years ago I had a vision of myself as an ox going round and round, running a grain mill. It's a very accurate picture. The energy is thrown into the mill. I go around endlessly grinding it down, finer and finer.

※ ※ ※

"On another trip when Swami Muktananda was making things as difficult as possible, I began to get to the point where I thought I would go crazy. I couldn't give up and I couldn't go on. Finally I decided to continue working until something gave way or I dropped dead.

"And then suddenly I had a vision of a great dragon extending a half mile along the ocean floor. It had endless strength and was completely untouched by anything that was happening to me. I realized abruptly that the dragon was my inner nature. All the torment I was experiencing was on the surface of the ocean. It was just the play of the waves. It had no reality. I was free! Do you understand what I am saying?"

"I understand how it applies to you," I said.

"It isn't your experience," said Rudi. "But it should help you begin to realize the limitation you put on your own work. You cannot coast on what was done last year. There is only one way to coast, downhill. Everyone wants to be comfortable. Rats, birds, people — but that is the addiction which stops any creative growth. You have to make the choice, to pursue your own destiny wherever it leads or make the best of a bad bargain. But by far the worst thing that can happen to anyone is to get caught in the middle. Don't let that happen to you! The door is open. You can leave any time. But if you stay it won't be out of habit or the lack of any real alternative. I don't want you as a booby prize."

"I understand," I said. "But if I told you I am going to work ten times harder, it wouldn't be true, and you wouldn't believe it. So what can I do?"

"You can work," said Rudi, "to find a new depth in yourself, and from that place you can make a new commitment to your own growth. This is essential for you to do at this time. Otherwise, you will get left behind. I don't want that to happen, and I can accept it if it does. Others will come to fill the vacuum. But for you it would be the end of your opportunity for this life. And I don't intend to be around for the next one."

"All right," I said. "You're finally getting to me."

"All these years that you have been with me," said Rudi, "you hardly touched the surface of what might be possible. The hardest thing I have to bear is that no one really can begin to take from me what I have to give. That is the reason more than any other that I will have to leave here. It isn't my personal preference. I eventually must go where people have the capacity and the need to take from me very deeply. Now go take a walk around the block and let it all sink in."

I left reluctantly. I should have been happy to get away from the battering I had been taking. But I was afraid that if I walked through the door it might disappear behind me. I had felt that only once before, the first time that I met Rudi.

Before The Sun

PHOTOS: INDIA

Photos: India

Before The Sun

Photos: India

Before The Sun

Photos: India

All photos courtesy of Bruce Joel Rubin

Chapter Sixteen

THE MARTIAL ARTS

The next time I appeared at the store it was with some reluctance. But Rudi greeted me as if nothing had happened.

"Greg was in before," he said as he poured us both some coffee.

I had known Greg for a long time. He had first appeared a year or two after I met Rudi. I had watched him change from a smart-aleck who had endless confidence in his own foolish judgment, to a gradually evolving, more serious person interested in both Rudi's work and Eastern martial arts. Rudi encouraged his interest in the latter, and Greg devoted a great deal of effort to studying Aikido and Tai Chi. After he had studied Tai Chi for a year, Rudi allowed him to give classes for those of us who were interested. We met once or twice a week wherever it could be arranged. I was never much for athletic activities, but the sense of controlled slow motion, so much a part of Tai Chi, interested me.

Greg was patient. He had to be. People seemed to forget the movements as quickly as he taught them.

"The man I study with teaches one new position in each lesson," he said. "You watch what he does. Then you do it. He doesn't tell you what is wrong. You have to gradually discover it for yourself. At that rate it takes a year to get through the basic series of movements. At five dollars a lesson it becomes a big investment, but it is worth it if you are really serious about learning Tai Chi."

The work progressed fairly well. Since most of the students were also working with Rudi, they had some conception of inner discipline. On the other hand they did not get as deeply involved in the Tai Chi as they otherwise might.

Rudi's own work had relatively little to do with any physical activity beyond the flexibility, relaxation, and control required to sit quietly for thirty to forty-five minutes at a stretch. He encouraged Tai Chi partly for Greg's sake to help his understanding grow through the process of teaching what he had learned to others. He also felt that Tai Chi would help to break down some of his students' physical tensions that interfered with the flow of psychic and spiritual force in his own classes. It was an experiment.

I also went at Rudi's urging to the Aikido Zendo where Greg was studying. I had always been afraid of physical combat since I was a little kid growing up in New York City. I had gone to private schools where the need rarely, if ever, arose. Presumably I was lucky, but as a result I had never learned to physically defend myself. The age of thirty-five didn't seem a very likely time to begin.

The Aikido Zendo was severely Japanese in character. The mats were carefully arranged. All the students wore the same basic clothes designed for freedom of action. The only difference was the color of the belt showing the level of proficiency of the individual.

I knew nothing and was in comparatively poor physical condition. I was shown basic exercises for strengthening my wrists and introduced to preliminary tumbling maneuvers. I promptly forgot everything I was shown within five minutes. But others, noticing my predicament, showed me again.

The first lesson was endless. When they announced that you could stay for the next class if you wished, I politely declined, thankful that I had survived with no more than a slightly sprained ankle. Actually I was rather proud of myself. I bought a book on Aikido which I proposed to study. Like most books that attempt to describe physical actions, it raised more questions than it answered. But at least I was becoming confused about new things.

On the surface Aikido was totally dissimilar to Rudi's work. It was physically active, fast, and violent. Rudi's work was apparently passive, gradual, and totally inward in its effect. But on another level there were similarities. Both involved gaining control of one's own inner mechanism — Aikido for purposes of self- defense, Rudi's work for the purpose of absorbing higher nourishment. Both involved an awareness of inner flow and concentration on psychic centers. In particular, Aikido, along with other martial arts, put great emphasis on being centered in the lower belly. Rudi also emphasized this area. But the greatest similarity was that both worked with a psychic force. The *Ki* of Aikido, like the *Chi* in Tai Chi, was not physical at all. It was a life vitality that flowed through all things, similar to the Hindu *prana*. The physical technique in Aikido was designed to direct and redirect the flow of this force so as to enable the practitioner to defend himself against direct physical attack.

All of the preceding helped to interest my intellect, but did little to quiet my fear. I continued to come intermittently to the Aikido classes. I learned something about tumbling and a few of the basic exercises. But when I finally strained my back I was happy to quit.

All of this was in the background as Rudi told me of his most recent encounter with Greg.

"He is such an idiot," said Rudi in disgust. "His uncle offered him a job in Paris, and Greg said he wasn't interested."

"I don't understand why that irritates you," I said.

"Greg's uncle happens to be a millionaire. He is a very difficult character. Consequently he has a hard time finding anyone he can trust. When he offered Greg the job it was really offering him an opportunity for a new life, if he can gain his uncle's confidence. I'm not saying Greg should take it if he isn't interested. Yet what's he doing now? Not much. His spiritual work is not going to fall apart if he takes a year to live in Europe and learn his uncle's business."

"What kind of business is it?" I asked.

"Manufacturing cashmere garments. His uncle travels all over the world buying the wool. There are endless possibilities to a situation like that. And Greg almost said nothing about it. He didn't think it was important. God, what a schmuck!"

"I'm sorry I missed seeing him," I said.

"Don't worry. He'll be back," said Rudi, lapsing into silence.

Finally I asked, "But what is Greg going to do now?"

"He's going to think things over, that's for sure," said Rudi. "I told him he was a fool for throwing away such an opportunity without talking to me about it first. What am I here for anyway? I sit in the store eight hours a day. I'm not hard to find. He bothers me for every idiotic thing that comes into his head. But for something important he doesn't ask me. Stupid! Stupid! Stupid!"

I stayed quiet, glad that it was Greg and not me that was absorbing Rudi's wrath. Generally he saved his temper for his mother, but it was never far from the surface. The intensity of the forces working within him kept him in an emotionally volatile condition. He had learned to control it only through severe inner discipline.

"I would have thought that going to Europe would appeal to Greg," I said.

"It does. If he went he would be supervising a factory of women. It sounds like something he would enjoy. But he doesn't like his uncle. So he said, 'No'. Jesus. If his uncle was likable, he wouldn't need Greg in the first place. But it's out of my hands now. We can only sit and wait."

We didn't have to wait long. After an hour Greg wandered in, looking like a dog that had made a mess on the living room floor and was slightly ashamed.

"I guess you have a point," he said to Rudi.

"So what have you done?" Rudi asked.

"I phoned my uncle. I made up a story about my parents not wanting me to leave the country. Anyway, I opened up the possibility again."

"What did he say?"

"I guess he believed me."

"Is that all?"

"Well, no. He said he thought my original reaction was stupid."

"We have something in common then," said Rudi. "How do things stand now?"

"I'm going to see him tomorrow and talk some more."

"Good! Do me the favor of not coming to an immediate decision. Listen to what he says. Ask for what you think is reasonable, and then come back and tell me what happened."

"Is that really necessary?" said Greg. "I'm pretty sure I'll be going."

"I'm pretty sure, too," said Rudi. "But nevertheless you don't have to agree to his terms without question. Find out what he wants and then come back. That way we can negotiate. He doesn't have to know who your advisor is, though if he did, it might increase his respect for you."

"Okay. I'll be back tomorrow afternoon," said Greg. He got up and left as if he didn't have a care in the world.

As the door closed behind him, Rudi made a wry face and shook his head.

"Greg has one saving grace. He's a fanatic. Once he gets into something there is nothing he won't do. You could use some of that, John. But stupid! I'll never get used to it."

* * *

In the coming weeks all was arranged, and Greg flew to France. I would occasionally hear of him through letters he sent to Rudi.

He wrote about visiting some exotic places where cashmere wool was raised, the nature of the work, his uncle, and an Aikido master he discovered in Paris. It was impossible to tell what was really happening from the letters; but he seemed content, and Rudi felt better about him at a distance than in person.

Then one day I walked in the store and Rudi said,

"Guess who was just here?"

Since there were about a thousand possibilities, I just shrugged.

"Greg," he said. "He had an argument with his uncle. He intends to quit."

"Is that it?" I asked.

"Not quite. But you will hear what happened yourself. I sent him around the corner for some coffee. Sit back and await developments."

We talked of other things and then, sure enough, the door opened and a slightly more sophisticated Greg appeared. We greeted each other as long lost brothers and then sat down to coffee and cake which Rudi produced from a hidden drawer. He was never at a loss for food. People were constantly bringing him fruit, cookies, and cake.

"So," said Rudi, "what happened?"

"I suppose the accident had something to do with it," said Greg. "My uncle had a Citroën. The whole hydraulic system failed at the top of a hill. He couldn't steer. He couldn't brake. Even the shocks ceased functioning. He was very lucky. The hill had no curves. He finally came to a stop when he hit a tree. He wasn't seriously hurt, but it didn't improve his disposition."

"That didn't really have anything to do with your leaving, did it?" asked Rudi.

"No," said Greg. "He's just impossible. I've had enough. I'm not getting anywhere."

"Just where do you think you are going to get if you return?" asked Rudi. "You'll be starting all over at the bottom. I didn't send you over there to have a party. Look, Greg. It's the same opportunity it always was. Just because the novelty has worn thin and it doesn't fit your fantasy of what you want is no reason to quit. I want you to go back, make it up with him, and give it another chance."

"Do I have to?" said Greg.

"You didn't have to go in the first place. You made the choice. Now it is up to you to make it come out right. You're learning how to supervise people. You've found a martial arts master. You have the opportunity to travel. And you can always come back here. But if you do, come back with something, not empty-handed."

Greg looked like a convict who thought he was up for parole, only to discover there were six more months to go. But he kept quiet, which was hard for him. A minute of silence passed. Rudi looked at him and suddenly smiled.

"Okay?" he said.

"All right," said Greg. "I don't want to do it, but I will because you say I should."

"You're a real hero," said Rudi. "I tell you what. On my next trip, I'll stop over in France and spend a few days with you."

Two months later, Rudi fulfilled his promise.

"Greg's uncle invited me to stay at his house," he told me on his return. "I thought it would be very pleasant. The first night I fell down a flight of stairs and hurt my back. For the rest of the time I had to listen to his uncle arguing with everyone in sight. I was really happy to get out of there. If I hadn't told Greg I would come, I would have flown right from England to India."

"How is Greg doing?" I asked.

"He's all right, but I think he will be coming back next spring. He's having a good time. He has a girl. The Aikido man he found is excellent. He knows acupuncture, Zen archery, and a couple of other things. Maybe he'll come over in a few years. Anyway," concluded Rudi, "the experience has been good for him, even if he doesn't want to admit it."

※ ※ ※

A month or two later Greg suddenly reappeared. He was in the country for a few days to conduct some business for his uncle, see his parents, and say hello to Rudi.

Rudi smiled at some hidden joke as he told me of their latest meeting.

"You missed Greg by a half an hour."

"Is he coming back?" I asked.

"I don't think so. He has heard enough for one day."

"Why? Did you tell him he should stay there?"

"No. That experience has served its purpose. It was something else."

Rudi paused enigmatically.

"So what was it?" I asked curiously.

"He wanted some advice on his love life. He has gotten involved with an Algerian girl. He wanted to know how to end it. I asked if he had a photograph of her. He showed me a picture of the two of them together. I worked with the picture a little bit to get a sense of the girl. She was very good inside. So I said to him,

"'You want to know how to handle the situation. It's very simple. Marry her!'

"I thought he would fall through the floor. He asked if I were joking.

"'I'm very serious,' I said. 'She's a wonderful girl. The only trouble with her is that she's too good for you.'

"That was a little more than he could take. He had decided he was tired of her and was trying to be what he considered kind in finding a way to drop her.

"'You can't be serious,' he said.

"'You asked my advice. I'm telling you. Marry her.'

"'But I don't have to, do I?' he asked with faint hope.

"'You can do what you want. You didn't have to go to Paris in the first place. You went because of the opportunity. You don't have to marry her either, but it has a wonderful potential for you. It's one of the reasons you went to Europe.'

"We argued about it for ten minutes. That is, I told him what to do and he tried to find a way out. But I expect it will happen. He could use the responsibility of a permanent relation."

"How can you be so sure from just a photograph?" I asked.

"I can see her essential nature in the picture, and I know Greg very well. But the one thing you have to understand, John, is that my loyalty is to Greg. You can't be on everybody's side. My students are my family. When I told Greg she was too good for him, I meant it. But, from his point of view, to get someone better than he could have expected is a wonderful thing. It may not be so wonderful for her. If I was her teacher, and she had met Greg, I would advise her to drop him immediately.

"But my commitment is to Greg's growth. Anything that can help him, I support. You have to be prepared to fight for the people who are close to you. That is your first responsibility. It's an illusion to try to support the whole world. It is an act of someone who cannot take care of himself. If you look in any religious tradition you see that development occurs over a long period, and as a result of great effort. A teacher makes a big investment in his students. If one or two emerge as completed human and spiritual beings, he is usually more than satisfied. In the last analysis all that is necessary is to produce one person who can carry on the work. The rest is background. It does not matter in whom the full flowering occurs. That is up to an individual's work, his potential, and in the end, cosmic justice which goes beyond anything we can see with our logical minds. Just think of me like a father. Greg is my son. I want the best for him. He should be returning in a few months."

Chapter Seventeen

A SEARCH FOR MANHOOD

While Rudi worked on my basic psychic mechanism, my ordinary life remained much the same, a vague arena of job and family that functioned with little effort on my part. Sooner or later it was bound to change. When it did it was more the result of my professional work than direct contact with Rudi. But he was always there in the background, affecting the outcome when it was most vital for my future.

I had for many years been interested in the study of small groups and personality change. During the 1960s I became involved in the Human Potential Movement. It hardly existed as an organized expression, but was more of an informal network of people who shared the common aim of releasing the vast reservoir of human potentiality which all agreed was masked and untapped. This emphasis did not differ from Rudi's work, but the level was more interpersonal and psychological rather than the psychic and spiritual. In a sense the two orientations were complementary.

In the course of developing a human potential project I was assigned to work with a woman executive who was attractive, but afraid of men. I began to feel drawn toward her.

I told Rudi about the woman. He responded by analyzing her character. He described qualities in her that I had never recognized until he mentioned them. Finally he got to the point.

"The main problem," Rudi said, "is that you don't know the difference between sexuality and creativity. They are related, but they are not the same. It's not your fault that you don't understand the distinction. No one has ever explained it to you. For most people the only positive attraction they ever feel is emotional or sexual, or often both in some peculiar combination. Even if they experience something truly different, they unconsciously assume it is the same and force it into that mold because it is all that they have ever known.

"There is something between the two of you, but it is not sexual.

It is not love. You feel the flow of creativity which comes from the work you are doing together. That is the whole thing. If you make it anything else, it will all disappear. She could not accept it, and even if she could, it would change what you are doing because the energy you feel was not meant to be used personally. It should be applied to your project to produce concrete results. This is what others expect, and what is right in this case."

"I hear what you are saying," I said, "and I can intellectually see a lot of truth in it, but I'm not completely convinced. It is simpler to do what you say but I want to know the truth, not just do the easy thing."

"You have heard the truth. But you have begun to build a fantasy around it, using the energy that flows between you. You have to stop feeding it."

※ ※ ※

A few days later the woman and I happened to eat in a Chinese restaurant. At the end of the meal we got the customary fortune cookies. Mine said, "She will grant whatever you request." While I thought mine over I asked her, "What does your fortune say?"

She was slightly reluctant to answer. "It just says, 'Give him whatever he asks!' What does yours say?"

"You'll never believe it," I said, silently passing it to her. She was slightly embarrassed and concerned about what I might ask next. I was thankful that I had talked with Rudi about the situation, otherwise I would have interpreted it as the fickle finger of fate. As it was I shrugged it off as a test and carried on with an extra cup of tea.

※ ※ ※

My work with this particular woman grew to involve a number of other people from different corporations and service agencies. We worked together in the preliminary stages of creating a National Center for the Exploration of Human Potential.

In my search for financial support for the Center, I was led to pursue a particular gentleman who was the director of a foundation. He was a difficult man to see, but I discovered through a mutual friend that he was going to attend an encounter group weekend. I decided that it might be a good place to meet him.

I contacted the leader of the encounter group, Bill Schutz, who admitted me to the weekend. I appeared ready to meet the Foundation Director, but totally unprepared for what was to come.

The major theme of the experience was the expression of love and hate. On both scores I found myself wanting. I couldn't express what I felt, and I didn't feel much. I had never really had a good relationship with a woman. As these realizations hit me, the need to meet the Foundation Director receded into the background.

Such insights are not unusual in a successful encounter group. The dynamics of the underlying process cause personal weaknesses to surface under conditions in which they are difficult to deny.

The crucial issue is how one reacts when they occur. The typical response is to be greatly affected for a short time. One gets a taste of a freer and perhaps more fulfilling existence. Then a counter-reaction sets in. The whole fabric of one's existence, all the relationships and responsibilities, reassert their hold. In a short time most of the initial impetus is lost. That is the typical course.

In my own case I found myself abruptly hurled into a region that was unfamiliar or long forgotten. I was faced with the clear recognition that I had never become a man. I had successfully evaded it out of indifference, cowardice, and a general inability to come to terms with the issues involved.

It was equally clear to me that there was no one either asking or expecting me to do anything about it. I was married, had a family, a good job, and was working on my future spiritual development.

What did becoming a man have to do with all this? Where would it lead? I realized at the beginning that it would take me back into the adolescence I had partially aborted. It would threaten the pattern of life I had built around me.

It has never been hard for me to act when the lines were clearly drawn. I looked at myself as a human being and was disgusted at my cowardice and lack of deep feeling. I did not care about the price. I knew that if I buried the insight the opportunity to make a new start might never come again. If it did come again, it might be too late for me to do anything about it. It might be too late now, though I did not really believe that. I would not have had the realization if it were too late.

I chose to take up where I had left off, perhaps twenty years before. It was a quiet decision. I shared it with no one, but it was real.

I started by attending a series of encounter weekends run by Bill Schutz over the next four months. I grew somewhat stronger, and developed a little more respect for myself.

In the end Bill Schutz left New York to work and live at the Esalen Institute in Big Sur, California, which was at that time the fountainhead of the human potential movement. My own professional work and personal need caused me to go there several months later. One of the driving forces behind my visit was to have an experience with a woman. It was implicit in my original sense of what I must do to complete myself as a man.

In a place like Esalen there were many opportunities for people to come together. The whole atmosphere fostered the possibility. But something always got in the way. At the crucial moment an invisible glass plate would come sliding down between me and the woman in question. It must have happened on nine different occasions. I began to get fatalistic.

Esalen was known for its hot sulfur baths. Rumor had it that the bathing was coed and nude. I found the whole idea pretty threatening. I kept putting off going there. After the first workshop was over, I finally got courageous and went down the steep path to the baths. It was almost deserted. I steeped in the steaming sulfur water for forty minutes and let the tension, confusion, and stimulation of the workshop leave me.

When I finally emerged I felt very relaxed. I started up the path that led from the baths to the main houses. As I came to the mid-point, a girl who had been descending arrived at the same place simultaneously. We paused. I looked at her. She looked back. I don't know quite what I expected, but without knowing how it happened she was in my arms, though I had never seen her before. I held her, feeling completely natural and with a sense of contentment in the moment that I had not known for a long time. It lasted for several minutes. Then we parted without a word. I saw her later. The warmth was still there, but the original moment never returned. It wasn't necessary.

An hour later the next workshop began.

At intervals, as the pressure grew, we were urged to go off by ourselves. I went into the redwood forest adjoining Esalen. It had a remarkable other-worldly atmosphere. As I wandered between the great trees, I gradually worked myself up into a kind of frenzy. A Nazi character emerged from within me and started screaming and wanting to kill people. I always knew I had the potential, but I had never felt the reality. It was frightening, but I felt freer when I had finished.

***

I left Esalen shaken, but still unfulfilled. I decided to stop off at the University of Utah and visit Herbert Otto. He and I were working on the development of the Center for the Exploration of Human Potential at the time.

A day later I was in Salt Lake City visiting one of Herbert's classes in Human Potential. I didn't particularly want to be there. It seemed rather anticlimactic after what I had just been through at Esalen, but it was moderately interesting. After the class the students usually went to the cafeteria. One of the girls whom I hadn't really noticed invited me to come along. Herbert seemed to want to go, or at least felt that he should, so we both went.

In the cafeteria I sat opposite the girl who had invited me. Her name was Janis. She was a friendly, curious type. She was particularly interested in Esalen, and kept asking me questions. I didn't want to go into it, but slowly I started talking.

My words sounded hollow to me compared to the experience I had been through, so I finally said to her, "The best way I can tell you about it is if we do an exercise together."

"Go ahead!" she said eagerly.

"Then touch my hands," I said, "and look at me. Just be conscious of your own sensations. No words. Use your hands to communicate what you are feeling."

It was a simple exercise. We had used it in a creativity workshop. She was immediately responsive. After a few minutes everyone stopped talking to watch us. They didn't know what was happening and were vaguely embarrassed. I didn't care, and wasn't about to stop in order to explain.

Without knowing how or why, I found myself locked together with this woman inside a field of emotion and energy that flowed around us and through us. It was not a totally unfamiliar feeling to me, as working with Rudi had made me used to experiencing strong encompassing forces. But it had never happened with a stranger. Everything else faded. We were aware only of each other. Vaguely I knew Herbert was near and not quite sure what was going on.

It continued for ten to fifteen minutes. When it was over neither of us said anything. Someone asked, "What was that all about?" I mumbled something. They were glad to drop it. I was shaken, but felt wonderful.

A few minutes later the group began to break up. The girl and I stayed together with Herbert, walking slowly out of the building. We stopped to hear some music. Nothing was said. Finally, I asked,

"Would you like to come with us for awhile? I'll be leaving for New York first thing in the morning."

"I'm really sorry. I can't," she said. "I have to go home."

My fortune seemed to be running true to form. But I didn't really care at that moment. It was enough. It was more than enough.

I walked her to her car. We paused, kissed, held each other for a minute. Then I said,

"I am not going to write to you so you won't feel under any obligation to reply. But I'll give you my address if you want to write to me."

She took it and silently departed. I went home and spent a sleepless night at Herbert's. We left the house at 6:15 for the airport. The plane took off at 7:00. It was a fitting end to the trip.

✻ ✻ ✻

I came back to New York and took up the familiar threads of my life. I told Rudi a little of my experience. He made no direct comment, but encouraged me to expand my professional contacts.

Two months later I received a letter from Janis.

Dear John, I want to tell you what happened to me the night we met. I returned home after leaving you in the parking lot. I was up the whole night. I didn't sleep at all. The experience just kept going in me all the time. I was really sorry that I hadn't come with you. I phoned at 6:30 the next morning, but you had gone. The experience was one of the most wonderful things that has ever happened to me.

As I read the letter, the whole trip rose up inside me and flowered.

Chapter Eighteen

BECOMING A LITTLE TEACHER

"The greatest mistake you can make is to sit and wait like a bump on a log," Rudi said as he talked during an evening class. "All that will ever overtake you is old age or death. It is one thing to surrender. It is another thing to be passive. Surrender is active and difficult if you are attached to what you are trying to surrender, or afraid of the unknown. Passivity may be good for meditation in the mind, but it will never get you anywhere in this work. If there is something you want you have to reach for it. You have to ask from your heart. You have to demand that it happen.

"When I really want something, I go up into heaven and begin to knock on the gate. I keep praying and sending messages and requests until they get so annoyed with me that they take action just to get a little peace.

"But most of you just sit here, absorbing a little of the force and thinking that your life will come marching through the door to find you. Maybe a little will happen that way, but not much. You have to be waiting for it, watching for it, longing for it. I am giving you notice. If it doesn't come and you don't ask inwardly or talk to me about it, you can only blame yourselves."

I couldn't ignore that. At the next opportunity, I spoke to Rudi.

"I've been thinking about what you said," I began.

"What was that?"

"About not just sitting and waiting, but needing to ask."

"So?" He was not going to make it easy.

"So I want to ask about teaching."

"What about teaching?" he said obstinately.

"Not about teaching, about my teaching. It's been a long time since my thirty-third birthday."

"That's true, John, What have you been waiting for?"

"I guess some indication from you."

"What is it you really want?"

"I want to be able to begin teaching."

"You could have begun several years ago. But nothing in you cared enough to ask for it. You just waited. Basically, you didn't want the responsibility. To become a teacher is to take on some of the karma of your students. It isn't glamorous. It doesn't satisfy your ego. You can't do it for any reason like that. You have wasted a lot of time."

"I admit all that," I said, "but I can't spend the rest of my life regretting the past. What should I do at this point?"

"You should go home and work on your wish. Be sure that you still want it and are willing to sustain the effort. It is better to wait than to start prematurely. Beginning to teach is like opening Pandora's box. You never know what will come out."

"All right, I'll do that," I said. "But I'm sure right now. I'm only ashamed about all the time that has gone by."

Rudi said nothing more, so I left.

During the next two days I asked myself when I worked whether I was really sincere and prepared to carry through wherever teaching might lead me in the future.

The general answer I got was that I would never be entirely sure, but that time was running out for me. I had to make my move or forget about it. I decided that I would pay the price, whatever it was.

It was autumn. The eight acres around my house in the country had one quantity in excess: leaves. They covered the grass in thick layers. Even under good conditions, it was a major operation to burn them.

But this year, most of the leaves were wet. They wouldn't burn. I decided on desperate measures. I began to gather them in front of the house on the gravel driveway. For several hours I did nothing but collect leaves. The pile reached six or seven feet high and was very wide around. My plan was to pour gasoline on it, stand back, and throw in a match. I felt that if the flame got hot enough the leaves would dry and burn.

I poured on plenty of gasoline, got the kids to move away, and stood back myself about eight feet. I lit a match and threw it toward the leaf mountain.

The next thing I knew there was flame behind me. Since I was facing the leaves, that was quite alarming. I could feel my eyebrows singeing, and instinctively turned away, putting my hands up to my face.

My children told me later that I had set off a great exploding fireball.

They thought it was wonderful. I staggered back more shocked than injured, though the left side of my face was very red. The leaves burned merrily. That aspect of the plan was a great success.

The next day I looked like a war hero halfway through plastic surgery. I went to the city because my work required it. I didn't feel too bad, but I looked terrible. People stopped on the street to stare. My colleagues were full of curiosity and sympathy. Finally I concluded my business and went to the store.

Rudi made no comment on my appearance. I was vaguely irritated. At least he could ask, "What happened to you?"

Finally, after ten minutes I couldn't resist bringing the subject up.

"I really did something stupid," I began.

"What was that?" he asked casually.

"I ignited a whole pile of wet leaves with gasoline. It set off a huge explosion."

"Was anyone injured?" Rudi asked. It seemed a pretty stupid question under the circumstances.

"No," I said, "just me."

"I think it's great," said Rudi.

"What's great?" I asked, sincerely puzzled.

"What happened to you! You got a real answer to your question. Do you accept it?"

"I'm not going to ask whether you're serious, because I know that you are, but Jesus!" I said.

"Listen, John. When you left here last time, you were going to decide whether you wanted to become a teacher, regardless of the price. I assume that the answer was yes."

I nodded my head in agreement.

"So the explosion was the next thing that happened. It was your baptism of fire. I think the symbolism is wonderful." He began to laugh.

I decided if there was a joke, it wasn't on me, so I laughed too. And at the same moment I recaptured the feeling that I had had during and immediately preceding the explosion. Something in me had known what was going to happen. If I had been consciously aware of what I was about to set off I wouldn't have had the courage to do it. But something had known. It had the fatality of a ritual.

"Well?" I asked. "What should I do now?"

"Find a student and start teaching."

"But how?"

"Finding the student is up to you. As far as teaching, just start! It will come to you. If you have any questions, ask me. There is a great deal of material stored up in you from all the years we have been together and the efforts you made before that in other kinds of work. It will all return as you need it."

"But give me some concrete idea of what to do," I pleaded.

"I'm giving you the right to begin. The rest is up to you."

As I left the store my mind was occupied with the question of finding a student. I went through the catalog of possibilities, and being of a courageous nature, I decided that Janis would be the least threatening person I knew. I called her up, explained the situation, and invited her to come to New York for the next weekend. She was delighted.

※ ※ ※

My first class, which was the culmination of eight years of work with Rudi, was given in a small motel room. The only decoration was a sculpture of a serpent which seemed like a good omen at the time.

Janis sat in a chair and I sat on the edge of the bed. There were several delays. But finally, I took a deep breath and began.

At exactly the same moment a one-man band started to play in the next room. There were drums, cymbals, a harmonica, and diverse other instruments. I began to crack up, and then realized that I couldn't afford to let anything stop me.

Janis took her cue from me. We worked for perhaps fifteen minutes. The band played for fifteen minutes. When the moment came that I decided "I've worked long enough" the band instantly stopped. The timing was unbelievable, but it didn't seem funny any longer.

There are some things that remain of lasting significance, regardless of their particular quality, just because they happened at all. The first class I had with Rudi was such an event. It opened the door to my life. The class that I gave to Janis that night was the same. If I could go back and see myself as I was then, I would probably find the whole effort somewhat ridiculous. But it was a beginning. One from which I have detoured, but never lost the way.

Chapter Nineteen

SACRIFICE

My contact with Janis continued mainly through the medium of long distance telephone calls. The climax came about six months after my initial trip West. I was attending another Encounter Workshop in California. But this time Janis was joining me. It was the fulfillment of her initial interest in Esalen on the night we had met.

I arrived first. To my surprise Bill Schutz was distant and unwilling to let us in his workshop. No one was really friendly. Since Janis was coming specifically for the workshop I had to try and stop her, but she couldn't be reached immediately. I went to the office to find out about transportation to the airport. There was a station wagon going into Monterey in a few hours. I was at loose ends until then. I paused uncertainly on the bench outside the office. A large man sat down beside me. I knew his name was Daniel, and that he was a Resident who lived at Esalen for nine months and attended all activities.

"How's the program going?" I asked, with no particular interest.

"I'm not in it any more," he said quietly. "I quit."

"What happened?" I asked. My curiosity was aroused.

"Hasn't anyone talked to you?" He was incredulous.

"Not really. Esalen feels more like an armed camp than a center for developing human potential."

"That's exactly what it is," he said.

I talked for an hour with Daniel. He described a fascinating mixture of personal conflict, mysticism, and political intrigue. What he told me fit the mixed paranoia with which I had been greeted. If I had not spoken to him I would have left without the slightest understanding of the situation.

My openness to Daniel was related to my long experience with Rudi. I felt both the presence of fierce energy and inner understanding. Daniel had gone through a recent mystical experience which I immediately felt to be genuine. Others had also accepted it at first, but when he had turned the results of his insights on the people around him, they quickly discovered that believing in truth in the abstract was not the same as hearing the truth about oneself. They moved from awe to suspicion, to a conviction that Daniel was crazy. He was too strong for them to overcome, so they had ostracized him. But he refused to leave. His continued presence in the environment mocked and threatened their efforts at personal growth.

I listened to the story, fascinated by the inherent conflict of a community devoted to human potential trying to eliminate someone in whom such growth had occurred.

Daniel finally told me how to approach Bill Schutz so that he would let us in his workshop. By the time Janis was to arrive, everything had been arranged. Daniel lent me his car to pick her up at the Monterey airport, and for the next five days my attention was mainly focused on the encounter experience in which Janis and I were put through an emotional baptism of fire. We emerged stronger than before and with our relationship in full bloom.

On the last evening we walked up the path from the hot sulfur baths on which I had met and hugged the unknown girl six months before. I stopped Janis a little above the same spot. A feeling of acceptance and gratitude flooded through me. We held each other with the stars shining down from above, and the ocean breaking on the bare rocks below.

✳ ✳ ✳

I returned to New York with a sense of fulfillment very rare in my life. I looked forward to seeing Rudi and telling him something of what had happened.

He was, as usual, casually pleased to see me.

"How was your trip?" he asked, as if I had just been around the corner for coffee.

"It was wonderful, like something out of a spy thriller. I met a remarkable man."

I told Rudi something of my encounter with Daniel. I ended with a question.

"Do you think he is genuine?"

"Yes," said Rudi. "But you dramatize the whole thing too much.

He had a genuine experience. It gave him a capacity he didn't have before. But to see the truth is no great achievement, or even to know what other people ought to do. That really isn't difficult. The important issue is what he does with himself. Will he try and develop what he has been given, or let it fade away? If he uses the experience as a new beginning, it could be wonderful. Probably it will fade. But in any case, John, you are a fool. You meet someone with an unusual quality, and what do you do? You bring back a good story. Instead of talking with him, you should have absorbed his energy."

"I never thought of that," I said.

"All the work you have done with me has taught you how to do it. You get the chance, and you don't make the connection. But I shouldn't be so critical. Most people wouldn't have even recognized him for what he was. Evidently you were the only one who did. But if you ever run into a situation like that again, don't worry about the drama. There is only one thing that matters. Absorb him! It is possible to digest the inner structure and experience of another person whole, like a python swallowing a pig. You take in everything and expel what you can't digest. Then you have his essence in your own energy system. You got something from him, but you could have gotten a hundred times more."

The conversation turned to other matters that had occupied Rudi in my absence. I gradually absorbed what he had said to me.

After a few minutes he casually asked, "Did anything else happen on the trip?"

I perked up. "Yes. Janis and I were in an encounter group together. Every conceivable weakness between us was brought out, but we emerged much stronger. I feel better about her now than ever before."

Rudi paused before speaking. It was not like him to hesitate.

"You are going to have to make a choice, John. Janis or this work. You can't have both."

I could not immediately comprehend what he had said, though it could not have been stated much more clearly. I looked at him with complete disbelief.

"What do you mean?" I said, relatively quietly.

"I can give you a number of reasons," he said, "and I will. But it won't change anything. You can continue the relationship with her if you wish. But then you must leave this work. Or you can end the relationship and continue the work."

There was no way that I could immediately encompass what was happening. How could Rudi give me such a choice? Why, if it were ever to happen, should it be now? I asked him this without really feeling anything yet.

"That is precisely the time to do it," he said, "People always wait until something starts to rot before cutting the connection. The time to do it is in full flower. It is the hardest time, but the best."

"But why?" I was beginning to feel something: sorrow, rage, bewilderment.

"The simplest thing I can say, John, is that you have to choose between whether your roots are going to be in yourself or in her. If you are going to continue working, your roots must be in yourself."

I didn't say anything. Rudi was quiet. Someone walking in at that moment might have mistaken the scene for one of intense inner abstraction.

Nothing in me accepted what had been said. But at the same time I knew what I would do in the end. Given the choice I would choose the work.

There was nothing personal in Rudi's action, I could sense that. It wasn't his objective to tie anyone to him, certainly not me. He was a surgeon performing an incision.

At the same time the whole turn of events was utterly incomprehensible. It had struck at the least likely time.

All of this is recalled through the mist of the past that softens the shape of events. It was different then; stark, brutal, with muted hate. But I never really wavered. Long before, I had decided that the work came first. I knew where I had started from and what had helped me to find my way back from darkness and death into the beginning of life. Janis herself had been attracted by the work functioning in me with the added impetus of my experiences at Esalen.

After a long pause, Rudi said, "Go and think it over, John. You are completely free to do what you want."

That sounded pretty hollow to me. The freedom to commit inner suicide was not something on which I placed a high value.

"I already know the answer," I said. "There is nothing I can do but end the relationship."

I wasn't sure if Rudi believed me.

"What should I do?" I asked.

"The quicker you get it over with, the easier it will be," he said.

"You mean I'm supposed to just pick up a phone and tell her?"

"It's the best way. It will be simpler than you expect. She will understand."

"I don't believe that," I said.

I left. Perhaps I was more in shock than I knew, but I decided to act immediately. I found a phone in the Times Square subway station. There, between the shuttle and the Seventh Avenue subway, with people passing on every side of me, I put through the call. The endless movement of humanity helped to distract me from what I was doing.

"Hello, Janis," I said. My voice shook slightly.

"Hello, John." She was delighted to hear from me.

"I don't know how to put this..." I said.

"What's wrong, John?" she asked. She was not concerned. What could possibly be wrong?

"I have just come from talking to Rudi."

"How is he?" asked Janis in a friendly tone.

"He's fine," I said. "But he gave me a choice. I have to give up the relationship with you or the work with him."

"I don't think I heard correctly," she said.

"You heard."

"What are you going to do?" asked Janis, as if she were inquiring about my next lecture at NYU.

"I don't have any choice," I said. "Our relationship is over. I don't want this to happen. Nothing in me wants it to happen. But I trust Rudi with my life. I don't trust myself. I have never known him to be wrong."

"You are really serious, aren't you?" said Janis.

"Yes!"

"There's nothing that I can say?" her voice trembled.

"There's nothing that either of us can say." I paused. It was quiet. "You don't seem all that upset."

"I'm not," she said. "Probably after you hang up I'll get hysterical. How can I believe that I'll never see you again? But right now I accept it. I guess something inside felt it was too wonderful to last. I don't know. I can't talk anymore."

✷ ✷ ✷

I saw Rudi a day or two later.

"It's all done," I said, feeling numb.

"Good. It's much better that way," he said.

I came over to him and my sleeve caught on a small vase. It fell to the floor and broke. It wasn't terribly valuable, but I offered to pay for it.

"Do me a favor, John," he said. "Don't come within six feet of me for the next two weeks."

I thought he was joking.

"I'm very serious," he said. "Regardless of what you may feel consciously, you hate me unconsciously right now. Give it some time to wear off, or next time you will break something really valuable."

The next few weeks were bleak. I kept my distance from Rudi, though I continued to stop at the store. For most of the time he talked about other things. Business went on as usual. After a time the barrier between us relaxed. But everyone without exception who knew of my relation with Janis thought Rudi was wrong. None of them could understand why I listened to him.

Their opinions made the situation more difficult, but I didn't waver. I had made up my mind, heart, and soul about Rudi long before. I may have had many limitations and thrown away many opportunities, but I understood the truth. He was fundamentally in a place more real than I. If I didn't accept that basic premise, there was no reason to work with him.

In talking about it later, Rudi said, "I think you know, John, that this whole thing gave me no pleasure. It had to be done, I could see into the future. You couldn't."

"What would have happened?" I asked reluctantly.

"You would probably have married and moved West."

"I don't see that," I said.

"How can you at this point? But you ought to be able to feel the possibility of marriage. You had already made a big step in that direction on your last trip. Isn't that true?"

"Perhaps." I couldn't be sure, but it was possible.

"Even if you hadn't moved West, I would have been forced to ask you to leave sooner or later."

"I suppose it will make sense eventually," I said.

"You would never have attracted the situation if you hadn't been working inside," said Rudi. "Therefore the inner work comes first. There can be no exceptions. Anything of an outer nature that has the power to come between you and your inner development has to be removed.

"You would have come to this point by yourself in a year and a half. By then the relation would have faded. The problem would have been how to end it gracefully. This way it is cut down in the prime of its life, which is harder but much better.

"But the crucial thing that determined my action was that I saw you putting your roots into her. It is all right to put branches into relationships, but your roots must be in yourself. Otherwise you will only be each other's limitation. It might be enjoyable. It might provide security. But in the end it will only be a haven in which to protect yourself from the very things you need to face.

"Don't worry, John. I am prepared to do the same thing in my own life. I already have. I'm sure I will do it again many times. Perhaps you can begin to appreciate how difficult it is for me, like performing surgery on myself without an anesthetic because I have to be conscious to do it.

"Janis was a gift, someone sent to help you fulfill yourself as a human being and as a man. She is very sentimental, but she truly loves you and would do anything for you. That is what you desperately needed. It had to come from a woman. Now she is doing the last thing she can for you, leaving you alone. That is the best thing you can do for her!"

Then when I didn't attempt to talk about it any further, Rudi smiled, as if he was about to share a great secret and said,

"Besides, John, in the next ten years you are going to marry an heiress and begin a totally new existence."

"That's nice," I said. I was not too enthusiastic. I figured he was trying to distract me.

"She will truly love you," said Rudi, "and free you from the life you have known. You will think you are in paradise!"

I began to believe him. But ten years was a long time to wait. At that moment I couldn't have cared less.

Chapter Twenty

ATTEMPTED MURDER

A month later, just before a projected trip to India, Rudi received a letter from an old student who was staying at Swami Muktananda's ashram.

"Dear Rudi," the letter said, "I am reluctant to write what follows because I don't quite know what attitude to take. For the last year and a half a man has been trained here at the ashram to kill you. I thought you should be aware of this before you came."

Rudi was deeply shocked by this information. He could not believe that his own teacher would do such a thing.

"Why should he want to destroy me?" he said to me the next day. "Isn't my life hard enough without something like that? But at least I am forewarned."

"Why should he want to destroy you?" I repeated his words. "I don't understand."

"Maybe it's his idea of a test," said Rudi. "What does it matter? I haven't gotten this far by running away. When I first went to India I didn't know anyone. Every door was closed. Believe me, I was scared then. But I went, and over a period of time made my way. Now I have friends. Perhaps they will help me. There is nothing to do but go."

Rudi left! It all happened so quickly that it was hard to get concerned. Finally he returned, shaken, but basically in good condition. He spoke of various side aspects of the trip. Then with some reluctance he got to the point.

"I might have been out of luck if I hadn't been warned," he said and then lapsed into silence.

"In what way?" I finally asked.

"I might have been psychically destroyed before I knew what hit me. Anything that builds up consciously over a long period of time has got to have a lot of force behind it. That was the secret of the Pharaoh's

Curse. An incredible amount of energy was accumulated in the pyramids over the centuries. When they were opened, this force was released. That is what killed the archaeologists. There was no curse.

"Anyway, being forewarned I was on the lookout for my assassin as I walked through the door of the ashram. I spotted him quickly. He seemed in a strange, somewhat crazed condition. Others told me that he had been brainwashed to believe that I was evil and that it was his mission to destroy me. If he could do that, he would receive a great inner reward.

"I put off any confrontation with him to give myself a chance to build up strength and support. When it came, I wanted it to be his move.

"A few days later I was working hard within myself, having almost forgotten him, when suddenly he was there psychically, threatening to attack. My impulse was to respond, and I knew that would be a mistake. He wanted me to fight back. He counted on it. That would reduce me to his level where he would be strongest. Instead, I made an effort to rise higher. He was there immediately. I surrendered that level, took in more energy and rose beyond where I had been. He was there again. I repeated this several times. He was still there, threatening, preparing to attack. I went out as far as I had ever been. I was beginning to get scared. I didn't know what he had been trained to do. By the time I found out it might be too late.

"He was still there. I was tempted to fight then, but I had resisted the temptation so far. This was no moment to give in. I gathered all the energy I could find and projected myself beyond anything I had ever known. I didn't care if I could get back. I went into infinity.

"When I became oriented, he was nowhere in sight. I had won!

"Afterwards, Swami Muktananda acted as if nothing had happened. It was a test as far as he was concerned. I had passed. The other man had failed. He was no longer interested in him. The year and a half of effort was concluded."

"But how did you feel?" I asked.

"Not good," said Rudi. "It was horrible for me to have the man in whom I put my trust consciously set out to destroy me. But I went to him to grow stronger. I could not deny that he made me put forth a tremendous effort and overcome obstacles that I otherwise might have avoided. It wasn't for me to judge him. If I didn't like it, I could go elsewhere. Right now I don't feel that there is anywhere else to go.

Swami Muktananda and Rudi in the streets of Ganeshpuri

"One thing I learned a long time ago was that saints are not necessarily kind, altruistic people who wander around loving God and spreading goodwill. If you study their lives, you will see that they worked incredibly hard to achieve their relation to God and that, in many respects, they were pretty odd people who might have been judged insane in Western society.

"In the East a saint is expected to be somewhat strange. He is a law unto himself. The only real concern is whether he is genuine. This is not so easy to say. Some saints will refuse to talk. Others will hide. They may live in graveyards. These are just some of the obvious odd aspects. They are also quite capable of fulfilling your expectations if they desire. But they may do this only to distract you, to see if you can find your way through the picture they create to the reality that is inside them. There are so many semi-phony yogis wandering around. Begging is a religious art in India. It is very hard to judge by any outward sign. Even a glowing sense of beauty and well-being doesn't necessarily mean much. Most of the people I have seen who fit my image of what enlightenment should be had just surface attainments. Scratch the surface a little and there was only an ordinary human being underneath. I remember a gorgeous holy man I saw along the Ganges. He looked like Mr. Yogi of 1967. He filled every image I have ever had of a spiritual person. But then I made the mistake of talking with him. He was very conscious of his looks and very superficial in his attainment. It was a good lesson for me. Real change of being requires working in great depth for a long period of time. There is no substitute or short cut. If there were I would have found it.

"I am saying all this so you won't just think I am stupid or a masochist for putting up with something like I have just been through. I have undertaken to work with Swami Muktananda. I have grown a great deal through being with him, particularly in combination with my spiritual relation with Nityananda. I will see the relationship through to the end.

"And in all fairness, there is another side to the situation. Swami Muktananda has great respect for me or he would not create such a terrible test. I present too great a challenge for him to overlook. I give his life added purpose. You can't imagine how boring it can get being an idolized guru in an ashram. It is a totally self-enclosed little community. Everyone needs a challenge beyond themselves. I am his challenge. We are stuck with each other. I accept it. He can do with me as he wants. He is my teacher."

Chapter Twenty-One

THE NATURE OF KUNDALINI YOGA

Rudi's whole life was a continuous ferment of forced growth. He would not accept anything less. In a talk for an evening class, he said,

"We always think of growth as something pleasant and light, like a flower petal unfurling in the sun. That is just the final stage. How does the seed feel when it is buried alive in the ground? What are its sensations as something begins to stir within its being? Probably uncertainty, fear, maybe even panic. That is growth!

"Even if it sends out a root and begins to germinate, how would it be, after getting used to the warmth, closeness and safety of the earth to have to face the prospect of breaking through the surface of the ground into a totally unfamiliar realm, facing the vulnerability of moving into the open, exposure to the elements, the blinding light? The seedling doesn't know what is happening. It grows unconsciously but also on faith, otherwise it would wither away very quickly.

"All of this is exactly paralleled by what occurs inside an evolving person. The only difference is that inner growth can only proceed through conscious suffering. It never occurs otherwise.

"When I rented my first store, which was made of pieces of tin nailed together, I was running wild. I sat myself down in the store and consciously decided to use it to tame my inner nature. I chose to have no heat. I got so chilled that it took until mid-summer before I began to feel warm. There was no bathroom. I peed in a pot which I emptied in the street. I could have afforded a heater and a bathroom. But I vowed to sit in that store day by day until I either broke down or gained control over myself. It was strong medicine and I had to take it for two years, but it did the job.

"I couldn't protest about it or feel sorry for myself. I wanted it that way, but anyone going through such experiences has the right to complain occasionally. It's like being a recruit in the Army. You can bellyache about the long marches, the food, and the officers, as long as you do what you're told."

"Its hard for me to relate to such experiences," I said. "I don't feel that I suffer all that much."

"You don't, not consciously and not yet," said Rudi. "You are still very dead to your own inner state. But there is suffering within you. What else keeps you working? The sense of emptiness that haunts you is suffering. You don't experience it as a physical pain because you keep it at a distance. But you can't escape it either.

"For most people inner work is like a paraplegic learning to walk again. Each step takes a great deal of conscious effort and must go against the physical pain and emotional discouragement which he feels. But we are not trying to restore a function which was destroyed through a physical injury. We are trying to reactivate a capacity that most have forgotten and everyone has lost.

"When something dead, diseased or non-functioning is being brought to life, it hurts physically. It is disturbing psychically. It is threatening emotionally. How can it be otherwise? Enlightenment is not sitting under a banana tree waiting for a fruit to fall into your mouth. It only comes after working and working and working to gather enough energy to break through the walls that surround you. As this happens the energy which was bound up is released in a sudden surge. It carries you onto a new level and gives you the experience of enlightenment.

"The classic picture of meditation is the Buddha quietly sitting under the Bo tree. But remember what he went through during the years in the forest, the constant obstacles that finally culminated in his refusal to rise again until he had achieved his goal. And even after that he was subjected to every temptation that could be thrown against him. All of this before the dawn of understanding began to break. That is the way it happens. You cannot imitate his life. The culture of which it was a part has vanished. Even the Buddha said that a century after his death his influence would diminish, and what remained would be a relic rather than a living force. The past can be a footstool. It is certainly nothing to idolize. You absorb it and move on. Christians who make a God of Christ only put an obstacle in their own way. It is much easier to do that than recognize that Christ represents a level of attainment, not the ultimate level, but the ultimate at that time, a man born into the world already in a totally cleansed state.

"The basic reason that real growth does not occur is that no one wants to feel pain. We are animals in that respect, conditioned to seek out things that bring us pleasure and to avoid those which hurt. Pain must occur in the growth process. When we avoid pain we avoid growth. That is what stops 90 percent of the people dead in their tracks.

"Then there is a more subtle obstacle for those who remain. Some of them are willing to sacrifice their time, security, and relationships for one overriding goal in their life. Unfortunately they reserve the right to pick this goal which removes most of the value which such dedication might have. No one is in a position to understand what is really good for them when they start to pursue their own fulfillment. They are flying blind. The major contribution which a teacher can make is that, having survived much of what the student must live through, he can put his own experience, understanding, and sympathy at their disposal. He can act as a guide to the further shore. But a guide is useless if you don't listen to him. And it is the major characteristic of a fanatic that they will listen to no one. They have the determination but not the humility to succeed in inner work. You can learn a lot from such a person, but you would not want to follow where he goes. His success is ultimately a prison from which he has neither the flexibility nor the inclination to free himself.

"Anything which is built on one level of experience may have to be torn down again in order to enter another. It is easy to accept something like that in principle when you don't have much to lose. But as you begin to grow more rapidly you will attract people and situations that you will not want to surrender. At that time it is only the action of an impartial force that wishes for your growth more than you wish for it yourself that can intervene and save you from what you have attracted. And as most of you already know, I don't hesitate to do that," said Rudi, concluding his talk.

Though Rudi spent long hours in the store and occasionally glanced through magazines and mystery stories, he avoided reading anything about spiritual subjects. When a new student asked for something mystical to read he recommended Agatha Christie. That usually ended the conversation. But once a very puzzled young man returned two hours later to say,

"I went to the biggest bookstore in the city and looked through every spiritual book on the shelves. There wasn't anything by Agatha Christie."

Rudi nodded and handed him a copy of her latest mystery which he happened to have on his desk.

"When you have a teacher," he said, "you don't need any books."

For the first five years that he taught, Rudi was so disinterested in spiritual writings that he didn't know the name given to the kind of work he was doing. Finally he indicated that it might be called Shakti Yoga. Shakti is the Hindu goddess of creative energy. Several years later he mentioned in an off-moment that we were now doing Kundalini Yoga. These were evidently equivalent efforts, though Kundalini Yoga was a more advanced version. It was never entirely clear as to the nature of the difference. He himself was not much interested in the distinction or the name and certainly read nothing about either one.

"I have left copies of *The Serpent Power* all over India," he said. "It is the classic text on Kundalini Yoga. People keep giving it to me, thinking that they are doing me a favor. As far as I am concerned it can only get in my way. All books on spiritual subjects either lie intentionally, i.e., the author pretends to knowledge he does not really possess through his own experience, or they lie unconsciously by giving the impression that the experiences recorded are either easily come by or almost impossible, neither of which is likely to be the case.

"Spiritual books generally feed the illusions of the people concerned. So, for me they are obstacles. I don't want to know other people's experiences until I have my own with which to compare them. If I know what is supposed to happen at a certain stage, it will make me try to force the result to that pattern. It can't possibly help. That's why I limit my serious reading to mystery stories.

"For a long time I never even knew that what I was doing had any relation to Kundalini, the serpent power. One day when I was at the ashram in Ganeshpuri, someone made a remark in English that I happened to overhear about serpents. I didn't know exactly what they were talking about. Maybe someone had seen a serpent around the garden, or maybe they were referring to the Kundalini power. I still don't know. But five minutes later one serpent after another started to run up my spine. Then I didn't need to read any books or listen to anyone else to believe in the reality of the force. I knew it was there and why they called it the serpent power. It was the serpent power!"

* * *

One day Rudi received a short article written by Swami Muktananda on *The Chakras*. It was the first time Rudi had read anything on the subject even though he had been working through certain chakras for many years. Perhaps he read the article because it was written by his teacher, though he had resisted reading anything Muktananda had written before. Perhaps it was something he needed to know at the time. In any case, it immediately influenced his basic description of the work he was teaching.

"Most people absorb about five percent of what they read," he said. "In a few months they forget even that. I don't read much, but what I read I absorb totally. I keep working and working on it, extracting more meaning than was almost ever there. I don't stop until I have connected it with everything I already know so that it is completely assimilated."

Before this time Rudi had emphasized the need to absorb force by drawing it in with the breath, and feeling it come down the center line of the body until it reached the sex organs. From there it was shifted backwards to the base of the spine, eventually awakening the Kundalini. The force then began to flow upward through a channel in the center of the spine, finally reaching the back and top of the head. Now the description became more elaborate as his own experience with the separate Chakras clarified the process for him. He described it in a series of talks to students.

"The basic process involved in doing inner work is one of absorbing and refining the nourishment needed for growth. Ordinary life feeds the personality. Higher energy is required to nourish the inner being.

"Just as there is a physical digestive system for taking in, breaking down, and absorbing the energy of food, there is a psychic digestive system that attracts, transforms and absorbs higher energies directly in a non-physical form. There have been various descriptions of this system. All of them are, to my knowledge, partially incorrect or incomplete. Either the writers didn't know what they were writing about, or they were consciously making it difficult for the reader to apply what they were describing. This was certainly done in various Tibetan writings where gaps were left that could only be filled in orally by a teacher. This helped to preserve the purity of the line of teaching, and served to prevent the student from attempting advanced work before

The Nature Of Kundalini Yoga

the proper foundation had been laid.

"Beyond all this, you have to understand one basic principle of spiritual work. The process of putting a method on paper makes it accessible beyond any immediate point in space and time, but the energy that is required to start the process cannot be transmitted by printed words. One must receive instruction from someone in whom the process is already functioning.

"There is fundamentally no way to steal it. Someone else must give it of his own free will. You can read books, listen to lectures, and share opinions with your friends. None of this can lead to any real result. It may, in fact, serve to confuse your mind with misguided expectations.

"One of the things that has always disgusted me in the various ashrams that I have visited, and there have been many, is the tendency of people to sit around comparing experiences. It encourages a subtle form of competition that is extremely undesirable. People do not, and should not, have the same experiences. There is no one to compete with except your own best effort in the past. But even worse, people lose the energy of their experiences by gossiping about them. That is the greatest stupidity. Experiences should be discussed only with your teacher, and then only if you have a real question about them. Otherwise they should be absorbed and forgotten.

"Every experience you have ever had, or will ever have, should likewise be absorbed and forgotten. This is the only path leading to inner freedom. Otherwise you may become a living memorial to some past enlightenment.

"All of these things I have said before in various forms, and I will undoubtedly have to say them again. It takes hundreds of repetitions for certain things to sink in. But today I particularly want to describe the working of the psychic system as I am coming to understand it. This is not to alter what I have said before, but to fill in certain gaps. What we were using in the past was a crude sketch. It was sufficient for the purpose, but incomplete.

"The simplest picture of the psychic digestive system is a line drawn from the point slightly above the eyebrows down the center of the body, ending in the region of the sex organs. Located along this line are a series of psychic centers, or chakras. The center line itself is a natural streambed for the flow of psychic and spiritual force. The chakras are like flowers along the streambed. When they are open they permit energy to pass through, drawing from it the nourishment they need, just as the digestive juices work on physical food to change its original character. All of this takes place naturally when the chakras are open. But, under normal conditions the chakras are closed. They almost never open spontaneously. It must be done through one's own conscious efforts. Even when they do open they quickly close when the conscious effort ceases. There is no way for the spiritual force to circulate while the chakras are closed. In parallel, one must look into the connections between the chakras. These connections are like the plumbing in a long-deserted house. There is no telling about its condition until you begin to run water into it again. There may be leaks or obstructions. Parts of the pipe may be rotted away. This must all be corrected for the system to function.

"In order for the force to enter into the first chakra, and to pass all the way down the front center line of the body, the pathway and all intervening chakras must be open. This may happen quickly and naturally as energy is fed in and brought down the pathway, or it may occur gradually, depending upon the individual's inner condition when he starts to work. But this process is only the first phase of the digestive process, even though it may involve great patience and persistence to activate it. It has no significance in and of itself, though each chakra is associated with its own function which emerges when the chakra opens. The total purpose of this phase of the work is to absorb cosmic energy from the surrounding atmosphere, progressively refine it, and draw it down until it strikes the chakra in the sex center. There, a transformation occurs which has been described in alchemy as changing lead to gold.

"The highest, most vital energy ordinarily available in the human organism is sex energy. When cosmic energy is related to sex energy in the manner I have described, a transmutation of the sex energy occurs. It is very real. You can feel it as gentle warmth and tingling of champagne bubbles in the sex center. It produces a force within the human organism that is never present under ordinary circumstances. This force is the normal stimulant for the higher creative energy which rests dormant at the base of the spine. Nothing else will activate it in a natural manner.

"When the transformation process has started and the attention is then shifted to the base of the spine, the higher sex force is brought to the site of the Kundalini energy which does in fact lie curled around the lowest vertebrae like a sleeping princess waiting for the kiss of the transformed sex energy to awaken it. As this happens the second major part of the total cycle begins. It usually takes place gradually and gently, though occasionally there is a fortunate person who feels the Kundalini activated strongly and quickly. Such people are objectively lucky, but they are usually more frightened than appreciative, and fail to do the necessary work to stabilize the inner process that has begun in them. But for most of you it has been, or will be slow.

"You can think of the spine as a thermometer, open at the very top. As the energy is directed from the sex center to the base of the thermometer, the fluid in the tube slowly warms and rises. Any obstacles it encounters will, of course, interfere with the process, but gradually these blocks are removed. At a certain point the energy fluid reaches the top of the tube and overflows. It is normally stored in the thousand-petal lotus chakra that corresponds to the bump on the back of the Buddha's head. This is not a natural bump. It develops only through inner work. As the energy of the Kundalini force is raised and overflows the chakra in which it is stored, it ripens and expands. It is like a large bud. After many years it begins to open naturally in the form of a great flower. It is then that the thousand-petal lotus earns its name. The higher energy that is released in the process is of a level and quality that the inner being has not known before. It flows into the brain, fertilizing and nourishing higher spiritual mechanisms, and then is drawn into the psychic digestive system so that it can touch each chakra in turn and provide it with concentrated nourishment. It is at this point that each human function begins to work at a new and almost totally unknown level. But there is no need to go into that now.

"Different mystical systems describe various numbers of chakras. For our purpose we will deal with eight of them, though there are additional chakras in the hands and feet, as well as in the head and beyond the head.

"The first chakra is the third eye. Its basic function is to act as a psychic mouth. When it is open, it is the natural entrance point for energy from outside, particularly as you receive it from me in a class. When Christ said, 'If thine eye be single thy whole body will be filled with light', he meant that when the third eye opens you can absorb energy directly.

"The second chakra is in the base of the throat. The third is in the center of the chest. It is the heart chakra. The physical heart is on the left side, but the heart center is in the middle. Below that, though usually ignored, is the solar plexus. Further down is the center emphasized in Zen Buddhism, located about two inches below the belly button. All the way down and slightly under the body is the sex center. The seventh chakra is located at the tip of the spine and the eighth at the top and back of the head.

"The total digestive process involves taking energy in through the third eye, bringing it down the front through each chakra in turn, like stringing a necklace, and then backward to the base of the spine, upward along the center canal of the spine until it reaches the top of the head. The only significance of the total process is when the energy reaches the top of the head. Until that point everything is preparation. It does no permanent good. But when the total system functions in a complete manner, the higher energy that is required for the conception and nourishment of your own rebirth begins to be manufactured and accumulated.

"Please do not begin to read books about what I have said. While some of my own most recent experience has been stimulated by the article Swami Muktananda sent me, if you start to read all the garbage that people have written about chakras, what they look like, how they function, the number of petals they contain, et cetera, you will only drive yourself crazy. It is totally unnecessary. But if you have read such stuff in the past, whether it was from Eastern or Western mystical literature, you will realize from what I have said that every description that has ever been written says nothing, or almost nothing, about bringing the force down the front. They speak only about drawing it up the back. Unfortunately there is no way in which that will ever happen naturally until the sex force begins to be transformed.

"There are a variety of technical means for opening the chakras. Some of them have been mentioned before, and I will certainly go over them again because people have an incredible capacity to misinterpret the simplest explanation when it applies to their own inner functioning. These methods include such techniques as directing attention, conscious breathing, visualization, inner asking, and supplying energy to a particular chakra through the use of touch. But there are also a variety of specific actions that are helpful in opening particular places in the psychic digestive system. For example, the best way to open the throat chakra is simply to swallow. The most effective means I know for opening the heart and lower belly chakras is the double breath. I'll go over that again in case you haven't received it before.

"You breathe into your heart to the count of ten. Hold for the count of ten, begin to breathe out but immediately shift your attention to the lower belly. After having expelled a small amount of air, begin to breathe in again for the count of ten, hold for ten, and out for ten. That is the double breath. It takes a while to get used to it, but the results can be quite remarkable. However, you shouldn't try it often because it supercharges the system. Once or twice every ten minutes is enough.

"There are many further examples. It helps to rotate slightly on the base of the spine to release the Kundalini energy. The head may twist back and forth as the energy reaches the level of the neck. There are an endless number of such techniques and manifestations with which you must become familiar. They are really priceless gifts, but only of value if you are doing the work.

"You might prefer that there be another internal arrangement, or believe that there is. But the question is not one of belief, but reality. You cannot eat food through your nose or digest it with your lungs. Your physical mechanism doesn't function in that manner. The relatively unknown psychic mechanism is no different. Each part is designed to perform an assigned function in a certain order. The problem is to learn what they are and apply this knowledge to your own shifting sensations of the inner environment in which you live. Gradually you can learn to relate an idea you may hear to an experience you actually have. But it usually doesn't happen quickly. We are clogged, not only with waste and negative energy, but with wrong ideas that we will not surrender. We cling to these because they make us comfortable or glorify our condition.

"The truth is all too simple. We are all of us trade-ins on a colossal used-car lot called the earth. We are here because we have damaged chakras. We do inner work in order to be reconditioned. The earth is not a good place on which to live. The vibrations are heavy and negative. Higher forces from the cosmos can barely penetrate the gloom. A fool tries to fix up his cave to make it more livable. A wise man will find a way out into the light. That is the purpose of all spiritual systems. Each of them has a partial answer. All of them serve as vehicles when they are at their zenith, and all become rigid and dogmatic in time, forming a prison more than a refuge.

"Astrology gives us an advance warning of psychic weather conditions. We can then take appropriate action to counteract these general influences. If we are not working internally, such adjustments are impossible and the knowledge does us no good whatever, except to add to our sense of fatality. Or in a positive case, it gives us a false sense of confidence that lies not in our own ability to overcome resistance, but in some external source where no security can ever be found. The only way to test one's understanding and security is to be stripped of everything one possesses. Then you will discover whether you have lost anything vital, and whether whatever remains is sufficient to sustain you. This is the meaning of surrender. We grow by reaching up and out. Inevitably we attach to things. That is what they are there for. Then we surrender and are free. It is a pruning process.

"When your work evolves to that point you will begin to realize who the people are that surround you, that is, who they were in past lives. It will throw the apparently superficial pattern of your everyday life into quite a different perspective. But such knowledge also has no value unless you can absorb it into your work. It too easily transforms into a novelty to relieve the boredom of your present life. That is not its purpose. You understand something of the past only when you have at least the possibility of correcting the mistakes you have made before. It is better not to know than to be tortured by knowledge that you cannot use. That is why you don't remember.

"On my next trip to the East I plan to stop over in Italy. I have never been there before, but I remember it. I was once a Roman monk who was stoned to death by an angry mob. I even know where I am buried. I may put some flowers on my grave.

"I wouldn't be saying all these things if I didn't feel that some of you were ready to receive them. I can't wait for everybody, or I would never speak. You must understand that what I say is not, in any sense, intellectual. I don't pass on ideas. I try to give you the raw flesh of my own experience. It may be slightly messy at times, but the blood is still warm. It is not for you to evaluate what I say or write a critique. I can't stop you if that's how you want to use it. But it is not why I talk to you. I am trying to open a doorway to the unknown. It is your response to the situation which will determine not only what you receive now, but what you will receive in the future.

"Some of you have been here many years. Others a few weeks. It is all the same. When something is given, it is open to everyone. Relate to it as best you can. If a new student can take as much as an old, so much the better for him. I am human. I feel differently about each one of you. I enjoy giving to some more than others, I can't help that. But I give to all. It is limited only by your capacity to receive and use it well.

"Whenever you or I act only from personal attraction, there is always a great price to pay. Work is increasingly objective. None of us can know exactly what or for whom we are working for in advance. There is a cosmic justice that operates in these matters over long periods of time. We see only a short scene in a vast panorama and jump to all kinds of conclusions. This is not a minor little drama enacted for your personal benefit, designed to make you feel a little better or give you a taste of understanding. There is an endless chain of people stretching into the abyss of time who have worked with higher energy and with whom you connect when you pursue your own work. You may not be aware of the chain of effort to which you are connecting. But it is very real.

"God does not need to reach into this distant arm of creation for your sake. It is part of a much vaster conception. In the same way, you do not live for any particular red corpuscle floating in your blood. If it disappeared you would not even be aware of it. It partakes of the general economy of nature. The difference between the corpuscle and ourselves is that we have a choice. We can choose the current in which we flow and the energy to which we have access. The ordinary person flows in the vast tide that sweeps humanity out to sea toward the inevitable dissolution of death. But to those who have the need and are willing to make the effort, there is another possibility. Every human being possesses the psychic mechanism which, if activated, can enable him to digest and transform the higher energies of life. As this occurs, he can slowly work himself loose from the tide of organic life into a higher stream of creation to which his soul is naturally related.

"Higher energy is the most precious commodity in the world. It is the basis of all inner development. Accurate teaching on how to obtain it is almost unknown at the present time. We often think that the East is the place to go for instruction on inner work. But its spirituality is fading. It has lived on its inheritance for fifteen hundred years.

"The people of the United States may lack cultural sophistication, but there is more freedom in this country than anywhere in the world. And the human soil is richer, unspoiled by centuries of abuse. It is here that the greatest development can occur.

"Two hundred years from now spiritual techniques may be taught in kindergartens. That doesn't matter. The period of the pioneer is the most wonderful time to be alive. The challenge is greatest and the discoveries that wait to be made are the most fundamental. I would not have wished to be born at any other moment."

Chapter Twenty-Two

DEATH AND REBIRTH

Rudi worked continuously in every situation that he found himself. Only the intensity of his effort varied. He also talked a tremendous amount and loved to be surrounded by people. He had been born with an open heart. In contrast to almost every other human being I have ever met he occasionally had to work to close his heart so that he could take certain actions which required cool objectivity.

The words that he spoke, however casual, usually had a purpose which emerged if one stayed around long enough to see the pattern. It is difficult to determine in retrospect when certain ideas first emerged, nor does it really matter. Rudi seemed to express what was occurring in him as it happened, more or less to whoever would listen. Watching this endless overflow it seemed to me that either his experience was so continuous that talking about it did not diminish it's content, or that he could not control this tendency in himself, and so decided to make the best of it. His friends and customers grew to expect it. And by giving them direct access to his latest experience he was allowing them to make contact with the possibility of joining his spiritual work.

It was only after more than a decade that I realized that there were certain aspects of his experience that he never mentioned to anyone. This threw his apparent expressiveness into quite a different light. He was doing what he consciously intended. There was nothing compulsive about it.

While Rudi was interested in the inner experiences of his students, he did not encourage them to talk with him about them unless they had a particular question. In any case he had a pretty good idea of where they were. He could follow the flow of the force within them and see various psychic manifestations functioning through them when they worked in class. It was harder to see them in himself. He did not particularly want to know too much about what was working through him lest it cause him to identify with it.

Once, at about the time I first met him, he was observed by members of another spiritual group. They described to him what they saw, the people who appeared, the strange creatures that manifested, the lights, colors, etc. It was all very dramatic. He was interested, but he didn't look for such information again for a long time, lest it create patterns and expectations in his work. Whatever appeared did so as a function of his surrender. It was not him, but that which worked through him. There was no reason to record it or analyze it as far as he was concerned.

I was not particularly distracted by these manifestations because I could not see them. But I gradually admitted to myself that they must exist. I had to believe it when Rudi described an experience that had occurred to him in class and then someone else, who had not heard him tell about it, describe the same experience later.

It is hard to select a particular manifestation. They were continuous. Each one set the stage for the next. If Rudi had worked less hard the time between experiences would have lengthened considerably. But he was always building toward the next breakthrough.

※ ※ ※

For a number of days he had been feeling odd stirrings in his brain. Occasionally he felt as if feet were scratching his head, but it seemed so strange to him that he ignored it. In one particular class the sensation grew much stronger. It finally came to a climax as a bird emerged from out of his forehead. It stood there for a time, took a few steps, and started to fly around the room. Afterwards Rudi said,

"It was all I could do to keep the class going. I just wanted to stop and watch the bird."

Other people described it also, both in the same conversation and independently. I had to assume it had really happened. When Rudi spoke of the bird afterwards, he said,

"What I saw was a phoenix. I never get used to the strangeness of such manifestations. They obey logic of their own. Most people never have such experiences because they are threatened by them. They can accept exotic birds as poetic or unconscious expressions of universal desires, but not as reality. No one has ever seen a phoenix flying in the sky, but it exists in the astral realm. Its significance is exactly what it is supposed to be, death and rebirth.

"That was exactly what I felt. When the bird appeared, something in me died. After the class I felt terribly empty. I didn't understand what had occurred until a few days later when life began to return like green shoots in the early spring.

"Everyone dies once in a physical sense. But the most remarkable thing about a human being is that he can die many times before his physical death. Such psychological and psychic deaths must occur before any rebirth experience is possible. You are all very naive. You assume that circulating and transforming the force will bring you enlightenment. There is not time enough in eternity for it to occur. The only hope of getting out of the web which you have created around yourself is to die to the level of experience you have known.

"When I look back on my life I see a string of corpses trailing behind me. They are all different aspects of me that I have shed. I have never found dying to be enjoyable. But by now I recognize the symptoms and know how to react to it. Whenever I sense a great withdrawal, as if the tide was going out never to return, I begin to suspect the process has started. Everything that seemed full of significance is hollow. The objectives I had seem pointless. The relationships closest to me have no meaning. I feel surrounded by an endless fog. Voices call out to me. Temptations appear to attract my energy just when I need it most. A man is very vulnerable at such a moment.

"The most crucial thing is that he sees the process through, and that others around him understand what is happening so that they can support him. Unfortunately that rarely occurs.

"You have to understand the subtle dilemma involved to appreciate the difficulty of successfully dying.

"First of all, the person himself either grows afraid of his condition or ceases to care about anything.

"Second, those who are closest to him will either be anxious about his state or feel rejected by him and reject him in turn. This is terribly unfortunate. A person needs to be helped through his inner death with understanding and love. All of his energy is absorbed by the inner process. He cannot communicate. Unless this is understood and accepted, those around him can't respond properly.

"As a result, the chances of dying successfully are not good. Usually the process aborts. Then the person feels better. Others feel better.

Death and Rebirth

None of them know that the fruits of his inner labors have just been totally lost. It is really tragic.

"When you work for your own development you cannot nourish selectively. The energy you attract causes everything to grow, the plants and the weeds. Therefore the process of death is the key to growth. It is the moment in which the weeds can be destroyed. As this occurs, there is room within the individual to attract a higher level of being. It is this level that is the expression of rebirth. It is not to exchange one personality for another, but to drop off a crude expression of energy for one that is more refined. The phoenix is the living symbol of this process and one to which, if you continue to work, you will come in due time.

"In another sense rebirth means the conception within the physical individual of a new being. The male and the female coming together in sex may create another physical being that goes through the various stages of growth with which we are all familiar. This involves a great investment of the parents' physical, emotional, and psychic energy. But all of the investment that parents make in a child usually walks away from them as the child matures. Many parents are rejected by their children. They are lucky if they end as friends. Society encourages fantasies about the endless joys of parenthood. The only thing that is endless is the work.

"Most of what I do with you represents a completion of what your parents failed to accomplish. It is a very rare parent who understands how to raise a child properly without crippling his potential in the process. We do not know how to feed anything in the way that it requires. We nourish it according to our own needs, which are not the same as the child's. Most people never recover from the effects of their upbringing,

"Spiritual work can only be done by healthy human beings. Such natural development is a relatively rare attainment even though it has nothing to do with spiritual growth. But when it occurs, then it becomes meaningful to work for rebirth, i.e., the conception and development of a completely new level of being.

"This conception occurs in the seeds of your potential. It can only be fertilized by a higher energy. This happens more often than you think. I have had students who left after working for only a week and then contacted me nine months later to say how strange they were feeling. I can't tell them that they have been spiritually knocked up, but that is what happened. The power of the initial contact fertilized something in them. It follows the physical parallel closely. Nine months later they can't help feeling the effects, even though they haven't worked at all since that time. If I told them what had happened it would only make them feel bad, or more likely, they wouldn't believe it. So I say, 'Don't worry. The sensations will vanish in a few days.' And they do. A psychic miscarriage occurs. The individual never knows what he has lost. If he did know he probably wouldn't care.

"Conception is nothing you can control. By opening to the force with which we work you are allowing for the possibility. What you can produce is a proper inner climate for the development of the seed that has been fertilized. That is the purpose of our work. A higher level of being requires higher energy for its nourishment. By activating your psychic digestive mechanism you are doing the one essential thing, creating the food for the spiritual fetus within you.

"I am not being fanciful. It is a concrete process that takes a long time. That is why no one should enter this work unless they can make a commitment toward the longevity of their effort.

"If the conditions are right and the inner embryo is created within the physical adult, it goes through the various stages of maturing like a normal child. During all of this period our ordinary self must act as the parent. Beyond the responsibility involved, the process is complicated by the fact that the child who is growing is on a different level of being from the adult who is taking care of him. The adult must serve him like a steward, as suggested by the parables in the New Testament. Over and over the steward is placed in charge until the master returns. Where is the master? In one sense, hidden and buried in the depths of the creative unconscious. In another sense, elsewhere in the cosmos. But in the present sense, he is not yet there because he is still growing up. He is at our mercy until he comes into his maturity and takes on his inheritance.

"It is a demanding task that we undertake when we experience rebirth. We never really understand who is reborn and at what cost until it begins to happen. As we are, we cannot be reborn. Our personalities are the husk from which the seed detaches. If we are attached to the husk, the suffering involved is greatly increased and we fight rebirth rather than help it. It will seem to us as if an alien being is absorbing our consciousness. This is extremely threatening if you have the illusion that you know who you are. But none of you even know who you were. Your only real opportunity for growth lies in the fact that you cannot know who you will be. When you feel this as clearly as the taste of a fresh lemon, then you will be in a position to surrender in the right way. It is very threatening from one viewpoint and a great adventure from another. No one has the right to ask or expect another human being to undertake such a transformation for any external reason, including the preservation of an existing relationship. Seeking this kind of inner growth is too consuming and subtle to be based on anything external. It does not justify giving up one's external responsibilities, but these responsibilities cannot form the foundation upon which the inner effort is built.

"There is in every person a masculine and feminine side. This is well known in modern psychology. You must learn to experience it for yourself without fear or concern. During a class you will at times manifest as a member of the opposite sex. If you deny the possibility you cannot receive the nourishment which the particular manifestation contains. This may stop your growth dead in its tracks, since this particular energy may form a vital psychic vitamin that is essential for the process that is occurring at the time.

"Similarly, any inner rebirth requires both mother and father, not only for conception, but to take care of the child during its long maturing. In Hinduism the Kundalini force is viewed as the basic feminine creative principle in the universe. The thousand-petal lotus into which it rises is the highest masculine power, Shiva. When the two are joined through the flow of higher energy up the spine, the child is conceived. It is only as this flow is maintained that the nourishment for the child is provided.

"A pregnant woman acts in various strange ways during her pregnancy. There are new hormones and energies at work in her system which produces these changes. The same thing occurs in spiritual pregnancy, except that since no one believes in the existence of the process or recognizes the signs, the person involved may be alarmed and think he has committed some fundamental error in his work. Look at it in ordinary human terms. If we did not know about pregnancy, a woman would have cause for anxiety about her experience. She may be sick in the morning. Her moods shift abruptly. She craves strange foods. And beyond all of these symptoms she detects signs of a foreign being within her. It is subtle. For some time she cannot be entirely sure. But at a certain point, it is undeniable and beyond that, the creature actually comes to life, moving and kicking her. If we were not conditioned to look on this as the process of maternal fulfillment it would be more understandable to think of it in terms of

some lethal disease.

"This is very similar to the situation after spiritual conception. The unsuspecting person may feel what he believes to be the symptoms of imminent mental illness. What, after all, is one of the major aspects of psychosis but the feeling that there is a foreign presence inside affecting you and gradually taking over?

"You probably have never thought of it that way. The trouble is that no one ever thinks of these things as if they were happening to them. It is someone else's experience. It does not have the continuous impact of reality like a child in the womb.

"Time is necessary to prepare for the event. The basic psychic system must be healthy in all its parts. The emotional stability of the individual must be secured. His sense of commitment must be tested and confirmed. Only then is there a reasonable chance that, should conception occur, it might lead to some fruitful result.

"I don't think that what I am saying is different from the indications given in various religious traditions. The mystical marriage of man and woman is always an inner experience, the consummation of which is a spiritual child. In the process of its growth, we are consumed. Our personality and past experiences become the fuel that is burned or transformed to provide its nourishment. We do not entirely disappear. There is a certain personality shell which may remain as our face to the world and our protection from it. But as the inner current grows stronger, our need for protection decreases.

"A slow moving stream is easily polluted. A rapid stream, with a broader bed, sweeps away anything that enters it almost instantly. In the human being it is more like a stream of fire. At first it is easily extinguished. But as the stream grows and the temperature rises, it burns whatever it contacts. In the end even metals will be vaporized. Then no protection is necessary from the situations that we attract. It is the other people who will need protection from us. They will instinctively stay away from the heat unless they are reaching out for the energy it contains.

"It is good that our culture has become more open to experiences that would have been denied or condemned without understanding a decade ago. But experience itself cannot be the motive. Pleasure maintains the bondage. It does not erase it. We are no different than the rat in the maze in that respect. It is the capacity to accept pain, to persist in spite of results, not because of them. It is to move with growing awareness toward a goal that others may find invisible or meaningless, which is necessary in order to achieve any permanent result. And the achievement will be our own partial destruction so that someone much greater than we are today can appear.

"It may sound grim, but it is actually the only approach to freedom. There is nothing wonderful about us. We are a patchwork of self-protective fantasies.

"To get out of prison you must begin to suspect you are in one. Then you must accept the hard fact that you yourself, not your parents or other strangers, have constructed it. And then you must tear it down. No one from your past is likely to help you. They will fight the inherent threat to their security contained in what you are trying to do. That is the hardest thing to overcome. You cannot hold onto them and work to escape. You must get out of prison first. If they are more concerned with staying inside their cells than having a life, you may discover they have disappeared if you succeed in getting free. Or they may be free also, waiting for you. Or you may go see them on visiting day. It does not really matter.

"I cannot say that the chances of escape are very good. But then what is the alternative? There is no parole but death. And the chances of success are better than they used to be. Ten years ago, and before that, when I was in the Gurdjieff work or wandering the streets at night going crazy with the energy running wild in me, there was almost nowhere to turn. Knowledge was in fragments. Immediate help hardly existed anywhere. A few great souls broke out of bondage, but they were the end of an old age. They left no real inheritors among their loyal followers.

"It is different now. A new energy is beginning to flood the earth, associated with the initiation of a new age, but it will only appear very gradually. It is the passing of the old age that has the greatest significance. That is what we are experiencing.

"Such a time is characterized by great, abrupt, largely destructive changes. The best image is of an earthquake that brings to the surface layers of geological history that are usually deeply buried. When this occurs the psychic heritage associated with ancient cultures is released into the atmosphere. It is not the full flowering of these traditions that is exposed. That is gone. This is a dying memory, but it is real nevertheless. For those who understand what is happening and know how to relate to it, the opportunity to absorb these fragments of human effort made throughout the last cosmic period is uniquely wonderful. These conditions will last for perhaps fifty years. Then all the energy treasures will be buried permanently as the new age takes shape.

"I have not spoken of this before, but you should realize the possibility now. It exists for whoever can open to it in the right way. But the first requirement is to know it exists. Now you know.

"We are always stupidly sentimental about the wrong things. We are forever concerned about world conditions. We never stop to think that the very circumstances that bother us are releasing opportunities that did not exist before.

"When Tibet was invaded by the Chinese, those with mystical sympathies for the Tibetans were greatly disturbed. Not only humanitarian considerations were involved, but the Buddhist tradition which the Tibetans had maintained in a relatively pure form during the last twelve centuries was being destroyed.

"What no one seemed to realize was that their loss was our opportunity. We were in no way responsible for the acts of the Chinese. We tried to stop them. But the Tibetans had previously cornered the market on spiritual energy. Through the purity and dedication of their religious system, they had earned the right to work with high cosmic force in the only way anyone ever earns anything, by using it well. Since there wasn't very much higher energy available in the first place, anyone living in the rest of the world didn't have much of a chance, regardless of the efforts they were willing to make. Even if they traveled to Tibet, the likelihood of getting in and being accepted was very small.

"Consequently their loss is our gain. The energy which they had monopolized was largely released during the invasion of the country. It may seem ironic to you that your opportunity for spiritual growth is given to you by the conquest of atheistic Chinese communists. But life is built on such ironies. You could breathe deeply until you fell over on your face from too much oxygen. It would do you very little good if the quality of *prana* in the air was impoverished. Nothing grows in poor soil except sickly weeds. So feel sorry for the Tibetans, help them if you wish. Understand also that they had their opportunity, and as with all things, time slowly ran out on them.

"There is such a thing as cosmic justice. Many of the actions on the earth that we cannot understand do not really originate on the earth. They are astrological in character, or they represent the working out of patterns of adjustment over long periods of time. We see the result but not the cause, or the causes we are aware of do not seem to produce the expected effects during the period we watch them. But they will, only later. You must either forget about it or take it on faith. Only when you begin to remember the past will the nature of your own development in the context of history be made visible to you. Then the centuries, the hundreds of thousands of years that you have invested in denying the reality of what you have done, will be revealed as total waste and cowardice. That is really the symbol of the last judgment. There is no escape from anything except confronting it and going through the door which led you into the situation in the first place.

"Whatever you wish to accomplish, whatever direction you want to go, you will need to be strengthened inwardly. Otherwise, even if you get there, it will be a twisted dwarfed being that receives the reward. He will not know what to do with it and his success will be hollow. This work can strengthen and complete your inner development. That is the first major phase in which we are engaged. It is a big effort which most people have the illusion is not necessary.

"When a person has reached the first level of attainment it doesn't bother me if he moves away. But he must earn the right to do it or there is no freedom in his choice. Roy Burnes worked for a time, developed certain inner gifts, and finally attracted an opportunity on the earth level that interested him, so he left. He didn't have to leave. He was just beginning and I wasn't surprised when it happened. His need for growth was not great. It came to him too easily for him to fully appreciate the opportunity he had.

"I had another student who left recently. He worked hard, both in his business and spiritual work. His wife owned some property down South in the middle of nowhere. A major corporation decided that they wanted to build on precisely that spot. It was incredible. Suddenly he was rich. He had never had money in his life. He left the work in order to enjoy it. Getting rich is no reason to leave. It could free a person to work more. But it was sufficient for him. It was a reward for his efforts which he could accept. Personally, there is no material payoff in this world that would tempt me. But I don't expect other people to have my fanatical viewpoint. I respected him for his honesty when he left.

"Unfortunately most people leave too soon. They have achieved nothing that can permanently enrich their lives on a level that is real and important to them. They leave for many reasons, and with many rationalizations. Usually they don't really know why. The work is too difficult. The reward's too distant. They must face something in themselves they have always tried to deny. What does it matter? There are thousands of reasons for not doing. Only one for doing! To grow! To transform! To die and be reborn! It is a stern, vast, and unknown realm of experience. But it is very real.

"For me it has been wonderful, painful, and very lonely at times. It has wrenched every bone, muscle, and nerve in my body. There are many paths, each for different types of people. Most of them wind gently around the foothills of the mountains. Some of them end on the edge of a cliff on a dark night with beautiful music urging them on. A few are for those who wish to climb mountains. And one or two are for those who want to use the mountain top as a launching pad into the cosmos.

"What we are doing has no end. Total enlightenment is the illusion and limitation of people who have gone before. They had a remarkable experience and did not wish to work anymore, so they called it ultimate and settled down on that level of attainment.

"People talk of 'God' with the illusion that by using the term they are somehow raising the level of their own existence. In older times, men were wiser. They treated the spoken or written symbol for God with reverence and fear. If nothing is sacred to us, how can something that is of a totally different nature enter our experience? We would not let it. It is precisely what our whole personality is designed to prevent. Contact with a higher being tears us apart because we fight it, or it reaches us only very gradually as we learn to tolerate it, like fish learning to crawl on land.

"The sign of God's love is often pain, not rose leaves and soft music. How could the love of something infinite be soft and sweet to a finite, fearful little being filled with millions of stupid illusions? It is the nature of light to reveal the truth. On the physical level, the truth is bound up in various tensions. On the psychological level, the truth is a system of lies we have glued together. On a spiritual level, the truth is an existential hopelessness for people who have the misfortune to understand without being able to act, or the illusion of attainment by those who can do but do not see the effects of their actions. Even if God approaches quietly as a good parent in the night, the effects are

bound to be devastating.

"When I was younger, before any of you knew me, I felt the need for a sign. I asked and asked for a few days. Then I got an answer. The left side of my body was suddenly paralyzed. It took several months for me to get back to normal. I could hardly walk, but I continued my business. And during all that time, when any normal person would have been frightened and overwhelmed, I felt happy. This was a sign I could recognize. I experienced it with every step I took.

"But the purpose of work is not to feel pain, but to be free. You work to experience a higher level of reality, the flowering of chakras, and the opening of unknown spiritual mechanisms moving into greater simplicity, abstraction and fulfillment. All of this brings happiness that is real, not just the overflow of a good day, but the dawning of a new era in your existence.

"I have worked for too long to be surrounded by psychic malcontents, psychological cripples, blinded enthusiasts who claim everything is perfect but cannot see the stone in front of their way. I want simplicity, dignity, respect, and finally, love as the flowering of maturity. Perhaps it is too soon for it to come, but bliss is not something abstract. It must begin to be available now. Open your hearts. Feel gratitude for the opportunity to work and to serve a cause that is unknown to you, but in which you nevertheless enlist through your own efforts to grow. And then ask to taste a drop of bliss. Feel it on your tongue or in your heart. You have the right to the experience. It is only a foretaste of the future."

Chapter Twenty-Three
TWO MOVES

All of the events that have been described occurred when Rudi lived and had his business in West Greenwich Village. During that period he traveled widely, maintaining a large number of contacts with people across the earth. But his home base was the Lower West Side of Manhattan.

When the time came for Rudi to shift the center of his operation to the East Side, it heralded a new and expanding period in his life. The immediate impulse for the action was his growing business and the need for a larger meeting place for his classes. It was inevitable that he would move in any case. His nature required that he shift his setting frequently, whether there was an outer need or not. But the two usually came together.

Rudis East Side Tenth Street address

Two Moves

I had been working with Rudi for seven years. During that time a process of inner transformation had gradually begun. There had been many delays and detours, inside myself and in others around me. But I knew that all of this was somehow necessary. If I thought that there were any other practical alternative my attitude might have been different. There wasn't. I had read books, visited various groups, and invested eight years of work in other approaches before meeting Rudi. If I had attained few positive results at least it helped me understand my own situation realistically and gave me the capacity to endure.

The energy which I steadily received during the long hours at the store and from the classes was going into a deep, almost bottomless pit. I was not discouraged, nor was Rudi.

"It took a very long time, John, before anything began to happen for me," he said in a moment of empathy. "All I could see inside myself was inky blackness. When I first noticed a tinge of dark gray it was a turning point in my life. People grow at different rates. The longer it takes to begin to break through to the light, the deeper your foundation in the earth will be rooted."

During this period the landmarks with which I was most familiar were removed. Rudi shifted the location of his store, his house, and the scale of his business and spiritual efforts. The new store was at least five times as big as the old; the new house was twice as large. Starting at first with a small group of students, and later expanding, he formed a household around him. The group lived together and, for the most part, worked together, either in Rudi's art business or in other businesses that he sponsored. They constituted the beginning of the first ashram.

I was not a part of this inner group. It was not practical, since I had a home in Peekskill and a job at New York University. But, otherwise, things followed their familiar pattern. There were generally five Kundalini classes a week which I attended. I sat in the store often, but not as often as before.

Every Saturday morning all available students spent a few hours cleaning the three floors of the brownstone building where classes were held. The first floor was the meditation room. The second floor was an extended living room and bedroom for those who lived in the house. The third floor was Rudi's bedroom. Since the house was saturated with art the cleaning had to be done carefully. It was supervised by one of Rudi's older students, Jack Stewart. Jack had a real sense of

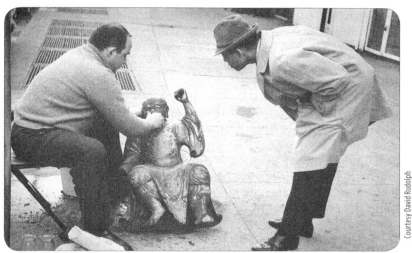
Rudi cleans a statue outside his store

identity with dust or dirt, wherever it might be hiding. If you missed any he would unerringly point it out.

In parallel with all of these developments the current of activity around Rudi moved more swiftly. The new store attracted a greater variety and quantity of people than the old. For the first time there was enough space to begin to see the art in a proper setting. Rudi laid flagstone on the floor and put in an extensive lighting system. He was not after an Uptown decorating effect, but the store was impressive and beautiful in its own way. It was at that point the largest Eastern art gallery in New York City, which meant in the East. In the next few years it became one of the largest in the world. As the supply of goods dwindled for others, Rudi accelerated the pace of his buying. He was able to get items that no one else could bring out of Asia. It was a constant source of amazement to other art dealers who came to the store to buy from him what they could not buy directly for themselves.

It also surprised them to discover that Rudi usually didn't know or care that much about the history of the art works which he sold. He didn't have the time or inclination to carefully research them. Over the years he learned enough to identify their period and type, mainly as a basis of pricing. There his interest ended. If he wanted to know more he entered into the piece by working with it as he did with a student. He never studied oriental art in any formal sense. Occasionally this led him to undervalue a piece. But more often he would find a special value amidst a shipment of varied quality that the seller had himself overlooked. The two tendencies balanced out over time.

"Even though I began many years ago," Rudi said, "I came in at the end of the business. It was the same in my spiritual life. It is the twilight of everything that existed during the last age.

"All the sources of great Eastern art are drying up. It becomes more and more difficult to bring art out of these countries, even when it is available. In many areas it is simply all gone or the cost is so prohibitive that it might as well be gone. Most dealers go on a trip to look for a few pieces of a specific type and period with a special customer in mind. That's one reason their prices are so high. If you select just one thing you pay a premium. I would rather buy the contents of a whole warehouse.

"A decade ago the countries in the Far East didn't appreciate their own art. It was only after Westerners began to import it in quantity that they began to change their mind. Even then, it was more from a sense of nationalism than any aesthetic appreciation. If you walked into the house of a rich Indian you would be shocked. They would just as soon have a plastic Shiva in a shrine as a twelfth-century masterpiece carved in stone. To them it is all the same.

"There is one exception, the Japanese. They are a nation of collectors. More and more I find they have been there before me, buying up everything they can. Sometimes I could sell my goods at a higher profit in Japan than in this country. But I would be in competition with some of the people from whom I buy in Japan, so I don't do it."

As I listened to Rudi my thoughts shifted to the last piece I had bought from him, which by coincidence, he had purchased in Japan. It had happened almost by accident. I had been sitting in the store when a mutual friend dropped in to talk with Rudi and inspect the latest shipment. She usually didn't buy very much but she had excellent taste.

While Rudi was busy with another customer, she said to me,

"Have you noticed this piece, John?" pointing to a rather haunting Chinese-looking feminine goddess.

"If you look at it for a minute, something really remarkable happens."

I had sufficient respect for her opinion to invest a minute. At first nothing occurred. I was distracted by the noise in the store. Then it hit me. The statue was moving forward. It didn't make sense, but I was impressed enough to buy it.

A few days later Rudi said to me,

"The last piece you bought from me, John, was a real coup. I was visiting dealer in Japan whom I have known for many years. We were having tea. I had already seen his stock. Then a servant passed by on his way to the courtyard. During the moment that he opened the doorway I saw a statue outside.

"'What is that?' I asked immediately.

"'What is what?' said my host.

"'I saw a statue in the courtyard.'

"'Must have been mistaken, Mr. Rudi,' my host said with emphasis.

"'I couldn't be mistaken about something like that. Why didn't you show it to me?' I persisted.

"'I show you everything for sale,' he said firmly.

"But I continued to pursue the statue like a hound after a bone. Finally he said,

"'Did not show you because already sold. Man comes from museum tomorrow. Is national treasure. No can sell.'

"'Is it a national treasure yet?' I asked. In Japan, once a piece is declared a National Treasure it is against the law to let it leave the country.

"'Man come tomorrow. Cannot sell. National Treasure.'

"'Is the man coming from the museum to declare it a National Treasure tomorrow?' I persisted.

"'Yes. That is so,' he finally admitted. 'Very special piece. Cannot sell. Sent by Emperor of China as gift to Emperor of Japan.'

"I ignored that. It wasn't going to help my case if I believed it.

"'It hasn't been declared a National Treasure yet,' I said reproachfully. 'So you could sell it to me!'

"'So sorry, Mr. Rudi. Is not possible.'

"'After all the years we have done business together,' I said. 'what could they do if the piece were gone? In the name of our friendship.'

"He began to waver. The end of the story you know, since you now own the piece."

"Is it true about the Emperor of China and Japan?" I asked, amazed.

"Yes. He assured me it was true after I had bought it. I have no reason to doubt him. It moves forward as you look at it. Have you noticed that?"

"Yes," I said.

"And it has a gift in its hand," said Rudi. "That is probably why it was selected by the Emperor of China for the purpose."

Rudi stopped talking and moved off to work on crating a large and beautiful Japanese figure. It was obviously old, authentic, and valuable.

"I am selling it to the Zen Center in San Francisco," he said with enthusiasm.

"It is beautiful. It must cost a fortune," I said with my mouth watering.

"It should," said Rudi, "It is worth fifty to a hundred times what I am charging them.

"Did you get a great bargain?" I asked.

"No, I want them to have it. They need it right now."

"I don't understand," I said, puzzled.

"Their Zen master has died. A younger man, an American, is taking his place. I am sending this piece to him as an expression of my love. It is my way of telling him that I believe in his capacity to carry on."

"But their work is so different than ours."

"Sure, it is different," said Rudi, "But it is real in its own terms. That is what I respect. Most spiritual work is fantasy. People kid themselves and each other into thinking that they are really trying to grow. Even when they make a serious effort, they are usually doing what they think is right, not what they should do. There is a difference. You can't just listen to your own ideas and ever expect to get anywhere."

He finished the packing in silence.

The next time that I returned to the store there was a huge stone statue of Vishnu reclining on the cosmic sea. I looked at it in silence. Rudi smiled as he saw me eyeing it speculatively.

"Forget about it, John, it is a gift from the finest Eastern art dealer in the city. I am really amazed that he gave it to me. Especially since there is nothing that I can do for him in return. He never gives anything to anyone. He isn't the type. I am going to place the stone in the courtyard behind the house and build a Japanese rock garden around it. Stones grow better than plants in New York City," he concluded.

* * *

As Rudi gradually settled into his new existence, my life took an unexpected turn. I was offered the Chairmanship of the Sociology Department of the State University College at Geneseo, located near Rochester, New York.

I immediately discussed it with Rudi. My main concern was the distance that the job would take me from him.

"It's a natural progression," he said, "Don't worry. You can come down for weekends. It's not the amount of time you are here that matters, but the intensity of your effort. I'm at the ashram in India for only a week to ten days in the whole year. But I spend the rest of the year preparing for it or digesting the results of the experience.

"You should definitely take the job. It will be a chance for you to expand yourself and try out some of your ideas. You can start a Kundalini yoga group up there. It can by your spiritual kindergarten."

With the ending of summer, I made the move to Geneseo and started a new life upstate.

* * *

When I returned to the city on one of my early visits, Rudi spoke at an evening class about the necessary conditions for inner development.

"If a person is growing," he said, "everything is relative to that. There are no universal principles. At one phase he may need a lot of meat. In another, none at all. The essential thing is to cultivate sensitivity to your own inner condition, particularly to the changes that are occurring. You must learn to evaluate each situation by the effect it has on you inwardly and be guided accordingly. This is not easy. There may be certain obvious actions to take, such as getting enough sleep or avoiding places with heavy negative vibrations. But there are always exceptions. There are times when you really need to stay up all night to break through a crucial resistance.

"When we were painting the front of the new store, I had the men work through the whole night. The job had dragged on long enough.

Courtesy Barry Kaplan

It was really necessary to finish. So we rigged spotlights and worked non-stop. Anyone who didn't like it had to overcome his resistance. If they said, 'The hell with it,' and quit, they would have left anyway a little later. Better to get it over with now.

"But beyond such simple acts is a world of subtleties. We have to examine each experience to learn how it affects us. Many people have the illusion they are having a meaningful and nourishing relationship because they feel a strong flow between themselves and another person. What they don't know is that the flow may be one way, in which case, they are losing energy. One way to discover the truth is by sensing how you feel after leaving the other person. Are you tired or invigorated? If you are usually tired the conclusion is inescapable, you are being drained. Such situations are dangerous, particularly if our emotions are strongly involved. In conscious work, love should be mutual. We lose too much otherwise, regardless of what we feel.

"The best guide is simplicity. The fewer our choices, the clearer they become. I don't recommend simplicity for its own sake. I lead a very complicated life, but I understand what I am doing for the most part so that I can keep the various contradictory elements separate and avoid being caught between them. Most people that I meet also lead fairly complicated lives. But they don't know what they are doing or why they are doing it. They seek to reduce their tensions through various partially destructive means which have sometimes worked for them in the past. When they are temporarily at peace, they are satisfied. None of this has anything to do with growth.

"The more aware you are of how the various situations in your life are affecting your efforts to refine your own vitality, the more responsible you become for the proper use of your own energy. Everything real is either a test or a source of nourishment. We overcome the test and absorb the nourishment. The more we do it, the more we have at stake. The reward of work is more work.

"Even when a person achieves a state of being that is illuminated in comparison to the level on which he began, it is not freedom or the expression of freedom. After a while he grows attached to that level and it becomes only a more beautiful prison than the one that he left.

"I am not working to go to heaven. I would be bored out of my mind. Most people's vision of paradise is some glorified suburban country club with wings. I can't stand the suburbs. Middle class people just drive me up the wall. They are almost totally dead and completely sure that they have it made. There is nothing you can do with such an attitude. It is hopeless.

"So, to retire to a glorified old folk's home run by angels is not my ideal. I want to get beyond it to the next frontier. No artist ever paints his last picture, nor does he do it just for the applause of the critics. It is a projection of an inner need. It is the same with our work. The satisfaction of growing through the work is its own reward.

"But none of you have begun to understand the amount of effort involved. You all take it very easy on yourselves. You don't want to know how to work five and ten times harder, because then you will have to do it. That is why everything takes so long.

"On the other hand, the level of the work can only rise as the expression of the continuous refinement of energy that is consciously occurring within me. Those who start now meet a different force than those who started five years ago. Their diet is richer so they can grow faster. This may not seem just to those of you who have been here a longer time, but how can it be any other way? Nothing stands still. There is only one choice, grow or leave. There is only one kind of competition, with yourself. I do not compare you to each other. That is meaningless. Each of you comes from a different situation, and with a totally different series of past lives. These things cannot be equated. Even if I could do it, it would be a waste of time. Everything from the past is either a source of nourishment or a burden that needs to be dropped. Breathe it in or let it go.

"Each phase of the work has its own dynamics. There is a time when a new wave of people is attracted. There is a time for these people to develop. And there is a time of harvest when the wheat is separated from the chaff.

"When I look back I see countless numbers of people who have come close to me and left for various reasons at different times. I loved many of them. I did not want them to go. But there was nothing I could do. It is the force working within me that attracted them in the first place. It is the acceleration and refinement which caused them to leave. The power of my own growth began to drive them crazy.

"And so, again and again, I have to surrender someone to whom I was attached. It never ceases to hurt. But I have to learn to accept it. It is only the willingness to detach from every situation that makes growth possible. First the situation develops. It crystallizes into a pattern. After that it must be melted down and burned away. The image of rebirth is the phoenix rising from the ashes of its own destruction. This is what we are working for. If it doesn't appeal to you, perhaps you better reconsider what you are doing here.

"Several years ago I had a recurring vision. I was walking up a lush green hill to a modern glass house. Seated inside was a man who I was to meet. It was a wonderful image.

"A few months ago Robert walked into the store. He was the person I had seen in my vision. Naturally I was deeply affected. But I shortly began to discover that Robert was a bull in a china shop. He had an extraordinary physical vitality combined with a childish and erratic nature. He demanded a tremendous amount of my energy and attention.

"It took me a while to see the negative side of the situation. I was too entranced by my vision coming true. But when various friends whom I otherwise respected began to warn me against Robert, I started to get worried. I couldn't afford to let anything stand in the way of my own growth, regardless of what lifetime it came from or how appealing it might be. I was faced with a choice: either to cut the connection with him, or to make a much greater inner effort so that I had enough energy to maintain the relationship and do everything else my life required.

"I decided, with some misgivings, to try the second alternative. I figured at the very least that it would force me to work harder. Once I decided to do it I was shocked to discover that the energy was there. I only had to reach for it. I could take care of his needs and everyone else's. I would never have believed it if the situation hadn't created the demand. I found myself having to sustain two worlds, like a boy with his finger in the dyke, keeping the water and the land apart.

"Then a new problem arose. I was going to take a trip to India, and for that I could not go divided. And so I did what I had never done before. I deliberately set out to destroy the relationship. If I had any doubts about the wisdom of my action, they were immediately dispelled when I told Robert of my intention a few weeks before the trip. I was suddenly faced with an emotional hurricane. You can't reason with such a force. It is pure destruction. But in dealing with the situation I was able to reabsorb everything I had put into it, as he in his wildness and immaturity poured it out in anger, hate, and frustration.

"As you can see he is gone, and I am still here working and growing. It was a colossal test based on my own need and vulnerability. If I had given in I would have lost much of what I have attained over the years. You can be thankful that it turned out well.

"Those of you who watched the process at the time may not have doubted the outcome, but it is one thing to watch and another to be in the battle.

"You listen to many of the things I say and think you understand," said Rudi as he concluded the story. "But there is only one way to really understand. To work until you find yourself in my position. Then these words will take on a different sense and urgency. There is no reason why some of you can't be where I am now in a couple of years. But don't look for me when you get there. I will be gone."

✻ ✻ ✻

About this time, Rudi began to attract a new quality of student. One example of the new breed was Michael Austin. The most striking characteristic about Michael was the intensity with which he took to the work. He would grab an ax, figuratively and literally, and dispose of anything in his way in a few minutes. He was driven. He needed only to be guided. He quickly became close to Rudi and filled a gap left vacant since Robert's departure.

Rudi and Michael in India

Michael was something of a military figure. He was not particularly warm, but he charged ahead with energy and determination. He was the first to study Hatha Yoga seriously while taking Rudi's classes. Rudi encouraged him in this. After a time he authorized Michael to give Hatha classes for those interested in them.

"You should try it," Rudi said to me, "It will help break down some of your physical tension."

I was somewhat reluctant; I didn't know what I was getting into. I was still recovering from the memories of Aikido.

"When you see what Michael has done in a few months," he persisted, "it should help you to realize all you could have done in these years."

"I know," I said, "but I am not Michael, I just don't function that way."

"You can believe that if it makes you feel better," said Rudi, "But it doesn't excuse you, particularly in the future."

Chapter Twenty-Four
SWAMI RUDRANANDA

"My teacher has given me the title, 'Swami Rudrananda'", said Rudi on his return from a recent trip to India.

"I hope I can still call you Rudi," I said, not certain how to take the announcement.

"Sure. It's going to take me a while to get used to the title. But whether I use it or not, don't take it casually. It would never have happened at all if I hadn't refused to accept any other alternative. I have paid for it in blood. You meet some white people who are swamis, but it doesn't mean much because they receive the title from a very minor person. But I have been playing with the big boys. Bhagavan Nityananda is worshipped as a living god by his followers. Swami Muktananda is considered to be a great saint. When he travels, people wait all night just to see his railroad car pass in the moonlight. They hope to receive a blessing from his presence. They are both, in different ways, at the top of the echelon of Hindu religious life, though they represent very different quantities.

"After my test with the man who was supposed to destroy me, I resolved to achieve certain recognition to symbolize the whole process of growth that I had achieved during the last decade. I went on my last trip with the objective of becoming a Swami. Muktananda hasn't initiated anyone into swami-hood. He does not give anything easily, except a touch of enchantment to keep his followers happy. He must have sensed my objective because from the moment I arrived he kept a certain distance between us. I made a special effort to bridge the gap, digging more deeply into my heart to find a greater sense of love for the man. I also expressed my desire to become a swami to others knowing he would hear it through ashram gossip channels.

"He smiled at my efforts, but it was like squirting perfume on a sheet of glass, nothing was getting through. On the occasions when

Swami Muktananda and Rudi in India

his guard was down there was always an interruption, a visiting saint, an immediate minor emergency about which he had to be consulted. I watched all this with a mixture of amusement and desperation. The charade was diverting, but I was never going to become a Swami if I went along with it.

"To make matters worse, most of the attention in the ashram was devoted to a rejuvenation experiment. Swami Muktananda was testing an ancient scripture that described how an old man could be made younger if he was put into total isolation and fed a special diet. A house had been prepared, and an old man had been placed in it for several months on the prescribed diet. He was supposed to emerge in a week. Everyone was excitedly awaiting the results. Personally I couldn't have cared less about the whole thing. It just created one more diversion for me to overcome.

"There is only one answer for a situation like that, put your life on the line and refuse to be halted. I started digging inside myself until I came to a rock foundation that I knew nothing could alter. Then I began to work outward. I had only a day and a half left of my stay. I asked Swami Muktananda for the opportunity to speak with him. He begged to be excused. He was ill. A recurrent fever had reappeared. He needed to rest.

"It was true. He did not look his usual self. I sympathized, but persisted. 'Baba,' I said. ('Baba' means 'father' in Hindi. It's a familiar form of address, like calling me 'Rudi'.) 'I will be leaving tomorrow. Let me only sit near the doorway of your room. I feel myself in a very crucial condition. I need the power of your spirit to help me!'

"It was true enough. I had been working with mounting intensity for over a week. I felt both strangely dissociated and burning with fever. Something had to be resolved.

"He looked annoyed, but did not refuse. 'I cannot go away in this state,' I continued relentlessly. 'I shall wait until you are asleep and then sit quietly near you, if you will permit it.'

"He looked at me keenly for a moment and motioned me closer. I approached, with more arguments ready. He shrugged his shoulders and said, 'You are dumb like I am dumb!' Then he touched my forehead. I was in a very finely balanced condition. The force that had been building in me like a static charge in a huge transformer broke loose. I was overwhelmed with it, and I fell to the ground.

"For the next hour I was wracked by spasms and surrounded by strange visions. I felt unknown areas opening within me and was completely disoriented.

"I recovered slowly to find myself back in my room. Someone had just come in. He motioned for me to follow. Evidently Swami Muktananda wanted to see me.

"I stumbled into the dim light of his quarters. He was entertaining a visiting saint.

"'How is our new Swami?!' he said jovially. I was shocked. I had achieved my objective. 'I have been thinking of your new name,' he continued. 'Do you know the god, Rudra?'

"'Not exactly,' I replied, still in a daze.

"'He was a primeval form of Shiva, a wild man,' Baba broke into laughter and slapped his knee. The thought seemed to appeal to him. 'So you are now Swami Rudrananda, the bliss of Rudra.'

"It all felt like a scene out of an exotic children's party. Everyone was festive, as if an idiot son had just made good in grade school. I was happy too, but I did not forget what all this cost me or take any of it for granted.

"I left the next day with many expressions of gratitude and friendship. Swami's last words to me were,

"'Now you are really going to be an independent person.'

"As I got away from the ashram I began to understand the significance of his last words. There was no doubt in my mind that Baba had withheld the title as long, or longer, than humanly possible in order to maintain his control over me. I didn't mind that as long as I was growing. But how long can you keep an infant in a crib? When he gets beyond a certain size, it's ridiculous. Now that I had been certified there was no telling what I might do.

"Before I left the ashram I asked to know more about the nature of the god, Rudra. I was told that Shiva stands on a dwarf, but Rudra is surrounded by thousands of people. I was also told that the next nine months would be very painful for me. Many people and situations to which I was attached would be torn away as a major transition occurred in my life. I could feel it starting already.

"I don't know what is coming next. But I have the increasing conviction that my studies in India have concluded. The energy of that tradition is all inside me now. I do not know how it will manifest, and I sometimes think that enlightenment in Hinduism is a single flower on the top of a great tree. It is an imposing and wonderful event, but I don't want to settle for one flower. In Islam they produce a low bush with many blossoms. I would like to graft the bush onto the tree and have the best of both cultures.

"If that is what God wants, it will happen. Whatever I want I will have to surrender anyway to allow the future to emerge from the depth of my own being. So that is what I am doing," said Rudi as he rose from his chair to wait on a customer.

Rudi, now Swami Rudrananda

Chapter Twenty-Five

BIG INDIAN

As Rudi began to settle into the next phase of his life, he started to look again for a house in the country. There was no immediate need for such a place. He had more than enough space for his teaching and his business. But he lived not only in the present, but continually projected a year, two years or a decade into the future.

In the fall of 1969 he began to spend his Sundays searching in rural areas to get a sense of what might be available. By late winter he was growing impatient to have the matter settled. He almost made an offer on a satisfactory place, but a friend who was with him insisted it wasn't good enough. So he continued looking, and in this way stumbled on Big Indian. I heard about his discovery on my next trip to the city. Rudi was overflowing with enthusiasm. I remembered the last country place near Woodstock and reserved my judgment.

"It's just beautiful," he said, "It used to be a small Catskill resort. It's got a completely equipped kitchen, a walk-in freezer that must be 15' x 12', endless space, and loads of bedrooms. But the most remarkable thing is the setting. It's on a dead-end road enclosed on both sides by mountains and down the road are only more mountains. There is a stream and a swimming pool fed by the stream, and lots of other smaller buildings. And it costs, John, just what you paid for your house in Peekskill, only this has a hundred acres and I can get an option on the whole valley."

"How long does it take to get there?" I asked.

"Two and a half to three hours. There is even a bus right to the town of Big Indian. You don't need a car."

"It sounds great," I said, more or less believing it.

"It is," said Rudi. "It really is."

✳ ✳ ✳

About a month later I took a detour on my next trip from the college to New York City to see the place for myself. It was late March. There was still snow on the ground. Rudi had told the owner I might stop by.

I left the main road, turned onto a bridge across a snow-clogged stream. From there it was a short distance to a crossroads. I took the branch marked "Dead End". It was bordered by another stream and pine trees brilliant against the snow. A half-mile up the road I came to the house. It was larger than I expected and looked somewhat run down. But that didn't surprise me. If it had been in first-class condition the price would have been much higher.

I felt vaguely self-conscious about bursting in on the owners, but they were friendly. They showed me the walk-in freezer and the professional kitchen equipment. I didn't bother with most of the house because it wasn't heated. But I could see there was a tremendous amount of space.

I was impressed. The setting was gorgeous. The surrounding woods were unspoiled, the air totally fresh. And on every side were the mountains, watching and waiting for what was to come.

A few weeks later Rudi officially acquired the property. He started to spend his weekends there, leaving the city Friday night and returning Sunday night or early Monday.

For most of Rudi's students, Big Indian was a new beginning. The day started at 6:00 a.m. The physical work at Big Indian was endless.

Big Indian, the old hotel

When the work finished, the classes began. Nobody needed to be persuaded to go to bed at night.

The main building needed renovating. The wiring was insufficient, the plumbing quixotic. Endless painting was required. There were other buildings on the property that needed similar attention. Nothing had been done in two years. There was even a separate theater that had been used for dancing and musical performances when the place had been an active resort. We took it over for a classroom.

Working in Big Indian

Our first project on the land was to clear a place for an orchard. This required cutting down trees, removing the stumps and stones that littered the land, and finally planting little apple trees. Anyone who considered himself Rudi's student came to Big Indian and worked. There was no escape.

While the country itself was beautiful, I shuddered whenever I approached Big Indian from the north. I didn't want to work as hard as the situation required, nor did I really feel at home. I came alone as a stranger from upstate. Everyone else came in groups from the city. Also, as Rudi had predicted, the newer students were better than the old. It made me glad for him, but uneasy about my own future. I had been used to my shadowy existence sitting in his store and attending classes. But Big Indian was more out in the open and the competition for Rudi's time was continuous.

The first few weekends were memorable. Everyone got sick. Some got headaches and fever. Others threw up. Still others couldn't sleep. If someone escaped all the obvious symptoms, they simply reported a state of total exhaustion.

The situation became clarified one Sunday morning when Rudi asked Stuart Perrin, a serious student who had been studying with him for several years, how he was feeling that morning.

"Really terrible!" said Stuart.

"Yes," said Rudi. "I feel awful, too. Everyone is paying a price. But it is very necessary. Whenever you enter a new situation, particularly when you buy a piece of real estate, it sucks your vitality. I don't expect anyone to enjoy it, but it is an honor. We are helping to bring Big Indian back to life by feeding it our blood. Once it begins to function, it will feed us. There is a wonderful vitality here. The earth is saturated with energy. That is why I bought the place."

Occasionally everyone would be enlisted in some concentrated effort such as removing rocks from the potential garden. A vast human chain was formed to move the stones to the road where they were being stacked. Each rock was passed from person to person without a break for five hours. It went on all afternoon. No one could stop for a moment, even to go to the bathroom, without disrupting the whole line.

One day a young man who lived in the area offered to assist in any way he could. Since he was experienced with heavy machinery and farm tools we were delighted with his offer, and equally disappointed when the promised help failed to materialize.

But Rudi didn't seem disturbed. "When I first saw the man," he explained, "he appeared to be dressed like Harlequin, the clown. I couldn't understand it. Then I realized that the dress was a symbol of his character and nothing real could be expected from him. His subsequent action has only confirmed my initial vision."

From the start it was evident that a group of people were needed as permanent residents of Big Indian. A couple, who had been Rudi's students for several years, became the first caretakers. They had wanted to get out of the city for a long time, but had never visualized anything like this.

"One reason I bought the property," Rudi said, "was to give Earl and Roz a place in the country."

It was hard to tell whether he was entirely serious. I had no doubt that it was one of the reasons. There may have been a hundred others, but the reasons no longer mattered. Once Rudi made his move he extended his situation and then dug inside himself to find the energy to sustain it. In this way he maintained a steady pace of forced growth. I had known very ambitious people who acted like that to attain some goal in the world, but not anyone who did it simply to encourage his own development, irrespective of the practical implications. None of them really cared that much about growth. Rudi didn't really care about anything else.

Late-night conclave in the Big Indian kitchen

If Big Indian was initially hard on most of the people, it was terribly difficult for Rudi. The pain was both physical and psychic. He did not complain, but when it got too intense he hid in the woods until the worst of it had passed, He had lived like that for years. It was the one aspect of his work that people appreciated least. They were interested in his experiences, but no one wanted to know about the pain. Occasionally, however, he talked about it,

"One day many years ago," Rudi said in a lecture given at the end of the summer, "a woman came into the store. I was in agony at the time. She asked me how I was doing, and I told her in graphic detail. She immediately started to leave.

"'I come here because you are cheerful,' she said as she walked out. 'I'm not interested in hearing your problems.'

"At first I was angry and resentful. Why did I have to put on a show for her sake? But as I thought it over I decided she was right. She came for some warmth and I gave her shit. No one is making me go through this suffering. There is no reason I should inflict it on innocent bystanders.

"Everyone suffers, even movie stars. The only difference is whether you take it like a dumb animal being led to the marketplace, or open to it as the means of attaining your objective — inner growth.

"One of the reasons that work takes so long is that people believe there is a loophole. They will do almost anything to avoid suffering if only it holds out even the slightest hope of being a way to growth. There is no such way. The obstacles within us must be faced and broken down. This has to be difficult. If it weren't so, they would not still be there. But no words will convince you. Not even mine, not even after all these years. Each of you will try to outwit yourself until you finally discover you are paying as much as ever and getting nothing for it. Then you may begin to approach your growth with a little maturity, accepting the cost and paying as it comes due. It is hard, but it is real. In time you may even begin to respect yourself, and then you can grow faster.

"There are only two forces that can motivate a person toward growth. One is to glimpse a higher state. This is a very powerful inducement as long as it lasts, but it doesn't last very long. Normal human consciousness does not have the capacity to remember a state beyond itself.

"The second force is the recognition of our own condition, which of necessity involves suffering. When the moment of truth occurs, we all think we are uniquely stupid, crazy and awful. Actually it is the thing we have in common, that we are all in trouble. The earth is more like a hospital than a lost paradise. The only paradise we have lost was on another level of experience, not here.

"You can stall the suffering for years, even for lifetimes, but you can never avoid it. When you have forgotten even its possibility, it will spring on you in an unsuspected form. It is a sign of maturity when a person begins to open to things inside him which hurts to recognize. It gives him the motivation to work," said Rudi, concluding his talk.

***

The summer had passed. The leaves were falling from the trees, and we resumed our normal schedule in New York City. Rudi continued to visit Big Indian every other weekend. But the people who remained in Big Indian were fundamentally on their own as the first snow storm of the season struck. They quickly limited their amount of living space and began a continuous struggle with antiquated plumbing, insufficient heat, and a temperamental water supply.

A number of these people hardly knew the basic nature of Rudi's work. They had simply appeared at the right time and he had sent them up to stay the winter at Big Indian. One group had come from Los Angeles, bringing with them a lifestyle more appropriate to California than the Northeast. They settled in and proceeded to survive in their own manner.

Rudi generally ignored the difficulties of the situation when he came to visit and concentrated on giving his energy and inspiration, leaving the students to work out their differences with each other.

Most of them had little or no money. Rudi personally underwrote the major expenses. Eventually a small baking business was started to help defray costs, but it was always a losing proposition.

To save fuel, class was conducted in a small room in the main building. But conditions were impossible. The door to the room squeaked loudly every time it was opened. The fluorescent lights in the room were blinding. Each person who entered either turned them on if they were off, or off if they were on, to the distraction of everyone. There was no organization, little discipline, and very little heat.

There were also only a few cars. Many students stayed on the property for months. When they left it was generally to make a bread delivery to New York City.

The winter was unusually cold and snowy. At times the temperature fell to thirty below. But if there was a great deal of snow, there was at least a lot of sunshine. And even though Big Indian nearly burned to the ground from a fire started by the ancient kerosene furnace, it remained intact. With the coming of early spring, the survivors congratulated themselves and each other as they began to prepare for the return of the city students who were completely unaware of the ordeal that they had undergone.

Chapter Twenty-Six

THE INVITATION

One evening Rudi made a general announcement to his class in New York City:

"I have invited Swami Muktananda to come to America. And he has accepted!" He paused to let the message sink in. Then he continued. "For years he has wanted to come, but I always put him off. We were not ready to support the effort it involves. We needed a place like Big Indian for a proper setting. But now he is coming, probably in the early fall. He should be here for the Labor Day Weekend. It's not that any of you are ready for him, but you have six months to prepare."

Rudi paused again.

"The basic difficulty which you will face as a group is that you have not been trained to know how to behave with a Hindu saint. I don't know what Baba will expect, but whatever it is, he had better receive it. I'm serious! If he gets off the plane and someone looks at him the wrong way, he is perfectly capable of getting right back on the plane and leaving. I have seen him do it. It doesn't help to think, 'What kind of a nut would do something like that?' He doesn't need us. We need him! Therefore, whatever he does, whatever he wants, is right! And if you aren't prepared to act that way, then forget about being around when the time comes.

"But all of this is a side issue. The important thing is that he is the real goods, a genuine Indian saint in the ancient tradition. He represents a species that is almost extinct. In meeting him you will be meeting the whole line of Indian spirituality that he represents. None of you would normally ever get to meet such a person in your lifetime. They almost never leave India. If you went there you would be ignored or palmed off on some lesser person. But when Baba comes here he will be available to you if we treat him right.

"I don't mean to scare you. Perhaps he will be on his good behavior

The Invitation

and make things very easy for all of us. However you have to realize that the guru is an absolute dictator in his domain. His word potentially governs every facet of ashram activities. One either accepts it or leaves. It is hard for an American to understand the mentality involved. It is not like a head of a monastery that is selected for his experience, understanding, and general capacity. The Indian guru is chosen because of his other-worldly attainments. He exists on another level of being and is treated accordingly. You don't have to believe it, but you better be prepared to act as if you do. You all can start by learning a little manners.

"Americans have the lousiest manners in the world. We are all used to it, so we take it for granted. We even enjoy it. But every gesture we make could offend someone brought up in a more traditional culture. I am no great example in that regard. I don't care very much about how some of you look, dress, or what you say to me. But when Muktananda is here you will have to take the attitude that we are entertaining visiting royalty.

"In a few weeks I have invited a Swami to visit us. He is a very sweet old man who is considered saintly in India. Some of you may get something from him, but that isn't why I'm asking him to come. I want you to have the experience of greeting him and being in his presence. You can treat it as a rehearsal. We will make wreathes of flowers, and each of you will present a gift to him and receive whatever blessing he might want to confer. You can bring your children if you wish," Rudi concluded.

Several weeks later the Swami arrived, an elderly man with a flowing white beard and a kindly twinkle in his clear eyes. The hall was filled. The day had been spent in preparing garlands of flowers and gathering small presents. Some people had brought their children. I brought a few of my own, including Lisa, the youngest. She was five or six at the time.

No one knew exactly what was to happen. The whole occasion felt slightly strained. It was so totally different from anything we had done before. Rudi was naturally suspicious of ritual as a substitute for honest effort. He had successfully instilled this attitude in most of us. Now we had to undo it.

Rudi had talked about how to behave on the previous evening.

"I can't tell you exactly what to do," he said. "It is for the Swami to set the pattern. He is the guest. We must accommodate ourselves to him. But don't worry too much about it. Be serious. Stay quiet. Then open your heart to the man and make contact with him. It may take you a while to get a sense of his quality, but when you do, draw it inside yourself. However, you shouldn't stare at him. It might make him uncomfortable. Use a little discretion. You can be open, receive, and still make him feel at home. It is not just a question of politeness. If he does not feel welcome he will stay closed. Approach the situation as a kind of love affair. Your warmth must open him and his must open something in you.

"Most of you are too emotional about such things. You only respond if you feel like it. If I look good to you one day, your heart expands. If I don't, you stay away from me psychically. You can't get what you need that way. Sometimes it is harder to open than others. It may be an inner change that I am going through that makes it difficult for you. More likely it is some resistance in you. I have learned to open under almost every condition, including acute torture. You must not tolerate anything less than a full flow between us. It is your work to dig until you find it or release the blocks preventing it.

"It will be easier for you to consciously open to someone new. You all know me too well, or at least you think you do. But this man is a visitor and unknown. Personally, while I like him, he doesn't do that much for me. But some of you may find more in him than you find in me. It doesn't matter. Whatever you find, expand on that. Whatever he gives or does not give, you should not leave empty-handed."

With those words echoing in my mind the occasion began. Rudi gave a short introduction. The Swami responded graciously.

"I am so happy to be present with you all today and especially happy to visit Swami Rudrananda's ashram."

He went on for a few minutes being pleasant, but saying nothing in particular. Then he smiled at us all in a genuine manner and sat down. It was time for people to present their garlands. I discovered that mine was in a pretty sad condition. It had not been much to begin with, but my daughter Lisa had succeeded in getting it all tangled up as she nervously played with it. I tried to sit quietly and open to the occasion, but I found myself having a small anxiety attack. People were going up one-by-one, bowing down, presenting flowers, fruit, receiving the Swami's blessing and perhaps some gift from him in return. It was all rather beautiful, but my necklace of flowers looked like they had just been trampled on by a small parade. Finally I said to myself, "This is

The Invitation

Students greet and gift Swami Chitananda

crazy. I have to relax. I'll just sort of bunch them together. They won't look too bad."

Shortly thereafter my own turn came. I went forward, bowed down, presented my dubious gift, and was given some fruit in return. I returned to my seat slightly shaken. It was the first time in my life I had ever bowed down to anyone.

A little later some of the children came forward, either to give gifts or to receive them. It was charming. Lisa was holding some flowers. I urged her gently to take her turn. She became stubborn. I knew that pushing her would only cause her to completely freeze, so I shrugged my shoulders and stopped urging. But her light blonde hair and bright blue eyes had caught the Swami's attention. He smiled at her. She looked down. He motioned her to approach. She tensed up. I could just see her breaking into tears. That would be great. He held out a tempting fruit to her. She looked up dubiously and shook her head firmly. She was not going to have any of it. I was a little embarrassed, but what could I do? The Swami had the good sense to pass on to other children.

Rudi finally expressed his appreciation for the visit. The rehearsal was over.

At the next class Rudi shared his reaction with us.

"You did all right," he said. "The Swami enjoyed himself. He found you attentive and friendly. Of course he didn't know you were trying to drink his blood. That must have been a new experience for him.

"At the same time I must tell you it was terrible. If you have ever seen the real thing, this looked like a play put on by the inmates of a residence for retarded children. You meant well, but it was very inadequate.

"The Swami is basically a gentle soul. It would be hard to offend him. He wanted to be friendly. But Swami Muktananda is a very different kind of being. He is as complex as a three-dimensional chessboard. He might seem friendly, he might be friendly, but he has more things going on inside him than you could ever imagine. He will appear to you how he wants to appear. If you are taken in by that, it is too bad for you. At the same time he expects you to accept what he shows and react accordingly. If you don't, there will also be trouble.

"I'm not trying to give you a nervous breakdown in advance, just some sense of perspective. What you are preparing for is a once-in-a-lifetime opportunity. Probably the only reason he is coming is that he trusts me to do right by him, which I certainly will, and also because he is chronically restless.

"He is a caged tiger. Nothing occupies him for very long. He goes through an experience and moves on. Like any creative person he needs new material. Even when I go to his ashram in Ganeshpuri, and I am probably his best and certainly his most challenging student, the relation between us begins to bore him after a few days. That doesn't bother me. It is a relief. It makes it possible for me to leave without offending him.

"There are plenty of you. He should not be bored. But even one day or one pointless hour could cause him to take off to California or Texas if he has been invited. Instead of staying with us a month, it could turn out to be only a week."

When I had the chance I talked with Rudi further about Muktananda's visit. Or rather, I brought up the subject and let him talk.

"He can't wait to come," said Rudi. "He keeps writing me about it. I think he wants to turn it into a world tour. I'm not a travel agent. I just want to get him here and keep him here for as long as possible. But there is one hell of a lot of work to be done before that.

"The trouble is, John, that I am the only one who realizes it. If he came next week, you would all get excited and think it was great. He would leave. You would be satisfied. You would never know that you hadn't touched the surface. But I would know! I have spent ten, twelve years, I can't remember how long, working with the man."

The Invitation

"The thing that puzzles me," I said, "is that you are building him up so much now. At other times, some of the things you have said certainly weren't so favorable. How can it be both ways?"

"Very easily," Rudi said. "I contradict myself a lot. It generally doesn't bother you. I'm sure it bothers some people. Often opposites are true. Or I am speaking about myself at one time and students another. It involves two different viewpoints. The average person avoids contradicting himself if he can, because it doesn't sound logical. I am not very interested in logic, I want results. I am trying to stir people into making an effort, into facing certain sides of themselves they would rather ignore. I am prepared to do anything that accomplishes this aim. If it requires love, I'll give love. If it needs strength, strength. If it takes scourging, then that. It's all a question of what you want to achieve. Once you know that you judge everything by whether it helps you attain that goal.

"As an example, the most important aspect of Swami Muktananda's visit isn't anything that will happen while he is here. It is that he is here. Once you understand this, it clarifies the whole situation. If he can be persuaded to stay put in Big Indian or New York City for a few weeks, he will inevitably not only put his own energy, but the whole line of Indian teachers whom he represents into the atmosphere. No one may be directly aware of this process as it occurs. But the energy will remain behind and continue to enrich the ashram. So the important thing becomes to keep him here for a sufficient time for this magnetizing effect to occur. Anything that aids the process is good. If he wants special foods, we get them. If he wants to give lectures, we listen. If he wants to sing, we will love it. And with all of this, he has to believe that there is a need for him that he is interested in fulfilling. He can't be fooled about that."

Chapter Twenty-Seven

PREPARATION

In a completely unprecedented action Rudi began to allow other people to teach his work in New York City and Big Indian. Michael Austin was the first. A little later, he was followed by Stuart and Calvin. Both of them had been with Rudi for several years. They were very different types. Stuart was quiet, slightly distant, and seemingly gentle. Calvin was much more ebullient. He had a theatrical background. But none of this mattered when they taught. The being that emerged was different from the person one had known in the past. It was always surprising, like trying to anticipate the color of a butterfly from looking at the caterpillar.

During this period Greg returned from Paris. He got married at Rudi's suggestion and began to work for a computer firm. With the coming of spring it became evident that someone was needed in Big Indian to supervise the situation. Rudi spoke to Greg about it. Greg decided to give up his well-paying job for the rather shaky prospects at Big Indian. It was a courageous decision on his part, but also a definite opportunity for him that might never have come otherwise. Rudi made him a teacher early in the summer. His first class made a memorable impression on me. I had known him so long, first as a happy schmuck, then as a martial arts fanatic, and as a dedicated student of Rudi's. It had been almost ten years. But the moment he started teaching it was obvious I had never seen him before. He emerged strongly Japanese in spirit, the embodiment of the martial arts he was interested in, but without the personality of a Jewish nebbish that was usually visible.

* * *

While I accepted Rudi's actions without any difficulty, I had to speak to him eventually of my own position. I found the opportunity on a quiet moment one Saturday morning.

"I have been teaching Kundalini yoga at Geneseo for more than a year," I said.

"Sure. So what?" he replied, in a rather discouraging manner.

"I have no illusions about the value of what I am doing, but it must represent something or you wouldn't let me do it."

"True,"' he said, ready to drop the matter.

"What I want to know is what I have to do to be able to teach down here," I persisted.

Rudi paused as if he had something difficult to say and was not quite sure how to put it.

"It is possible that you could start by the end of the summer," he said. "But the problem is, John, that there are certain pieces missing in you. If you can get them, then you can teach."

"How would I do that?" I asked.

"It is basically quite simple. Stuart, Michael and Calvin each have some of these missing parts. What you have to do is to acquire what you lack from them."

"But how? I don't understand."

"First, spend time with them. Get them to open to you. That shouldn't be too difficult since they are supposed to do that as part of their teaching. But even more important, you have to open completely to them and ask to receive those aspects of their inner nature which you need. If you ask deeply enough, it will occur."

"But how will I know?"

"Maybe you won't know. I will know. That's what counts. But I can't do the work for you. It is part of the price you must pay for the chance to teach. I have replaced psychic parts in you in the past. I won't do that anymore for you or anyone else. You have come a long way. But that no longer matters. If you want to teach you must fill in the gaps by your own effort. You have the rest of the summer in which to do it."

I left, still not sure what Rudi meant. But I had the distinct feeling that if I didn't make it this time around, it would be far more difficult in the future.

On my subsequent visits to Big Indian, I concentrated on opening to the teachers. I talked to them, worked with them in the fields, anything that I could think of. It wasn't so bad, but I didn't have the slightest idea whether I was succeeding. At the same time I had a fateful meeting which enormously complicated the whole process of preparing for the fall.

※ ※ ※

I walked into my first summer school class in late June. Sitting at the opposite end of the room was a beautiful blonde girl, seemingly intent on blending in with the background. My first thought was, "What is she doing in Geneseo?"

I was giving two three-week courses back to back. She was enrolled in both of them. During the first three weeks I fought my attraction to her. I avoided looking at her or talking to her very much. Regardless, I was falling in love; it was completely inevitable. She was beautiful, exotic, very intelligent, and had a quality of untouchability that I found totally irresistible.

After the first course was over I went on a two-week publicity tour in connection with my book *Encounter* that had recently been published. In the course of a radio interview I was asked,

"Dr. Mann. What happens if the leader gets involved with a member of his group?"

"I'll let you know in about six weeks," I said, "if you want to invite me back."

"What do you mean?" the interviewer asked.

"That is exactly the situation I am in at this time."

"So what are you going to do?" said the interviewer, warming to the subject.

"I don't know," I said, and I didn't.

I returned to give the second course. It would have been simple if she had dropped out, but she hadn't. Each day that we were together became a link in the chain that was being forged between us. Toward the end of the course I made a move. The group was over for the day. She was walking out of the room. I caught up with her and said,

"Could I talk to you?"

"Sure." We walked out onto the quadrangle around which most of the college buildings were placed. It was probably the most public spot on the whole campus.

There was a preliminary silence.

"Well?" she said.

"I have been fighting my feeling for you since I met you," I said.

Preparation

"I know," she said in a matter of fact, but slightly tense tone. "What made you change your mind now?"

"The group is coming to an end," I said. "You are graduating. It seemed like I should talk to you now or forget about it."

"I'm glad you're saying something," she said. "What made you hesitate?"

"I can think of a couple of good reasons. But anyway, all I want to say is that when you graduate and settle down, I want to see you. How do you feel about that?"

"I want to see you too," she said.

I smiled and felt very happy. There was nothing more to say. She left shortly thereafter. I felt very much in love.

As the term drew to a close, we decided to take a trip together. This was not an expression of my better judgment, but the course was over and she was about to graduate. I felt like Adam with a ten-day pass to the Garden of Eden.

The trip was set for the following week. The weekend before, I went to Big Indian. On the way there, Dora, an old friend who was driving with me, announced,

"I'm going to tell Rudi about what you are doing with Melanie."

I was shocked, but I knew there was nothing I could do to stop her, so I just said, "That's your privilege."

When we arrived I decided I had better get to him first. I found Rudi between the main house and the class hall.

"Could I talk with you a minute?" I asked hesitantly.

"Sure. What's up?"

"I wouldn't bother you but I know Dora is going to say something, so I want to give you the background."

"What have you done now?" he asked.

"I've fallen in love," I said. "I wanted you to hear it from me first."

Rudi looked at me without expression, I waited. He didn't say anything.

"Is there anything you want to know?" I asked.

"No, I'll talk to you after I hear what Dora says."

On those less than reassuring words I went back to work, removing brush from what was to become an orchard by the end of the season. As the hours passed, I became more nervous. I began to remember the time several years before when Rudi had ended it between Janis and me. I compared it to the present time, with Muktananda coming and the issue of my becoming a teacher very much up in the air. The more I thought about it, the less I liked the situation.

In the afternoon, Rudi came by. He motioned to me to drop what I was doing. I walked over nervously, like a school boy caught in the act of cheating on an exam. He didn't waste any words.

"What is wrong with you John?"

I didn't say anything. One thing I had learned was that there was no defense. Whatever came, it was for me to open to it and absorb the impact. Any decisions could come later.

"First of all," said Rudi, "this girl is a student. How can you do such an idiotic thing?"

"I haven't done anything yet," I said.

"But you are going to."

There was nothing I could say to that. I began to have the horrible feeling that I would not be visiting the Garden of Eden.

"Don't you have any sense of responsibility?" Rudi went on relentlessly. "You can't expect to be protected for the rest of your life. How many times do I have to save you from the edge of a cliff?"

I couldn't resist defending myself a little.

"I don't really see what is so terrible," I said. "I love the girl. She is graduating. It may not be entirely right, but how can it be that wrong?"

"Listen, John. All you see is the beautiful girl in front of you, a sparkling enchantment. But when it's over, what will you have? Nothing! A waste of energy. I can understand how you feel. You have had so little in the way of real human relations for so many years. You have no resistance to this sort of thing. But it is still wrong!"

"What am I supposed to do?" I asked, knowing the answer in advance.

"When you go back, see the girl and tell her it is over. Maybe she'll understand. But whether she does or not, that is what you must do."

I looked at it, hated it, recognized a certain inevitability in the situation and agreed. If I hadn't, I could kiss being a teacher goodbye. I cursed Dora inwardly, though at the same time was peculiarly grateful. Her influence might have saved me, if I needed saving.

Finally I said, "After she graduates in September, is it all right then?"

Rudi paused for a moment and then said, "Even then it would be better if you didn't."

He walked away and I went back to work. I would have fought if it was possible, but I had too much at stake and I knew that what Rudi had said was more or less true.

* * *

The next time I returned to Big Indian, Rudi asked, "Did you end it?"

"I hated doing it," I said, "but I did it."

"Good," he said, "You really had no choice."

"I know," I said.

"It was the effect it would have had on you that was crucial."

"What do you mean?" I asked, not sure I really wanted to know.

"You certainly would not have become a teacher. At another time perhaps the whole thing wouldn't have made too much difference. Right now, the timing is crucial. If there is a miscarriage the time and effort you have invested would be largely wasted. Inwardly I think you knew this. That's why you did what had to be done. I'm sure it was hard for you. Better it should be hard and done than to lose all you have a worked for. It was a test and you passed."

He paused and looked at me speculatively.

"Don't feel sorry for yourself. Be glad for the girl's sake."

"That's a hell of a thing to say," I answered, taken aback.

"Two years ago," said Rudi, "we went through a scene like this in regard to Janis. I never fully explained my actions to you, though I think you accept them now. If you had not broken off with her you would have been married and gone West with her in a year. It would have been the end of the work for you."

"You've already told me that," I said.

"That is just the beginning. In a year or two, you would have grown tired of her. Then you would have moved on, looking for someone else to repeat the same pattern. Over the years you would have left a trail of broken situations and lives behind you, and you would have nothing in the end."

I sat very still, feeling the cold chill of these words.

"Why didn't you tell me this earlier?" I asked.

"You wouldn't have believed it. Enough time has passed for you to be able to see things differently. To go into a Garden of Eden, as you were going, leads nowhere except to the back exit. You blow a great amount of energy on the illusion of paradise. There is nothing real about it but the emotion you feel at the time. You don't grow in paradise. You can't! If it were only necessary to follow one's desires in order to become enlightened, you wouldn't need to be here with me today. Nothing is attained without sacrifice. And no one is in a position to know what he should sacrifice until the answer falls on him, usually unexpectedly. God chooses what he wants from you. If you pay you receive an unknown gift in return. That is where faith is required. It is the bridge between unknowns."

There was a pause. Rudi looked at me and through me, and then started to speak in a different tone.

"You are a monster, John. You are a vampire sucking the blood out of situations and then leaving them dead. You have been doing it all your life. For a long time it didn't matter. You were too dead yourself to have much effect on others, and people instinctively shunned you. But I have been bringing you to life. You are getting to the point where you can attract other people to you. It isn't you doing this. It is the force working through you. That makes it my responsibility. I am Dr. Frankenstein."

I was shocked. Rudi had never said anything like this to me before, not in eleven years. What had I done to deserve it? I had given up Melanie. I was working hard.

"If you asked to be my student at this point, I wouldn't take you," Rudi continued relentlessly. "You are a menace to me and could be a menace to the work unless something is fundamentally changed in you."

"Is this what you always thought?" I asked as I tried to recover my balance.

"Yes. I always saw these things."

"But for eleven years you never said anything. I can't understand that."

"It would have done no good. You would not have been ready to hear it."

I felt a growing sense of numbness. The implications of Rudi's words seemed to spread in all directions, like black ink in a blotter. So many years of experience were being recast in a different light. How could he have felt such things and never said them? I sensed that I had been cut in half with a psychic meat cleaver. It was a clean cut with little blood, but I could imagine the two pieces just falling apart. I couldn't say anything. He was silent. Then he resumed.

"Perhaps you think I don't mean what I am saying, or that I am exaggerating it. You couldn't be more mistaken. I haven't made you a teacher here because I dared not turn you lose. You couldn't do much harm up in Geneseo. They aren't sensitive enough for you to hurt them. But unless something changes in you drastically, you will never teach down here. I have nothing personally against you. It is my responsibility to protect others from the result of my own efforts where you are concerned."

I left slowly. It had been relentless torture from the least expected source. I walked up the road, along the brook, past whispering trees. But I was blind to the scene around me. I felt like the picture of Dorian Grey come to life. I had escaped from the mirror and there was nowhere to hide. It was horrible! I had met with a taste of such an experience when I was alone in the redwood forest at Esalen. But this was different. It had happened in the full light of day, delivered from both barrels by the man on whom my future most depended. If he thought those things, what chance did I have?

But I did not care what he thought at that moment. My own nakedness came before anything else. I sat down on a secluded rock by the stream that bordered the road and began to cry. They were deep hopeless tears. I cried in the merciless light that shone on me in all directions. It was one of the most awful moments of my life. Every rationalization and excuse had been stripped away. If anyone else had said it to me, I would have doubted their words and muted the effect. But I had gained an extraordinary admiration for Rudi's ability to see to the center of a situation. I had watched his insight operate on others for over a decade, continually revealing things that were obviously true once pointed out and invisible until then.

Crying brought little relief, but it gradually exhausted me. I walked for a long time. I didn't know where I was. Gradually it grew dark outside. Whatever had happened seemed to be over. It was time to return to the ashram. I made my way back, feeling exhausted and defenseless. If I had wept my soul out of my eyes I would not have been surprised.

It was quiet in the main house. I wanted to be inconspicuous. I walked towards the stairs to the upper floor where I was staying. At the base of the stairs Rudi was deep in a poker game. It was one of his less spiritual forms of relaxation. I tried to walk by inconspicuously. Usually, if I wished to attract his attention, he ignored me. But this time he stopped what he was doing to give me a searching glance.

Poker night at the ashram

"You look good, John. Your eyes are clearer."

"I feel totally exhausted and empty," I said, and stumbled up the stairs.

That was the beginning of a process that extended through the rest of the summer. Every time I worked deeply it was followed by tears of sadness and remorse. I could not have said for what I was crying, other than my own inner state and the seeming hopelessness of ever doing anything about it. If it had not changed in all this time, what hope could there be? What I did not know was that the change was occurring as I cried. In every bitter harsh tear something was leaving me that had been deeply buried under forgotten layers of my experience. I might never understand what I had done in the past, or only after it had ceased to be a problem to me, but the effects that had haunted me were being purged from my system.

When it was necessary, Rudi continued to scourge me. He was utterly merciless. I had always thought of him as relatively easygoing, inclined to think too well of people. I never assumed that again. He saw people for what they were. He focused on their positive aspects by choice, not blindness. He reached for the good because growth and nourishment lay in that direction.

A month later I saw Rudi alone after lunch as everyone left to go back to work. I gathered up my courage and took the opportunity to approach him.

"At the beginning of the summer," I said, "I asked you about becoming a teacher at Big Indian. You told me I needed some missing pieces that I could get if I opened to several of the teachers. I have tried. I am going to keep on trying. But time is passing. The summer is more than half over. I want to know how I am doing."

"You are doing all right," he said.

"That isn't terribly definite."

"At this point, it is up to you. It is possible for you to succeed, but certainly not inevitable. How much do you want it?"

"I want it. I wouldn't have given up Melanie if I didn't want it."

"Have you given her up?"

"Yes."

"Good."

Rudi was quiet for a very long time. Then he broke the silence.

"There will be ten teachers produced this year. You have been with me longer than anyone. You certainly deserve a chance. But you have to understand something, John, I am basically detached. Each person who becomes a teacher requires a great effort on my part. It is like having a child and I am willing to make that effort."

His eyes took on a stern but distant glimmer that focused beyond me." It makes no difference to me who the ten people are. They will emerge in terms of their preparation, need, and capacity. I certainly want you to have every opportunity, but at the same time you must realize that if you don't make it that will be all the same to me. The ten teachers will come through whoever they are. I will have fulfilled my responsibility and my commitment."

I sat there experiencing a cold chill. I knew I had heard the truth. It was just. I would not have wanted it any other way.

He saw I understood and had accepted it. Then he smiled slightly.

"There is no reason why you shouldn't be one of the ten if you do what you have to do."

"If I should make it, when could I begin?" I said, wanting to pin him down before the conversation ended.

"On the Labor Day Weekend," said Rudi. "Remind me about it if I should forget."

He got up and left. I sat there somewhat stunned. Labor Day Weekend! That was when Swami Muktananda was due to arrive. It was the first weekend he would be at Big Indian. It seemed like an incredible time to begin. I left in a very thoughtful state.

One of the major tasks at Big Indian during this period was to finish the outside of all the buildings. This included repairing the roofs and gutters, and repainting the houses. I was involved in the painting. The main house was three stories high. We had extension ladders, but they were not fully adequate. Standing on the next to top rung I could still reach only within ten feet of the peak of the roof. I worked with another fellow who was afraid of the wasps that had built their nests in the eaves. Slowly we worked our way up. We had to cover a huge area. But inevitably the effort converged on the relatively narrow strip at the top. My partner didn't want anything to do with it because of the wasps, and I had always been afraid of heights. One of my nightmare fantasies was to have to cross a fragile hand bridge over a high mountain pass in the Himalayas.

Now as I climbed higher up the ladder, my legs and shoulders became increasingly tense. I had to come down to rest with increasing frequency. During one of these periods Rudi appeared.

"Where are you working?" he asked me.

Getting ready for Swami Muktananda's visit to Big Indian

Preparation

"Up there," I said, pointing to where the fully extended ladder came to an end.

He nodded and said, "Good."

"What's so good about it," I said.

He didn't reply.

"If I fell from there," I said, "that would be the end."

"Don't worry about it, John," he said. "You won't fall. You weren't meant to have such an easy way out." And on that note of sympathy, he departed. But I felt much better. He was aware of what I was doing and was unconcerned about it. I felt that I would get through somehow without a serious accident.

At the end, I had to stand on the last rung of the fully extended ladder using a paintbrush tied to a long broom handle. Wasps were swarming around me. I didn't mind getting stung, but I was really afraid of falling off the ladder. My legs began to quiver, I was very tempted to quit and let someone else worry about the last few feet. It could hardly be noticed from the ground.

I came down the ladder to rest and think it over. My partner had disappeared somewhere without telling me. That was really great! He was supposed to be holding the ladder. All my laziness and fear urged me to walk away, at least for the time being. But I felt that the situation was not accidental. If I ever wanted to teach, I'd better get my ass up that ladder and finish the job. I reluctantly forced myself to return. In the end, it wasn't so bad. My partner came back after I had finished.

"Oh," he said, "You did it without me."

I was tempted to hit him, but my legs were still shaking and I was thankful that the job was over. The wasps were swarming angrily above.

***

As the work on the ashram proceeded, there was word from India to spur us on. Swami Muktananda was getting excited about the trip.

He wrote that he would like to bring fifteen people with him. Rudi was shocked. He had accepted responsibility to underwrite the expenses of the trip. He wrote back a tactful but firm letter:

Dear Baba,

We all look forward to your arrival. Excitement is mounting...

Fifteen people are out of the question. Much as we would like to have them, the facilities are inadequate and I do not have the money. I am not a millionaire, regardless of what you may think. Please limit the party to three.

"That way," Rudi explained to us, "he will probably limit it to five or six."

For the first time since I had known him Rudi began to collect money from his students. It was not for the expenses of running the ashram, but to help cover Muktananda's visit. Even then, he was apologetic about it.

"He is really coming for all of you," he said in class. "I can go to India to see him. But very few of you will ever go to the East. And even if you did you would not have the opportunity that will exist while he is here. Endless stupid obstacles would be placed in your way unless you went with me.

"But this time you will have a remarkable opportunity. He wants to make the trip, so he will make himself available. His own people will not be there to occupy him and insulate him from outsiders. That is the real reason I would not accept his bringing fifteen people. If he did that he might as well stay home. I don't care about the money. If I really thought it was necessary I would raise the money for twenty-five people. But the problem with any teacher is that you have to get through his advanced students to get to him. It is like trying to see the head of a corporation. The difficult part is to penetrate the layers of protection that surround him. The man himself is usually accessible if you have a real reason to talk with him."

During the three months before Muktananda's arrival, various new classes were instituted. An American girl who had spent time in Ganeshpuri gave lessons in proper behavior at ceremonial occasions. For the first time we learned to chant. Rudi had previously discouraged chanting. He felt that it too easily produced a superficial effect that gave people the illusion of working without doing much work. But Muktananda approved of it. So we would chant.

An Indian lady named Droupadi, who had been with Baba a long time came ahead to help prepare the way. She was very gentle and inwardly dedicated to her master in a manner that I had not seen

Preparation

before.

On one occasion Droupadi was scheduled to give a class. When I arrived she was alone. There should have been twenty-five to thirty people in attendance. I later discovered that Rudi had started to talk in the dining room at about that time. Everyone had stayed behind to listen to him.

Droupadi waited a few minutes and then began. We went through a basic routine of chanting and brief meditation. When it was over, I continued to sit for a while. Suddenly I felt Rudi's presence. I knew he was not in the room. There was no one there but Droupadi. But I began to burn and feel that I had been absorbed into Rudi's belly. I didn't think much of it. If I had I would have doubted the reality of the experience. But later in the day I casually asked him about it.

"Did it have any reality or was I having a daydream?"

"Of course it had reality," Rudi said, slightly irritated with me. "How do you think a teacher is created? He has to be born. Who is the parent? The guru. I am carrying you inside me, John. The fact that you didn't realize it until now doesn't mean it wasn't going on. Now that you know it should help you have more faith in the reality of the process.

※ ※ ※

As part of the general preparation Rudi decided to celebrate an Indian holiday devoted to the guru. It was in the nature of a birthday party for all gurus, regardless of when they were born. I arrived at Big Indian without knowledge of what was to occur, and consequently was totally unprepared. Rudi himself was ambivalent about the ceremony since he resisted situations that placed him in too high a position. Nevertheless he accepted it as part of the preparation for Muktananda's visit.

My first inkling that anything unusual was occurring was a sign on the kitchen doorway listing persons who were fasting for the day. But even then I didn't know it was in preparation for any particular event. It didn't begin to dawn on me to ask about it until I noticed several people making gifts.

"What's going on?" I asked.

I received surprised looks. "It's the Guru's Day. We are having a ceremony after lunch."

"What does that involve?" I was totally at sea.

"No one knows exactly, except that we each give gifts to Rudi."

Lunch passed. I volunteered to help wash dishes with a crew of seven. It had been a festive meal and had generated an endless number of dirty dishes. One by one people began to disappear. I gathered the ceremony was due to begin at 2:00. It got to be 2:15. I began to feel slightly sick. I had no present and would be late besides. I knew I shouldn't leave until the dishes were finished, but that didn't solve my problem. I couldn't say, "I'm sorry I didn't know about it and have nothing to give." Such an excuse might be reasonable, but psychologically it would cut no ice. I continued washing the dishes, getting more and more upset. Finally I took myself in hand. I had survived when the garland had gotten all tangled up in the previous ceremony. I would live through this also.

The dishes came to an end about 2:35. And then I had an inspiration. For some reason I had brought my checkbook. It was in the back of the car. I ran outside like a madman— couldn't find my car keys, finally located them, opened the trunk, and ripped off the strap on my briefcase in my excitement. Inside was the checkbook. I wrote out a check, started for the theater, stopping only to pick one orange flower that was growing in a window box. I folded the check around the stem of the flower. I was ready! I arrived in the theater a slightly nervous wreck, only to discover that there was no hurry. There was a long line of people waiting to present their gifts, old and young, one at a time. They approached the front of the stage where Rudi was sitting, bowed down, gave their gift, and waited to receive his blessing. The ceremony had been going on for at least thirty minutes and more than half the people were still in line.

I waited, enjoying the opportunity to relax and absorb the scene. It was quite beautiful. Whatever Rudi's initial misgivings he was radiantly happy. His presence filled the room. Each person approached him differently, quickly or slowly, with a half bow or a complete prostration. He looked on each serenely, accepting what they gave him, sometimes giving one of the gifts he had already received in return, or touching the person in a blessing.

Slowly the line shortened. I moved toward the front. As one or two were still ahead of me, I began to feel strange. Was my gift appropriate? I thought it would be all right. In any case I owed Rudi a lot of money. He could use it as needed. The thought of bowing down to him didn't bother me, though I had known him for so long and never

Preparation

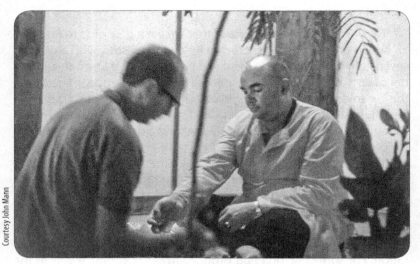

John Mann offers his gift to Rudi

had done it before. But this was not the Rudi that I had known.

The person before me moved ahead. I watched, waited with a sense of anticipation, though I did not expect anything in particular. Now it was my turn. I moved forward and came down on my knees. At that moment, a picture was taken, though I did not know it at the time. I presented my gift, bowed to the floor, came up and waited. Rudi looked at me seriously for a moment and then gave me a garland and smiled happily. I smiled too and moved away to rejoin the rest of the group. Shortly thereafter the last of the people passed before him and were seated.

There was silence for a few minutes as Rudi sat within the vibrant spirit that filled the room. Then he spoke briefly.

"I know that these gifts are for the force that works through me, not for me. It is in this sense that I have accepted them. It makes me deeply grateful to have experienced this day. I want to share my happiness with you.

"A few of you will find yourselves in my position in the future. When it happens, remember it is not for you. Otherwise you will be in danger of believing in yourself instead of knowing always that it is only through your nothingness that the force flows."

He looked around the room at each person separately, mirroring in his own face what he saw before him. The atmosphere shone. Then quietly but abruptly, he left, leaving his presence shimmering in the air.

Later when photographs of the whole day were shown, it turned out that the moment I had been with Rudi was the only picture taken during the actual ceremony. When Rudi was shown the picture he said, "John must be coming up in the world."

※ ※ ※

A few weeks later it was announced that we would have a *puja*. No one understood what was involved but Rudi. He had witnessed the ceremony on a recent trip to India.

"It was," he explained, "a week-long fire purification ritual during which many holy men gathered to renew their inner commitment to God."

Rudi had some doubts about the wisdom of attempting to duplicate such an ancient ritual under Western conditions. But again he was urged to do so by others as part of our general preparation. He described what would happen a day before the ceremony.

"In my last letter from Swami Muktananda, he gave Big Indian the title *Shree Gurudev Rudrananda Yogashram*. It is a great honor but it is also just a name. It represents a possibility, not anything that really exists. The purpose of the puja is to begin to make it real.

"Today we are going to dig a great hole in the upper field. Tomorrow it will be filled with logs and in the evening after dark we will have a great fire. There will be a full moon. It is the right time. I cannot tell you exactly what to do beforehand. I do not even know whether anything will happen."

I had no doubt that something would happen. Rudi never did anything that didn't work. If it didn't happen easily, he just worked harder until something gave way by the sheer intensity of his effort.

As the day of preparation stretched out, expectations mounted. A vast pile of logs was thrown into a large pit that had been gouged out of the earth with a bulldozer.

At eight in the evening we met in the theater. While we worked it rained briefly, a good sign. At the end, Rudi said,

"As you leave here, walk quietly up to the field. A puja is a ceremony of ritual purification. It represents the nature of our work. It is also a means of attracting the attention of great beings who must be enlisted in the atmosphere of the ashram. As the light of the flame ascends, we also can rise to attract the spirits down on us. The fire itself is not important. It is only a visible symbol. It is the burning within your heart that attracts the cosmic energy with which we work. Just as a statue is dedicated through a ceremony designed to make contact between the image and that which it represents, so this experience has the potential of making contact between the whole physical structure of this ashram and great powers in the universe. I can't be sure that this will happen, but I have seen something very like it occur during the puja ceremony I witnessed in India.

"For each of you it is an opportunity to deepen your sense of dedication and surrender. As I talk, the wood is already being lit. We will shortly begin to walk around the fire. If you wish you may hold burning branches. That is not important. But as you walk, ask to place in the fire everything within you that is obstructing your own growth. Throw in your whole personality if you wish. It's an opportunity to get rid of a tremendous amount of garbage from the past. Each step can be a different item. Each great circle around the fire can be a whole phase of your past. As for the rest, follow my lead."

Rudi got up and walked out the side door into the night. Slowly, we followed him. It was quite light outside. The ground was damp but the full moon threw the scene into relief. The mountains surrounding Big Indian loomed as dark organic presences. The air was cool, and the great fire was already visible in the distance. The figures around it were silhouetted, and the sound of the damp wood crackling, spitting, and sparking filled the atmosphere.

As I reached the pit, the heat of the fire was overwhelming. The scene looked vaguely infernal. People were chanting as they walked slowly around the blaze. I felt awkward, but I tried to surrender. There were certainly things in myself that I wanted to drop. As I thought of them or felt them, I threw them in the fire. I could imagine them sizzle and disappear in the huge swirling flames. I didn't know what anyone else was doing or whether anything was actually happening, but there was certainly an intense mood.

After a few minutes Rudi paused, took off one of his shoes and threw it in the flames. I was tempted to follow suit, but it seemed stupid to throw away my shoe to imitate him. I thought about a sock, but that really seemed ridiculous.

The moon appeared and disappeared behind gentle clouds. The fire roared and the light stretched into the heavens. People stopped moving. I stared into the flames for a time. I looked at Rudi. His eyes were reflecting the orange light. He was in some kind of abstract state. I walked over to be closer to him. He sat facing the fire for a time. Others sat down around him. He did not look at them. It was not an ordinary class.

The vastness of the outdoors combined with the intensity of the inner effort seemed to be converging in some invisible direction that I could not see. I asked to be a part of whatever was happening. Rudi went into some kind of spasm that often occurred when the force became particularly intense for him. Shortly thereafter he stood up and walked off into the darkness. The puja was over.

Later he said, "A vast figure of Shiva appeared. It stretched up several hundred feet into the sky. We always think of higher beings on a human scale. But that is ridiculous. They are huge.

"If we can build on what happened tonight, Big Indian can become a place that attracts such beings from the astral, and is enriched by their energy. It is a great and important possibility that people scarcely understand. If we can bring down the energy of another level of existence, the quality here will rise beyond anything you can imagine. That is one reason I wanted Muktananda to come. Everything he has within him can be absorbed by the atmosphere and remain behind after he goes."

All of this was somewhere in the background as August ended. The necessary work at Big Indian had been accomplished. It had been a huge job. A special sign had been made in copper for the classroom which said *Shree Gurudev Rudrananda Yogashram*. The stage was set. It remained only for the protagonist to appear.

Chapter Twenty-Eight
SWAMI MUKTANANDA COMES

Swami Muktananda arrives at JFK Airport

I had lived in the shadow of Swami Muktananda for over a decade. But the reality of the man was unknown. I awaited his arrival with hope, curiosity and uncertainty,

I was not in the city when he came. But I knew that he was going to be in the country ashram at Big Indian for the long Labor Day Weekend.

I arrived at Big Indian early in the evening on Friday. It seemed deserted. I looked in the theater. No one was there. I entered the main house and heard the distant sound of chanting to the accompaniment of an unfamiliar stringed instrument. I followed the sound into the small living room which was overflowing with people. In the front of the room was Swami Muktananda singing and chanting as if he had always been there. He seemed the essence of friendly power. I sat down quietly in the back of the room to absorb the scene. It was an overwhelming impression because it was so totally different from anything I had expected.

Swami Muktananda Comes

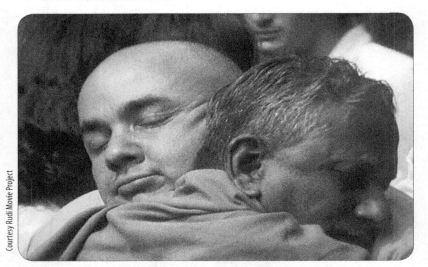

"You can't judge him by your standards," Rudi had said. "You will see what he appears to be and get involved in what he appears to be doing. But Baba is perfectly capable of doing a number of things at once, some of which you can't see. He has more angles than a hall of mirrors. If you get involved in trying to understand what is going on, you will go down and never come up. None of it matters. Absorb what you can use. Let him worry about the rest."

But as I sat there I forgot about everything Rudi had said as Baba's singing transformed his surroundings into an Indian temple. After fifteen minutes he stopped and said through his interpreter,

"I am very pleased to be here and will see you all after supper." He smiled happily as if he had made a subtle joke and quietly made his way out of the room. The weekend had begun.

Swami Muktananda's arrival in the United States had received a good deal of advance publicity. By Saturday two hundred and fifty people, representing several different spiritual groups, had assembled in Big Indian. Swami Muktananda seemed to accept, and probably enjoy, the activity and excitement surrounding his presence. He gave classes through his translator and led chanting in a generally festive atmosphere. Watching him totally at ease before all these people, one was tempted to think of him as a kindly elderly yogi, full of love and charity. But if you looked more closely the effect was more of a smiling tiger, or a friendly serpent, whose actions might completely change at any moment. However I was far enough back in the crowd not to have to worry. And as Rudi said later, "He was on his good behavior."

One of the puzzling things to me was to reconcile his appearance with so many of the stories Rudi had told me about him over the years. At Big Indian on that weekend and later he was kindly, captivating, and patient, at least in public. I didn't see him in private. But on that weekend everyone seemed different as we were gathered up in the energy and excitement of the occasion.

Rudi spent a good deal of his free time with an Indian gentleman whom he had just met. He treated him with great affection. It was beautiful to watch them together.

"It is a very strange feeling," Rudi said to me later. "Both of us are mature men, but I was his mother and he was my daughter in another life."

In the context of the occasion, nothing seemed strange to me, not even that.

During the first day after one of Muktananda's classes, Rudi started to work with some of his students in a totally new way. At first all I noticed was people approaching Rudi and then collapsing onto the lawn. Then as I watched more closely, I saw that he put his fingers on the person's forehead, and shortly thereafter they seemed to become dizzy and fall to the ground in some kind of fit. It was scary. I stood

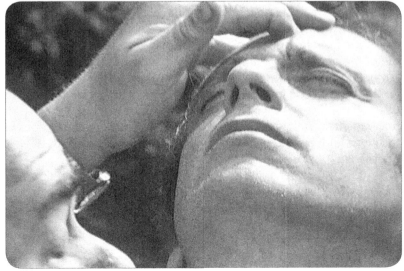

Rudi works on John Mann

Swami Muktananda Comes

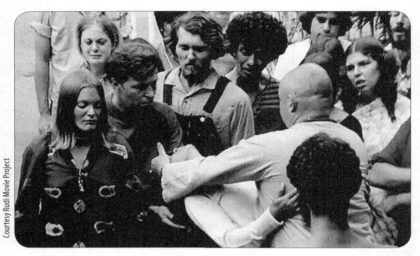

Rudi working with students in a new way

around in the narrowing circle, watching with mixed emotions as he worked with one person after another. And then Rudi turned toward me. I had no idea what to expect. Two of his fingers burrowed into my forehead. My hesitation had no power over them. I closed my eyes and began to feel dizzy. I didn't know why. Was he pressing on a nerve? My head went back. He touched my heart center, and then the base of my spine. Without knowing quite what was happening I felt myself arching backward and falling to the ground. Someone caught me to break the fall. I lay still, occasionally racked by a spasm. It reminded me of the occasion so many years before when Rudi had raised the kundalini in my spine during the great Northeastern blackout. I lay on the ground for a minute or two, conscious of great energy moving through me. Then I slowly got up. The whole scene looked like a spiritual battlefield with people strewn across the lawn in various stages of recovery. Rudi was slowing down. He had worked with about twenty people. He took on one last person.

Shortly thereafter an Indian man who had observed the situation took me aside to ask, "How did it feel to be in samadhi?"

I wanted to reply, "I didn't know that I was in samadhi," but I controlled myself. I figured, *a)* it was none of his business; and *b)* if he thought that was samadhi he didn't know much, so I just smiled enigmatically and moved on.

As evening approached I realized that the Labor Day Weekend was proving to be the least likely time for me to start teaching. There were so many people moving in so many directions. Rudi seemed to have forgotten ever having said anything to me about it. Why should he remember? It was up to me. I got sick at the thought. He was terribly busy and constantly involved with Swami Muktananda, as was natural. I could imagine the response I would get if I could find the opportunity to talk to him. But I also knew that the situation had to be clarified. So I bided my time, afraid but determined.

My opportunity came after dinner in a crowded hallway. Rudi was rushing past on some errand. I reached out to catch his attention.

"Could I speak to you for a moment?"

He obviously didn't want to speak to me or anyone else. He had something on his mind. But he halted.

"What is it?"

"A month ago you said if all went well I could start teaching on the Labor Day weekend. Is that still true?"

He looked at me as if I were some particularly loathsome bug that he had just uncovered under a rock, I didn't care. It was no time to hesitate.

"I felt that if I didn't say anything," I pressed on, "the opportunity would just go by. I know you have a lot of things on your mind,"

"Remind me tomorrow if I forget about it," said Rudi. "Perhaps we can do it after class in the early afternoon."

He didn't wait for my reaction but disappeared in the direction he had been going. I stood there shaken but happy that I had apparently achieved my objective.

That evening Rudi heard that Baba was disturbed about movies that were being taken of the weekend. Bruce Rubin, one of Rudi's older students, was the cameraman. While Baba had given his permission for the filming, Bruce, in his enthusiasm, had been taking a good deal of footage of Rudi as well as of Muktananda. This Baba did not like.

Rudi took the matter very seriously as he spoke to Bruce about it.

"I don't care how you do it, but go to Swami Muktananda and apologize. Don't be misled by his apparent egotism. He is the honored guest. He has the right. No one told you to start taking my picture instead of his. Your future is at stake. Obtain his forgiveness."

Bruce didn't argue. He went to Baba's room. After a lengthy wait by the closed door he was informed that Swami was not to be disturbed. He waited for several hours more. Finally he was told the Swami had retired for the night. Bruce was grim, but not discouraged.

※ ※ ※

The next day, Sunday, was varied and exciting, but I couldn't get involved in it. The question of what would happen in the afternoon haunted me. Swami Muktananda gave a long class. Everyone was absorbed in his words. Everyone but me. I was scared of teaching and scared that the opportunity would get lost in the shuffle. Finally, after an hour and a half the session began to break up. Rudi stayed with Baba. I waited. Some people approached Baba for his blessing. He gave it. Rudi drifted away slightly. I moved up to him. He looked everywhere but at me. It might have been intentional, but I didn't think so.

"What about it?" I asked.

He looked puzzled. Then he smiled.

"This is the time, isn't it."

"Yes."

"See if you can find Lucas, Natalie, and the others who are preparing to teach. You can all start at once. Tell each of them to round up a few people and give a class somewhere on the grounds."

I waited to hear more. But Rudi had no more to say. I started off. Somehow I accumulated twelve to fifteen people. They sat in a semi-circle near a large tree in the middle of a field near the entrance to the main house.

I had taught many times before at Geneseo. But this was the big time and these were all students who had studied directly with Rudi. I knew it had better be good.

I would have found a reason for delay if I could, but there was none. I started working! Once started, everything else was forgotten. I was only aware of the flow of energy.

After class, I hugged each of the students as was customary. Rudi always compared it to burping a baby. As I did it I felt a totally new sensation in my chest. My heart center was opening for the first time. It seems incredible, in retrospect, that I could have worked twelve years with a closed heart. Some people have their hearts open the first time they work. Others, after a relatively short time. I had heard Rudi talk of the importance of opening the heart, not only as a means of relating to other people, but also because of the treasures hidden in the heart center itself. Now it had finally happened. Jack Stewart who was in the group and was one of Rudi's oldest students told me later, "You came on like a tiger."

I left the group feeling deeply content. Then I discovered that my wrist watch was missing. I began to look for it in the grass. After a few minutes one of the people who had been in the class joined me. But we could not find it.

"It was a cheap watch anyway," I said, getting up to leave the scene. But to my surprise the man took off his own watch and said, "Here, take mine." My immediate inclination was to refuse, Why should I take his watch? I hardly knew him. But then I paused. I was being stupid. He was trying to give me some kind of repayment for the class. It was not for me to refuse. I thanked him and took it.

Later that evening I was talking to another student. It was getting chilly, so I said, "I think I'll go upstairs for my sweater."

"Here. Take mine," the man said, starting to pull it over his head.

"No, I have one in my room," I said.

"No, no," he persisted. "You can have it. I have another just like it."

Then it dawned on me that he was not lending it to me. He wanted to give it to me. It was absurd. But it was too much of a coincidence. I stopped being a fool and said, "Thank you very much. That is really wonderful of you." It was a heavy knit orange sweater, the traditional color worn by teachers.

On Monday morning, people began to disperse. Some left early to avoid the holiday traffic jam, but classes continued and the general festival atmosphere persisted. I left after lunch for the trip back to Geneseo. The incredible mixture of Rudi, Muktananda and the sense of climax of all the effort and heartache that had preceded the weekend, rose up in me and then began to settle. Beyond all the varied impressions, the crucial fact for me was that I had been allowed to teach. It had been squeezed in as an afterthought, but it would not be taken away from me unless I did something really terrible. And I had no intention of letting that happen.

Shortly before leaving I had bowed down to Muktananda and he had blessed me in his slightly abrupt way. Then as I had walked off I heard someone calling my name. He wanted me to come back. I returned. Then to my surprise, he gave me a rose. I still had the flower in the car as I drove away from the ashram. I didn't know what it meant. But an increasing sense of inner contentment pervaded me.

However, back at Big Indian, Bruce Rubin was still seeking an audience with Baba. As the weekend drew to a close, he grew desperate. He decided to put all that Rudi had ever said about accomplishing a goal to the test. He sat down by Muktananda's door, determined not to leave until he was forgiven.

Soon thereafter, the door opened and he was ushered in. Bruce quickly went into his prepared speech before anyone could interrupt.

"I have come to apologize for anything that I did which caused Swami any displeasure. It was the last thing I intended. It was only my own ignorance. I will destroy the film if you wish."

Swami followed the translation with interest, smiled slightly, and waved Bruce away. It was the nearest he would get to forgiveness. Bruce left with relief to tell Rudi that the mission was accomplished. Rudi was very pleased.

"You see," he said, "it wasn't very difficult. All you had to realize was that you had no other alternative. If you can keep that attitude Bruce, your success in this life is assured."

Before The Sun

PHOTOS: BIG INDIAN

Photos: Big Indian

Before The Sun

Photos: Big Indian

Before The Sun

Photos: Big Indian

Photos courtesy Rudi Movie Project

Chapter Twenty-Nine
NEW YORK CITY

Rudi in the NYC classroom

On my next trip to the city I was immediately struck by the intensity of the atmosphere in the ashram and the increased number of people. I was thoroughly lost in the crowd.

Swami Muktananda was holding four meetings a day: in the early morning, at noon, in the afternoon and in the evening. In between these Rudi, Michael, Stuart and Calvin squeezed in a few Kundalini classes. It was a marathon, sometimes not ending until after midnight.

I saw relatively little of Rudi during this period. He was exceptionally busy attending to his normal business and all the additional demands created by Swami Muktananda's presence. It shortly became evident that he was being prepared by Baba for some kind of extraordinary ceremony that was to take place in Ganeshpuri later in the year. He spent several hours a day receiving the necessary background in

Hindu tradition and spiritual understanding,

Swami Muktananda never expressed any particular interest in the nature of Rudi's teaching. His own approach was very different. He did not work directly with anyone. He told stories, chanted, wrote letters, received gifts, gave blessings. From all this, those present received his energy. The nearest approach to any direct contact that he made came in the form of what he called *shaktipat*. It involved his touching a person briefly, usually on the head or heart in order to start a psychic or spiritual process that was on the verge of unfolding.

Most of us were prepared to draw from Muktananda through the methods Rudi had taught us, but it was hard to see how someone without that knowledge could obtain much from him. Probably they couldn't. But the aura of energy, music, chanting, and stories with which he surrounded himself was enough to keep most people interested and enchanted.

In his lectures he described a new form of inner work which he called Siddha Yoga. It had to do with the mere presence of an enlightened soul as sufficient to confer blessings on others. It was this that he seemed to practice.

* * *

During this hectic period I made a fateful decision. Melanie had come to New York. I knew where she was. I decided to renew our relationship even though Rudi had told me during the summer that it would be better if I did not.

I had never gone against anything he had told me before, but in this instance I was prepared to take the risk.

Our reunion had the intense and wonderful quality of two lovers who never expected to meet again. But almost immediately I could see a potential problem which I attempted to resolve at the first opportunity.

"Before anything else happens," I said to Melanie, "maybe we better have a talk."

We were taking a ride on the Staten Island ferry. It was a late fall day, clear, and still warm. A gentle wind was blowing. There would not be many such days left.

"Nothing has happened has it?" she replied.

"Nothing that couldn't be stopped," I said. "Do you want me to

Before The Sun

leave again?"

"I never wanted that."

She smiled and was happy to look out at the passing ships and the receding silhouette of Manhattan. But I continued to think. I was caught in two separate streams — my work with Rudi and my love for Melanie. Perhaps they could be brought together. I had the feeling that if they weren't, they would pull me apart. One solution might be for her to enter the work. It might serve to make the whole thing more legitimate.

I said nothing for five minutes. But as the boat neared the Staten Island shore I asked,

"Would you be interested in knowing more about Rudi's work? You were its victim. You might as well know what hit you."

"Sure," she said. "I guess so. What would it involve?"

"I would work with you. Then you would understand what it is and we could go on from there."

"That sounds simple."

"Perhaps we can find a quiet place on Staten Island in which to try," I said.

That did not prove easy. There was nowhere to sit down near the ferry landing that had any privacy. Finally we came to an overgrown piece of land choked with weeds. It didn't seem to belong to anyone. We climbed through the underbrush, thorns, and poison ivy. There was only one spot on which to sit comfortably. It slanted downhill. I sat above Melanie. I could see the Statue of Liberty over her left shoulder.

It seemed an auspicious symbol. I started to work with her. At first she was puzzled, but shortly she entered into the flow. I had some doubt as to my motives in all this, but if it was wrong nothing would be lost but a little energy. However if it did take then she could go with me to the ashram and the two streams could blend. It was worth a chance.

We worked for ten minutes. It felt good. The next day I worked with her again, this time in Central Park under a tree. I thought it was a quiet place. But as soon as we started to work, people appeared from every direction. I had to ignore them even though they stopped to stare at us.

It was at that moment that I saw Melanie in a new light. At a casual glance she was a gorgeous creature. Occasionally I would look at models in fashion magazines and think, "My God, she is more beautiful than they are." It always came as a shock. She wasn't very interested in her beauty. She tried to be inconspicuous, but it was hard to hide. However as we worked in the park all that faded away, and a starved and hungry face emerged from behind the enchanting mask. It shocked me, and I ignored it. If I had been able to understand what I saw I could have saved myself an extraordinary amount of heartache. It was there before me at that moment. But I chose to put it aside as an impression and let the beauty return to blind me.

Many new people were attracted to the ashram by Muktananda, so I knew it would be easy for Melanie to come also. The doors were open to all as far as his classes were concerned. The next day I brought her down. She sat quietly. Muktananda was dictating letters, meditating, opening presents, and carrying on his daily routine while we worked with him. It went well. She liked the atmosphere. She had not thought of herself as interested in spiritual work, but she recognized that it and I came in the same package.

When the class was over we discovered that we had nowhere to go. I didn't feel like dropping by the store with her. That was asking for trouble. The next class was in three or four hours. It would take forty-five minutes to get back to the place where she was staying. So we wandered the streets looking for somewhere to sit down, to talk, and to wait. We ended up on a battered bench in Sheridan Square.

Sitting with her in the transient anonymity of New York City was not very romantic, but it beat walking. I still could not really believe that we were together. Something in me was waiting for the ax to fall, but it hadn't. Everything seemed fine. We were getting to know each other slowly. I was deeply in love with her. She obviously cared about me. Nothing is as sweet as the resurrection of love that had been lost. Still it was vaguely idiotic to have nowhere to go, two lost children wandering the streets of Manhattan waiting for a Hindu saint to give his next class.

Shortly thereafter, it was announced at the ashram that those who had come to hear Swami Muktananda should speak with Rudi if they also wished to attend Kundalini Yoga classes. I decided that the announcement would offer a natural transition for Melanie. She had already started the work with me. The sooner she became a part of the ashram the better for both of us. Thus, taking my heart in my hands, I sent her around the corner to see Rudi in his store. He had never seen Melanie. He didn't even know her name. There was no particular reason for him to identify her as the same girl Dora had talked to him about. But I also knew that he could read minds at times. What would prevent him from instantly seeing through the whole thing, and what would he do if he did? I had reason to be nervous!

She returned in about twenty minutes and smiled reassuringly at me. But maybe she was trying to prepare me for a shock.

"Everything was fine," she said. "He was very nice. I would have been back sooner, but he had some customers."

"What did you say to him?"

"I just said that I wanted to begin Kundalini classes and understood that I had to get his permission."

"Then he said, 'you're a friend of John's, aren't you?' I couldn't say 'No.' to that. And then he looked at me for a few seconds."

"How did he look?" I asked, fearing the worst.

"It's hard to say. No one ever looked at me just that way. But anyway, after that he smiled and said, 'Of course. You can begin right away.' Then I left, and here I am."

I wasn't entirely reassured, but he had let her in. There was nowhere to go but forward. I took it as a sign that even though I wasn't following his advice it might somehow turn out all right.

At one of his evening classes Rudi made the public announcement, mostly at Muktananda's subtle insistence, that henceforth he would be a vegetarian and observe sexual continence. I was not greatly impressed by the announcement. Rudi had always maintained that one could and should be able to eat anything, but that it must be adjusted to the particular phase of growth occurring at the time. As far as sexuality, he had been relatively quiet in that sphere for a number of years. He felt it necessary for his growth during that period, but he had never looked at it as a general principle.

All of these things went through my mind as Rudi announced his pledges with Muktananda's obvious beaming approval.

"I have never," Muktananda said, "demanded that Rudi give up anything, but I am happy and proud that he has decided to do so."

A month before Muktananda's arrival Rudi had talked to us about the significance of the relation between student and teacher. He made a particular point of telling us how we should relate to him (i.e., Rudi), during Muktananda's visit.

"A student's loyalty is to his own teacher. Your loyalty is to me. Baba is my teacher. My loyalty is to him. You honor him because of the level that he represents and because he is my teacher. But do not forget that I am your teacher, and that without me you would never even meet Baba."

All of this seemed fairly obvious. It was hard to see why Rudi made such a point of it. But he knew Muktananda. We didn't.

The closest person to Rudi at the time was Michael Austin. During a momentary lull at the store, Michael approached Rudi and said,

"I have been talking with Baba and have arranged to go to Ganeshpuri to spend a lengthy time in his ashram and receive his training."

Rudi described the scene to me a few days later.

"I said nothing to Michael. I couldn't. I was too shocked. He had taken it on himself to do this. He hadn't come to me beforehand. Maybe he was afraid of my reaction. But, in any case, it was an absolutely wrong thing for him to do. That Baba went along with it was his business. But Michael is my student. He had to have my permission for anything of that nature.

"There are certain things that are totally wrong. This is one. But Michael doesn't know it. He thinks he has pulled a fast one. Let him think so. He may change his mind when his romance with Baba wears off and he wants to return. Then I will say to him, 'I don't know you.'"

I listened in paralyzed silence. Michael had done so beautifully up to this point, but he evidently just walked off the side of a cliff.

Chapter Thirty

THE WEST COAST

Late in October Rudi went with Muktananda on a trip to Texas and California. Classes continued in New York, but the spiritual focus had moved elsewhere. No one knew precisely what was happening. Rudi's own communications were brief. He was evidently going through an intense and painful experience.

By a strange coincidence I found that I needed to fly to California on business and return at virtually the same time that Rudi was scheduled to leave Muktananda and return to New York. I left word with his mother to tell him what plane I would be on. The opportunity to be on a transcontinental flight with Rudi just after he had been traveling with Muktananda seemed like a wonderful opportunity to me. But our paths did not cross. I returned to New York on Sunday evening. He had left Saturday afternoon. Later he apologized for not waiting.

"To tell you the truth, John, it wouldn't have been any treat for you. I felt I was getting seriously ill. I had gone beyond my own endurance. So I just excused myself and took the first plane back."

On his return Rudi was very subdued. He stopped giving Kundalini classes. He lectured and encouraged chanting and meditation with eyes closed. I was amazed. The whole nature of the work had altered.

Rudi himself said little. He seemed to be recovering from a spiritual operation and wanted to conserve his strength.

But gradually, as we sat in the store, part of the story slowly emerged.

"When Muktananda was in New York," Rudi said one day in a quiet moment, "he generally made himself agreeable and captivated almost everyone. But I was going crazy working with him, doing my business, and keeping the ashram going. When we went West I thought it would be easier, but that was naive on my part.

"He had begun by asking me to give up meat and sex. As we left

New York behind us he proceeded to systematically deprive me of other aspects of my life.

"A number of my students had followed him down to Texas. He told them that they should leave me and come with him. I didn't mind because all of them were old students who had been dragging on for years. If they left I could accept it as long as they went of their own free will. But the situation didn't give me a very good feeling.

"Though I was the traveling host I was treated as if I was not even a member of Muktananda's party. No place was saved for me at the table. I was often ignored in the conversation. I had been through all this before. I didn't like it, but if this scourging was part of the preparation I had to undergo I welcomed it.

"If you don't accept what the guru does unconditionally, there is no basis for the relationship. I accepted it. I had created the situation by bringing him to this country. It was not for me to question him. My present life was being dismantled so that something new could be built. It was brutal, but I did not protest.

"In the end, he demanded that I surrender Nityananda. I can't really explain to you what that meant. For many, many years Nityananda would come to me when I needed him. In the depths of my loneliness he would descend from heaven to give me strength. He was Muktananda's guru, but he lived in me. We even grew to look alike. Nobody could avoid seeing it. But Muktananda made me give up this inner connection. It was a horrible experience. The Indians in his group were really amazed that I was willing to do it. They had never seen anyone go through such an ordeal of inner destruction of every living tie. But I want to grow. It has always been my central objective. I have never bargained about the price. I was not about to start now.

"After that connection was destroyed I could not conceive that anything remained to be sacrificed, but that was just because I failed to see the obvious. Muktananda's last demand was that I give up my form of teaching. He said it would be replaced by something much greater after my next trip to India. That was the hardest thing I had to do. My teaching is closer to me than any person. But I did it. There was nothing left, except my life.

"The last thing that Muktananda said to me before I got on the plane to come home was,

'The next time I come to America, I will do to everyone what I have done to you'. It was scarcely a reassuring statement."

Before The Sun

Bagavan Nityananda

Almost two years later, Stuart Perrin, who had been on the trip with Rudi, filled in some additional details.

"I remember one day when Rudi was soaking in the bathtub. I sat nearby and, as I watched, he turned into Nityananda and back to Rudi and back to Nityananda. It went on like that for maybe ten minutes. I was used to seeing Rudi manifest in all kinds of ways. When I started with him two years before, I watched him turn into weird space monsters and various ancient creatures. But somehow this was different. It must have been about the time that Muktananda asked him to surrender Nityananda.

"The climax came for me", Stuart continued, "when Muktananda began to ask me to come to study with him in Ganeshpuri. Every time he asked I would put him off with some polite response. But he was insistent. I finally did what I usually do when I need an answer. I went deep inside and found Nityananda in my heart and asked him. The answer was simple. The next time Swami Muktananda approached me, I said,

"'I would certainly like to come, but I cannot do anything like that without asking my guru's permission.' He looked at me with sudden respect and never brought up the subject again. He knew what Rudi's response would be."

* * *

During the next few months Rudi recuperated. He was inwardly preparing for the ceremony that was to occur early in the spring when he returned to Ganeshpuri.

At the same time I thought that my own situation had stabilized until one afternoon in December when Melanie said she had a presentiment that our relationship was ending. That very morning Rudi had discussed my own future with me. He had spoken again of the heiress I would marry in about seven years. He had even said she would look like Jane Wyman.

Thinking to reassure Melanie that no break was imminent between us, I mentioned this forecast to her. She was strangely silent when I finished. Since our own relationship was uncertain from month-to-month it never occurred to me that what was supposed to happen seven years hence could possibly disturb her. Marriage did not appeal to her as a general idea, and we had never talked about it specifically. Nevertheless the atmosphere instantly clouded.

"There really isn't any point in our being together if that's what is going to happen," she said tensely.

"What?" I couldn't believe her attitude.

"Maybe you think it's funny. I don't," she said.

It went on this way for the next half hour. Finally we dropped the subject. Her last words were, "I think we're through."

It was such an unsuspected disaster that I couldn't adjust to it.

In the course of the next few days she wavered but did not falter.

She refused to come to a final decision, but seemed to feel that a decision was necessary.

Then she said,

"I'll tell you what I want to do. I'm going home for Christmas. I'll be gone for two weeks. When I come back I'll have made up my mind. I know it will be hard for you to wait. But I am asking you to do it."

I reluctantly agreed.

On the 28th of December Melanie returned. I met her at the hotel where she was staying. But she almost immediately had to rush out to look at an apartment.

When she returned, I asked her hesitantly, "What have you decided?"

"About the apartment? I'll take it if I can get it," she replied.

"No. About us."

She made a face, shrugged her shoulders and said, "I don't know. While I was away I decided that it should end, but now that I see you again I'm not so sure."

"Melanie!" I said in desperation, "you're driving me crazy! Decide one way or another!"

But she didn't. She couldn't. Two days later I was at the breaking point. I couldn't stand the thought of entering the New Year in that state.

"I don't care which way it goes anymore," I said, "but I want something definite by the end of the afternoon."

She agonized for a few hours and finally said, "If you are forcing me to decide, then it is over." I was almost relieved.

"But one thing I want you to know," she added. "I will always be deeply grateful to you for introducing me to the work. I know that may not sound very convincing right now, but I really mean it."

I shook my head, but said nothing.

The next day was December 31st. I decided on a strategy of desperation.

"All this time," I said to her, "we have hidden our relationship from Rudi. But now that it's over, I would like to go and ask him what he thinks. Would you object to that?"

"No," she said. "If you want to."

I phoned Rudi and arranged to meet between class and the big New Year's Eve party he was going to throw in the evening.

We were both pretty nervous when the time came. Talking with

Rudi was what I had been avoiding. I never knew what problems might be created. I still wasn't sure if he knew who Melanie was. I wasn't about to tell him, but maybe he had known all along. After class we both approached him timidly on the second floor where he was waiting to meet us. He was still dressed in bright orange, the traditional teaching colors. He seemed very happy but slightly preoccupied with the details of the party that was due to start in a few minutes. He stared at us for a moment and asked,

"What is it? Do you two want to get married?"

I didn't know whether to laugh or cry.

"No. It isn't exactly like that," I said.

He was silent, waiting for one of us to speak. Melanie said nothing, so I took the lead.

"In two sentences," I said, "we are in love but Melanie doesn't feel it is going to work out. She thinks it should end. I don't."

Another pause.

"Is that right?" Rudi asked Melanie.

"That's what I feel," she said.

"Then that's it," said Rudi.

"What's it?" I said, pretending I didn't understand.

"It's over. There's nothing more to talk about."

"But," I started, "we have felt differently at different..."

Rudi interrupted me. "John, just be quiet. Don't drag it out. Over is over. There is nothing more to say. Both of you enjoy the party."

Melanie moved away.

"It'll be like attending my own funeral," I muttered.

Rudi smiled at me and gave me a hug.

"You don't have to enjoy yourself if you don't want to, but give it a chance. The world hasn't come to an end."

Objectively the party was fine. A group of young kids from Texas that Rudi had met on his trip with Muktananda had come up for the party. They had taken over the entertainment, singing old country ballads to the accompaniment of a guitar. The atmosphere was very warm. Melanie and I stayed at opposite ends of the room. The happier everyone else got the more miserable I felt. But I kept my mouth shut.

About 10:15 Melanie approached me to say she was going. I didn't blame her.

"Do you want me to stay with my parents tonight?" I asked.

"It doesn't matter," she said.

"In that case I'll be along in an hour or so." I went back to the party and suffered through other people's happiness. About an hour later, Rudi crawled out of the center of the circle of people that surrounded him. I followed. He looked at his watch and said,

"My God, It's only 11:00. I'll never make it."

I took advantage of the moment to say goodnight. He was very warm. He knew what I was feeling.

I left the house and went to the subway. There was a strange feeling of hectic celebration in the air. I wanted to hide or shoot somebody. I arrived at Melanie's hotel shortly before midnight. She seemed happy to see me. She had gone to bed and was trying to sleep. I read her Eliot's Four Quartets as the New Year came in.

There were two beds in the room. After I had finished the poetry reading, I started to get into the other one.

"You don't have to sleep in that bed if you don't want to," she said. I could hardly believe my ears. But I didn't stop to analyze her motives. Perhaps she was lonely. Perhaps nothing mattered any more now that we were definitely parting. We ended up making love in a distant, bittersweet manner, and then went to sleep in each other's arms.

We stayed in bed all the next day. By 7:00 in the evening, we were starving. We got up and had a huge Chinese meal. When 8:30 came around, we were still together. The subject of my leaving never came up. I didn't know what to think, but I didn't ask questions.

The next morning was Saturday. I went to class. Melanie said she would stay home and clean up.

After class Rudi said to me,

"Come to the store, John. I want to talk to you."

I couldn't begin to imagine what he wanted. When I got there he motioned me to come outside on the street where we could talk privately.

"I know you pretty well, right, John?" he began.

"Yes. You do," I said uncertainly.

"Then if my estimate of your character is correct, you have somehow succeeded in patching the whole thing up as if nothing had happened." He paused, waiting for me to respond. I wanted to disappear but I had to admit the truth. I mutely nodded my head.

"When Melanie spoke to me two nights ago," Rudi continued relentlessly, "I was shocked. There was nothing in her that was willing to fight for you. It is completely wrong. Somebody should love you deeply and want to be with you without any qualifications. Regardless of your feelings."

I couldn't say anything. It was like being hit with ice water. It took my breath away.

"Therefore I am going to put it as strongly as I can. Not only should you break up with her immediately, but I don't want you seeing her outside of class. I don't even want you to say 'hello' to her in class. Absolutely nothing. You are not to be trusted."

My house of cards had tumbled. There was nothing to do but agree.

"I will do exactly as you say," I managed to get out.

Rudi was silent. He studied me for perhaps fifteen seconds. Then he said, "It's all right."

"What's all right?" I didn't know what was happening.

"You can do it," he said.

"Do what? What are you talking about?" I felt slightly hysterical.

"You can stay with her. It's all right."

Right there on Fourth Avenue, I collapsed to the pavement in relief. I wasn't angry. I was beyond such an emotion. I picked myself up and said,

"This isn't your idea of a joke, is it?"

"No. I wouldn't joke about such a thing. It doesn't make that much difference. If you really like her then stay with her. But let me ask you, 'Do various wines taste that much different to you?'"

I hadn't quite regained my balance. I thought I had missed something.

"What are you talking about?"

"Different wines," he said.

"No, I suppose they don't. I don't know much about wines."

"Neither do I," said Rudi. "They're all alike to me. That's the way it is with women. Making love to one is like making love to another. It's all basically the same thing. If you don't take it too seriously, it can't hurt you."

I couldn't believe my ears, but I wasn't going to say anything that might make him change his mind. Shortly thereafter I said goodbye. My last words to him were, "She'll never believe it."

As I rode home on the subway, I had a chance to think about what had happened. There was only one possible explanation. I had convinced Rudi that I was one hundred percent willing to give up the relationship. It was true. I was. Therefore, he was allowing it to continue. If I could surrender it, there was nothing there that could really hurt me.

I returned to the apartment. Melanie was busy cleaning up.

"How was the class?" she asked over her shoulder.

When I didn't answer, she stopped what she was doing and looked at me.

"He said it was all right," I said.

"What are you talking about?"

"Rudi."

"Rudi what?"

"Said it is all right for us to be together. He approves."

Melanie stared at me in disbelief. She grew pale.

"If you don't believe me," I said, "go down and talk to him yourself."

"I just can't comprehend...."

"Me neither," I said. "How do you like them potatoes?"

"I'm not sure," she said. With a pained smile she returned to her cleaning.

Chapter Thirty-One

END OF THE AFFAIRS

During the next few months Rudi was inwardly preparing himself for his return to India. In parallel with this effort, the number of people living with him in the ashram steadily increased. A small group from Bloomington, Indiana, came about this time. I met them along with everyone else but paid no particular attention. One Saturday morning after an early class as I was walking to the store, one of the men from Bloomington passed me going toward the house. I glanced at him and was very struck by the intensity of his gaze. That was the moment when I first became aware of Michael Shoemaker.

When I got to the store Rudi was reading a letter from India, but he did not disclose its contents. While he was working ceaselessly to ready himself for the unknown events that were to come, most of it was behind the scenes, I was not directly involved.

My own life was very full and it required most of my energy to keep it in balance. It is hard to say at what point that it began to unravel. Perhaps Greg's diet was partly responsible. He had been studying natural foods and acupuncture with Rudi's encouragement. He recommended a strange six-week diet to help me purge my system of physical poisons.

It was during the last week of the diet that Melanie finally asked me to go.

"I can't take it anymore," she said. "I feel like I am choking to death. I may never meet anyone that I love as much as you, but I can't stand having you around."

I tried to talk her out of it. How could this be happening? I had won every battle but was losing the war. When I became convinced that there was nothing I could do I talked to Rudi about it.

"If you put half as much energy into your spiritual work," he said, "as you do into screwing around, you would have remarkable success."

"I come here with my heart bleeding and you kick me in the ass."

"You have to be a man. This is the way it's worked out. Accept it and go on. Be grateful for what you have had."

"That doesn't help. I feel like my life is being ripped apart."

"Good," he said. "Maybe you will really learn something. Melanie is a very rare type of person. She does not want to be physically or psychically touched by anyone. I am sure she feels as much for you as she can for anybody, but she has very little to give you or probably anyone else. She is very beautiful. She is young, intelligent, cultured. But what does it all matter? You are much better off without her. It was all right up to now. But it had to end. She herself did not want to grow. She stopped coming to classes. You are still growing. It is a hard lesson, but that is the real reason you are parting. Your growth is choking her. Would you rather not grow and keep her?"

"No."

"Then accept it. I have had this problem all my life. I attract people I love. I grow and grow. They move a little bit and then stop. My growth forces them to leave. It's like a great spinning vortex that throws them off the edge. Do you think I want them to go? These are people I love. Strong as your emotions may be at the moment, mine are generally much stronger than yours. It always hurts. But you get used to it. The alternative is much worse. In time you will be grateful."

I left the store feeling better. I went back to Melanie's and moved my things.

"We are still friends," she said. "You just don't live here anymore."

I kept my mouth shut and left.

✳ ✳ ✳

It was about this time that Rudi went on his long-awaited trip to India. On the eve of his departure he announced that he was going to be honored as Muktananda's spiritual son before a great gathering of Hindu religious dignitaries. A statue of Nityananda was also to be dedicated in a Hindu ritual designed to bring it to life.

Rudi was scheduled to be gone for a month. After two weeks he cabled his mother: "I have left Swami Muktananda's ashram! I shall never return!"

There was no further word. Everyone was in a state of suspended animation. The feeling was of a great formal marriage that had been

Rudi accompanies Swami Muktananda to an early morning meeting in India

arranged, only to have the groom walk out of the church at the end.

Rudi flew in a little ahead of schedule. He looked good. He sounded good. He seemed much younger. He had worked with Swami Muktananda for more than twelve years. Now it was over. I knew he would talk about it when he was ready. It didn't take long. He began in the first class.

"There will be no further chanting in this ashram," he said. "There will be no meditation with eyes closed. We will resume the work that we did formerly, starting today. All connections between this ashram and Swami Muktananda are formally severed. All pictures of him should be taken down. I will say more about it in time, but these are the things that should be done immediately."

✸ ✸ ✸

Rudi was very peaceful. Buford, who had gone on the trip with him, seemed quite detached though excited about some of the places he had seen.

"I went directly to Ganeshpuri," Rudi began one day when he felt like talking further about the experience. "Swami Muktananda had told me there would be a great festival. Thousands and thousands of people were to attend. All of the Hindu hierarchy was to be represented. He had been building it up for months.

"But when I got there everything was quiet. I didn't know what to make of it. Then he started to treat me like dirt. I was used to that from the past. But now I was supposed to be coming as a Swami to receive a high honor. It didn't make sense. I was willing to be ignored and insulted if it served some useful end. But what did this serve? I had already surrendered everything. Why kick a dead dog?

"But the final blow came with the dedication of the statue of Nityananda. That was supposed to be a crucial event. I kept asking when it was to occur and was told, not to worry. I would be informed.

"One day I went into town for an hour. When I returned I discovered that the ceremony had just occurred. It was totally incredible. Inside me something gave way. They had no love for me here. No respect. No sense of brotherhood. To them I was some kind of strange beast to be eternally kicked and prodded to see how much I would take. They would find out. My twelve years with Swami Muktananda had made me very, very strong. Now it was over. I was ready for a higher and more merciful approach. I told Buford,

"'Pack your bags. We're leaving.'

"He didn't ask any questions. In five minutes, we were ready. I told someone who was passing, 'Say goodbye to Swami Muktananda for me,' and we left. I'm sure he still doesn't believe what has happened. I expect letters from him to start arriving. But there is absolutely nothing he can do. And the irony of it is that he has cut his own spiritual throat."

"What do you mean?" I couldn't help asking.

"He was counting on me to get him out of this world."

"How?"

"He isn't stupid. He knows this is my last life on earth. When I go up he plans to go with me. I would have taken him too. But now, I don't know..."

"Do you mean," I persisted, "when you die that you could have carried him up with you?"

"Yes. When I am quite old the force will become so incredibly strong that I will burn alive and my energy will explode into the atmosphere. That event will constitute the basic energy on which the Aquarian Age will be built."

A psychiatrist listening to such a statement would nod in agreement and motion for an attendant. I did not feel that way, even though

I had clinical training. Rudi, like all saints, could not be evaluated by every-day standards. He was beyond me when I first met him. He was only further beyond me now. My whole contact with him depended on my acceptance of that basic fact.

"When this happens," he continued, "there will be many highly evolved people there, students who have worked with me for decades. I must have mentioned this vision before. It is one of the things that has made it possible for me to go through all this suffering. I know how the story ends."

I had always wanted to know, but had never dared to bring up the question "Will I be there?" I asked hesitantly.

"Yes, John. You may have died by then, but one way or another, you will be there."

In spite of my immediate situation with Melanie, I felt very happy. If I followed the road I was traveling, I would find fulfillment in the end.

Chapter Thirty-Two

ASTRAL FLIGHT

As Rudi settled back into his familiar routine, he was faced with a mounting pile of correspondence. For the first time he hired a secretary and spent an hour or two a day answering letters from across the country and around the world. As he got used to dictating he discovered that he could easily extend the process to include a description of the experiences he was undergoing at the time. Such dictation became a regular feature of his day.

A visitor to the store might interrupt him in the middle of a sentence. He would pause to deal with a customer, wave a student to an inconspicuous seat, take a swallow of cooling coffee, and fifteen minutes later continue with the sentence where he had left off. To an observer it looked like total confusion. But Rudi loved to have a number of things going on simultaneously, preferably in different dimensions. He always seemed to have sufficient attention for all of it.

As his dictations accumulated he conceived of the idea of a book. He was attracted and repelled by the prospect. He preferred to keep a low profile for as long as possible. But he was human enough to want to see himself in print.

He started looking for a publisher.

※ ※ ※

With the first signs of spring he began to talk of advanced work that would be given in the summer. He referred to this work intermittently and urged us to prepare ourselves for the opportunity. During the same period he began for the first time to tape-record his lectures.

In mid-June, he announced that on the July 4th weekend he would teach Astral Flight. I had no idea what that meant. If I searched through my memory I could recall Rudi talking about being "far away" or "in a different place" occasionally, but he had never explained how or why, nor did he suggest that it was important. I took it, as I did with most of his experiences, as something unique to him. Consequently I waited in limbo, having no idea what to expect.

When July 4th came, it began like any other long weekend with a full day's work. In the evening Rudi walked to the front of the classroom amidst growing expectation.

His first words were,

"Please don't record what I am about to say."

The tape recorder was hastily turned off.

"Nothing that is given here tonight must ever leave this room. You must never share it with anyone. If you do I can assure you that you will live to regret it. I have never said this before about any of the work that has been given, though no student should ever give anyone else what he has learned here without express permission.

"But this is quite different. If you attempt to give to another what I am giving to you tonight, you will take on yourself a responsibility beyond anything you can realize and you could fatally injure your own spiritual growth.

"If this seems too strong a statement, it isn't. I can't put it too strongly. Some of you are unbelievably stupid. You won't think I really mean it unless I put it this way. I really mean it! If you can't accept these conditions, please leave."

No one stirred.

"What I am going to give you has not existed in the world for many centuries. When I announced that I would teach Astral Flight I had no idea how I would do it. But I knew that if I obligated myself a means would be found. In order for me to be able to give it to you at all I have had to reorder the whole universe. The cosmos is a vast combination lock. For this work to be transmitted all forces must be in perfect alignment.

"Some of you who read spiritual books are probably puzzled why I make such a large production of Astral Flight. You have heard of it before. Why all the secrecy? Right? But I am not talking about traveling out of the body to different places on the earth. That might have been useful before modern communications were developed, but it really has nothing to do with growing. Conditions on the earth are pretty much the same over the whole surface. The whole point of Astral Travel is to get off the earth to a better place where the energy is richer,

purer, and cleaner and of a more refined character. Symbolically we all live in the slums. The air is contaminated, the streets filthy and cold. People are crowded together. It is very difficult for anything of a higher nature to penetrate into such a setting. But if you can take an airplane, in a matter of two minutes it is all left behind. The view is endless, and the pure radiant energy of the sun shines above the clouds.

"Then you can realize the significance of the saying, 'You are what you eat.' The higher the source on which you feed, the greater your growth will become. It is the lack of availability of higher energy that constitutes the major barrier for most people in fulfilling their potential. Certainly there are other difficulties. We are full of psychic and emotional barriers and tensions. There are inner leaks that cause us to lose most of what we absorb. Nevertheless if all of these conditions are corrected, a person would still be limited by the quality of energy he could obtain. There is plenty of low-level energy lying around, constantly being wasted. But higher energy is like a rare trace element. It almost doesn't exist.

"You have all learned how to absorb the energy that is available. What I am going to give now will enable you to go where the quality of energy is a hundred times more nourishing than anything you can presently obtain by yourselves. It is therefore the greatest gift I can give to you. I have never given it to anyone. I have never even talked about it before to anyone. But I have been using this work myself for the last decade and even before. This is part of the Tibetan inheritance that I received at the age of six. It has not existed in the world since the early days of Tantric Buddhism."

I was shocked by Rudi's final words. To those who had been working a year or two, it was just a general statement. To me, it threw Rudi in a totally different light. I had been with him for twelve years. I had long ago concluded that he shared everything that happened to him with anyone whom he thought would be interested. I had heard him talking endlessly to total strangers about the details of his current spiritual experiences. I had come to take it for granted. He had done it with me the first evening we had spent together.

But now I was being informed that he had been engaged in a totally secret work throughout that whole period. Such control was awesome!

I didn't sleep very well that night, but neither did most of the people who were present. The energy flow was too intense.

The next day we put in a full day of physical work. In the evening Rudi took up where he had left off.

"Astral flight is not sending part of yourself elsewhere while you remain behind, as most people believe. It is leaving the earth totally. It is not imagining you are somewhere else. You are somewhere else, flying through the cosmos at a vast speed. Physically your body remains where it is. It is still visible to other people. But when the process is working strongly, you will have only the slightest contact with your physical presence here. Perhaps all you will feel is a slight pressure on your bottom. And even that may go and you will be totally flying with nothing left behind.

"Until today your work has consisted of using the basic psychic digestive system to refine energy. Your system has grown stronger and your inner being has been nourished. Astral Flight uses an entirely different mechanism. It does not supplant the basic work, but greatly extends it by taking you to places in the cosmos where the force content is much richer than anything available here. When you absorb there you get ten times more, a hundred times more, of a higher force than you can get on the earth. Consequently you can grow at a greatly accelerated rate. What would take you ten years of effort on the earth can be accomplished there in one."

He then transmitted the basic Astral Flight experience. It is not given here, in accordance with his instructions, and also because inner work cannot be given through the printed word. It must be passed from teacher to student.

At the conclusion, Rudi said,

"The experience has begun in a number of you. I am very pleased. When you receive a gift it is extremely important how you treat it. This is a new and highly powerful mechanism that has been put in your hands. It must be treated with great respect. You should not attempt to activate it more than once every two weeks, and then only at the end of your normal inner work period when you are functioning at your best.

"The psychic muscles that are used must come into play gradually.

If you go too far too soon you run a very real danger of burning out your mechanism. Then you may have to wait six months before you can begin again.

"Any higher work depends on an excess of energy. When you are reaching above yourself, you are stealing from your own vitality on one level in order to invest it on another. This is fine if you have an excess. You are simply reinvesting the interest elsewhere. But if you dip into the principal you will get into real trouble. That is why your basic effort must always become greater to support a higher level of work. You are building a structure. It can be a great structure that stretches from earth to heaven. But the higher it goes, the sounder the foundation must be.

"Astral Flight is not meant as an escape from everyday problems. If you use it that way, you will live to regret it. Everything is important, the everyday and the extraordinary. The everyday is the foundation for the extraordinary. You cannot repair your foundation if you get yourself in a spaced-out condition. Even if you succeed you will end up a freak, unable to function in this world and suspended in another.

Rudi paused. A student raised his hand and said hesitantly, "I felt very frightened while I was working, as if I was being swallowed up and lost. I was afraid I could never come back. What should I do?"

"Go on," said Rudi. "That you are scared only shows that you have some sense of reality. I was terrified when I began this work. You are lucky. You have me to guide you. I had to dig the experience out of my own flesh and then use it without any idea of what it would do to me. I was scared shitless. But if you are going to live the rest of your life in fear of what might happen to you if you take a step into the unknown, you might as well move to Florida and stake out a nice chair by the ocean. Certainly you have no business being here."

"I know this sounds stupid," said another person, "but when I started I felt I was in a rocket pulling away from the earth. I could see the earth getting smaller and smaller. I kept thinking, 'This is really corny.' I suppose it was all a fantasy."

"Not at all," said Rudi. "It is natural that you would think it was because it doesn't happen to fit in with your ideas of the possible, but it was quite real. The unfortunate thing is that if you hadn't asked about it, you would have discounted the whole event. Right now most of you are wondering whether the flight experience has occurred for you or not. Give it time. If you don't think it has happened, try the exercise once a day until you are sure. When that happens, do it once every other week for ten minutes."

"How can we know if it has taken?" someone asked.

"If you feel yourself rising and rising, if you almost totally lose contact with your earthbound body, you can be pretty sure it has taken," said Rudi. "But if you have any serious doubts you can ask me later."

"Won't this work interfere with sleep if we do it late at night?" a student asked.

"It might," said Rudi. "So what? Which are you more interested in, sleeping or growing? And furthermore, if you can fall asleep within the exercise it will continue all night. It is a natural time to work. The personality is quiet. We are in touch with a larger reality. A child understands this. He basically sleeps on the ceiling. As he gets older he slowly sinks down into the bed.

"The further you get, the more you realize that inner work has to be endlessly expanding to support the mechanism you are building. It is not a question of this or that, but this and that."

"How does it feel to work in your sleep?" someone asked.

"There are different experiences. I don't want to go into all that now. But, basically it's simple. You fall asleep flying and your first experience on waking is also flying. When that happens it is reasonable to assume that in between you were also flying.

"Astral Flight is not a spontaneous condition. You have to work to activate the mechanism. But once it is going it can go on and on and on and on. God is forever. The limitation is in our own conception of what is possible.

"But flying is not an end in itself. The purpose of Astral Flight is to go to a better place in the cosmos, absorb the energy content there, and return. It is no use exploring if you don't bring back the essence of the experience inside you."

"Won't this work interfere with our ordinary sense of reality?"

"No," said Rudi. "Not if you do it as I have indicated. As you grow stronger you will find it entering into your everyday existence more and more. The purpose of spiritual work is to get you off the earth! You don't have to be on the earth in order to accomplish your everyday tasks. I can talk to any of you in the store, conduct my business, and have 95% of myself in Astral Flight without any of you even knowing the difference. I have been doing it for years. On the other hand if any of you experienced my ordinary state for a few minutes, you would probably become thoroughly disoriented and incapable of doing anything. It takes getting used to.

"It is incredible under what conditions you can learn to function. But it is only possible because ordinary life takes very little effort if you begin to act with a little consciousness. It is not so much a question of simplifying life as learning how to handle more things simultaneously. That is the hallmark of an evolving man. Most people are no place. They wander around in a chronic daze and go through a mechanical routine. Occasionally a man appears who is someplace, pursuing a goal that has enough meaning to him to help him push through the resistance which life creates. He usually succeeds because there is so little competition. Very few people really want to work at anything.

"But the rarest of all is an evolving individual who sacrifices his own personality as he pursues many levels simultaneously. He knows that they are all important to the structure he is creating. Up until this weekend you have only been working on the foundation. With this work you literally move into the vertical dimension. That is not an end. Beyond what you are given, there is always something else."

Without allowing time for further questions Rudi quickly departed, leaving a strangely suspended feeling in the room. Later the next day I managed to find the chance to talk to him.

"I don't feel I can judge," I said. "Is the Astral Flight taking hold in me properly?"

Rudi looked at me for a moment. "Yes. It has started, but it will take a few days before you feel it strongly."

I walked away, content. My only fear was that I might not be able to relate to it. As long as the process was starting I could afford to be patient. I worked on it again that night before going to sleep. It seemed a more complete experience.

The next morning while I was weeding in the garden, Rudi came over to where I was working.

"I am still trying to absorb the magnitude of what you gave," I said. "I have the feeling it goes far beyond anything I can sense now."

"You are so right!" said Rudi. "You feel the exposed tip of the iceberg. This is a whole new beginning."

"How could you walk around with this inside you for twelve years without saying anything to anyone?" I asked. "That is really incredible."

Rudi just smiled. "You don't know everything about me, John. I did it because no one had worked long enough or hard enough to be trusted with the experience. I still don't know what people will do with it, but there comes a time when something must be shared or its fertility is lost. This is the time!"

I waited to see if he would say more. He looked slowly around the garden in which I was working and then said,

"Every great religion and philosophy has believed that the world is an illusion. But that is only an idea and, to some extent, an emotional reaction. It can't be a real experience to anyone who lives on the earth. But in Astral Flight you experience the truth of the belief. While you are moving in a vertical direction the ordinary horizontal activities of the earth are seen for what they are, an endless dream from which you temporarily begin to awake."

I listened in silence. Rudi looked at me for a moment from a distant place and then moved on.

Chapter Thirty-Three

THE PRICE OF TEACHING

After the July 4th weekend my summer was suspended. I was only scheduled to teach at Geneseo through the middle of July. The rest of the time was open. In a moment of unguarded enthusiasm I said to Rudi,

"My summer is totally free. I don't know what to do with it." As soon as I said it, I was sorry. I was sure he was going to tell me to go to Big Indian and work ten hours a day. But, to my amazement, he said,

"Why don't you go to Europe for a month?"

"Are you serious?"

"Sure. It would be good for you to get away. You will have a marvelous time."

"When should I go?" I asked, afraid he would change his mind.

"As soon as you can. There is nothing to wait for. If you miss anything while you're gone I'll give it to you when you return."

Perhaps Rudi was sorry for me and thought I should go away to recuperate. I couldn't be sure. Whatever his reasons I went right to work planning a tour of Spain, Portugal and Morocco that wasn't actually confirmed until the day before I left.

I was never overly enthusiastic about the trip. The thought of going alone to a strange place without knowing the language gave me pause. But I moved ahead on schedule.

The plane trip was tolerable. I struck up a conversation with a lovely blonde girl from Georgia while going through Spanish customs. But she was being met by a family, and my itinerary was planned weeks in advance. That was perhaps the last best moment.

For the rest, I found myself totally isolated from every familiar contact, thrown together with a strange group of people, none of whom I would have ordinarily chosen to know. Three-fourths of them did not speak English. The rest didn't want to. They had come to practice their

Spanish. There was almost no one my own age. This was the group I was to spend my time with as the tour bus took us inexorably from one sightseeing spectacle to another. We ate only in hotels. I constantly had to make friends with people who were already together and were not eager to know me.

As the days passed I began to feel marooned on a forgotten shoal of time. There was no escape except leaving the tour, and they were not about to give me a refund. I began to regress. Every bit of progress I had made with Rudi was gradually stripped away. My old fears recurred. Every effort I made to reach out to anyone ended disastrously. I gradually recognized that this was what I was supposed to go through, and nothing I could do would really change it. In the back of my mind I kept wondering, "Why did Rudi tell me it would be so marvelous? It is awful. Maybe he figured I wouldn't go if I knew the truth beforehand. If so, he was right. And maybe there is something wrong with me that I don't enjoy it."

Every day I felt worse. Toward the end of the trip I began to forget where I came from or who I was. Rudi himself seemed a figment of my imagination.

I arrived home after a month. Sick, unhappy and angry. I purposely did not phone Rudi for a few days. I wanted to calm down before I talked to him. When I got around to it he was very cheerful.

"How are you, John? Did you have a good time?"

"I feel sick," I said, "and it was awful."

"Really. What's wrong with you? I send you to Europe and you come back full of complaints. You have no capacity to enjoy life. I am thoroughly disgusted with you." He hung up.

I must have held that phone in my hand for three minutes. I just couldn't believe my ears. I was angry and puzzled. Maybe there was something wrong with me! Maybe I was supposed to enjoy it! But one thing I knew for sure. It had been horrible and I felt sick. But I didn't have much time to think about it.

✻ ✻ ✻

It was almost Labor Day Weekend, a year after Muktananda's arrival in America. I didn't want to go to Big Indian for the occasion, but I had missed so much. I knew I should go.

I appeared on a Friday afternoon like a thief in the night. A few people greeted me casually. "Hi John. Haven't seen you around." They obviously didn't know I had been in Europe. I didn't tell them. The whole situation felt very strange, as if it was out of a lifetime I had half-forgotten. I said little to anybody, and was more or less totally ignored.

When Rudi arrived early Saturday morning he greeted me enthusiastically.

"How are you, John? Recovering?" He paused to look at me intently. "You're in better condition than you think, and less miserable than you feel. The trip did you good."

Before I could respond, he moved on. I was puzzled, but pleased that he thought there was something good about it, even if I still felt like a stupid failure. I went to sleep that night like a psychic invalid who was just beginning to recover.

The next day after lunch Rudi started talking to one or two people who were sitting around him. Shortly, the numbers began to grow as other people came over like flies attracted by a sweet left in the open air.

He was talking about teaching and teachers.

"A great period in my own life has concluded," he said. "Swami Muktananda's last gift was to rip Nityananda out of me so that God could begin to come in. That is the way it happens. One attaches oneself to a great being and becomes one with him. When that has gone as far as it can, it must be destroyed. Into the resulting void God can enter. It is almost the only way. Many people talk about God. But they are expressing only a word or a feeling. They lack the capacity to endure any experience of him, any more than they could survive a live wire being placed in their bath. It is truly beyond human endurance." He paused, looked out the window at a pine tree stirred by the wind and continued.

"My Indian period is over. I have grown enough to assimilate the total content of the culture within me. Some of you have been with me many years. John, you have been here the longest. Perhaps you know a little of what this means."

I nodded mutely. I was surprised he had brought me into the conversation.

"We always get involved in the packaging of a situation and forget the content," he continued. "It is not the teacher who is important. He is a servant to the force that flows through him. In honoring a teacher you praise the force for which he acts as a satellite and a magnifying glass, not his personality. Never forget that! Whoever teaches, whether it is Greg, Stuart, or John, they should receive the same love and honor as you would give me. It is basically the same force, only limited and filtered in different ways.

"It is a great joy for me to see others able to take over the work that I have done, and free myself to walk in the woods or sit by the stream. Most teachers hold onto their situation as long as possible. I want to give it away as soon as there is anyone who is capable of sustaining it. I am very grateful that it is beginning to happen," Rudi concluded.

I sat there quietly, feeling slightly stunned. My teaching in New York and Big Indian had been virtually non-existent since I had started just one year before. But there was Rudi, including me in the list of people who should be honored as we honored and loved him. It was unforgettable, at a moment when I felt a general failure as a human being.

Later in the afternoon, Rudi continued his talk before the total group.

"Nothing remains as it was if it is part of a growing situation. You cannot find your security in the familiar. The only security is in God. He exists. Everything else is uncertain, relative. It is hard to speak of anything universal because it so completely eludes our every-day experience. It sounds almost totally abstract. It is invisible, silent and alone. We can never find it by our own efforts. But it doesn't mean it is not real. How can a dream creature, such as we are, find our way to reality? It is almost impossible, like getting out of a vast hall of mirrors.

"Sooner or later, almost everyone sells out to some version of reality. They crystallize on that level. Anything less than the ultimate is an unworthy objective. Nothing and no one has ever tempted me to strive for less. Nothing ever will. The whole purpose of our existence is to complete every situation that we attract. When all our karma has been burned away, then we will find ourselves alone with God. It may be that two or three of you sitting here today will attain that in the course of this life."

✻ ✻ ✻

I saw Rudi briefly later in the evening. He continued to be encouraging. I was grateful, but puzzled.

"The trip was really wonderful for you, John."

"Maybe it wasn't as bad as I thought," I said, "but how could it have been wonderful?"

"I judge by how you look inside," said Rudi. "You are reacting to what it revealed to you. I'm sure that wasn't very pleasant. But you needed to know it. How would you have ever found out if you had stayed home?"

"I have to admit, that's true," I said. "I would never have allowed myself to get into such a situation."

"That's why I had to put you there," said Rudi.

I was stunned. All my anger and resentment, my loneliness and deep disgust with myself dropped away. There had been a reason! He had really done it for my own good. It was like the previous summer when he had attacked me with a psychic meat cleaver. I started to cry. Rudi hugged me and smiled.

"I love you, John. Longevity is everything. You have survived so many people who had more than you to offer. You are here and still growing. They are gone. I really have great respect for you."

That only made me cry more.

"I want you to teach the late afternoon class tomorrow."

"What?" I did a double take. "Do you really think I can do it?"

"Get a good night's sleep." He left me.

I had never taught a major class. The largest group I had worked with was about fifteen. This would be more like sixty to eighty. I didn't even begin to know how to approach it, but I slept well.

The next day I kept myself in a state of suspended animation. I concentrated on the work I was doing, nailing panels on a wall. I didn't allow myself to think of anything. I feigned amnesia. When that didn't work, I just said to myself, "Rudi wouldn't have me teach if I couldn't do it. It doesn't matter that I feel totally inadequate." Somehow I got through the day.

A half-hour before the class I ran into Rudi coming out of the kitchen. He stopped and began to work with me. He touched my forehead and my heart. When he finished he said,

"Now you are programmed. You will have to be good." I wasn't sure if he was kidding but it gave me more confidence. The half-hour passed. I entered the theater and saw a horde of people, all facing toward the front. If I wanted to run away this was the moment. But my feet carried me forward. I was trembling as I bowed before the pictures of Rudi and Nityananda, and seated myself on the couch used

The Price Of Teaching

by the teachers. I faced the multitudes. I closed my eyes for a moment to come more deeply into myself, and also to avoid the situation for as long as possible. Then I opened them and began the class.

I found myself as a conductor seated before a vast orchestra. Each person was an instrument that sounded as I focused on them. But what I had never realized before was that in a large group it was impossible to work with individuals, I had to deal with a total situation. Sitting there I worked as hard as I ever had in my life. Every moment, every breath, was completely exposed before a fiercely attentive group, all of whom were focused on me. There was no place to hide. Even Rudi was in the class. Others might be deceived but he would instantly see through any lack in me. I worked as if even a fraction of an instant's distraction would bring down the entire house of cards crashing on me. After twenty minutes I stopped and asked everyone to use what they had received to help them open to Rudi, as he walked forward to give a short talk. I moved toward the back of the room. Rudi smiled at me as we passed each other. I sat down, shaking with the after effects of the class and listened to his talk.

Afterwards I couldn't remember anything he said. I was too numbed by the impact of what I had done and very relieved that it was over. I felt it had been quite good, but I wasn't sure. The verdict wasn't in.

Rudi concluded his talk and left. I got up and followed.

"Very good class John. It was like watching a thousand-year-old Chinese egg open and seeing something wonderful emerge. It was really gratifying after all these years."

I felt like crying again. "Thank you," I said.

"Now you are a real teacher. You can teach here and in New York. You can teach wherever we have ashrams."

It was so unexpected. I couldn't directly respond. But Rudi could feel my reaction. It was such an incredible reversal of everything I had felt about myself as a result of the trip. At that moment I was glad that I had gone. It had been necessary as a preparation. It had burned out any sense of superficial confidence I might possess. It had shown me what I could revert to if I was removed from the environment in which work was possible. I could never forget it; I drove back to Geneseo feeling marvelous.

✳ ✳ ✳

The next weekend I went to New York City. On Saturday morning I visited Melanie at her invitation. I hadn't seen her in three months.

As she opened the door, I thought, "She is more beautiful than I even remembered." We quietly shared coffee and cake together. As we talked she seemed happier and lighter than before.

"I have really been crazy, John. I don't know how you stood it."

I could hardly believe her words. But she meant it.

"There was no one I wanted to be with since you left. You know what I am like, John. Nothing happens quickly for me. But when it happens, it is for life."

I believed her. She was completely faithful in her own way. She went on, "Whether I marry or whatever the circumstance, I will always be open to you!"

I told her about the Labor Day Weekend.

"That's really wonderful," she said. "I have never seen you look so good. I had the feeling, before you said anything, that you were everywhere in the room at once. Only your body is sitting on the couch."

I left her, feeling like Job, who having been deprived of all, had everything restored to him. I took the subway down to Rudi's and spent the afternoon with him at the store.

"You said I could go to any of the ashrams to teach," I reminded him. "How would I arrange something like that?"

"Just call them up. If they have any questions, tell them I said it was all right."

"I was thinking of going to Bloomington," I said. "It's the nearest."

The group from Bloomington had come to stay with Rudi in New York the previous February. After six months Rudi had sent them back.

"I suggested they start an ashram," he told me later. "Within two or three days of their return to Bloomington they located a house and started a restaurant on almost no money. It was amazing."

There was a pause.

"Did I miss anything while I was away?" I asked. It had been at the back of my mind.

"I gave an exercise in working with angels."

"Yes?" I said. Rudi had promised to give me anything I missed as a condition of my taking the trip.

"It is basically very simple. Angels are servants. You call on them when you need their help. If one isn't enough to handle the job, you ask for more. Just because they look holy or have wings doesn't mean you should get involved with them. Keep your sense of proportion and remember your goal. Otherwise they can lead you astray like any servant."

"Okay!" I said. "I get the idea. But what do I do?"

"It's a very simple process, but don't be deceived by that. The important thing is that it works. Start by opening your heart. Then hold your arms in this position and ask from your heart center for an angel to come and help you with whatever you particularly need in connection with your work. Don't overdo it, or they will cease to take you seriously. Now try it."

I did what he said and to my great surprise I felt something happen.

"Try it again when you are alone," said Rudi, "until you feel more secure with the experience. That is all. Otherwise you didn't miss a thing except a lot of work."

※ ※ ※

Toward the end of the day Rudi asked me, "Are you going to visit your parents after you leave the store?"

"Yes," I said.

"Are you going to take the Seventh Avenue subway?"

"Yes."

"Would you like me to walk you over?"

I was surprised. He had never done that before.

"Sure!" I said. If I had known what was to come I might have been less enthusiastic.

We crossed Fourth Avenue and walked down Tenth Street.

"Whatever happened to that girl?" Rudi asked casually.

"What girl?" I asked, surprised.

"The beautiful blonde one."

"It's funny you should mention her," I said. "I just saw her this morning. Things were terrible for a while, but the tide has turned. They are going to be better from now on."

"It is over, John!" Rudi said quietly.

It was as if a shoe that had been held aloft for over a year had just been dropped. Perhaps I hadn't understood.

"That's what I thought too," I said. "But whatever she has been going through has finally lifted. We are friends again. She told me today she would stay open to me for the rest of her life."

"Haven't you suffered enough?"

"Why is it wrong if I love her?"

"At this point John, she is beginning to hold back your future."

That scared me. "How do you mean?" I asked.

"All your emotional energy is tied up in her. If she returned it in kind it would be good, I would be happy for you. But she won't, and the trouble is you don't care. It truly must end."

"All right," I said, feeling a sense of pained relief.

"You have paid a terrible price in suffering. And your growth has been poor during the last year."

"Anything else?" I asked.

"You must walk away and never even look back."

"Can't we even be friends?"

"No. You can't handle it. You care too deeply. Write her a simple letter and say goodbye. She has style. She will accept it. Probably she will be relieved. You want so much. It must be a strain on her to have you around."

"All right," I said.

"You agree, but you don't really believe me. You think about what she said to you today. It opens the door to the future. That, more than any other reason, is why you have to end it. Otherwise she will bleed you for the rest of your life."

We walked on in silence. "If I had known what was going to happen I wouldn't have been so eager for your company," I said.

"Why do you think I offered to come?" said Rudi.

I felt stripped to the bone. How could you deal with someone who was all around you, looking in every direction?

"One of your troubles, John, is that you don't think enough of yourself. And so you accept shit. That must stop! For the rest of your life, you should never be near anyone who does not either love you very deeply or honor the work very highly, preferably both. You must insist upon it, even if emotionally you don't care. The time for anything less has passed. If anyone does not appreciate what you are inside at this point, leave them."

We had a drink together in a small deserted bar and parted.

That night I wrote a short note:

Dear Melanie,

It is all over. I am never going to see you again. I wish you

The Price Of Teaching

every happiness in your life.

John

I sent it and opened the doorway to the future.

Chapter Thirty-Four

EXPERIENCE AND FULFILLMENT

While I was still in the city I decided to phone Michael Shoemaker, the teacher in Bloomington. I dialed his number with some inner uncertainty. He knew who I was, but was obviously taken aback when I said,

"I would like to visit and teach at the ashram." Before he could think too much about it I added, "Rudi said to call him if you have any questions." Michael had no questions. A tentative date was set for several weeks in the future. I put down the phone, feeling good, but also scared. I would be very much on my own out there.

Several weeks later when I arrived in Indiana, Michael met me at the airport. The first few minutes were slightly strained. Finally, he asked me,

"Just why have you come?"

"I wanted to experience what you were doing, and to teach," I said. "That's all."

"Then Rudi didn't send you?" he asked suspiciously.

"No! It was my idea. What did you think I was, a spy from central headquarters?"

"That's pretty close," said Michael.

"Well, you can forget it. As far as I know, Rudi is very happy with what you are doing."

After that the atmosphere cleared and everything went smoothly.

Even in those early days the spirit in Bloomington was totally new to me. There was a quality of dedication and simplicity that the people in the East simply did not have. I had lived among New York City neurotics for so long that I took them for granted.

I shortly discovered there was a real need for my presence. The group had done truly remarkably in a few months, but the intensity of the effort, particularly on Michael's part, inevitably created certain tensions that someone from the outside could help to clarify and reduce. This I proceeded to do.

I taught class, talked endlessly to people, went to see a rock concert and ended up feeling that I had always been there. When it came time to leave I did so with the intention of returning again soon. But that did not occur for more than a year, and then under very different circumstances.

It was by then early in December, 1971. The trip to Bloomington had changed my perspective about my teaching, and my own life.

"Maybe I was a real idiot to ever move out of New York," I said to Rudi on my return.

"Not at all, John. Life doesn't stand still. You had to move on in order to have a larger responsibility and gain a different perspective."

"But what I am doing seems so fruitless," I said. "I have been working with a group for four years. There is almost nothing to show for it."

"You don't understand," said Rudi. "It is all preparation. You are ready to stop putting effort into it, but you should put much more than you have. Are you coming into the city over Christmas?"

"Yes."

"Well, stay through New Years and then I want you to go back and work with your group for six weeks. Stay away from here for that period, except for my birthday."

"I'll probably drive them all up a wall," I said.

"Not at all. You'll learn how much work there is for you to do right there. You have never put enough energy into these people to understand what is possible. Stay there for six weeks and see what happens."

"All right. I'll try, but I think it would be better if I spent the time with you."

※ ※ ※

I returned to Geneseo and announced,

"Starting with the New Year I am going to give classes every day, several times a day for six weeks. Twice a week I will go into Rochester for people who live in that area. Once or twice a week they can come to Geneseo. It will be a great opportunity for you if you want it. By working intensely for a long but limited period, you can really break through to a new level."

To my surprise, everyone was quite enthusiastic. Maybe Rudi knew something I didn't know. Or maybe the intensity of the schedule appealed to them. How they would react when it started a month hence remained to be seen.

During the early autumn, I had met an intense and slightly crazy girl who was in the process of getting separated from her husband. Month by month I watched her becoming increasingly haunted by a mounting sense of anxiety. I was puzzled. There seemed no reason for it. She had come to class several times, and then began to fade. We were still friends. However she wouldn't listen to me or anyone. She became convinced that her fellow teachers in the school where she worked were conspiring against her. One weekend in December when I returned from New York I discovered she had been checked into Strong Memorial Hospital, diagnosed as acute schizophrenic breakdown. I was shocked, but not surprised. I had seen it coming, like a train approaching a cliff in slow-motion.

I visited her in the hospital. She didn't know who I was, though she had been asking for me. I wondered whether her starting the work had anything to do with her sickness. I asked Rudi about it over Christmas vacation.

"It is not your fault," he said. "There is nothing you could do. If this had happened a few years from now, you might have been able to handle it, but not now. We are all in love with death. This was her expression of it."

"Did anything that I did, or anything in the work, act to push her over the edge?" I asked.

"Don't flatter yourself, John. The problem was that you didn't have the power to resist the force of her insanity. How well did she work while she was in the class?"

"The first two times she was good. Then she began to wander."

"There is your answer."

"What should I do now?" I asked.

"Be a friend. Visit her once a week, no more. If the doctors want you to cooperate, do it. But, John, don't feel bad. You know that if it was even to a small extent your fault, I would certainly tell you. It wasn't. It may be sad, but the world is full of people who would rather destroy themselves than take the responsibility for their own inner condition. You can't be concerned about that. Living in New York City I am surrounded by every sort of insanity, most of it is walking the streets. It doesn't matter. I draw a line at the entrance to the store no one crosses unless I allow it. Inside the store is a different world in which I can grow and flourish. I cannot change the whole earth. To try would be an endless waste of energy poured into a situation which is meant to be exactly as it is."

※ ※ ※

On New Year's Day as I drove back to Geneseo, I was ready to begin working intensely with those close to me. I did not know where it would carry me, but as I gave the first class that night I had a sense of satisfaction and excitement. Some of the students I had known for three or four years; others, a matter of weeks or months. Whatever the case I was determined that regardless of their previous experience, they would not emerge the same.

I began to work with students alone, in pairs, in small classes or larger classes. It became a marathon. I loved it, and I was also caught by it. I had never worked so hard or continuously before. By the end of the day I was burning with a fever of no physical origin.

Inevitably some people received much more than others. They were more available, had a greater need, or were more open. I just kept pouring it out and let the results take care of themselves. I began to get a different sense of what it meant to be a teacher, the extent of the commitment, and the endlessness of the effort. The teacher accepts the responsibility for the inner growth of the student if the student is willing to give it to him. He cannot do the student's work for him, but he must see what is possible and feed that potential.

Many things began to happen. People who had sat endlessly began to move. One unexpected effect was that a woman whom I had known and overlooked for a long time began to emerge. As she did, the love she felt but had never expressed began to shine. I did not quite know what to do. It was obviously such a direct result of the intensified work that I felt there was a special meaning or possibility in it. I began to see her as a space woman, not a creature from another galaxy, but a woman explorer. I had the sense that we could travel together beyond the earth into different levels of the universe. It was just an impression, and I had little to guide me. But the intensification of our relationship seemed to draw us not only together, but upward simultaneously.

※ ※ ※

About this time Rudi celebrated his forty-fourth birthday. He had been anticipating the event for a long time.

"Fifteen years ago," he said, "the Shankaracharya of Puri told me what a wonderful life I would have, the incredible happiness and the force that would come pouring out of me. Then when I began to get enthusiastic, he said, 'Of course you are going to have to go through fifteen years of hell first.'

"On my forty-fourth birthday, the fifteen-year period will be over. I have been working toward this moment for so long that I can hardly believe that I have survived to see it occur."

I had searched for several months to find an appropriate present for such an occasion. When I had almost given up I came upon a great woven rope hammock that was designed to hang from the ceiling. That seemed adequate. I wrapped it in bright orange paper and started out for the city.

When I arrived at the house Rudi was resting. I asked Buford, who was going upstairs, to tell him I had come. The word came back that I should join him. I took my present and walked to the third floor. I had rarely been there before. Rudi was sitting on a large covered oriental bed. He was doing some new form of work with a student. I didn't know what was happening, but the effect seemed very strong. After a brief period the student left and we were alone.

"Two days ago," said Rudi, "I found the root of the third eye. If you feed energy into the root, everything else develops from that." He repeated what he had done with the student on me so that I could experience what he was describing. It was like a probe being introduced between my eyebrows. Then after a few seconds Rudi took a deep breath and relaxed.

He had a big night ahead of him. I felt reluctant to bother him, but I certainly wasn't going to leave unless he threw me out.

"What's in the orange package?" he asked when it caught his eye.

I handed it to him silently. He ripped off the paper and looked at the contents somewhat puzzled. "Is it a hammock?" he finally asked.

"Yes, it hangs from the ceiling; I hope it will fit into your new life."

He smiled. He was pleased.

"It has been a long time, hasn't it, John? I am glad you are here to be part of tonight. It is a wonderful and important day for me."

"I am deeply grateful to be here," I said. He put his hand on mine as he lay down. We remained that way for half a minute. Then he said, "I am really tired. I'll see you downstairs a little later."

The party was a major event. Hundreds of people came from across the country to be together with Rudi for that day. The food was lavish and overflowing. The current winner of the Chopin Festival had been invited and he performed in an atmosphere of singing silence. But the most remarkable aspect of the occasion was the palpable sense of happiness that sparkled between people and created warmth and peace wherever it came to rest. It felt as if five planets were lined up for the only time in a century.

✳ ✳ ✳

When I returned to Geneseo, one of my students told me that she had not slept at all the whole night. Great musical sounds and beautiful patterns of light rained endlessly down from above. She had never known anything like it.

I resumed my intensified six-week period of work. Several of the students achieved breakthroughs into new levels of functioning. I was very pleased, though I couldn't help but wonder what was going to happen when the six weeks were over. They had made a commitment to themselves to work hard for that period. I suspected that afterwards there might be a reversal. But that wasn't my worry. I had been told what to do. I was doing it.

One of my students was a fellow named Josef. I had introduced him to the basic work almost four years before. But he had quickly dropped it and stayed away from me thereafter. Eventually he went to England and was hurt in a motorcycle accident which kept him in the hospital for several months. When he returned to Geneseo he became interested in Zen. Occasionally, we met to discuss Zen in relation to Rudi's work. I suggested that he might want to do a Directed Study comparing the two disciplines. It was on that flimsy basis that he began again to work with me. Once started he worked hard and even desperately. He took to following me around wherever I went for six to eight hours at a stretch.

On a certain crucial day he complained that he could feel pressure at the base of his spine. He seemed to expect me to do something about it. I wasn't sure what to do, but I recalled the night so many years before when Rudi had first raised the Kundalini in my spine. Now I was being asked to do the same thing. The only difference was that Rudi knew what he was doing; I did not.

At first I tried working in the usual manner, thinking that if the overall pressure in his psychic system were increased, the spine might open spontaneously. It didn't. It only made Josef more frustrated. I told him to lie down and completely relax. I led him in a semi-hypnotic series of suggestions to achieve full relaxation. It helped a little, but he wasn't satisfied. Having started the process nothing was going to make him stop. I had to admire his persistence, even though I was beginning to wish he would go away.

I tried to feed in energy with my hands directly to the place in his spine that was blocked. It seemed to help slightly, but he was in a kind of agony. The energy wouldn't rise and the harder he tried, the more constricted he felt. Then I discovered that my own back felt increasingly tight. That proved the key. Somehow by working with him my own system was picking up his tension. I started working on the tension in myself as an indirect way of releasing the blocks in him. I continued all of these approaches more or less simultaneously.

As if in slow motion the energy began to rise, vertebra by vertebra. It took about half an hour, but it finally reached his head. It was like delivering a baby. In the end Josef was too exhausted to be thankful, but I had a taste of teaching differently from anything I had known before.

Another significant moment occurred with a student named

Harold. I had known him for some time. But two years had passed from our first meeting until he began to work. Though he was not to be hurried he had a tremendous capacity to draw from me when he chose to access it. A year after he started to work he vanished. I didn't know where he had gone or why, I just shrugged my shoulders and forgot about it. Students were forever coming and going. Six months later he suddenly appeared at my back door. He wanted to return to the work. I thought it over and agreed.

On one particular night, all of the effort of the past suddenly came into focus. Instead of an uncertain sheepish man, there appeared a great Indian chieftain, powerful, sure, beautiful to behold. I asked him how he felt after the class.

"Absolutely wonderful," he said.

At last it seemed that he would really begin to move. But a month later he disappeared again and never returned.

Chapter Thirty-Five

ACCELERATION

By the middle of February I concluded my six-week marathon and went to New York. When I sat down next to Rudi in the store once again, he said,

"I am happier, John, than I have ever been in my life. Ever since my Birthday, spiritual gifts have been raining upon me. I wake up in the middle of the night and feel my heart chakra opened way beyond my body. I am so grateful.

"The new students who are coming are wonderful, not just here, but in the other ashrams. A new man from Bloomington is visiting. I love him very much. He is engaged and I had the feeling that the girl might be threatened by his relation with me. So as we were walking on Fifth Avenue the other day, I saw a coat in the window. The moment I saw it I knew it was meant for her. I went in and bought it. He will give it to her when he returns to Indiana. A new relationship should enrich everybody."

I thought about that for a while, and then said,

"You were certainly right having me stay in Geneseo for six weeks. I learned a lot."

"That's what I told you. Now you can go back and work your way out of the situation. That is what I am doing."

"The only thing that bothers me," I said, "is that I feel most of them aren't prepared to continue working with anything like the present intensity. If they quit or go backwards, what's the good of it all?"

"The good of it is what it is doing for you," said Rudi. "What it does for them and how far they go with it is their choice. Don't worry about it. If some fall away, others will come."

"What did you mean," I asked, "about working yourself out of this situation?"

"In a year or a year and a half," said Rudi, "I feel I am going to leave

New York for the Middle East. There will be others here who will carry on. It will be the start of a totally different life for me. But don't worry, John. I'll let you know where I am. You can visit me once or twice a year and get what you need. Believe me, by that point it will be enough."

I sat there trying to digest what he had said. I had mixed feelings. Was it all coming to an end? I knew that Rudi was more than capable of leaving. I was worried, but I also felt a kind of relief. I always had to run just to keep up with him. If he assured me that I could get what I needed by visiting him twice a year, I was partially ready to believe it. I knew it was stupid. I didn't really believe it. It might be possible with the proper preparation, but I doubted my capability to do the necessary work.

In any case there was nothing I could do to affect his decision. It excited him to think about a major change in his life, and he was obviously trying to prepare us for the transition by talking about it so far in advance.

But sitting with him in the store any such possibility was hard to accept. He so filled the moment that everything else seemed a dream. He shone. The world circled around him. I didn't stay long that morning. I had to meet my children who were coming in on a twelve o'clock train. Rudi walked me to the door of the store. He paused at the threshold. Then he said,

"'I am the sun and you are the moon."

He didn't say anything else. I stood there paralyzed. It was so completely true. It was his radiance that brought me life.

※ ※ ※

At the next class he talked about his next trip.

"In a few weeks I will be going back to the Orient. While I am away try to prepare yourselves to receive more deeply from me when I return. None of you have used me well. None of you have been willing to make the effort and the commitment to begin to get from me what I have to give.

"The energy that is flowing through me now is too powerful or too subtle for you to take unless you have worked long enough and hard enough to prepare the ground within you. It will dribble through your hands. You are all much too easy on yourselves. You think there is all the time in the world. You are wrong! There is a certain time available for a given piece of work. If you finish it sooner, so much the better. But if you don't finish within the allotted time, you are out of luck.

"The longer you work the more you have to lose. The longer you work the more you realize nothing and no one is worth the sacrifice of your own inner growth.

"I will be in this country for another year or so. Take advantage of it. Afterwards, other people will take over. They will certainly be competent, but it will not be the same.

"If even three of you could work hard enough I would never go anywhere. But all of you combined can't begin to do it. That is why I have begun to establish ashrams across the country. I am not interested in numbers, but my energy has to be used. I create other ashrams to draw on me and force me to continue to grow.

"You have a month while I am away to prepare to make a new effort. It is for me to make you aware of the opportunity. The rest is up to you."

I accepted what Rudi said. I remembered eight years before when we had talked together at Woodstock.

"You are the only one," he told me, "who might have a chance to receive some of what I have to give. It is really up to you, John. If you work harder, much harder, then I will fulfill my promise."

I knew that on the whole I had failed. If this was a new opportunity, I hoped and prayed I was in a better position to utilize it. But I couldn't assume anything.

※ ※ ※

Rudi went on his trip. Usually he planned to go for a month and return in less than three weeks. This time he returned exactly on schedule. By intent and good fortune I was present in New York on that day. Buford, who had gone with him, had little to say and seemed to be exhausted. I did not expect to talk with Rudi since he went right upstairs to his bedroom. I waited around and finally decided to take a walk. As I started out, I heard him descending. I paused.

"Hello, John," he said. "It was a wonderful trip. I am supposed to go back in the early fall and meet an incredibly holy man who is seven hundred years old."

I didn't think he was joking, but I looked at his expression to make sure. He wasn't.

"Would you like to come with me?" he added quietly.

I had known Rudi fourteen years at that point. But I had never really gone anywhere with him.

"Whom do I have to kill?" I asked.

"No one," said Rudi. "It will be wonderful for you. It is the beginning of a major cycle. The last one started when I met Nityananda as I was on the way to New Zealand. This is the next. I want you to be there so you can get the immediate impact of the experience."

He smiled at my expression. I was so totally taken aback. Then he motioned for me to follow him as he walked into the living room. Rudi had some tea, and talked sparingly with those present.

"During the first few days," he said, "Buford and I enjoyed the new situations in which we found ourselves. We sunbathed on the beaches in Bali and played with the native children. Then I noticed that Buford gradually seemed to be withdrawing. I asked him if anything was wrong. He said, 'No,' but there obviously was.

"As this trend continued, I began to get upset. Here I was, not only allowing him to come along, but paying his way. And everything seemed to be turning to dust. I began to resent it. I was getting ready to blast him for his lack of sensitivity and gratitude. But something made me hesitate. I decided to get a better perspective on the situation.

"I sat down and started to work. It took quite a long time, but I kept at it until I felt that my frustration and anger had fallen away. Then, and only then, did I look at Buford. What I saw really shocked me. He was surrounded by a thin brown membrane that completely enclosed him like an unborn baby in a sack. He was going through a rebirth experience.

"From that point my whole attitude changed. What he needed was nourishment. What I had been about to do was deprive him of the energy of our relationship. If I had done that he would have been screwed since he didn't have enough energy in himself to complete the rebirth process.

"I have gotten through such experiences myself because I could sense their symptoms from the inside. But to see it in someone else was different. And to feel how my whole emotional reaction was to kill it off in him helped me to understand how difficult it is for most human beings to come through such a process successfully.

"When I understood the situation I began to pour energy into him.

There was little direct reaction on his part until the membrane broke. But then, like a chicken from the egg, he began to emerge.

"The crucial point came when a phoenix appeared on his forehead."

"How did that happen?" I asked.

"I performed a psychic operation that allowed the phoenix to emerge," said Rudi. "I have had it appear on my own head many times, but I have never brought it out on anyone else."

"Could you do that on me?" I asked, striking while the iron was hot.

"Yes," said Rudi.

"Would you?" I persisted.

"Perhaps over Memorial Day Weekend. Ask me about it again in a few weeks. Right now I am going to bed."

He went upstairs. Shortly thereafter I left, slightly in shock from all that had occurred.

***

From that day until the end of September, I lived in expectation of the trip to India, though numerous events occurred to raise doubt about whether it would take place. For Rudi it was a period of unparalleled development. Each time I returned to New York something fundamental and unexpected had occurred.

The first innovation, which had begun before the trip, was the development of a new kind of class specifically keyed to Buford's particular abilities. It was called a tantric class, though it was not like anything in the tantric literature with which I am familiar. The major point of similarity was the emphasis on Tibetan ritual instruments; the *dorje* (thunderbolt), *purba* (ritual dagger) and other ritual instruments associated with tantric deities, such as chimes, human skullcaps, and ritual bells.

While I was at the store Rudi talked a little about the background for the class.

"During the last few months, I have been noticing that higher manifestations have been appearing when I worked. It made me feel that a new type of class should be created as the natural vehicle for these forces.

"I'll give you an example. On the flight home from Europe at the end of my last trip, I was followed by a great cloud of energy. It accompanied the plane. I don't mind telling you, it was more than a little strange to look out the window and see this cloud of intelligence. I wasn't sure if it was friendly at first, but when it left us somewhere over the ocean I ceased to worry about it.

"We have such a remarkably limited concept of life. Energy manifests in every conceivable pattern. If it doesn't wear a familiar face we refuse to recognize it. When astronauts look for life on another planet they probably won't see it because they won't know what to look for. Life is energy. It can take any form."

My first contact with the tantric class was indirect. Buford asked several of the teachers to come with him to participate in a brief ceremony. We went upstairs and worked before Alfred, the Tibetan god of Astral Flight. Then each of us in turn placed his hands above the flame of a large orange candle and asked to surrender to the force with which we worked and be consumed by it. The effect was powerful. I immediately began to burn.

From the beginning I felt that the only way I would possibly understand the tantric class was to teach it. This did not seem immediately practical since no one was giving it but Buford. But I wasn't shy when it came to something I really wanted. I approached him after one of the early classes and said, "Is there any way I can help you give the class, Buford?"

He was a little diffident.

"I'm not sure," he said. "Keep attending it when you can. I'm thinking of teaching Walter the use of the purba. If I decide to do that, then I could train you at the same time."

I happily agreed, and settled down to wait for the opportunity to occur.

The tantric class was Rudi's creation. It was, in a sense, his gift to Buford. I didn't have the illusion that I understood much about it, but that didn't bother me. That was my chronic condition. All I knew, and all I needed to know, was that it was a higher form of work like Astral Flight, to which it seemed to be indirectly related. It had to be more than a coincidence that the class was conducted directly before Alfred. Also it was given in Rudi's bedroom, where otherwise few came except to dust and clean.

On my next trip to New York I asked Buford when he thought I could begin, just so he should realize I was really interested. To my surprise he said,

"Tonight! I have already started with Walter."

Later that evening the three of us assembled in Rudi's bedroom with the unknown surrounding us.

"First," said Buford, "let's wash up and change our clothes. Anything that helps to make a break from the routine of the day is useful."

I washed with care and a mounting sense of inadequacy. Buford continued to talk.

"I can tell you a few basic things, but a lot of what happens I don't really understand myself. Each class is different. I see a pattern developing, but it is still very fresh."

That was not very reassuring, though I could well believe it was true.

"Though I will talk with both of you," Buford continued, "only one will work with me tonight. Otherwise, it would get too confusing. John can start, since he isn't here every week." He paused.

I was still waiting patiently for some concrete indication of my actual function in the class. Buford seemed to have forgotten I was there. I didn't want to interrupt his concentration, but finally I said, "You better tell me what I should actually do."

He smiled enigmatically.

"You use the purba to work directly on specific chakras. It is really an astral instrument given a physical form, a magic dagger designed to penetrate layers of psychic tension. The dorje, which I will use, is literally a force gatherer. It exists beyond time and space and is both a symbol and a manifestation of a higher force in the universe.

"I will work on your hands to start the force flowing before I give you the purba. Then you are on your own. You will have to discover what feels right. Each time you need to reconnect with the force, reach up into the astral and get what is necessary. When I do it I feel as if my arm extends upward, another arm comes out of that, another out of that, until I reach what I need.

"If you feel that the force is diminishing, you can also work with Alfred for a few seconds. That is about all I can tell you. Rudi didn't really tell me very much when I started. You have to sense it out for yourself."

I didn't know much more than I had before, but whenever I had been thrown into a new situation in the past it had usually worked out well.

I tried to relax as the students began to enter the room.

"Just follow my lead as best you can," were Buford's last words. He walked to the front of the room, bowed down before Alfred, and then lit a large candle and several sticks of incense. He motioned to me and we both put our hands above the flame, dedicating ourselves to the force and letting it burn within us. After that he consecrated the chimes, dorje and purba in the candle flame. Then he motioned me closer with his eyes. He took the purba and gently pushed the tip into my palm where the hand chakra is located. I felt a rush of force. He placed the purba into my hand and motioned me to start.

For the next forty minutes I was completely absorbed in using the point of the purba to directly inject energy into the heart, throat, and third eye chakras of each student. Buford was working behind me. As I finished with one person, he moved in using the dorje and his free hand. I heard strange sounds as people were affected by his action, but I could not afford to be distracted, so I didn't look back.

At the end I returned the purba to him. It was again purified in the flames. I sat down on the side while Buford went through the concluding section of the ritual. Then it was suddenly over. Buford relaxed and smiled. I felt like a shirt that had been pulled through a wringer. I hugged him and then staggered down the stairs and out into the street. I didn't know what had happened, but I knew that whatever it was I would pursue it until I understood how to relate to the force that was being invoked.

Though Rudi stood behind the tantric class, he took no direct part in it. He wanted it to be an expression of Buford's work and direction.

During the early stages the two consulted about the class, but later Rudi stopped taking the initiative, and Buford proceeded on by himself.

* * *

When Buford and Rudi had last been in India they had gone to an excellent psychic, Mr. Thomas. He had stated that Buford would be leaving Rudi in a few months to go to Paris. Rudi couldn't have been more surprised. Buford was, at that time, closer to him than anyone. The thought that he would leave for any reason was inconceivable. But afterwards, partly in jest, he mentioned the matter to Buford.

"He was generally a very good psychic, but your moving to Paris was remarkably inaccurate."

"I don't know about that," said Buford. "I have a feeling my karma is drawing me to Paris."

Rudi was speechless.

Later, in describing the event to me, he said,

"I was shocked, but if that was what he wanted to do, the only thing was to let him go. It wasn't right. How could it be right? But what good would it do to keep him here? Buford had begun to work more with Alfred than with me anyway.

"I know what Paris means to him. It is a chance to be free and fall in love. He is young. He has the right. But, what a waste! I can't say it doesn't affect me. But I have had so many people leave me in my life that I am almost used to it."

As the weeks passed, preliminary plans were made for Buford to go on a short visit to Paris. On the day of his departure, the two of them came down the stairs of the ashram on their way to the airport with Buford in the lead.

For a long moment a deep sense of waste and regret seemed to sweep over Rudi. But there was nothing to be done, and Buford never saw it.

After he left, the tantric work slowly lapsed, but not before I had the opportunity to give the class several times. And that was what I wanted.

* * *

The period following Rudi's forty-fourth birthday continued to be marked by unprecedented growth. Rudi began to use various psychic instruments such as a whip, a cleaver, and sword in working directly with people. I couldn't see them. They didn't exist on the physical level, but I could certainly feel their effects.

On one visit in mid-winter, Rudi said to me in a jovial manner, "I have been working on something new with my hands. Would you like to see it, John?"

I nodded, "Sure."

I was sitting ten feet from him. He opened his hand and I was hurled back several feet. I had known the impact of many forces over the years, but this was unprecedented.

Rudi described what was happening to his hands when I saw him the next day.

"It is as if there are thousands of spores borrowing into my palms, each containing a little reservoir of energy. When I set them off all at once they have an intense power, beyond anything I have had before. I can feel them digging into my psychic system deeper and deeper. They seem to be working their way up my arms."

Rudi's whole energy system seemed to be rapidly increasing and ripening. In parallel with this inner unfolding, he was surrounded by greater love than he had ever known, not only in New York and Big Indian, but particularly in the more distant ashrams where his appearance was more of a special event.

※ ※ ※

It was during this period that Rudi visited Boston for the first time. His trip had been preceded by an exchange of enthusiastic and imploring letters that indicated that there was a real and genuine interest in his work, and many people waiting for him to appear.

On the basis of these letters Rudi arranged a trip. He returned puzzled and a little disillusioned. His lectures were quite well attended, but there was no core group anxiously anticipating his arrival. He shrugged his shoulders and forgot about it.

A few weeks later the mystery was solved.

"It was all one man, John."

"What do you mean," I asked, not knowing what he was talking about.

"In Boston. It was all one man. Two weeks ago he showed up in New York. He was in a very emotional state. He explained to me that he had written all the letters. He had never seen me and he couldn't understand his own feelings. But after we met in Boston, he realized that we had known each other before and been very close. He felt we had been married in a previous life.

"I can accept the possibility. But it is not so easy for him. He does not have my detachment. But for me it is wonderful. The intensity and emotionality of the energy between us is very rich. I can quietly absorb it while doing whatever is necessary to keep him balanced. Life is really much stranger than anyone could ever dream."

On that evening, Rudi worked upstairs with his students as usual. Michael Shoemaker, who was visiting from Bloomington, sat on one side of Rudi. I was on the other. Rudi reached out and took our hands. It was like being grasped by an electric current. I was torn between wishing the experience would go on and hoping it would stop. But Rudi was inexhaustible. I went into convulsions that usually followed exposure to such intense energy. This was just the beginning. Over the next half hour Rudi worked with us using a variety of psychic instruments. I was reduced to a dazed electrified jelly.

The next afternoon I happened to visit my lawyer to pick up a slightly revised version of my will. I read it over casually, stuck it in my hip pocket and left.

My next stop was the store. Rudi was fairly busy. I sat inconspicuously in the corner until a quiet moment came. Then I said,

"You told me to remind you about the phoenix, so I am reminding you."

"Sure, John," said Rudi. "Maybe Memorial Day weekend. I need to rest and prepare myself first. Okay?"

"Of course," I said, dropping the matter. Memorial Day sounded like an appropriate time.

As I was sitting there I became aware of the will in my hip pocket and shifted it to my shirt so it wouldn't get squashed.

The store became busy again. I bathed in Rudi's presence and relaxed, glad to be in the rich, warm atmosphere.

After about twenty-five minutes, the store cleared. There was a pause. I continued to work with him whether he paid any attention to me or not. Then he began to look at me with a strange expression on his face.

"The store feels strong, doesn't it?" he said.

It did, but I said nothing. Then he got up and walked over to me.

"Shut your eyes and relax."

I didn't ask any questions. He began to work on my head with his hands. I tried to relax and felt like a piece of wood being chiseled by a sculptor.

After a minute or two, he paused.

"All right, John, Go sit in the back room. Be very quiet and don't touch your head."

I did as he said. I had a suspicion about what had happened, but I didn't want to think about it.

After ten minutes Rudi stuck his head through the door. "You can come out now."

I emerged. The store was empty. He looked at me and smiled.

"I have been wondering," I said, "whether you decided to go ahead without waiting for Memorial Day."

"Yes!" said Rudi. "It seemed like the right moment. The force was strong and no one was here. How do you feel?"

"Fine. But did it work?"

"It certainly did!"

At that moment, Michael Shoemaker and several others entered the store. Rudi motioned them over.

"Look at John's forehead," he said.

They looked somewhat uncertainly.

"What is that?" asked Michael.

"That is a phoenix. See the wings, the head, the feet." Rudi indicated the outline with his forefinger.

There was no doubt that they saw it. I felt rather strange, like a sideshow exhibit. I was happy that something had happened, but could not feel that I had anything to do with it.

Rudi's last words as I left were, "Be very quiet for the rest of the day."

As I walked down the street it struck me how odd it was that my new will was in my breast pocket, and the bird of rebirth was on my forehead. But the situation was even stranger than that. When I returned to Geneseo I discovered that my secretary had suddenly died during the same time that Rudi was working with me in New York.

✷ ✷ ✷

Shortly after his return from the last trip, Rudi began to undertake a serious diet for the first time since I had known him. He had always been overweight. Now he started on a grape fast. He gave various reasons for doing it.

"It is the right thing for my chemistry at this time. I need to be lighter inside. It is part of my preparation for the next trip. If I am going to meet an ancient holy man who is highly ethereal, I have to be in that state myself in order to relate to him."

I asked if I should do the same thing.

"No. It isn't necessary. It wouldn't hurt you to lose some weight, but not for that reason. I am the one who has to make the connection."

About this time Rudi met an unusual woman through a mutual friend. His relation with her had some bearing on the fast.

"I realized at last year's Christmas party," he explained, "that everyone was happy and fulfilled but myself. I began to ask for someone who would have the capacity to absorb what I have to give.

"A month later I met A. I was immediately struck by an indefinable quality in her. When I saw her again, the connection between us deepened. I became aware of the depth of the tie going back many lifetimes. She is a completely new quantity in my life. It isn't a romantic relation. I don't know what it is. One of main reasons for going on the diet is to be able to relate more fully to her level, which is one of great personal refinement.

"Then I discovered that she had cancer. I was deeply upset. Now I have to decide what to do about it."

Though Rudi could act as a healer if he wanted to, he had generally resisted the temptation. He was not interested in using the force that flowed through him for curing physical ills. His aim was inner growth. He assumed general good health in his students and never hesitated to recommend the latest developments of medicine if they needed it.

But there was always an exception. He worked once or twice with A. and then he left on a short trip to Japan. He didn't realize what had happened to him until he got to Tokyo. Then he began to experience the depth and intensity of the poison he had taken into his own system. He began to burn. It continued during almost the whole course of the trip. For ten to twelve hours a day he did nothing but perform the exercise to surrender negative psychic tension. It became a full-time occupation. He worked in his business activities on the side. If he had known what he was getting into, he might have hesitated. But then he would never have known the nature of the force contained in a cancer victim.

On his return he saw A. again. She reported her symptoms were somewhat improved. Encouraged by this initial result, Rudi decided to continue.

The next time I saw him he had tried a new approach. "Stuart, Michael and I went to the back room and formed a triangle with A. in the center," Rudi said. "I worked with her and they worked with me to intensify the experience. Then we left her alone. A half-hour later I stuck my head through the doorway to see what was happening. It was extraordinary. The whole back room was filled with people and forces that were beginning to emerge from her. I closed the door and let the process continue.

"Most people aren't interested in drinking cancer milk shakes," he concluded, "but for me it is a new quality of energy that I need for my own fulfillment."

Each time I came to the city I found that something new and significant had occurred. I began to take it for granted.

"I have never had so much going on inside me before," Rudi said. "It is almost endless. And my life has taken on a sweetness I have never known.

"When it started, I had a talk with God. I said, 'Listen God. You can take all this love and shove it for all I care. I haven't worked so hard for this kind of payoff. It's wonderful and I appreciate it, but this isn't where I want it to end.'

"I carried on this way for a while and then I began to understand what was happening. I saw the ordeal I would have to go through twelve years from now. I understood that it would be impossible for me to stand the intensity of the pain without some protection. The love and sweetness I am receiving now is the insulation from the pain to come in the future. After I understood that I felt better. I am being prepared for the next stage, I am not retiring."

※ ※ ※

A few days later Rudi said to me casually, "I am giving some new work on Sunday. Try to be there," I assured him that I would.

I arrived for the class a little late and was dismayed to find the room completely full. But on closer inspection I saw a small clearing near the wall in the back. I resolutely moved toward it, stepping over arms, shoulders, heads and pocketbooks until I arrived at the spot. People on either side made slight efforts to make room for me as I sat down. I turned my attention forward to listen to Rudi, who had just started talking.

"We usually think of chakras as static," he said. "That is a limitation. Everything in the universe is moving. When the Buddha set the wheel of the law in motion he was transmitting the energy of his message, which called for change on every level. In an inward sense you can do the same thing by beginning to set your chakras — which are another Sanskrit term for wheel — in motion."

He paused to let the thought sink in. As he did, I realized why the place where I was sitting had been left vacant. It was right next to a radiator. No matter how I shifted, there was no way I could avoid having my leg rest on the burning pipe.

Rudi continued. "Rotating a chakra is very simple. You simply reach into it psychically and give a twisting motion with your hand.

Don't think about it. Just do it." He paused. "How many of you succeeded?"

About a third of the people raised their hands.

"Good," said Rudi.

By this time my leg was burning and the sweat was pouring off me. I could hardly hear what Rudi was saying. I only wanted one thing, for the class to end.

Then Rudi said, "Now we will go through the chakras one at a time, setting each in motion as we come to it. After that, we will have a short class. Whenever you feel a particular chakra stopping, just give it another twist."

Most of my attention was on my leg, but I tried to do what Rudi had suggested as an exercise of will if nothing else. Something seemed to happen, but I still kept praying for the class to be over.

A half hour later I saw Rudi in the hall. He seemed pleased.

"That was a great class," he said.

"It was hard for me to tell. My leg was resting on the radiator. It was all I could do to continue to sit there."

"But it was wonderful for you, John. Sacred symbols kept appearing on your forehead. I was very impressed."

"And I didn't know anything had happened," I said in amazement.

"Well," said Rudi, "a miracle is of no use if you aren't aware of it."

Acceleration

I felt strange for the rest of the day and was sobered when I undressed and saw the great red welt made on my leg by the heat pipe. But if something wonderful had happened, I was grateful. Perhaps the pain had been the payment.

※ ※ ※

From time to time Rudi would refer to work beyond Astral Travel. He mentioned it and then passed on to something else. He did not answer any questions. In fact, he gave the appearance of not knowing what you were talking about if you asked a question. It didn't take long to get the message.

For example, he said, "The basic work is simply the foundation. You need a strong basis for advanced work, but there is nothing stupider than a man who spends his whole life building a foundation on which nothing is constructed.

"Astral Flight is not the end. It is a direction. It is no use asking 'toward what?' until it has grown strong in you. But it is toward an end that is entirely different from the means."

Or another time,

"It is a stereotype of people interested in Eastern mysticism to talk about past lives. I don't do that often because it too easily passes into imagination, and a way of avoiding what one should do in the present life. But however you look at it, one thing is clear. If your present life is lousy and a past life was better, it means you have screwed up. People who run around telling how they were a queen in ancient Egypt never think about that. If they were a queen then, what are they doing this time in some stupid job with crazy friends?

"There were very few privileged people in past times. Life was hard. Practically everyone had to struggle bitterly for survival. If we remembered past lives we would remember that. It would not tempt us or give us any sense of superiority.

"Nevertheless there is a reality to the past. We have lived hundreds of lives. But our unconscious never sleeps. It will not release these memories from our depths until it judges us worthy to receive them. When this begins to occur it can change our daily experiences in a dramatic way. We begin to understand for the first time not what we are, but what we have been. That is always bound to be a shock and to place a whole new quality on everything we do."

Nothing is ever quite what it seems in relation to other people. That is why it is always better to wait when you feel attracted to someone, particularly in the ashram. What we have in common is only a need to change and grow. That is a lot. It may be, in the end, all that counts. But until we have some sense of the nature and depth of our relationships in the past, it can be ludicrous or dangerous to be too prematurely open with anyone. The person you are smiling at might have been your murderer. The woman toward whom you are attracted could have been your daughter. It needs time to clarify. But be assured that if there is a real basis of attraction, delay will not cause it to disappear. It will be as strong in six months as it is now."

I could relate to what Rudi was saying because I had had such an experience with a woman almost a year before, who had been up to that point only a casual friend. We had been working together. Abruptly, without reason or preparation, I began to feel terribly sad.

"I feel as if someone had died," I said. "As if you had died. I can see myself standing at your funeral. You are quiet, cold, beautiful and dead. You look Chinese. I don't know the relation between us. I might be your husband or your father or perhaps your young lover. I can't really see myself. But I am in mourning."

At that point I had to stop talking. I cried bitterly for about five minutes. It was more than strange, because the woman was sitting with me the whole time. What affected me more than anything else was the feeling that she had come back to me from beyond the grave.

✳ ✳ ✳

As spring turned to early summer, the trip to India seemed to grow dimmer.

"So much is happening right here," Rudi said, "there doesn't seem that much reason to go. Besides, I don't think I'll be able to buy as well in India as I can in the States."

What could I say? I had seen so many plans change again and again that I knew better than to count on anything. The more I wanted the trip, the less likely it would be to occur.

In one of his talks at the time Rudi made a statement that not only constituted an epitaph for Melanie but explained so much in his attitude towards his students.

"Some of you," he said, "think that because you get away with something that you don't pay. You couldn't be more mistaken. I can't always be bothered worrying about whether you tell me the truth. I accept what you say, unless I am forced to do otherwise.

"There is no shortcut in spiritual work. There is no half-way effort. If you cheat me, you cheat yourself. If you lie to me, you lie to yourself. If you think that because I don't say anything, what was wrong becomes right, that's your privilege. But you will pay eventually. If in no other way, it will close the psychic connection between us without you even being aware of it. Your own guilt will do it.

"It is not for me to worry any longer about such things, I am preparing for the future and trying to absorb and assimilate the riches that are opening before me. I am happy to pass them on. But who is there to take them? You are too busy defending yourself and each other to let the truth enter your snug little world."

***

In June, Rudi began talking about presenting work on time and space on the July 4th Weekend. But as the day approached he changed his mind.

"There is no use in my doing it if no one is ready to receive it. I wanted to be able to share the work with all of you, but no one has worked hard enough. I am truly sorry. I will give Astral Flight again in a different form. It will be a chance for those who have started during the last year to receive the experience."

After the July 4th Weekend had passed, Rudi seemed to relax. It was as if he had absorbed the major impact of whatever was unfolding inside him.

"There was so much richness every day," he said, "so much work to be done. How could I think about another trip? I didn't have the energy, and there didn't seem to be any need. But now it's different. I am willing to consider another trip. When do you want to go?"

"I'll arrange it whenever you want," I said, delighted.

"Can you do that? Won't the college be upset?"

Having waited fourteen years for the opportunity, I was not about to let anything stand in the way.

During July and August I taught summer school at Geneseo. When I saw Rudi at Big Indian, he would refer to different aspects of the trip. I had always been curious as to how a man seven hundred years old could still be alive, but I got little information on this point.

"All I have to go by is that I am supposed to meet him along the Ganges or someplace close by. We will just go north from Delhi toward Hardwar, Rishikesh and into the mountains.

"What can I do to prepare other than what I am already doing?" I asked. "Nothing. Just try to open more so that there is a greater space in you to receive the contents of the trip."

"But," I said, "you seem to be going through all kinds of inner preparations. Shouldn't I do some of that?"

"Your trip and my trip are two different things. I am working to attract a great unknown experience. When it occurs I will pass on to you whatever happens to the extent that I can. If I didn't want you to get as much of the direct impact as you could, I wouldn't have invited you to come."

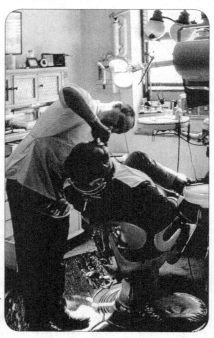

In the dentist's chair: no novocaine

* * *

The rest of the summer was covered by a veil. Perhaps my sense of anticipation put all else in the shade. Rudi certainly did not diminish his pace. He continued to present new ideas and new experiences.

In particular he began teaching a series of deeper psychic cleansing methods for surrendering negative psychic tensions.

"I am giving these methods," said Rudi, "as I work them out. They are coming through to me now because I need them. Before this time it didn't matter too much about the state of my own inner purity. There was so much movement inside that nothing could really poison me. But now I feel a need to grow much quieter. I am cleansing myself to be able to relate to the purity in the ancient man I will meet. Otherwise my chemistry will not adjust to his, and nothing will happen."

Three exercises were given. The first involved absorbing energy through the hands and feet and then releasing it after it had dissolved some of the accumulated psychic poisons of the past. Another consisted of approaching the psychic mechanism as if it were a complex huge toilet that could be completely flushed in one lengthy but simple operation. The third involved opening a valve at the base of the spine to drain the accumulated poison in the spinal cord. Each was very different from the other. All had in common that they worked in depth.

"When you are doing this work," said Rudi, "you must understand that you are not just dealing with the negative tensions of the present. As you use these exercises you will begin to loosen the accumulated debris and poisons of a lifetime and beyond that into past lives. It is hard to overemphasize how important this is."

Over the long Labor Day Weekend he continued to pursue this theme.

"I am giving you this work on inner purification to do while I am away in India," he said to the hundred-and-fifty to two-hundred people who were gathered in the theater. "It will prepare you to receive what I will bring back. If you don't do it, you will not have sufficient purity to connect with me when I return."

"How long should these exercises be done?" someone asked.

"Don't do too much at any one time," said Rudi. "But each time you work the force will begin to break up the poisons that are crystallized. It is like dissolving an ice jam. Sometimes only a little may be released, sometimes a great deal. For most of you it will be a slow and gradual process.

"But one thing you will realize as a result of this work is that you don't know who you are. People who devote a lot of time and money to psychotherapy may learn something about the crap that is in them. But that is not who they are.

"We are all petrified souls lying deep in the earth. If we succeed in breaking down the layers of poison, fear, and paralysis that surround us, we will eventually come to the living being at the center who is probably frozen. Then and only then do we need to decide how to revive him. All the work up until that point has been excavation. None of you can work deeply enough to let the energy get to the center, where it could begin to awaken this being who is really you. Most people spend their life creating conditions around them that make such an awakening impossible, and then wonder why it doesn't happen. It will never happen unless you want it more than anything else. It is not a question of words. The wish must be real, because it will surely be tested. If you say you want it, ten situations will appear to distract you from your desire.

"The difficulty is compounded by the fact that until a person forms some communication with the unknown being buried within him, he really can't know what he wants. If and when you ever get to that point you will cease to take two steps forward, one backward, three sideways, and then lie down and go to sleep. You will know what you need, and you will inwardly continue to pursue it in every situation in which you find yourself.

"Everything in your life is there to show you what you have so far refused to learn. When you begin to look at it in that way then those things you have avoided or thought pointless will reveal their secret. Mostly what they will show you is how stupid and weak you are. It isn't pleasant to see, but it is essential. To build on a weak foundation is the ultimate stupidity. It is bound to come tumbling down on your head sooner or later."

The talk ended with everyone doing one of the new cleansing exercises. Rudi sat quietly watching and looking beyond the scene.

Chapter Thirty-Six

THE GANESH FESTIVAL

Rudi decided to leave during the last week in September. I gathered the necessary money together and bought an airplane ticket. There were four of us in the party besides Rudi — Stuart, the principal teacher in Texas; Buford; Peter (who lived in Paris and was going to work with Buford in setting up a Paris ashram); and myself. Buford was not returning to the states after the trip, but was to fulfill Mr. Thomas' prediction by remaining in France. I was to travel with Stuart directly to Bombay. The others were stopping in several European cities on the way and would meet us there.

I thought I was calm on the day of the flight until I quietly locked my keys in the trunk of my car. I had to call a locksmith to get them out. After that I met Stuart at the New York ashram, and we were driven to the airport by Bruce Rubin who had spent six months in India, and was full of advice. I sat in the back seat and talked my head off, which was a good indication of my excited state. I was usually quiet. At the airport my own anticipation was absorbed by the impersonal shuffling of people and baggage until I was seated in the plane and the motors began to roar.

The flight was endless as the jet raced into the path of the sun. Life became a mixture of meals, movies, accumulated sweat, and the slow passage of time.

Several days later we staggered out into a relatively primitive airport at 5:00 in the morning, exhausted. The ride to the hotel was punctuated by the sight of people living in what looked like abandoned sewer pipes, cows sitting on the road that were reluctant to budge, and then the teeming, human incense smell of Bombay.

When we were briefly held up by a religious festival in the streets, I asked the driver, "What is the occasion?"

"It is the Ganesh Festival," he said, in exotic English. "It will go on

The Ganesh Festival

for the rest of the week. Today is the beginning."

I did not think much of it then, but later a pattern became clear that dominated the time in Bombay. Nityananda had been known as the incarnation of the "elephant God" whose name was Ganesh.

We got to the Taj Mahal Hotel, checked in, went upstairs and collapsed. We were grateful that Rudi and the others were not due until the next day.

When Rudi arrived he immediately began to contact people he knew. Then he proceeded to set a pace for which I was totally unprepared. In New York he was always inwardly busy, but he sat quietly all day long in his store. In India he was constantly running around and slept only three hours a night. This in itself would not have been so extraordinary but the nature of his inner work required a great deal of sleep. He always got at least eight hours in New York as far as I knew, and didn't hesitate to take more if he needed it.

The rest of us were drawn in his wake as he visited shops, friends and psychics. From the start Stuart and I felt we had to make a choice. Either we had to attempt to relate to everything Rudi was doing, or to forget all that and concentrate only on him. We decided on the latter. If he objected we figured he would let us know. So we proceeded to work with him under an extraordinarily diverse set of circumstances — in a store, during a dinner party, at the house of a friend, on the street. India became a stage set as we followed him around. Occasionally when he went away for a short trip, or to a place where he preferred us not to go, we either collapsed gratefully in a hot bath, or visited some of the local stores where the goods were extraordinarily cheap.

But when he was present the atmosphere was never restful. At any moment Rudi might stop what he was doing and start to teach. God forbid if you did not respond immediately.

"What the hell do you think you are doing?" he would say to the offending person who had taken five seconds to loosen his belt and cross his legs in preparation for the class. If the individual were smart he said nothing. But even if he kept his mouth shut, that was not the end of it. Rudi continued relentlessly.

"You are here to work. You have to be ready at any instant. It is for me to worry about all the other people. They have nothing to do with you. Sit up straight and stop feeling sorry for yourself."

※ ※ ※

Before The Sun

Rudi in India on a shopping trip for his store

India was a kaleidoscope. We were being exposed to first-class hotels, a variety of business establishments, or various forms of home life, some simple and others highly luxurious.

Watching him with art dealers filled in a gap in my own understanding of his operation. I had only seen the final results when the shipments arrived in the warehouse in New York. Now I saw him buying the art. I realized the degree of personal relationship that lay behind the commercial transactions.

To one man in particular who specialized in Indian textiles, Rudi talked at great length about beginning to buy folk art. They both agreed that art antiques had become too risky to import.

As part of the visit we were measured for orange shirts and *dhotis* by the dealer's wife. Rudi used these clothes as a teaching uniform for his work.

As we got ready to leave, the dealer placed his car at our disposal. Rudi gave the driver instructions. After ten minutes we stopped in the middle of nowhere and got out. We walked another five minutes to our next destination which turned out to be an antique dealer. It seemed like a striking contradiction to everything Rudi had been saying to the first dealer about the end of importing antiques.

"Why did we have to walk the last five minutes when we had a car?" I asked as we entered the next shop.

"So that the first man wouldn't know where I had gone. When I am with him," said Rudi, "I am interested in folk art. Now that I am here, I am interested in antiques. Keep your mouth shut, and wait in the store." He disappeared behind closed doors.

The next day we returned to the first man to pick up our clothes. We tried them on, had some adjustments made, and left amidst general excitement. Everyone in the garment factory seemed to have stopped work to bid us goodbye. Only Rudi seemed subdued.

When we were outside the front door he began to talk.

"People are so strange. I have known this dealer for several years. He and his wife are a truly beautiful couple. But this time when I saw them together I immediately sensed that something was wrong. Their marriage was dying in front of me. I asked the man about it yesterday in a private moment. He confessed something he had told nobody else, that he thought he was dying of cancer. His wife could sense that something was terribly wrong, but he had kept his fears to himself.

"I worked with him and could sense nothing inside him that corresponded to his fears. I told him that I felt whatever was wrong, it was not serious. He went to a doctor after I left and discovered I was right. He was too frightened to go before, so he put himself and everyone else through hell. Now he is very grateful, but the stupidity of it all. In a few months he might have talked his body into a real cancer, and then it would have been too late."

※ ※ ※

One of Rudi's oldest friends was a man named Mr. Japatti. He had been his personal forecaster at the ashram in Ganeshpuri. Rudi was anxious to see him. I had been hearing about him for ten years.

"When you meet him, John, you may not be very impressed," Rudi said. "He looks like an Indian Alfred E. Newman, but he really works for me."

We went to his house which was probably upper middle class by Indian standards, and yet would have been viewed as a slum dwelling in America. His wife was gracious, insisting we eat authentic Indian food and drink water of unknown origin. The food was super-hot. The water I didn't touch. I ignored all the social amenities, waiting anxiously to hear what Mr. Japatti would say to Rudi. Finally, he began to talk in a low voice that I could hardly follow.

"You have come through a great period," he started.

"I know," said Rudi. "But what should I be working for? What should I expect?"

"It will come like a lightning bolt," said Mr. Japatti. "You will form a cult that will involve millions of people. It is very soon that the change will occur that will make it possible."

Rudi listened to all this quietly. It was nothing less than he expected. I probably also expected it, though I had never projected his life in such terms. Perhaps I hadn't wanted to. It was enough trying to keep up with him from hour to hour as it was.

After two hectic days following Rudi through cross-sections of Indian life, we suddenly had a free day. He was flying up to a Maharajah's palace to look at some art. Stuart and I decided to see the caves at Elephanta, which were about an hour and a half from the hotel by ferry.

During the previous days we had continued to run into signs of the Ganesh Festival, but it wasn't until I was on the small boat, being tossed around with Stuart and a number of Indians who were making the trip, that I realized the connection. The Island of Elephanta was part of the same pattern! It was named for the elephant. As we discovered when we got there, it was dedicated to Shiva, of whom Rudra was an early form.

Elephanta was a tropic paradise, relatively untouched because of its status as a national shrine. The caves were approached by an endless series of stone steps carved into the steep hillside. I had seen pictures of the cave sculptures, but nothing could have prepared me for the reality. The caves themselves were carved out of solid stone. The central portion consisted of a series of pillars that led one inevitably to a shadowy place where they seemed to converge. As you walked toward it, you felt rather than saw that something was there. Moving nearer, a shape looms in the darkness. Then with a shock of recognition you see the colossal three-part head of Shiva, reproduced in every book on Indian art. It is perhaps twenty-feet high and completely dominates everything in sight, God as preserver, creator and destroyer. A photograph could not possibly capture it. It is beyond description. I stood frozen in place. As the shock wore off I explored the rest of the caves. One by one, I came to galleries of superhuman figures. The sculptures

The Ganesh Festival

had a harmony, power, and beauty beyond anything I had ever seen. Their essential quality was that they existed and were more real than I was. It was like looking into heaven and knowing for the first time that it was not a myth.

Eventually Stuart and I tore ourselves away and started down the stairs. We had just missed the boat back to Bombay, and would have to wait an hour and a half for the next one. We had a lukewarm coke and decided to explore the island.

For some time we had been hearing the beating of a drum in the distance. Stuart had to know what it was. We followed the sound down the beach approaching a small, very primitive-looking village. We walked around it, reluctant to enter since we were strangers. A young child appeared and motioned to us to follow him. He led us through the very narrow dirt path that was the street. The houses were mud huts with little or no space between them. He smiled and motioned us on. We followed. No one could be disturbed if two strangers were being led by a child. Eventually we came to a slightly larger building. The child pointed to it. The drums and other sounds were coming from within. The door was open. We entered.

Inside were about twenty people, mostly women and children with a few older men. The women and children were dancing. The men were drumming, someone was playing a primitive flute. Everyone stopped as we entered. Two chairs appeared by magic. We were seated in front of a Ganesh shrine and the dancing resumed. We smiled. They smiled. No one spoke English. We were total strangers. These people were obviously incredibly poor, but we received a total welcome. The room was filled with love and celebration. There was no disharmony, no complexity of modern civilization, though from somewhere two coca colas materialized. Women came and brought us flowers which we passed out to the children. Finally, they marked our foreheads with dye in the traditional Indian caste sign.

It all took about fifteen minutes. It was an enchanted moment out of time, strangely complementary to the Elephanta caves. They were the colossal expression of the height of the Gupta culture. This was the human reality of the celebration for the God.

We left amidst love, smiles, and happiness. It stayed with us all the way home. As we entered the hotel we decided to wipe off the caste marks lest any Indians be offended.

Before The Sun

***

The next day when Rudi returned it was again an endless mixture of stores, friends, social occasions, and work. Squeezed within this continuous treadmill of activities was a visit to several fortune tellers, including Mr. Thomas. My own experience with psychics was extremely limited. I had never been attracted to astrology, palmistry, or any other form of forecasting. I felt a personal distaste for pseudo-science. And in any case Rudi knew all that was necessary to know about me and didn't hesitate to inform me as the need arose. But I began to change my mind when I saw that he took these things seriously. I would not have been in India in the first place if a fortune teller had not told him of a possible meeting with an ancient holy man in the late fall of the year.

I was particularly keyed up to meet Mr. Thomas. Rudi spoke very highly of him as direct, simple, and extraordinarily perceptive. We arranged to have enough time together so that he could give each of us a reading.

Mr. Thomas was certainly not unusual in any obvious way. His manner, surroundings, and approach were almost matter of fact, which in the end only made them more extraordinary.

Rudi went first. Mr. Thomas repeated, almost word for word, some of the things Mr. Japatti had said. He talked of what Rudi had gone through and the extraordinary expansion of his work that was to come. He described the meeting that Rudi was to have on the trip and the importance it would have for his future development.

Stuart came next. He had little interest in predictions of the future. He looked on them as likely to produce more problems than they resolved if they were taken seriously. But his interest grew as Mr. Thomas began to describe certain of his qualities, all of which were essentially correct. Then abruptly he shifted into the future. He said that in six years Stuart would create a great ashram or series of ashrams.

"At the end of that time, it will all be destroyed," he said. "People who you thought were your friends will do it. Nothing will remain. For the next six years your life will be quiet. You will recover to do something greater."

Stuart was not disturbed. He was delighted to be told that he would achieve a great result, have it destroyed, and then after a period, produce something even better.

Buford had already seen Mr. Thomas on the previous trip. This time Mr. Thomas spelled out certain exceptional features of Buford's capacities, and then went into detail about a number of time periods that would prove particularly difficult for him.

Finally it was my turn. I was quite nervous.

"Life has been harder for you than anyone else here," Mr. Thomas began. That sounded very true in one sense, and absurd in another.

"But that is essentially over," he continued. "You will shortly enter a very important period of your life, starting in March through June. A major change may come. It can be a new beginning for you. There will be difficulty with someone close to you from February 15 through the 30th. It will be a rough period.

"During the time from March to June, you may have a possible marriage. You will meet someone whom you will know for four years, name of K. This will be in June. The opportunity to marry will exist until you are forty-nine."

At this point Rudi interrupted. He began to graft onto what Mr. Thomas had said, his version of the heiress who was to come into my life. Mr. Thomas was slightly taken aback, but shook his head in mild agreement. I didn't have the feeling that it was what he had in mind, but Rudi was very persuasive when he wished to be. Finally, Mr. Thomas continued.

"You are rarely appreciated. You are a genius whose ideas are not usually accepted. Only after you leave the scene will people begin to

realize your value."

"That's all right, John," Rudi interrupted again, "you don't give a shit what anyone thinks of you anyway."

That was essentially true. I smiled. Mr. Thomas paused to draw some diagrams, and then added, "You will have name and fame from the age of forty-seven through seventy-one."

"We are all going to have great lives," Rudi interrupted again. "I don't want to be surrounded by nonentities."

"There will be a return of something from the year 1958 into your life," Mr. Thomas continued. "A cycle that began then will be repeated. Someone you knew at the age of twenty-two will also return."

[As it turned out all of the statements that were time-coordinated have proven to be correct. I did have a difficult time with someone close to me at the end of February. The period from March to June was a great new beginning. I did meet K. during this period. We were eventually married for a time. The return of situations and a person I knew from 1958 is embodied in this book. It was the year I met Rudi. The return of a figure I knew at the age of twenty-two occurred with the recent death of Dr. J. L. Moreno, the creator of Psychodrama, with whom I have studied for five years.]

We all left the reading in a slight state of shock, except for Rudi, who took such things in his stride. He immediately began discussing with Stuart ten different ways that the destruction of his work in Texas

The Ganesh Festival

could be avoided six years in the future. Stuart wasn't too enthusiastic. The idea of a *Gotterdammerung* appealed to him.

On the way back to the hotel Rudi said,

"A little psychic reading can go a long way. For most people it only produces a great deal of confusion, even if it is true. You have to be very stable and work hard to take in what was said and not be disturbed by it. What will happen in a year depends on what you do now. If you hear about something wonderful in the future, you subtly begin to believe that it is about to happen or has already happened. Then you stop making the necessary effort. And then it never happens. But Mr. Thomas is very fine. Really remarkable.

"And tomorrow," he said, abruptly changing the subject, "we will get up at 5:30 and visit Ganeshpuri."

I absorbed his words slowly but with mounting excitement. After twelve years I would see the town that Nityananda had created, visit his tomb, and the places where he lived. It would also be the first time that Rudi had been back to Ganeshpuri since he left Swami Muktananda almost a year before.

I went to bed early and was grateful to be able to sleep. The next day had to be extraordinary.

I awoke in darkness to the ringing of a telephone.

"It is 5:30, sir," said a cultivated Indian voice. I grunted and put down the phone. By 5:45 we were all seated in Rudi's room having tea and buns. He had arranged for us to borrow a small station wagon belonging to one of his old Indian friends.

The car arrived at 6:00, complete with driver. We shortly were winding our way out of the maze of Bombay. It was still quiet. The sun was beginning to rise. Sleepy people were moving toward their daily tasks and those few who had been up all night were returning gratefully to their beds. The traffic conditions were relatively good at that hour, so we moved rapidly out of the city. Rudi was quiet. The rest of us took in the scenery and worked inwardly. I had never seen the Indian countryside. It was not particularly inspiring, and it was endless. As we progressed the road slowly deteriorated.

"Another fifteen minutes," said Rudi as we turned onto the worst road yet. The sense of anticipation was growing. I felt totally unprepared.

I asked, "Is there anything we should know before we get there?"

"Just stay close to me. Do what I do. Don't get distracted by anything, and open as deeply as you can to the atmosphere."

And then abruptly we were entering the town. We passed a temple but kept moving. It was Swami Muktananda's ashram. We drove on as far as the road went. Ahead was a marble building. We got out of the station wagon and entered Ganeshpuri. My initial reaction was one of disappointment. It was just another little Indian village. The only thing that set it apart was the number of holy men wandering around, and the stands selling garlands of flowers with pictures of Nityananda, Muktananda, and others. By Western standards it was almost primitive. But that was my prejudice. Nityananda had been indifferent to material values. He had lived his life in a mud hut, slept on a straw mat, and asked for nothing.

We bought some garlands of flowers and approached the building made of white marble. It was Nityananda's samadhi tomb where his ashes were enshrined. We took off our shoes and entered. Immediately I was engulfed by a radiant ringing sound. It was Nityananda's *shakti* filling the room. We approached the tomb, placed the garlands on it, walked around it several times, finally touching our foreheads to the casket holding his ashes. Then we withdrew and worked for perhaps ten minutes with the energy in the room. I could feel the presence, but couldn't really tell what or how much was happening. While I was trying to decide, Rudi, Stuart and Buford moved on. Peter and I rose to follow. They had stopped to buy some more flowers. We stopped also. When we had finished the transaction they had disappeared. Peter and I began to search. We walked down the street into a building that a passerby had pointed out to us. It was some kind of shrine, but Rudi wasn't there. We walked back the way we had come. Suddenly Buford appeared, and motioned us into a little building. It was where Nityananda had lived and taught. We were almost alone. I placed the flowers near Nityananda's bed, bowed down, and worked. It was a very different feeling from the shrine, much stronger and more intimate. Stuart said later, "Nityananda was sitting there on his bed working with us." I couldn't affirm or deny it. But after we left I felt slightly dazed. Rudi decided to relax in the town. We walked down the line of stalls, looking at photographs. Then we entered a crowded cafe to have a cold drink. Immediately people whom Rudi knew approached him.

"In five minutes," he said in a low voice, "Muktananda will know I'm here. I didn't want this to happen, and it will be interesting to see what he does."

We finished our drinks leisurely, found our driver, and slowly proceeded out of town.

As we approached Swami Muktananda's ashram, a figure moved out into the road and flagged down the car. It was an American whom Rudi knew. He had a message from Baba. He would like Rudi to stop and say 'hello'.

"No. I can't," Rudi politely declined.

"Baba has no bad feelings," he persisted.

"I am glad," said Rudi. "Thank Baba for me."

The conversation continued that way for a few minutes. The man was growing frightened. It became evident that he had been told to bring Rudi, or else. Finally, he took hold of his jacket collar.

Rudi looked at him coldly and said, "Please take your hands off me before I slug you."

The man was shocked by his own actions. In one last desperate effort he said, "At least come into the anteroom and look at the new statue of Nityananda we have just had installed."

Much to his and our surprise, Rudi said, "Sure," and proceeded to get out of the car. The man was delighted and went ahead of us to spread the good word.

"What he doesn't know," said Rudi as soon as he was out of earshot, "is that this is all we are going to do. After we see the statue, we leave. Don't look to the left or the right. Just follow me."

We entered. It was a large, partly darkened room. In one end was the figure of Nityananda. It was very impressive. We sat for three or four minutes working with it. Then Rudi got up. We followed him. A number of people had entered the room during that time. We ignored them all and made for the front door. They were too surprised to react. Before they had regrouped, we were back in the car.

The same man came running out. He started talking again. Rudi paid no attention, but nudged the driver, who did not respond. Perhaps he considered Swami Muktananda a great saint whose invitation should not be ignored. Rudi shook him. He hesitated.

"If you don't start this car and get us out of here," he said to him, "we'll dump you and drive ourselves."

That gentle urging seemed to convince him. He started up and we slowly moved away. No one said anything for five minutes. It was such an extraordinary mixture of impressions. Then Rudi began.

"What an incredibly stupid thing for Baba to do! What was he trying to prove, that he has power over me? He should have known better. All he has achieved is to lose face in front of his followers. Why didn't he just leave me alone? I had no desire to hurt him. We just came to pay our respects to Nityananda. Was it an anticlimax, John, after all these years?"

"No," I said, shaking my head mutely.

After a few minutes Rudi began again.

"That is a beautiful statue. I ordered a copy of it six months ago. Maybe when we get back to Bombay we can go see if it's finished."

Again, a few minutes passed. Then the atmosphere subtly changed and Rudi began to work on Stuart, principally using his hands. Stuart very quickly went into convulsions and arched backwards over the edge of the back seat into the baggage section of the station wagon. I turned to be able to face Rudi and absorb what I could, but he concentrated his attention on Stuart for about ten minutes. I looked forward to his finishing with mixed emotions. It was like waiting for a cosmic steamroller to approach. It came. Rudi placed his fingers on my forehead and began to bore inward. I found myself arching upwards over the backseat. Rudi followed me over, working on various chakras. The edge of the seat was quite sharp. But there was nothing I could do. All of the power that Rudi had drawn from contact with Nityananda was demanding to be exerted. When I felt I had more than I could endure it still continued, finally ending only after I had ceased to care.

I slowly settled back in my seat in a dazed condition. Rudi had meanwhile worked briefly with Buford and Peter, and was casually talking to Stuart about the experience at Ganeshpuri. I didn't pay too much attention until I heard my name mentioned. It had something to do with a book. Rudi repeated what he had said.

"I want you to write a book about me, John."

I still didn't quite take it in.

"It would be impossible," I said.

"No," said Rudi, "just write about your experience with me over the years, from your own viewpoint."

Perhaps it could be done, I thought.

"It is very important," he said. "It will teach you how to write, and give you a foundation for the rest of your life."

"If you are telling me to do it, then I will."

"I am telling you," he said. Then he turned to Buford and changed the subject. I knew at that moment that the book would have to be written. The circumstances were extraordinary. Anything said at such a time had to be accepted as binding.

The rest of the trip was intense, but quiet. We got back to the hotel, had an early lunch, and collapsed for a few hours.

※ ※ ※

In the late afternoon, we were off to see the statue of Nityananda which Rudi had commissioned.

The sculptor lived in a relatively small apartment. Almost as soon as we walked through the front door the statue was upon us. It was larger than life-size and overwhelming in power. It filled the living room as we sat down before it. No one said anything for a time. Then Rudi spoke to the sculptor.

"It is a great work of art. We were in Ganeshpuri today. I feel Nityananda as much in this statue as there. It is an extraordinary accomplishment."

We continued to sit silently. It was a totally unexpected climax to the day. Here, hidden in this room in the midst of Bombay, was the elephant God in human form, Ganesh. The pattern was complete.

We left Bombay early the next day for New Delhi. On the way to the airport we asked the driver if the Ganesh Festival was over.

"It ended yesterday," he said.

The statue in the Big Indian Meditation Hall

Chapter Thirty-Seven

NEPALESE INTERLUDE

From Bombay we went to New Delhi where we separated. Rudi went on to Indonesia, Hong Kong and Singapore to search for merchandise. The rest of us decided to go to Nepal. Rudi had never been to Nepal, even though he owned one of the greatest collections of Nepalese Tibetan art in America. He had never found the time. He hadn't even been to the Elephanta caves, though Bombay was his home base in India.

We watched him leave for the airport with mixed feelings. It would be emptier without him, but it would also be a relief from the pace he had set. We made arrangements to depart for Kathmandu, stopping over at Benares, which the Hindus called the "City of Light". As soon as I emerged from of the plane I understood why. The atmosphere was radiant. Everything shone with effulgence that was almost visible.

We spent a hectic day with a guide seeing corpses burning on the shores of the Ganges, visiting the market place and getting stranded in one of the worst traffic jams in the East. This was the India I had expected — exotic, religious, teeming with impressions, incredibly ancient. We met many beggars, a few yogis, and saw some beautiful temples all crowded together. We rode on the Ganges at sunrise, got lost in the winding alleys of the city, and were constantly surrounded by beggars and merchants. But in the end it was the light in the atmosphere that was most impressive. It penetrated everything.

We left Benares and flew on to Kathmandu. The first two days were spent in preliminary sightseeing and arguing about where to go. Buford had heard of a Tibetan monastery located at an elevation of 13,500 feet at the base of Mt. Everest. It was the highest monastery in the world. He wanted to visit it. There was a plane that flew within ten miles. From there you hiked for half a day.

The rest of us were dubious. I had once been up to 12,000 feet and found it very difficult to breathe. Going higher in unknown territory did not appeal to me. I didn't want to end my days on Everest. But Buford was not to be dissuaded. We bid him goodbye, and hoped that he would reappear in four days. It seemed vaguely insane that he should venture off alone on the highest mountain in the world, but no one could stop him.

Stuart and I decided to visit the Himalayan foothills. There was an outstation at about 7,000 feet that could be reached by jeep. Peter somewhat reluctantly came along.

"What is there to do up there?" he asked.

"Nothing," said Stuart. "That's what is so great about it!"

It took two and a half hours in the jeep to go forty-five miles. The road was primitive. But the panorama as we ascended grew progressively more impressive. The outstation was built of wood and concrete in a starkly simple manner. The food consisted of local produce grown on the mountains. It was organic and relatively bland. Peter, who was a gourmet, was less than enthusiastic. After a day or two he returned to Kathmandu. Stuart and I settled in. We started exploring the surrounding area. We discovered a shrine on the top of a small mountain with its own pool where we bathed and meditated.

The longer we stayed in the foothills the more tired we got. We felt like patients coming to a TB sanatorium. By the last day of our stay, we hardly stirred from our rooms. During all that time there was nothing to do but sit, relax and talk.

One day as we were resting on the porch, listening to the wind and wondering what Rudi was doing, Stuart said,

"I lived in the New York ashram for a whole year. Every single day Rudi burned me to the ground. He never missed once."

"What do you mean?"

"He would yell at me, humiliate me, and show me up before others. Everything everyone else did was good. Everything I did was wrong. It was an incredible training. I don't know anyone else who would have cared enough to do it.

"Then one day he said to me, 'Stuart, why don't you go down to Texas for a week or two. Those people I met there when I was traveling with Muktananda need a little help.'

"The next day I was on my way. That was two years ago.

"The last time he came down I asked him, 'Am I on the second week yet?'

"He smiled and said, 'You're getting into the third day.'"

Stuart lapsed back into silence, which was the main quality we shared.

Twice a day we climbed a great hill to observe the Himalayas at sunrise and sunset. The conditions varied but the panorama was always impressive, and sometimes incredible. Distant sounds floated upward — animals, bells, a snatch of some timeless chant. I knew that part of me would always stay in this place. It was a living memory from another lifetime.

Whenever Stuart or I meditated the natives were greatly intrigued. It was surprising to us that meditation seemed to be unknown among these simple, exotic mountain people. Certainly religion played an important part in their lives.

It was with a mixture of boredom and reluctance that we finally left. We were rested and prepared for what was to come. We still had two days to spend in Kathmandu, which proved to be a remarkable city. The artwork was completely unprotected. Priceless statues were mounted in small niches in the wall or on top of courtyard gates. I had never understood how high religious art could architecturally be combined with everyday functions. But here it existed.

Westerners had made unfortunate inroads in Kathmandu. I never met one that didn't make me feel ashamed. But the Nepalese were remarkably beautiful. The men were somewhat delicate for our tastes, but the women were extraordinary. In the West, perhaps one woman in twenty-five is really striking. In Nepal it was every other woman. The mixture of Indian, Chinese, Mongol, and other less identifiable strains produced a breathtaking combination.

On the next to the last day in Kathmandu the festival of the Living Goddess began. It was dedicated to Kali, the feminine goddess of destruction. There were many such festivals in Kathmandu during the year. The streets boiled with people. Everywhere shrines and statues were freshly decorated. The spirit of Kali was in the air, wild and chaotic. Her food was blood. In one huge bronze effigy, her hideous but irresistible face was held on high by priests. Men struggled to drink from the fluid that poured from her mouth like a water spout. There were animal sacrifices. Probably there had been a time when there had been human sacrifices.

※ ※ ※

Nepalese Interlude

The next day we were due to meet Rudi in Delhi. He was flying in from Hong Kong. We had bought a number of art objects which we were a little uncertain about getting through customs, but all went well. We flew back to Delhi on a Royal Nepalese jet, the only one in their air force at the time. It had been christened by sacrificing a goat a few months before.

The period in Nepal was completely self-enclosed. It did not directly relate to Rudi, but we were constantly aware of his presence and knew that when we came together, the climax of the trip would occur.

Chapter Thirty-Eight

MEETING ABOVE THE GANGES

Rudi was jubilant!

"I bought a million dollars' worth of goods for almost no money — fabrics, furnishings, rugs. It was the most remarkable trip I ever made. I just happened to go at the perfect time. A month from now is the international trade fair. The Japanese will buy up everything.

"It was a whole new beginning, particularly in China. India is more or less finished. The new laws require that every piece of art in the country must be registered by its owner. The government can ask him to account for it at any time. Under these conditions smuggling is almost impossible. But when something ends, something else begins. It always works that way for me."

We listened, happy for him and excited at the magnitude of what he had achieved while we were resting in Nepal.

"I brought you each something." He searched through his luggage and brought out various presents. We were surprised, but that was like Rudi. He never returned empty-handed.

Immediate arrangements were made for hiring a driver. The third phase of the trip was about to begin. We were going to travel north from Delhi up the Ganges, ending probably in the foothills of the Himalayas.

That night Rudi asked us about Nepal. We spoke enthusiastically of its exotic mountain beauty. Then Buford told of his time on Everest. He still looked a little shaken.

"They set me down on a landing strip in the middle of nowhere," he began. "The plane carried supplies for the monastery I wanted to visit and for a hotel that is being built nearby. It is supposed to be the highest hotel in the world. They give the guests oxygen tanks at night. I started out in the direction they showed me, but the going was slow. By evening I was alone under the stars. I pitched my tent and spent one of the most ghastly nights I can remember.

"I had altitude sickness. Every muscle in my body was in agony. But the real climax came when I staggered into the monastery the next day. Someone had a tape player going. You know what was playing in the highest monastery in the world? — the Beatles. I was really disgusted. But the setting was incredible. I am glad I went."

I listened, and was glad I hadn't.

After we had talked for a few minutes about what we had seen and the things we had bought in Kathmandu, there was a strained silence.

"What is wrong with all of you?" Rudi said finally.

We didn't know what he was talking about.

"Didn't it occur to any of you to buy me a present?"

"I thought about it," said Peter. "But I decided you already had everything. The last time I gave you something you gave it away."

"What I do with a gift is up to me. But that none of you should have enough humanity or sensitivity to bring me something is really terrible," said Rudi. "Don't you think I need it? Even if I don't, it betrays your total lack of awareness of the situation.

"None of you would be here except for me. If you don't feel this inside yourself, you are completely unworthy to receive anything. I don't care about receiving gifts. I would much rather give than receive. You all know me well enough to be sure of that. But it is absolutely crucial that you should have some sense of gratitude. You owe me. That fact gives me no particular pleasure. You can never repay directly. But you can give love. A gift is a material manifestation of love. Your failure to be aware of that limits you terribly."

Rudi stopped talking. We all slunk out of the room and tried to forget what had happened.

✱ ✱ ✱

The next morning we left at sunrise. None of us knew exactly where we were going or how long we would stay in any particular place, but Rudi was happy to get started. This part of the trip was the nearest thing he was going to have to a vacation. The night before was forgotten as we squeezed ourselves into a typically small Indian car he had hired for the occasion. The trip was endless. Most of it took place before we reached the Ganges. There was nothing to do but watch the endless panorama of Indian villages simmering in the heat.

As the hours unwound, any sense of destination or purpose began to dull. But finally the atmosphere altered, the temperature cooled. The road signs indicated we were nearing Rishikesh, a holy city along the Ganges where many ashrams were located. As soon as we pulled up by the river and left the car we were absorbed by a crowd of Indians intent on religious purposes. There were stalls selling beads, pictures, and various other religious articles. Rudi walked along the boardwalk. We followed. Nothing happened except that we were continuously approached by various beggars and tradesmen. We ignored them all and kept on moving.

Finally Rudi stopped to buy some malas. He sent Buford to buy more.

"All of you get some. I will bless them in the Ganges."

I had waited until last and had a hard time finding any. The nearby stalls were sold out. I had to wander several blocks away. When I returned I discovered that everyone had undressed and entered the Ganges in my absence. I quickly followed. Our nude bodies attracted considerable attention. Whether it was friendly or not was hard to tell, so we ignored it. After a few minutes the curiosity seekers began to disperse.

The water of the Ganges was remarkable. I had heard of its unusual properties and knew it was considered holy by the Hindus. I quickly discovered why. In the coldness of the rapidly moving water was an extraordinary vitality that went through one's body like psychic champagne. I gave the ten malas I had bought to Rudi. He touched them to his forehead to transmit his shakti to them and then dunked them in the river for a few seconds. As he handed them back to me, he said,

"These malas should only be given to future teachers. It has cost me too much to do anything less with them."

"But I'm not likely to train ten teachers," I said.

"You'll see, John. But even if it takes you ten years, what is the difference?"

We emerged from the river, cold and totally invigorated. We dressed and started to walk slowly back to the car the way we had come. Rudi would occasionally wander off, but very shortly return. It was about three in the afternoon. We got in the car and headed toward Hardwar, an hour away. Rudi was eager to visit the Divine Light Mission, the ashram of the late Swami Sivananda. The current director was a good friend. He felt he might be an important connection in

his quest for the ancient saint. We arrived. The Swami had left the day before. He was not going to return for three weeks. We stayed a half hour, sat briefly in Swami Sivananda's room, and departed.

"Sivananda was one of the last of the generations of truly great yogis to which Nityananda belonged. They died almost at the same time," said Rudi.

As we drove away the atmosphere in Sivananda's room continued to surround me with a sense of radiant awareness.

We drove on until we came to an arched bridge across the Ganges where we saw an extraordinary sight. Arranged in a curving line from one side of the bridge to the other was an incredible assortment of beggars. They all stood there waiting. Rudi took one look and said,

"It looks like the casting office for *El Topo*."

I didn't know what he meant at the time, but learned later that the movie *El Topo* dealt with every known form of human decay and deprivation. He approached the beginning of the line. An old beggar woman walked forward hopefully. Rudi smiled at her and said, "Do you take MasterCard, baby?" Fortunately she didn't understand any English. Rudi's attitude toward beggars was not sentimental. But at the same time he had Buford distribute some small change down the line.

We walked across the bridge to the other side of the river, looked around, bought a few trinkets and left. There were many beautiful temples, but none that we were seeking. We got back in the car. It seemed to be a temporary dead end.

"Let's go on to Mussoorie," said Rudi. "We can still get there by nightfall. It would be great to sleep in the mountains."

It was another two or three hours' drive. We settled back uncertain as to what, if anything was happening. As we came to the beginning of the foothills, Buford and Peter spoke of a Tibetan temple school they wanted to visit. We inquired and found that it was on the way, so Rudi agreed to seek it out.

When we finally arrived our reception was mildly ambivalent. The main teacher was busy. If we wished to see him we were told to come back the next day. Rudi shrugged his shoulders and began to play with the many Tibetan children who attended the school. In five minutes he was surrounded by thirty of them who were enchanted by his smiles, belly-blowing and ear wiggling. We left, followed by their enthusiastic calls and waving.

"Well that was a big nothing," said Rudi, sarcastically. "I guess they must be used to people from America, so they don't bother disturbing themselves. What fools!"

"Can we go back tomorrow?" asked Buford.

"We'll see. On to Mussoorie!" said Rudi.

The remainder of the trip was uphill on a winding mountain road.

The weather was clear and the temperature of the air cooled as we climbed higher. Nothing had happened, but it felt wonderful to be leaving the tropical plains behind.

We arrived as the sun was waning. A slight mist was rising from the valley, but the sky was clear. The hotel was marvelous — a great rambling structure obviously built for the English, and more or less kept up by the Indians. It was the off-season. There were only three other guests in the whole place. We settled into two large rooms with fireplaces, quaint baths and surrounded by well-trained servants who asked only to serve.

Rudi said to Stuart and me, "Get settled and then come back. We'll take a walk into town."

* * *

It was about 5:30 when we returned to Rudi's room. He was sitting on a couch and had started to work with Buford and Peter. We quietly sat down and joined the class. I could hear the gentle mountain wind and smell the pines around us. It was with a great sense of inner surrender that I happily sat in this old hotel room high in the Himalayan foothills, absorbing the force coming from Rudi. The air was highly charged, but that seemed natural. The setting alone could account for it.

Gradually it became obvious that something unusual was happening. Rudi was in great pain, or appeared to be. He started moaning and crying as I had never seen him do before. I watched, trying not to get emotionally involved while at the same time opening to whatever was happening. Perhaps it was only his own sense of disappointment. But this was just the first day. We had a whole week in which to search. If necessary we could go to the origin of the Ganges by jeep.

Rudi continued to be wracked by terrible suffering. I didn't doubt that he could come through anything, and would continue to work with us unless it temporarily became too much for him. But what was happening? Was he being attacked by some invisible being? Was he undergoing some kind of terrible spiritual birth pangs? The process continued for perhaps ten minutes.

When it receded he motioned to us to sit in front of him one at a time. He worked with us using his eyes and hands. Each of us in turn was set off into wild convulsions. It was completely overpowering, as if a dam had been suddenly broken and the vast water pressure released. When I finally got up off the floor where I had fallen, Rudi was sitting quietly with his eyes closed as if nothing had happened. We all sat for another few minutes. Then he said,

"Let's walk into the town, but stay very quiet."

We put on our coats. It was getting chilly. The town was quaint, exotic, completely out of the world. But we paid little attention to it just then.

I finally asked, "What happened? Are you all right?"

"Ask me tomorrow," Rudi said. Shortly thereafter we returned to the hotel and all slept well.

The next day Rudi looked very strange. That is, he looked like himself and someone else. It was hard to define.

"Can I ask you now?" I said.

"Yes," he began. "As I was working, a great human head of a very, very ancient holy man materialized near the ceiling. I worked intensely to bring it closer. Finally it came into me. Did any of you see it?" Rudi asked. No one spoke.

* * *

As the day wore on, we explored the town and decided to drive down the mountain to the Tibetan school. This time we saw the principal Rinpoche (teacher) who was quite high in the Tibetan hierarchy. He complimented Rudi on the discipline of his students as we all stared at him with concentration, attempting to draw out of him every bit of energy we could find. He had probably never been subjected to that kind of treatment before. Rudi and the Rinpoche talked for a time. Then the Rinpoche excused himself. He had to go to his meditation. We filed out. As we walked down the stairs Rudi said,

"The only thing he had to do was eat lunch. I saw them preparing it. It is really disgusting. He has no sense of what we are or our openness to him. He really doesn't care."

An assistant asked if we would like to visit the temple. We agreed. We sat there for a few minutes. Then Rudi rose, went forward, and left money in the offering box. We followed. Outside, every child in the place had somehow heard of Rudi's return. They were jumping up and down and shouting around him. It was a beautiful sight. As we drove away they were all going crazy.

"Where I was sitting in the temple," Rudi said sarcastically, "I noticed that we were being watched through a peephole in the ceiling. I left a hundred-rupee note in the offering box. I wanted to give them something to think about. Maybe the next time they won't take visitors so casually. I could have really helped that man expand his work if he had shown the slightest openness to me. Everyone is so intent in defending their own little pile of shit that life just goes right by them."

※ ※ ※

We returned to the hotel and had supper. Then we reassembled in Rudi's room. There was a fire crackling. The air was very cool. He began to work for a few minutes. Then he paused and announced,

"We will go back to Delhi tomorrow. I have told the driver."

I did a double-take inside. Had I missed something?

"What I came for has already happened," he continued. "There is no reason to stay."

I was slightly flabbergasted, but it was just like Rudi. The climax could come in a flicker of an eyelash. If you were looking elsewhere at the time, you missed it.

"I expected to meet a living person who was seven hundred years old," he said. "I looked. I waited. It never occurred to me until the experience began that it might be with the soul of someone who had died that long ago. The experience has been continuing all day. He comes in and moves out, comes in and moves out. Now he has begun to settle in me. My whole chemistry is completely disturbed. I have never been in this condition. It is tearing me apart, but I am deeply grateful. It represents a quantity above and beyond anything I have known before. I don't know where it will lead but I am certain it is the beginning of a totally new phase in my growth.

"But what really shocks me is that with all the Indian holy men devoting their lives to spiritual work, such a being should come to rest in me. I am not saying I am something great. I am what I am. But it doesn't say much for everyone else. I have just worked harder than anyone and am inwardly prepared for the fantastic jolt that such an experience produces."

Rudi was quiet for a time. Then he smiled at Buford and Stuart.

"Can you see it now?" he asked.

They nodded their heads 'yes'.

I did not expect to see it. I never saw anything, not even an aura.

"I am deeply happy to share this experience," said Rudi. "I could never go through the pain and effort that is necessary if I were doing it just for myself. It is too endless and brutal. It is my love for you that makes it possible for us to be together at the beginning of the next phase of our work."

I sat looking at Rudi with tears rolling down my cheeks. There was no weighing this man.

We left in a very subdued state. We drove back to Delhi without stopping, except for lunch.

* * *

That night Rudi decided to go to the movies. We hadn't done anything like that since arriving in India. He chose *The House of Dracula*. He always loved a good horror movie.

"Indians are movie addicts," he said. "They would rather not eat than give up the movies."

We got to the theater and discovered the truth of the statement. There were no tickets available. We were approached by a scalper. Rudi told me to buy the tickets from him. They were two and a half times the proper cost. We went inside and discovered that the tickets were not together. But the usher assured us that he could fix us up for a price. We waited around for half an hour in the lobby. Finally he reappeared asking about twice as much as the tickets had cost from the scalper. We were seated in time to enjoy the last two-thirds of the movie. It was a strange story under the circumstances. The Dracula theme of draining the blood of the living in order to achieve immortality was a sinister counterpoint to the whole experience Rudi was undergoing, but he enjoyed such strong contrasts.

As the climax of the movie approached, Rudi passed the word.

"When I say leave, we all leave. No questions."

Buford began to object.

"If you don't want to come," said Rudi, "you can find your own way home."

Five minutes later, when all the forces of good were about to descend on Dracula, Rudi said, "Now!" in a loud whisper. We all rose, Buford was obviously reluctant. Rudi grabbed him by the arm. We dashed out of the theater and hailed the first available taxi. Once inside, Rudi expressed himself.

"When I say 'move', move! You don't have to understand why. But I'll explain it. There is a law in India, everyone must stand at attention when they play the national anthem. If you sit or leave they can throw you in jail. The split second after they finish the movie the national anthem comes on the screen. Everyone has to wait while it plays, and then everyone leaves the theater at the same moment. The chances of our getting a taxi would be nonexistent. Maybe some of you feel like walking, I can't. I am in a very delicate condition. You have to accept the fact that when I say something, there is a good reason. I can't stand the tension right now of four different people each with their own opinions." We traveled back to the hotel in an unsettled silence.

The next day Rudi announced that he was going back to Bombay to conduct some business and to see Mr. Thomas. He suggested that Stuart and I stay in Delhi to rest up. We agreed, since that was obviously what he wanted us to do. We were going home in two and a half days in any case.

✳ ✳ ✳

On that last day Rudi took us apart, one at a time. First he spoke to Buford privately. When he came down to the pool edge where Stuart and I were relaxing, he said,

"I just gave Buford something to think about." We were silent.

"He is going to Paris at the end of the trip. I showed him how many opportunities he has thrown away, and how disgusting it is to have the ability to grow spiritually and not use it! I think he got the message. He was crying when I left."

Then Rudi started on Stuart. I listened, trying to be very inconspicuous. He criticized him for his egotism, for his not wanting to take from Rudi, but preferring to run his own show in Texas. He was completely merciless. Stuart sat there stony-faced until he finally began to break down and cry.

"And when I come down to visit," Rudi concluded, "I want to feel that I am truly welcomed and deeply loved, not some visiting power you have to tolerate." Stuart weakly protested. Rudi subsided. Then after a pause he turned to me.

"Don't sit there feeling superior, John. You have thrown away more opportunities than anyone else. The fact that you were too crippled at the time to benefit from them is not greatly to your credit. You leave death behind you wherever you go. That has to change. It doesn't matter whether I can accept it. You cannot afford to accept it any more. When you return I want you to start an ashram in Livonia. It is crucial. Then when you leave Geneseo something living can remain behind you for once."

"How about the book?" I asked. "Do you still want me to write it?"

"If you want to have a life," said Rudi, "then write it! Personally I don't care. There have been plenty of people eager to write books, articles, do interviews with me. I have always discouraged it. I have postponed fame as long as I could. It is better to delay something so that the foundation is strengthened, and one is mature enough to endure it. I want you to write the book for your sake, John, not mine."

"How have you ever put up with me all these years, Rudi?" I asked hesitantly.

He just looked through me. "It doesn't matter, John. The past doesn't matter. All that counts is that somehow you have survived. That is the test of time. I love you very much, John."

That did it. I was completely demolished.

Later in the day I ran across Stuart outside the florist shop.

"What are you doing here?" I asked.

"I was paying for some flowers I sent to Rudi. I wrote to thank him for what he said to me and to tell him that I loved him. I was just up in the room. He didn't say anything, but he had them in a vase. I asked him why he said that he wasn't welcomed in Texas. I really couldn't understand that. You know what he answered? He said, 'That was a great line, wasn't it?' I didn't know whether to slug him or hug him. It was like that for a whole year when I lived in New York. He just tears me to shreds."

The next day Rudi, Buford, and Peter departed. Stuart and I remained resting and growing bored by the pool. We were both eager to return to America when we finally got on the plane at four in the morning and entered the twilight land of jet travel.

Chapter Thirty-Nine

AFTERMATH

On my next visit to the city after returning home to Geneseo, Rudi filled in the missing pieces of the trip.

"I went to Mr. Thomas as soon as we returned to Bombay," he began. "He asked just when the experience with the ancient saint had occurred. Then he disappeared into his books for a while. Finally he said, 'It is remarkable that you could see what happened. It was extremely subtle. It marks the beginning of a great new cycle in your inner development. It will be a three-part experience. Each part will be clearer and stronger than the next. The second phase should be around your birthday. The third should occur in early spring.'

"Then he told me certain things about the future, which time will tell. But at the end he gave me a remarkable mantra. You know that I have never been very interested in anything like that. But this was quite different. As soon as I began to use it my head started to split open. It has been driving me crazy. But it is the first time that I have ever received anything spiritual without having to pay a great price. I hope that it is a symbol of how things will come to me in the future.

* * *

"About that time, Rudi gave a talk in Big Indian about his possible future departure from the United States, for the Middle East or elsewhere.

"I may go away," he said. "It could happen by boat or train or plane. If I go, you will be on your own. You should prepare yourself. Don't assume I will always be here to tell you what to do and straighten out every problem that arises. If I were gone you would find out what you have really learned. You don't own anything unless you are able to hold onto it."

Aftermath

* * *

When I was next in the city, I went to the store on Saturday morning. It was relatively deserted. Rudi appeared to be sitting quietly but from the first moment I felt that something was radically different. I sat for perhaps fifteen minutes trying to relate to him in the familiar way, but I couldn't connect. He was there, but he wasn't there.

Finally I asked, "Am I crazy or is something totally new going on?" Rudi smiled abstractly and said, "You're not crazy. I am working in time and space."

As soon as he said the words I resolved that this was a form of work that I must learn. Hesitantly I asked, "When are you going to begin to teach it?"

"Probably on the July 4th weekend," he said. "Maybe I will begin with a few people next spring. If you want it, John, prepare yourself. Work harder and more seriously than you ever have before. How is the ashram coming?"

"I am getting the house ready. The ashram should come into existence early next year."

"Fine. How about the book?"

"I'm thinking about it."

"Great. But do it!"

I shook my head in assent.

"I have found a publisher for my own book," said Rudi. "I thought of a great title."

"What's that?" I asked, thinking that nothing would surprise me.

Spiritual Cannibalism!

"That should get plenty of attention," I said.

Rudi just smiled.

Throughout this conversation the extraordinary quality in the atmosphere persisted. It fit in with my impression that Rudi was able to be completely normal and still not be there at all. Finally he stopped whatever he had been doing, and shortly thereafter I left.

* * *

November and December were relatively quiet. Rudi used the time to allow the crucial experience he had undergone in India to settle in him more deeply and to prepare himself for a stronger onslaught on or around his birthday.

I continued to visit regularly. Rudi always had something new to tell me.

"I was looking at Sam's head the other day while he was mopping the floor," he said. "I would never have believed it, but the whole shape is different than it used to be. If he can change anyone can. It gives me a great feeling of satisfaction to see some concrete results in other people.

"Speaking of heads, I am having Barry Kaplan photograph my own head every few weeks to document the changes that are occurring. One of my friends who is an expert in Eastern art and mysticism suggested it. I don't know how it will turn out but some of the pictures are really interesting. You can see different channels in the brain, shapes on my forehead, and a snake emerging from my neck. Remind me to show some of them to you next time."

"Don't worry. I will."

"Oh," said Rudi, smiling, "you will enjoy this. Alan Watts came into the store the other day. Someone must have told him about me. He looked around for a while and then we talked in between customers. The more I talked the more excited he got, which was all right, up to a point. But then he started to tell me how he could make me famous. That was when I stopped talking. But he didn't understand and only carried on more strongly about all he could do for me. I finally interjected that the main thing he could do was leave my store. He didn't like that very much. In the end I had to physically push him out the door. I don't need anyone to make me famous. I want to delay fame as long as possible. But I guess you know that."

Rudi paused to drink some coffee and cut two slices of fresh pineapple that someone had airmailed him from Hawaii. He handed me one and said, "I was at a party last week. During the main course the woman on my right asked the hostess whether she had put anything in the food. The hostess was puzzled.

"'You mean like special seasoning?' she asked.

"'No,' said the woman, 'like LSD.'

"At that point I realized the woman must be feeling the effects of sitting next to me. But I didn't think she would believe it if I told her, so I kept my mouth shut."

We both laughed and enjoyed the marvelous taste of the fresh pineapple. Then Rudi resumed.

Aftermath

Courtesy Barry Kaplan

"The other day an elderly black man came into the store. I didn't pay much attention to him. He looked around for a time. Then I noticed that he was crying. I asked him if anything was the matter. He said, 'No.' He was just very happy. He had seen my face in a dream. He felt there was a deep connection between us.

"It is probably true, but it doesn't excite me. I have had many such encounters. They can last an hour, a day, or a year. You can't tell anything from the initial reaction. What counts is whether it goes anywhere. I may never see him again, or if I do he may not really want to work. It is not in my hands. I can only surrender and wait.

"In the last few weeks I have been seeing people who belong to different periods in history walking the streets of New York. You can't imagine how weird it is to look out your window and see a knight in armor followed by a Roman in a toga. However I am getting used to it. You can get used to anything.

"When we were in India one of the psychics said I would have financial difficulty in this period. He was right. But it is not affecting me in any way. Five years ago I would have been upset. Now I can't afford to waste my energy on anything like that. I surrender, open, and realize the richness around me. I am the wealthiest poor man I know."

* * *

During that period Rudi and I took a walk in the East Village, He liked to get out of the store for ten or fifteen minutes to help break up his day. As we proceeded across Fourth Avenue, he said, "What are you doing inside, John?"

"Nothing in particular."

"That's what I thought," he said with a disgusted shake of his head.

"You are wasting the opportunity. How many chances do we have to walk together these days without a hundred other things going on?"

That was true. The last time I had walked with him he was so busy that I had to wait thirty minutes before I could ask him a simple question.

"What should I be doing?" I asked.

"First of all absorb energy through the top of your head. The lotus chakra can receive energy that comes from above. Bring it down into your heart and circulate it from there. And then let your hands hang down and keep your fingers open so that you can drop negative psychic tension at the same time."

"Is that what you do when you walk?"

"Sure. Do you think I am just killing time?"

I tried out what he suggested and immediately discovered that it worked. It made me feel pretty stupid.

"Can I ask you something else?"

"Anything you want," said Rudi.

"When you are talking to people in class you sometimes tell them their heart isn't open, or they are not functioning somewhere else.

How do you know?"

"It is very simple. I open my heart, then I psychically contact their heart. If they are closed the echo comes back to me like a dull thud. If their heart is open there is an immediate flow between us. Try it. It works."

I took a breath into my chest and began to feel my heart center expand. Then I went to sense Rudi's heart. The impact was immediate.

"It is so simple when you know what to do," I said.

"Like most things it is just doing them that is difficult," he said.

We were almost back to the store.

"How about psychic operations that you sometimes perform. Are those easy too?" I asked as I warmed to the opportunity.

"You'd be surprised," said Rudi, opening the front door to his store, "but that is enough for now. Ask me again some other time." The walk was over.

※ ※ ※

At the end of December I attended the usual Christmas party. It was quiet, warm, and peaceful. There was the deepest sense of fulfillment in the room of any such time I could remember. I felt thankful just to be present.

On the 30th of December I happened to stop at the store. Rudi said "hello," and motioned me to a chair. He didn't mind if I sat there as long as I blended into the background and kept quiet.

When he had a moment he came over and said,

"Nityananda's statue has arrived. I have it upstairs in my room. It is even more extraordinary than I thought. His spirit lives in the statue. I have tried working with it for a few minutes at a time. That is about all I can take. No one else has even seen it yet. In the future, I can visualize it being used as an initiation piece, helping to give hundreds and thousands of people the initial contact with the energy with which we work. It is really extraordinary."

At this moment a striking young man came in. I later learned his name was Tom. Rudi went over to talk to him.

I was not part of the conversation, but I was seated nearby where I couldn't help overhearing it.

"It is part of my nature to need someone close to me," Rudi said.

Tom nodded his head in silent understanding.

"There are riches in me no one has touched. It is just a question of whether you are willing to work.

"I want to work," said Tom.

"Each day you have to demand a fresh result and go beyond anything you did the day before," said Rudi.

Tom didn't flinch.

"There is so much going on inside that I have to give. There are thousands of souls in my being. There hasn't been anything like me on the earth in the last ten thousand years."

The last sentence froze me. I was perfectly willing to accept it.

At the same time I knew that most people would think such a statement was insane. I had never heard Rudi say anything like that before. I knew that I was in no position to evaluate it, nor in any position to really doubt it.

So I kept my peace.

Chapter Forty

SECURITY IN THE FUTURE

I returned to Geneseo to work on the development of the ashram. I had been giving classes in Kundalini yoga for several years. Many students had come and most had gone. But there had never been any attempt on my part to establish a school where a central core of people lived and worked together. I started working toward that objective in November. The situation finally crystallized in the middle of January. I gave classes every morning and evening, and experienced for the first time the feeling of being responsible for and living with people, all of whom shared the same basic aim. Then on January 24th I went to the city for Rudi's forty-fifth birthday party.

As a birthday present I had my lawyer prepare incorporation papers for the Shree Gurudev Rudrananda Yogashram, Inc. It was Rudi's non-profit corporation for his work in New York City and Big Indian. He hated legalities, but both situations were getting too complex to be anyone's personal property.

There were fewer people and less outward show for this birthday than the previous one. But the sense of achievement, closeness, and love was if anything fuller as we gathered together in the aura of our teacher whom none of us could really fathom.

"For the first time in my life," Rudi said, "I am out of danger. All along I have been following an unknown treacherous path with psychic enemies trying to attack me. That is over. I may still have to go through great trials, but there is nothing that has the power to stand in the way.

"The last year has been the greatest in my life, but my position wasn't stabilized. With this birthday, my foundation is secure."

As Rudi talked, his words were mirrored in the faces of his students which shone with happiness and gratitude. Everywhere was a sense of ripening in midwinter.

"I am having the second part of the experience that began in India,"

Rudi continued. "It is still growing and settling in me. I didn't realize its significance at the time. Everything I have done before is a prelude. What more wonderful realization could I have at this time."

※ ※ ※

The next day I stopped at the store. Rudi was sitting quietly working and waiting for whoever might walk through the door. Finally he said,

"A new channel has been opening in my temples during the last month. For weeks I felt like there were two oil drills coming in from either side of my head. Finally they met and the pressure eased.

"Last week Danny Cook was in from Texas. Even though I felt pretty strange, I worked with him. Gradually everything began to darken. It was as if the whole room was filling with black ink. But I didn't stop working. Then suddenly from a vast distance a blue light cut through the darkness. It slowly approached me and eventually connected with this new channel in my head. I have read of blue cosmic energy and seen it in pictures of Krishna and Buddha, but I thought it was just symbolic. Now I understand it is very real."

At this moment Tom came into the store. And as he saw him Rudi said, "Tom has been going crazy. He is around me so much that the channel has begun to open in him too."

I looked at Tom more closely. He seemed in pain and somewhat disoriented. While I was talking with Rudi he didn't say anything, but when he thought I was leaving he said, "Isn't there anything I can do for the pain?"

"Yes," said Rudi. "Be grateful!"

Tom shrugged and left. It probably hurt more when he was around Rudi.

"I no longer feel that I am going to the Near East," Rudi continued after a sigh. "I have grown so fast in the last few months that it has made a great bridge to fill in the void I needed to cross. There are so many new people now, and such activity going on inside me that nothing else is necessary. The Near East is right here."

Rudi paused again.

"I don't know if I mentioned it but the leading Tibetan historian from Germany has been visiting the ashram for the last week. He has studied with three or four Tibetan Lamas in the past, but he has been keeping his distance from me until he makes up his mind about my capabilities.

"Yesterday I worked with him for the first time. He has a remarkable inner quality. All I could see were a series of great doorways slowly opening, one after another.

There was another pause as Rudi put his hand on his head and rubbed it gently.

"You often hear people talk about the thousand-petaled lotus in spiritual work. In Kundalini yoga we treat it as the reservoir of the refined spiritual force. Once or twice I have heard people mention the ten-thousand petal lotus, but I never knew what they were talking about until a few days ago. Now I understand because the whole top of my head is beginning to open like one gigantic flower. I can feel it separating petal by petal. Each time I circulate the force and bring it up my spine, I draw the energy to the next petal and help it open."

Courtesy John Mann

He lapsed into silence again. Then he raised his arm, smiled and said, "Have you seen these Tibetan paintings?"

He pointed over to a vase holding several thangkas.

"I don't think so." I walked over and unrolled the largest one. It was a great picture of a thousand-armed figure, Avalokiteśvara.

"I had that upstairs in the house for a long time. Do you like it?"
"Of course. It's great."
There was a reluctant pause. I owed Rudi $20,000 at the time.
"I'd ask how much it is," I said, "but I can't buy anything more."
"It's $3,000. If you want it you can have it."
"But what about all I owe you?"

"That is the past. This is for what your life is going to become."

I stood there looking at the beauty of the image, feeling wonder and gratitude.

"Have you seen the Chinese tapestries I just got in?"

"No. Should I?"

"If you want to."

"Sure."

We went to the back. There were six huge, gorgeous dragon tapestries, hand-sewn and embroidered.

"They're incredible. I have never had anything like them," I said.

"I picked them up in an estate a few weeks ago."

"They must cost a fortune."

"No."

"How much?"

"I'll sell all six to you for $2,000."

I was staggered. I assumed that they were each worth that much.

"I got a bargain. I want you to have them. They will be in the Institute you form. All the art you have bought will be there. It will be wonderful. I can't wait to help you decorate it."

"Is this charged to the new account too?"

"Sure," said Rudi, starting to wrap up these latest treasures.

I left in a daze of gratitude to get my car and carry away my ransom to the future.

* * *

The next day I stopped at the store at about three in the afternoon.

We talked casually. Then Rudi asked me to get something from the house. On the way I met another student who asked, "Are you going to the concert?"

"What concert?"

"The one Rudi is going to."

"It's the first I heard about it."

I returned to the store. About 4:00 Rudi started to leave. He usually stayed open until 6:00.

"Where are you going now?" he asked me, "To your parents?"

"I guess so. Isn't there a class tonight?"

"No. I am going to a concert." As an apparent afterthought he asked, "Are you free to come?"

"Sure," I said. I was thankful to be included. If I hadn't known about it before I might have just left the store before he had invited me.

There were about twelve people waiting for transportation outside the store. Rudi motioned me into the car he was taking. Michael Shoemaker was visiting from Indiana. He and I were in the back. Rudi and Tom were in the front, along with Norman, who was driving. We headed toward Westchester to pick up Norman's wife.

Rudi talked for a time with Norman and Tom. He asked Michael some questions about Bloomington. Then he began to work with us as he had in the station wagon in India coming back from Ganeshpuri. He came to me last. He simply took my hand in his. It contained an incredibly strong force. I didn't want to let go, but it was like holding lightning.

When it was over I closed my eyes and settled back to absorb the aftereffects. Rudi began talking to Tom and Michael.

"When should we go? I was thinking of late June."

At first I didn't pay much attention, but it slowly dawned on me that he was talking about his next trip to India. Evidently Tom and Michael were going.

It was the first I had heard of it. Rudi talked on. Abruptly he turned his attention to me.

"Would you be free, John?"

"I'll make myself free," I said.

"You don't have to do that," he said, "Just tell me when is good for you and we'll go then."

A moment before I was overhearing plans in which I had no part. Now I was included and the departure time was to be arranged at my convenience.

The effects of the work and the invitation welled up in me. I started to cry. Rudi took my hand again and smiled.

"You are included in my future, John."

I cried some more. So many years of watching and waiting! So much time spent in half-hearted attempts to start moving, with so little result! All that seemed behind me. I cried for what I had been. I felt it return and fall away.

"No matter how many times the work has changed," said Rudi, "you have managed to change with it. That alone entitles you to a place. You have always felt insecure. I understand that. It has kept you moving. You are going to have to work harder and harder. But the place is yours. You have survived everything."

I settled back again, feeling a sense of great spreading happiness as the car moved on into the country.

Courtesy Dean Gitter

Chapter Forty-One

RUDI'S WORK

The following day, January 27th, Rudi asked me to drive him to the airport. He was going to visit various Texas ashrams. I had never driven Rudi to the airport alone. It was a special treat for me. I relaxed and decided to enjoy it, but that wasn't so easy. The traffic on Fourth Avenue was heavy, and the drivers unpredictable. I said to Rudi,

"I guess I don't have to worry with you along. Nothing could happen."

He smiled. "Nothing can happen to me," he said, "but that doesn't mean that someone might not hit your side of the car. Don't take anything for granted."

I was slightly dismayed, but I still felt protected. As we proceeded on the traffic began to thin, and Rudi said,

"I have been thinking some more about the Institute you are going to establish. I always assumed that it would have nothing to do with the ashrams. But last week I began to see how the two are connected."

"What do you mean?" I asked, intrigued.

"They can help each other. Certainly the Institute can help the ashrams. I'll talk to you some more about it another time. It is still forming in my mind. But I can't wait until you meet the heiress, and it all begins to become a reality."

I listened to him as I had done in the past, interested, but not terribly excited.

"Maybe there is something wrong with me," I said, "but I don't get bent out of shape in anticipation."

"That's all right," said Rudi. "You shouldn't live in the future. And maybe you find the thought of a permanent relationship a little scary. You won't be able to screw around once you meet her. She wouldn't stand for it."

"I know."

"And you can't assume that she will just appear and tap you on the shoulder and say, 'Here I am!'. You should circulate more. You could be in the same room and never meet if you aren't reaching out."

"Okay," I said. "I will."

There was a pause. Rudi looked at me keenly.

"Besides," he said, "after ten years she will die and leave you everything. Then you can do what you please for the rest of your life."

I started to laugh, slightly hysterically. When I got control of myself I said, "It's lucky there was no traffic when you said that, or I would have hit someone."

"I made sure there wasn't before I said anything."

"You weren't kidding, were you?" I asked, still bewildered.

"Of course not, I just never mentioned it before."

We both settled into silence, and not long thereafter arrived at the airport. Rudi grabbed his bags and jumped out of the car. My last glimpse of him was as he turned in the doorway of the terminal and waved goodbye. I drove slowly back to Manhattan, still digesting his words. He was leading me into, and freeing me from, the future simultaneously.

✳ ✳ ✳

Rudi settled down for the long flight to Dallas.

There were many different people waiting for him at the airport there. He worked during the flight to be ready for all of them, sensing the difference in their individual needs.

When he arrived a lecture was scheduled almost immediately. He raced to the auditorium and went to the washroom, washed his hands and face, and changed into a bright orange robe. Many of the members of the audience were prisoners from a local penitentiary. As Rudi glanced in the washroom mirror, his attention was caught by a blonde man with striking eyes. There instantly passed from him to this man a wave of energy, and Rudi felt his heart open. The man was probably a prisoner, but he recognized a karmic connection between them from the past which helped him prepare himself for the talk that was to come.

Most speakers present material they have previously developed. Rudi's approach was quite different. As he came before the audience, many of whom he had never seen before, he consciously opened himself to them. Then through his inner effort he began to absorb the energy that they were emanating, at the same time becoming conscious of its varied quality and content. He then began to gather together these themes and threads of energy into a kind of continuous fabric, using words as the medium of expression. He called himself a cosmic weaver and compared what he was doing to conducting an orchestra. He was not creat-

Rudi gives a talk in Denton, TX

ing the music, but integrating the notes into a performance. He talked in this way for two hours, and then left for the Dallas ashram. There he gave a Kundalini Yoga class.

At the conclusion he took Stuart aside and worked with him for another hour. It was like unspinning a cocoon of tension that had formed around Stuart since the last time he had been in New York. As the principle teacher in Texas he was under the most pressure. By freeing Stuart from his tension Rudi enabled him to work more deeply with others.

A little before midnight Rudi finally collapsed into bed.

The next morning, after giving another class, he flew with Tom and Madge to a new ashram they had just formed in Austin. During the flight he worked intensely to open himself to all those whom he would meet. He had to be ready to find in them a greater need to which he could respond. He did not stop until he felt that he was ready.

The situation in Austin was different from Dallas. The people were newer and less experienced. But the enthusiasm and devotion was real and it filled Rudi with a sense of gratitude. He gave a lecture that kindled the enthusiasm of many people who were coming for the first time. He was very satisfied.

Afterwards he went with Tom and Madge to see a building they proposed to buy with their own money as a home for the ashram. It was very suitable. It had enough rental units left over after supplying the needs of the ashram to help pay for itself. It was a healthy and mature situation.

In the early afternoon Rudi flew with Larry to a third ashram in Nacogdoches. He spent the entire hour and a half in the airplane dropping negative psychic tensions from his hands. There seemed to be no end to it. Suddenly he felt a strong pain in his third eye chakra. It continued to throb and expanded into an inverted triangle, about five inches across, with the point between his eyebrows.

On their arrival, Rudi asked Larry to stay with him in the meditation room as the pain in his head was intense.

Larry sat next to him and said, "I would like to be able to share whatever pain you ever have."

With this, Rudi's heart opened in gratitude and he was able to sleep for a few minutes. He awoke feeling better and able to give the lecture that was scheduled in the afternoon.

Immediately thereafter he headed for the airport. He was scheduled back in Dallas to give a lecture at 7:00 to about forty inmates from a state prison.

As Rudi walked somewhat uncertainly out of the plane, the triangle that had begun to form on his forehead in the early afternoon had changed into a cobra's head. It was very alive. If he simply glanced at someone, the energy of the Kundalini force immediately transmitted from his forehead. It was part of an extraordinary buildup of energy that had begun around his birthday, and which several astrologers had said would culminate about April 15 when Rudi's true spiritual life would begin.

There was only time for a quick sandwich, a shower, leaving hurriedly for the lecture. On his arrival he walked into a large, cold room and proceeded to face one of the most difficult situations he had ever encountered. The room was filled with violence and hate. He talked for an hour but felt that it was totally futile. Then several of the more hostile prisoners left, and communication with the audience became possible. The longer he talked, the warmer the atmosphere became. By the end many of those present spontaneously approached him with appreciation. Danny Cook, who was present, said "I felt as if my stomach had been torn out."

Immediately thereafter Rudi returned to the Dallas ashram. People were waiting for a class. He worked for forty-five minutes with all of them. Then he worked for another forty-five minutes with Danny Cook, and afterward for two hours with another man who was preparing to become a teacher. He did not sleep until almost 2:00 am, and was up again at 5:45 to give a final class before catching the 7:15 flight back to New York City.

On his return he said,

"I have never been happier in my entire life. It is with enormous gratitude and joy that I understand it is only the preparation for a much more intense period ahead," It was then January 30th.

Rudi inspects homemade Texas BBQ

* * *

Several days later, one of his early students from Texas visited him in New York. To his surprise Rudi felt somewhat cool toward him. This was perhaps explained by a painful experience that he was undergoing in his forearms since his return from Texas. They felt stiff and swollen, as if hundreds of rubber-covered wires were being put into them. He had students massage his forearms to ease the pain. Enormous amounts of energy shot out of his fingers in the process. A psychic rewiring process was occurring.

In the midst of this change Rudi asked himself why he was reacting differently to this visitor. He realized, to his own chagrin, that the many other relations he had formed had simply absorbed his energy.

As he looked at the reality with which he was confronted, he felt ashamed. He had always said that the new should encompass the old, not be stolen from it. He talked about the situation in a lecture and publicly acknowledged his own mistake.

* * *

He continued to be enormously busy, catching up on his art business, visiting Big Indian on the weekends, and more than anything, continuing to experience the acceleration and expansion of his own inner growth.

In the second week in February he began to sense an enormous increase in the life force that was flowing within him. He realized that a new inner mechanism was being evolved to handle it. This mechanism required much greater quantities of energy. The two were unfolding in parallel. He fought to open to the reality of the experience, and surrender that within himself which felt that he had already done enough.

* * *

During that week I was approached by an old student named Jim. He wished to return to the work but I was very reluctant to admit him. He had suddenly disappeared a year before to become involved in a fundamentalist Christian sect. As part of his initiation he publicly condemned his work with me as of the devil. Then after a few months he left the sect and had a mental breakdown. He was still on tranquilizers when he reappeared. I felt his request was sincere, but I didn't really want to have anything to do with him, if for no other reason than he was still on drugs.

In another instance Rudi had said to me, "If someone requires medication in order to get along, don't accept them. They are too unstable, not to mention what the effect of those drugs will have on you when you work with them."

But Jim was persistent. So I finally said to him, "My hands are tied. Rudi already told me not to work with anyone taking medication. The only thing I can suggest is to go to him directly. If he says it's all right, I will take you back."

I thought that would end the matter. But to my surprise, the next day Jim bought a round-trip ticket to New York and went to see Rudi. He returned the same night.

Listening to him talk about his experience, it was hard to separate fantasy from reality, but gradually an approximate version of the truth emerged.

He had entered the store, and Rudi had asked him to wait while he dealt with customers. Then Jim asked to be allowed to return to the work. Rudi had given him a mop and told him to clean the floor in the basement. During the early afternoon Rudi went down to inspect his progress.

"All right," he said, "come on upstairs."

They sat together for a few minutes. Finally Rudi said, "Okay. You can have another chance. But it is the last one." Jim left immediately thereafter and caught the next plane back.

As I listened to him tell the story, I wasn't entirely sure if it was true, but it sounded as if it were. In any case I could ask Rudi about it the next time I saw him. I let Jim return to class.

* * *

During the same week in February Rudi began to plan for a European trip that would be the basis for establishing several ashrams on the continent. Buford had been doing some spade work in Paris, and Rudi had various other contacts in Sweden, Vienna and elsewhere that were waiting on his appearance to be activated.

One of his major concerns was that such an expansion should not occur at the expense of the work that already existed in the United States. For this reason Rudi invited Stuart from Texas, Michael from Indiana, and Buford from Paris to come to New York for a week to reinforce his connection with them, and thus strengthen the foundation for his European venture which was scheduled for late February or early March.

* * *

On February 17th, Rudi left for a trip to Georgia. On the plane he realized that his attitude toward his students was changing. In his whole life as a teacher so many had come and gone that it was natural for him to almost anticipate that anyone he cared for would leave. But that no longer troubled him. The inner richness of the people who were coming was almost greater than he could encompass. It enabled him to open more deeply than ever before, and recognize in himself a commitment to his students beyond anything he had previously felt.

The trip to Georgia was not typical. No public lectures were planned. A small group of close friends had taken a house and wanted Rudi to simply be with them for the weekend.

As soon as he entered the house he was surrounded with love. When he took a shower in an unheated room, he felt only that he was home. The surroundings were very limited, but the care and love behind them were real.

Rudi's Work

On Saturday evening, after a quiet day, he worked with a group that contained many new people. Such a class was a wonderful experience for Rudi. It had all the uncertainty and excitement of a romance. At the same time, as the higher energy entered the new students, deep psychic poisons were released from within them. These entered Rudi during the class.

At five in the morning he awoke with a violent headache. He was drenched with sweat and discovered that he could not move his head at all. The psychic poisons he had absorbed were temporarily paralyzing him. The pain and sweating continued for three or four hours. By 9:30 he was beginning to feel better. At 4:00 in the afternoon, he was able to give a class that had been previously scheduled.

As the day drew to a close, Rudi wondered whether he should stay longer. But as he talked with the group he realized that they had absorbed as much as they could take. He left with a feeling that he would be working with them for a long time in the future, and that their growth and his own would be shared.

He arrived home on the 20th, tired, but immediately caught up by all the matters that awaited his return. It included the signing of papers turning over the property at Big Indian to a not-for-profit corporation which I had had my lawyer prepare at Rudi's request.

Chapter Forty-Two

THE END OF THE MEETING

On the next day, Wednesday, February 21st, I had a question about my inner work. There was nothing pressing about it but I decided to phone Rudi, which was unusual. I had only called previously when I needed immediate advice.

I dialed the number. He answered, sounding slightly distracted.

"Hello, John, how have you been? When are you coming in next?"

"I'm fine," I said, "I'm going to Bloomington this weekend. It's the first time I've been back there in over a year. I'll probably come down on the weekend after that. Are you very busy right now?"

"I'm always busy. What is it?"

"I wanted to ask you something."

"Go ahead," I could hear Rudi yelling at someone off the phone to do something or not do something. But I went ahead.

"When I was fifteen years old," I said, "I had an experience which is returning now in a different form. I want to know whether it has reality and how to relate to it."

He didn't say anything, so I continued.

"The original experience happened while I was walking along a country road. A voice began talking inside me. I knew it was inside but it was extremely real. The thing that struck me the most was the total alien quality of the person behind the voice. He could have been from another galaxy.

"The basic thing he told me was that I would be alone in a haunted house for a long time, and that there was nothing that I or anyone else could do about it. He said some other things, but it wasn't the content that held me. It was the realization that this alien being was me, and that everything else I had ever identified with had no existence. I am beginning to sense that being again more strongly. I have had a taste of it intermittently, but now it has a more permanent feeling."

The End Of The Meeting

There was a pause.

"What do you think?" I asked.

"I'm sorry, John," said Rudi. "There is a lot going on. Could you repeat what you just said?"

In all the time that I had known him I had never heard Rudi ask anyone to repeat themselves. Usually he interrupted them after the first few sentences, having heard enough. But I did as he asked. Then he said,

"John. I have been telling you for fourteen years. You have to work deeper. If you don't you will spend the rest of your life in a backwash of shit."

I said nothing. He continued.

"The experience was real. It was your higher self. That is what you have to try to bring into your work, your relations, your writing of the book. How many times have I told you this over the years? You never listen. You never try hard enough. If you don't do it now, everything you have done could be for nothing."

I was happy that he had confirmed the importance of the experience, but disturbed by what he said. I couldn't reply immediately.

"John. I wouldn't bother saying this if I didn't want you to have a wonderful future. The easiest thing for me to do is to sit back and watch you go over a cliff. But I won't do that. I care! But that isn't enough. You have to care too. You can no longer live your life on the surface. You must dig and dig until you get into contact with this being and begin to let him function. Then everything will be different for you. I have to go now. I love you very much. Goodbye." He hung up as I said,

"Goodbye and thank you."

I sat by the phone for a minute after I had hung up, silently digesting what he had said.

* * *

Late that afternoon Rudi boarded a small plane piloted by one of his students. He was scheduled to give a talk in upstate New York. As the plane took off in the waning winter twilight, Rudi relaxed for the first time in an otherwise hectic day. But after the flight was securely underway he began to dictate to Mimi, one of his students who were accompanying him:

2/21/73:

Today has been a particularly exhausting day. I knew I was going through a transition but could not quite determine where it would carry me.

I am now in route to Glens Falls in a small plane to teach a class in Ft. Miller, New York. It is a good way to travel.

I have been sitting for at least seven or eight hours today letting negative psychic tensions flow through my fingers which it continues to do unceasingly.

I seemed to doze for just a moment or two and could see the faces of several of the people whom I love deepest. A great warmth opened in my heart, and I felt positive energy move down from my brain to my heart and my sex organs. It immediately clarified the reason for the amount of the outflow of these negative psychic tensions. It was my system making room for the transfer of this finer energy and removing the heavier energy which previously occupied those areas.

Although it is just a few minutes since this experience took place, I feel refreshed and renewed and once again strong. It is exciting to look forward to the way the energy expresses itself, as all of these changes have the capacity to reflect a higher creativity. It is not within my mind to try to guess, but I am deeply looking forward to teaching the class tonight.

It has always been a great strength for me to do a simple exercise for a long period of time, allowing it to go deeper and deeper. Improvisation is not a substitute for discipline. It is continually the inability of students or teachers to do what is given to them that brings about problems. They wander through the basic exercises, not having the ability to sustain them. Involved and dramatic methods allow us to lose, in their elaborate nature, the basic responsibilities and discipline from which we receive our strength. It is the ability to check ourselves by our deviation from our constant that not only guides us but perpetuates the line of energy which makes for elasticity as well as an extraordinary deep strength.

I am leaving for Europe this weekend to begin a deeper commitment towards my European ashrams. Most of the teachers in the United States were brought to New York for additional work and strengthening of existing connections. I feel this exemplifies the above principles. I do not wish to exchange the loyalties in this country for loyalties in another. It is easy to look to the glamour of a foreign culture as a means to expansion. The success that our spiritual work has will be based on the depth and growth and love and reality between me and those with whom I have connected my life. From that, the integrity of our European ashrams and brothers and sisters will grow. It is the investment of those people who have been with me that allows me to consciously deepen and expand that which exists. It is not the neurotic need to go off to the glamour of other ashrams and countries. I feel I need to strengthen and simplify relationships with all of those close teachers that I have, before I leave. It is always a principle of growth that simplification conserves energy and allows it to rise to a higher level. I do not wish to see what will happen in Europe as anything except the rising of a total spirituality that reflects the maturity of my surrender to God.

I am deeply grateful for this opportunity and feel the last year of my life preparing me for the understanding that expanded consciousness can only come through expanded nothingness. This has to do with the ability to surrender tensions that bind and restrict our physical mechanism from expressing the power of creation. This is God flowing through us and showing us how we are connected to him. It is the expression of higher creative will and a deeper sense of surrender...

Rudi paused. The pilot suddenly cried out, "Oh my God!", as the plane came out of a cloud bank directly in front of the crest of a mountain.

* * *

The next day I was in an encounter group. During the meeting a woman described her dream of the night before. She had walked up to the attic of her house. The door was closed. She could sense spirits behind the door calling to her. She wanted to go in, but was afraid that if she went through the door she might not be able to return. Suddenly, as she described the dream, she realized who was on the other side. It was a man she had loved and their child, both of whom had died. I listened to her and started to cry. The sadness of it held me. Other people were also affected, but not to that extent.

During the group, I led a guided fantasy. Each person was told to imagine a door, which they would open and walk through. When I did, I found myself on a kind of airfield. I started to rise like a rocket, flying and flying and flying into the universe. I felt concerned about whether I could return and retrace my steps. Then I realized it didn't matter. There was nothing on the earth that could claim me anymore. I was launched and could go on forever. It was a wonderful feeling.

* * *

The next day was Friday. I spent it quietly in the country. I returned to Geneseo about 5:30, and for some reason decided to stop at my office. I spent a few minutes clearing up some details. Then the phone rang. I picked it up.

"Hello, John. This is Jack Stewart. (I had known Jack for almost ten years. He was one of Rudi's oldest students.)

"Hello, Jack. You're the last person I expected to call."

"We have been trying to reach you for two days."

"Me? Why?"

"I don't know how to say this. Rudi was killed in a plane crash Wednesday night." There was a blank pause.

"His plane hit the top of a mountain in the fog. Beau was the pilot. Mimi and Stuart were there. Rudi died instantly. His heart exploded in his chest. He was dictating to Mimi at the time. The others are all right."

Finally I said, "I'm sure you mean what you say, Jack, but it isn't possible."

"That was my reaction at first," said Jack. "I'm afraid it's true. I have seen his body."

He said more, but it was of no matter. Inwardly I still did not believe him for a moment. It might appear this way, but it would be shown to be entirely different in time.

"Thank you for calling, Jack," I said when he paused. "It must have been difficult."

"Will you be at the funeral?"

"Of course."

"Rudi's mother particularly asked that you come quickly."

"I'll be there tomorrow."

"She wants you to say something at the funeral as one of Rudi's oldest friends."

"Of course. I'll see you soon, Jack."

I stood there by the phone feeling rather detached, but realizing even then that the rest of my life had been altered in an instant. That evening I talked to the students at the ashram.

"Rudi has been dead for two days and nothing in me felt anything. That is really extraordinary. The nature of the work is such that whatever is happening to the teacher inevitably affects the students, even at a distance. I have seen that happen thousands of times. When Rudi has a headache, others do. When things go well for him, they go well for them. I don't know how I could be untouched when he died. But my strongest sense is that it makes no difference. His work was done."

* * *

When I got to New York City the conditions were such as to test my detachment. While everyone was attempting to remain calm, the situation was charged with disbelief. The immediate task was to prepare the funeral arrangements. On Saturday night a small group of us went to the Riverside Chapel to make the final arrangements.

"Would you like to view the deceased?" the director asked.

We nodded. He took us into another room. The coffin was open. In it was a large body. I remember it very clearly. There could no longer be any doubt in my mind that Rudi had actually been killed in the crash. But this was not him. It was a shell. I felt nothing toward it. No pang. No sadness.

The funeral was held in a large chapel that overflowed with people, most of whom I had known. They were a living cross-section of Rudi's life — students, customers, dealers, friends. Through it all my inner calm persisted. Perhaps it had begun with the experience of flying into the universe the day after Rudi's death.

Michael, Buford, Stuart and I sat together in the first row to represent the teachers of Rudi's work, along with Hilda and Tai San, a Zen Roshi, both of whom Rudi had known and loved for many years. Each spoke briefly. Michael said a few words for the rest of us.

In front of the room was Rudi's coffin, which even in death seemed oversized. The ceremony passed quickly. Finally each person came forward to say farewell to Rudi before they left the room. I watched the endless procession, noticing how each individual approached the coffin in a different way — standing up, bowing down, with tears, in a meditative state, touching their forehead to the closed lid, placing a flower upon it.

The farewells began to take longer than the ceremony. Toward the end people were asked to hurry so that preparations might begin for the next funeral.

When it came to my turn I bowed to the ground for a moment, remembering a similar occasion on Gurus' Day in Big Indian. But that was long ago. And the doors were closing.

Afterward, Buford accompanied the body to the crematorium. The rest of us returned to the ashram where we talked in muted voices and two teachers gave class simultaneously. It was intense and slightly crazed, but it was better to work than stand around and pretend that nothing had happened.

I returned to Geneseo that evening to face an unknown future.

Chapter Forty-Three
RETURN TO INDIA

In the wake of Rudi's passing my daily routine carried me on. I occasionally thought of the book, but felt partially paralyzed. On my less frequent trips to New York City I saw that a struggle for ascendancy was brewing. The City had been Rudi's home. Big Indian had been his country retreat. But the respective teachers in each ashram began to view each other with suspicion. Their students could do little but await the outcome.

Shortly after Rudi's death I went to Bloomington. The situation there was radically different. There was strength and love in abundance and no struggle for power. In a quiet moment Michael Shoemaker and I made plans to return to India in the late spring. He wanted to visit some of the places where Rudi had been on his last trip to India.

During this period Rudi's mother Rae gradually recovered from her loss. He had been the mainstay of her existence. On several occasions he had literally saved her life.

At the reading of his last testament the remarkable truth was revealed. He had left her everything. The will that I had witnessed a decade before was still in effect.

Rudi knew his mother would take care of his brothers. He seemed to assume that the ashrams would take care of themselves. Whatever he had in mind, Rae found herself in the center of a confusing empire that Rudi had been building. She inherited his art, his debts, his tax problems, his buildings, his customers (most of whom owed Rudi money) and all the complications that follow when a will is probated.

Two major issues of concern to her were the disposition of Rudi's ashes and the statue of Nityananda. Both were finally sent to Big Indian for safekeeping. Rae was afraid that someone might steal the ashes. This did not seem terribly rational, but it was possible. The room that held them was securely locked and only Dean Gitter, who had replaced Greg as principle teacher, had the key.

✳ ✳ ✳

In March I visited Big Indian. Michael Shoemaker was also there. I happened to be present when he was having a conversation with Dean. As I listened it slowly dawned on me that Michael was planning to spend the night in the room with Rudi's ashes and the statue of Nityananda. Without pausing to think about it I asked if I might join him. He agreed, but urged me to say nothing about it to anyone since a slight air of paranoia surrounded the statue and the ashes. It was understandable. Their future was uncertain. It was in Rae's hands and she was still partially overwhelmed by her responsibilities and her grief.

As night approached I borrowed a sleeping bag and, in a quiet moment, gathered with Michael and Dean before the closed door of the room in which we were to stay. Dean opened the double lock and let us in. His last words were, "Please speak softly."

I had seen the statue in India in the living room of its creator. It had seemed large then. Now it occupied three-fourths of the available space. There was only room for the two of us to stretch out in front of it, nothing more.

As soon as the door closed behind us I glanced at the statue. A torrent of energy struck me. I felt as though I had been grabbed by the shoulders and was being shaken. The thought of spending the night in the company of such intensity frightened me.

Michael proceeded to light a candle and burn some incense. He bowed before the statue and consecrated some tantric instruments that he had brought with him. I followed his lead silently. On one side of the room was a shelf with a small box of Persian design. I realized, with a chill, that it must contain Rudi's ashes.

As we settled down I said to Michael, "I don't know if I can take a whole night in here."

"I'm not so sure either, "said Michael, "but if it gets too much for you, leave."

I lay there in the dark, aware of the energy that continued to pour from the statue, wondering whether my system could absorb it without being injured. I was haunted by the box by the window. I knew that Rudi was dead, but it was hard to believe it in the presence of such energy.

I did not sleep that night but gradually the force receded, or I became used to it so that it was like resting under a waterfall.

We left as the sky began to lighten. The next time I saw Michael he looked radiant.

"Nityananda descended into the statue while we were there," he said. "It was a great honor, John. It wasn't just his energy. He was really present in the room to meet us."

I wasn't entirely sure what Michael meant, but I could certainly feel the energy burning in me for the rest of the day.

※ ※ ※

For several years before his death I had invited Rudi to come to the Rochester area to talk and teach. He had always put me off. He didn't feel the situation was ready to receive him. But finally in the beginning of January, he had agreed to come. I had made preliminary arrangements for him to talk at an ashram in Rochester. When the time came I had to appear in his place.

It was a fiery day. I could feel his energy upon me as I introduced his work. There were many in the audience who were to become my students in the following months. In particular was K. whom Mr. Thomas had said six months before I would meet at this time. He had further described this period as the beginning of a whole new phase of my life. I could not have visualized the circumstances, but there was no doubt that it was true.

※ ※ ※

One of the indirect effects of Rudi's death was that people began to visit psychics to get some sense of contact with the future. Rudi had used psychics to help chart his own possibilities, but he had done so carefully and with a conscious sense of skepticism. That was now abandoned in the search for emotional reassurance.

Chief among the psychics who were consulted was a woman named Beulah. Many stories began to circulate about what she had said. Different people were named as the inheritors of Rudi's work. Contact with Rudi himself was established. It was very difficult for me to sort these stories out. If anything they only made the situation more precarious, as they put fuel on the hopes and ambitions of different people and intensified their conflict with each other.

I purposely held back. I didn't want to be involved in the uncertainty and struggle that was occurring. But in late spring after the initial excitement had subsided, I made an appointment with Beulah, calling from upstate New York so that she would not connect me with Rudi in any way.

I duly appeared for my appointment on my next visit to New York City. She lived in a large suite in a West Side hotel. The living room was overflowing with objects and upholstery. It looked like she stayed there for days at a time without leaving, which might well have been true. But I didn't have much time to think about it as she quickly ushered me into her office. In an abrupt and business-like way, she sat down behind her desk and motioned me into an armchair.

I said nothing. She shrugged her shoulders and closed her eyes.

"I feel a strong presence. Someone you know. Very high energy. It is someone I have come to know in the last months. RUDI!"

I was shocked. I hadn't said two words to her since I entered the apartment.

"He greets you as an old friend," she continued. "He sends you his love. Do not be sad."

I waited. I wasn't sad.

"Is there anything you would like to ask?"

"Why did you die?"

"My work was done," was the immediate reply.

I had never believed that Rudi could die accidentally.

Beulah continued on.

"He is gone, but I hear singing. It is in a large place like a cathedral, many people. It is a ceremony for you, in your honor. You have completed your transformation."

Shortly thereafter, she concluded.

I didn't really want to think about what she had said.

Toward the end of May Michael and I left on our trip to India. There was nothing but time as the jet took to the air, and life became a succession of meals, naps and movies. During one of the endless intervals

I asked Michael what he thought of Beulah. I had gained great respect for him since Rudi's death.

"She said that I would inherit the mantle of Rudi's work."

"What do you think of that?" I asked.

"Time will tell," said Michael.

"Then you take her seriously?" I persisted.

"I just want to do my own work. When we get to India, I will talk with Mr. Thomas. I am not going to drive myself crazy about what to believe or not to believe. It will all take care of itself."

※ ※ ※

Two endless days later we were in Bombay. Michael went off to meet Mr. Thomas while I caught up on my sleep. When he returned he didn't want to talk about it, except to say, "Mr. Thomas is coming over later in the afternoon."

We took a walk around the neighborhood. It was all the same — the overcrowding, the decayed exotic odors, the shops, the beggars and the heat. But Rudi's name, like an unanswered question, hung in the air. To come halfway around the earth and see things that only reminded me of him was extremely strange. The ashes had not yet settled.

I stopped in Michael's room later in the day. Mr. Thomas had indeed come. He didn't seem to remember who I was, but in a lull in the conversation he started to make a few comments about me.

"You are the kind of person," he said, "on whom most of what you have gone through is wasted. But you will gain great benefit in sharing it with others. As you do that you will come to understand and appreciate what you have known. And others will benefit greatly also."

I immediately thought of the book. Mr. Thomas had shifted his conversation to other things.

Later in the evening as we consumed some papaya fruit, Michael said, "Mr. Thomas gave me the mantra he gave to Rudi on his last trip. It is very intense."

"I don't suppose..." I began.

"Don't even ask, John. Let me work on it. When the time comes, we will see."

※ ※ ※

The next day we hired a car and driver to retrace the route that Rudi had taken toward Hardwar, Rishikish and into the mountains. It rained continually. The roads turned to mud and the heat intensified. Finally we came to the Ganges, cold, vitalizing, bubbling with pure energy. But we did not delay. There was no seven-hundred year old man waiting for us in the foothills of the Himalayas, but our destination was still Mussoorie.

When we arrived the hotel was almost full. It didn't look like the same place.

I rested while Michael disappeared into the mountains. He wanted to be alone. I didn't really know why until later, but when he returned, it was with enthusiasm.

"I ran across a Tibetan who invited me to his village. There is a whole Tibetan colony nearby. The man's uncle is a famous thangka painter. I commissioned him to make some huge paintings for the ashram in Bloomington. He is going to send one of his best students to stay with us and teach painting. They are wonderful, wonderful people."

Michael went to bed early, complaining that his head was splitting open and that he couldn't see straight. I decided to take a walk in the surrounding forest. As the sun was setting I caught a glimpse of the Himalayas, but the mountain mists quickly blotted them out, and I turned home before I got lost in the dark.

The next day I went with Michael to the Tibetan village, but most of the people he had met were gone. We sipped buttered tea, ate small cakes, and decided to move on.

Our next stop was Benares. Our guide of the previous trip materialized to lead us through the maze of temples, shops and people. I listened as Michael talked to Indians about our work, describing himself as its leader. It was strange for me to hear him say it, but I discovered that I had already accepted the fact. Evidently Mr. Thomas must have reinforced the idea for him, though he hadn't specifically said so. But who else was there? Stuart had retired to Texas and took no part in any struggles. Buford was in Paris and didn't seem concerned. Richard, in New York, was untrustworthy. And no one else really had the strength. I had purchased a ticket to Bloomington before Rudi's death and accepted the transition easily. Therefore I said nothing. Michael's biggest problem was that he was only twenty-five years old, though it could become a great source of strength if he could survive the maturing process.

Finally I asked him directly,

"Just what did Mr. Thomas say?"

"He said that because I was starting so young I would grow beyond Rudi."

"How do you feel about that?" I persisted as we walked through the twisting alleyways, trying to keep our guide in sight.

"It sounds very impressive, John, but it is also endless work and a lot of pain. I don't think anyone else could stand it. Rudi and I have a similar chemistry. I loved him completely. A few weeks before he died he said to me, 'I know where everyone fits into my past lives. But I can't place you, Michael. You must be more ancient than anything I can remember.' Maybe it's true."

"Was he talking about time and space work when he said that?" I asked.

"Yes."

"It's a tragedy that it died with him."

"It didn't," said Michael. "He gave it to me a few days before his death. He said I was the only one who had worked hard enough to receive it."

I was stunned. I had assumed it was lost.

"Don't misunderstand me!" said Michael. "Like anything else it takes time to mature. But he gave me the basic method. The rest, I hope, comes with time."

"Is that something you are free to share?"

"Sure," he said. "I thought you would never ask. But don't stop dead in your tracks or we will lose the guide. Ask me about it when we get to Darjeeling...."

* * *

We flew to Calcutta and shifted connections to fly to Northern India. But the trip nearly was aborted when we discovered that permission for Darjeeling was difficult to obtain without long notice in advance. A customs official finally decided we were too naive to be dangerous, and waved us on.

The drive from the airfield to Darjeeling took three hours on a small mountain road that wound upward, continually crisscrossing a small railway that followed a similar route. It was rainy with intermittent fog. We could see very little, just enough to realize that our safety depended on the memory of the driver.

Darjeeling was a little like Nepal, a world of its own, peopled by a unique mixture of exotic racial types. The season was over. Fog almost totally obscured the view of the Himalayas for which it was famous. But the manager of the empty hotel was happy to see us as we settled in to explore the surroundings.

There was a large Tibetan settlement. Many monks had been forced to sell their most precious religious possessions to survive. When it became known that we were interested in such things merchants began to appear at the hotel, uninvited. We followed them in fascination through the fog to small huts and houses where their wares were stored. It was hard to tell what we were looking at in the dim light. They were very happy to mail or ship anything we might wish to purchase. In the end we bought some paintings and small statues that we could carry out by hand. It wasn't clear whether they would be seized by Indian customs, but as far as we knew, Tibetan objects were not of concern to Indians.

Michael then discovered a zoo at the end of town, and I discovered amoebic dysentery. With considerable reluctance I went to the local pharmacy where they recommended large brown pills which at least looked appropriate. The joy had gone out of the day.

After a few days I began to feel slightly better. By then time was running out. Michael was scheduled to return to Bombay to meet Danny Cook, the teacher from Dallas, who was coming over on business. And I had to return home.

✳ ✳ ✳

Seated in my room in Darjeeling, with a warm fire burning and fog obscuring the view, we talked of the trip.

"The night that Rudi crashed, I knew instantly what happened," said Michael. "Ever since then I have been paralyzed inside. During this trip I have begun to thaw. The immediate effect has been a terrible pain in my head. If I seem a little strange at times, that is the reason. I feel like a great wounded water buffalo charging around India.

"When I was in the mountains I began to let my grief emerge. It wasn't very pretty. I just wanted to pull some trees out by the roots. I had to come to India or I would have gone crazy.

Rudi's house, 10th Street, Second Floor, 1970

"The first time I met Rudi, I didn't know what to expect. One of my friends had told me about him, so I decided to go to New York to see for myself. I walked into the store. He was sitting behind his desk. All he said was, 'Hello. I've been waiting for you.' But inside I began to have incredible experiences. Voices started talking in different languages, images started flashing of other lives. It was something completely out of science fiction. I used to think that Rudi was Maitreya, the Buddha who is to come, but that no longer matters."

We sat in silence and listened to the crackling of the fire. Outside it had begun to rain. Finally I asked, "Are you still leaving tomorrow?"

"Yes, I want to meet Danny at the airport when he gets in."

"I think I'll stay," I said, "and try and get into Sikkim, even though the border is closed. The head of the Red Hat sect has settled there."

"The Red Hats originated the Lamaist tradition in the eighth century. You should have an interesting day. I'll see you for breakfast before you go."

He paused and looked at the pattern of the raindrops on the window.

"In Benares," I began, "you said that…"

"I know," said Michael, "Time and Space. I haven't forgotten. I'll give you the exercise now."

When he finished, I sat there feeling the characteristic sense of hovering in emptiness that the experience brings and thinking of what Rudi had written about it in *Spiritual Cannibalism*. In many ways he had explained the process. But he hadn't given everything. You needed all the pieces, or it didn't work. Now it was relatively complete.

"I don't know what to say," I hesitantly began.

"Just be thankful that it wasn't lost, and use it well," said Michael, dropping the subject.

The next morning he returned to Bombay and I left for the border of Sikkim which was supposed to be closed to Westerners. Much to my surprise I was allowed to cross. I spent the day visiting several Tibetan monasteries, and finally meeting the Chief Lama of the Red Hat Sect. He dictated letters and asked me questions through an interpreter.

Before I left he signed and presented me with a picture of Padmasambhava, the originator of Tibetan Buddhism. As I looked at it I suddenly remembered the first thangka I had bought from Rudi fourteen years before. It was a painting of the same man.

※ ※ ※

When I returned from India, the pattern of my life began to alter. I visited New York only infrequently. The next time I saw Rudi's mother a year had elapsed. She scolded me for having stayed away so long, but then forgave me.

Afterwards both of us went up to Rudi's old apartment where some of his Tibetan statues were still kept. On Friday night the apartment was open to old students who wished to go there to meditate. She wanted to arrive early to avoid the crowd.

We both ascended the familiar stairs. I had not been inside the building since the day of Rudi's funeral. The room that we entered was still alive. I sat quietly and opened to the energy in the atmosphere and all the memories that the room evoked. Rae closed her eyes and seemed to fall asleep. She was very tired.

After a few minutes she roused herself and said,

"I haven't felt Rudi's presence since his death! Now he just came to me and said he would return later to deliver an important message."

We left the room as others started to assemble. I gave Rae a big hug and returned to Geneseo.

Over the weekend, she had a heart attack and died.

AFTERWORD

Hello, John.

Where am I?

Where we can talk.

But you don't seem the same.

I'm not. Your personality is coloring my words. Try to surrender more deeply.

I'm not sure that any of this is happening.

You never were. That was part of your difficulty.

You seem impersonal.

No, John. But you must understand. This conversation is like a dream to me. I will wake up when we stop talking.

Don't you care what has happened to your work since your death?

It's not my work. It's the work that the creative spirit of the universe did through me. Use what was given. That is the only way to absorb it. Take my life. I left it to you in the only way I could. Isn't that enough?

But there is so much I want to ask.

Afterword

There is nothing to say.

Then why have I written this book?

To offer what you have been privileged to witness to an audience beyond yourself. You may not have appreciated it in one sense, but you knew from the beginning that it was basically extraordinary.

I'm still having difficulty accepting your reality.

That is your limitation. When you look at one of my photographs, do you feel a flow of force?

Yes. And it always surprises me.

Why should it? You have been working with statues and paintings for years.

I just don't know you anymore.

No one knew me. A hundred different books could have been written about my life, each by people convinced of their version of the truth. If I had lived longer it would have happened.

How could I be with you for so long and not know you?

You knew enough. My force is impressed on you indelibly. That's what counts, alive or dead. You must either feel yourself begin to burn or know that you are a dead hunk of shit. Which is it to be? Do you want to spend the rest of your life apologizing for your inadequacy in comparison to my example? That would be terrible!

I looked forward to talking with you. I was a little scared, but I needed to do it.

And now?

You keep backing me up against a wall. I have done what you asked. I have written the book.

Good!

Is that all?

Sure.

What do I do next?

Open to your own depth. It will attract the future.

I thought that seeing you would answer all my questions. But you are doing what you always did, pushing me in a direction I can't see. And I am fighting inside to hold back.

And it is stupid! Stupid! Stupid! I am not trying to prove anything. Every time you feel resistance and fear, John, take a stick and hit it. No one can inflict anything on you. Don't you understand that yet? You have to be a chorus of voices pleading for growth and energy. You have to get out from behind the clouds and live in the sun.

I want to.

Then do it. You can cooperate with creation by raising the level of energy in every situation you attract. If you do that, the rest will take care of itself.

I'm beginning to feel better.

You are starting to relax. You can't do anything unless you are very open and full of force. Work for that. It will keep you busy.

Isn't there more?

You haven't even scratched the surface and you ask is there more. What more do you want?

I don't know — fragments of the past are scattered around me, but I begin to feel resolved.

Afterword

Fine! I never wanted to burden you with my memories. Absorb their nourishment. Eat me.

I don't know if I want to do that.

You've been doing it for as long as you have been writing this book, dummy! Now aren't you going to ask me about the future of the work I left behind?

Do you want to tell me?

Sure. If I were vulnerable, it would bother me a lot to see what has happened since my death. Every personal weakness in the people around me has manifested. Some of it was terrible. But I knew it would happen. It was part of the price for my own freedom. And at this point, I am no longer concerned. A new generation is emerging. The work will go on.

Then what should I do?

Breathe me in. Put me in your heart. Feel my radiance as you have known it in my lifetime. We are all bubbles. The Rudi bubble may shine brighter than the John bubble, but it is the light that counts, and what does either of us have to do with that? Behind all patterns are atoms of vitality that bind us together and make us brothers. Accept the past and move on.

The only thing that anyone can leave behind is a pathway through the wilderness. Follow it. That will help to justify my existence. But don't expect me to be waiting at a turn in the road. I have never waited for anyone. Is there anything else? I can't stay here forever.

Are you on a schedule?

I have things to do. Don't you?

Nothing important. And I may not get this chance again.

You could have had the contact any time you really needed it. I wanted to help. All you had to do was find me — think of it this way: You have a friend in high places.

I would like to believe it.

I'm telling you!

Oh, Rudi! It is really wonderful to be with you. I was never able to remember what you were really like from week to week. You are more real than I am.

Then open to my energy. I have never tried to hide. It is not my nature. The problem is just the other way around. Who could take my radiance? It is still there. Can you feel it?

Yes. It is growing strong. I am very grateful to be talking with you.

It wasn't easy. You had to write this whole book to create the need.

Wasn't the book necessary?

I don't mean that. Its function will become clear in time. I mean, you could have talked to me before. But I got my message through one way or another.

That's what I figured.

And if you open more completely, I can manifest within you in the future.

That would be wonderful!

Then attract it. But don't get caught in that possibility either. Open and grow. Transcend everything you have ever known, including me.

And then?

And then, nothing — you will be free.

PHOTOS: RUDI

Photos: Rudi

Photos: Rudi

Photos courtesy Barry Kaplan

A NEW LIFE

Rudi's death was a severe emotional and spiritual shock to all those who were close to him — students, friends, customers and family. His contacts spread around the earth. The interlocking sets of ashrams that he had formed, and which were in various stages of maturity, were rocked to their foundations.

How could he be gone?

Rudi had described to me what his death would be like. It was not like this.

In an atmosphere of uncertainty and denial various explanations were offered:

It was a pure accident
Rudi had hinted that his death was imminent during a talk in Texas
His work was finished
He sacrificed his life to protect those who were with him in the plane
His accelerating spiritual development carried him right off the earth
Other gurus had put a death spell on him
It didn't matter because he would be reborn very soon

A period followed that resembled the aftereffects of the assassination of Julius Caesar. Competing centers of power were formed and struggles were fought that might be of real interest to a scholar of spiritual movements. I am too close to the persons involved to want to go into this history except to acknowledge that while those with the influence did the best that they could under the circumstances, it wasn't always exemplary. Rudi had selected and trained teachers who had strong energies and personalities. What they had in common was a willingness to be guided by him. They were not willing to listen to each other.

A New Life

Over forty years have passed since Rudi's death, half a normal lifetime. One thing is brutally clear. His passing was a profound tragedy. He was at the major crossroads of his own evolvement. His influence was inevitably going to spread across the earth during a time when true spiritual power and understanding was so vitally needed. This was clearest to those who were closest to him, and yet the greatest loss was to those who did not even know that he existed at the time, and might have met him later.

Rudi and I were born in the same year; now I have lived almost twice as long as he did. You may wonder what happened to me during the last forty years since his departure. Though it has been an endless journey in one sense, in another it happened only yesterday, and Rudi's influence remained throughout as the counterpoint to my existence.

The intervening time naturally formed the content of several books. The first was called *Ecstasy in Flight: the Tantra beyond Space and Time*.

A few months before the plane crash I began to experiment with a tantric form of Astral Flight in which a couple would ascend together. It seemed to have great possibilities. Before I could talk with Rudi about it, he was gone and I was left very much on my own.

During the following year the practice evolved into a tantric form of Rudi's last work which involved going Beyond Time and Space. At a certain point my partner and I decided to keep parallel journals of our daily experiences together. We were basically entering a condition in which we were eternally everywhere, fueled by the attraction between us.

All of this, preceded by a description of Rudi's basic work in the framework of the Tantric Tradition and followed by a series of poems inspired by the experience, constituted the material of the book. Here is an example of one of the poems:

> *After you left*
> *There was a blaze of light within the room.*
> *I sat and started to absorb its power.*
> *it was a goddess flowing with designs*
> *And filling them with blinding yellow lines.*
> *I could not ask her anything.*
> *I opened to the stream, from which she came,*
> *To take her into me.*
> *She spoke your name.*

I took the experience as far as it could go in the context of the personal commitments of the participants, which turned out to be a lot further than I could have imagined. And then human considerations intervened and the experiment came to an end. For personal reasons the book remains unpublished at this time.

The next major event concerned the death and rebirth of Big Indian. During his lifetime Rudi had underwritten the costs of operating Big Indian with the help of the members of the New York City ashram. After his death the situation decayed. Support was withdrawn from the city, and the people living in Big Indian were faced with an uncertain future.

Courtesy Robert Sink

During the next four years, despite semi-heroic efforts, their financial situation worsened and the bank threatened to foreclose on the property. When I became aware of the situation I offered to take over all existing debts. After a long and drawn out closing I became the owner of the Ashram property, and thus preserved Rudi's Country Retreat Center for the future.

The first thing that happened was that almost all the members of my little ashram in Livonia took to the hills, not wanting to be involved in the extra work that they were sure would be necessary at Big Indian.

I wasn't too disturbed because I had a Plan B. I would ask each of the existing ashrams around the country to sponsor one of their members to come and work at Big Indian for a month each summer so that the site would be maintained and available to all for visits and retreats. It would cost them very little, and preserve the site with which Rudi was so intimately associated.

They all agreed, but what they agreed to was to say NO. There was

A New Life

a variety of reasons, but only one general effect. I was there with a decaying property almost all by myself. For the first summer I ended up hiring two of my own children who, with me and my girlfriend, worked endlessly to begin the process of restoration.

※ ※ ※

As the repairs were completed I was approached by Stuart Perrin, the principal teacher of Rudi's spiritual work in Texas.

He began the conversation with a completely surprising question.

"How would you like to have a fifty-foot Stupa dedicated to Rudi built at Big Indian?"

I was shocked and said nothing. He mistook my silence as hesitancy and said:

"I'll raise the money and provide people to do the work."

At that moment my only concern was how such a structure might affect the real estate taxes. Otherwise it sounded like an offer I couldn't refuse.

"Thank you," I said. "It is extremely generous. Let me think about it for a few days."

My next step was to see the County real estate appraiser. I described the project to him and then said,

"I know that you can't tell me exactly how it would affect the taxes, but, completely off the record, could you give me some approximate estimate?"

"No problem," he said. "I can tell you exactly what the effect would be: NOTHING. Such a structure serves no practical purpose. It is just a memorial. It would have no effect on the taxes whatsoever."

I contacted Stuart with the good news and the project was underway.

For the next several summers, under the supervision of Ra Baker who ran a construction company in Denton, Texas, the work proceeded. He decided to build it using concrete so that it would endure forever.

This proved somewhat naive since neither he nor anyone else who was involved knew much about working with concrete. But somehow over the summers the Stupa grew to its intended height, which for a Stupa was almost unique in the United States at that time.

But somewhat mysteriously just at the time when it was physically

The Stupa is painstakingly built in Big Indian

complete those who had done the work withdrew. Since a Stupa is basically a Sacred Structure it needs to be properly blessed and ceremonially acknowledged. Fortunately Lar Short appeared with his group from Colorado and later New Mexico. He had been trained not only as a teacher of Rudi's work but in the higher forms of Tibetan Buddhist Ritual and Wisdom. He brought the work on the Stupa to its mystical conclusion, culminating with obtaining the blessings of His Holiness Dilgo Khyentse, a teacher of the Dalai Lama. That was in the mid-eighties. The story of the creation of the Stupa could be the basis of another book. Forty years later, it is still unfolding.

✷ ✷ ✷

It took five years to get the property to the point that retreats could be held there on a regular basis. By 1988 it was thriving. Big Indian had truly been reborn as a Spiritual Retreat Center.[1]

A year or two later I received a surprising invitation from the students of Da Free John to come to California for two weeks, all expenses paid, to give two talks about Rudi. I had known Da Free John as a student of Rudi's in the early 1960's, when his name was Franklin Jones. His experience with Rudi is described in his book, *The Knee of Listening*,

---

1 A brochure that describes the activities of that summer is given in Appendix A.

which was the first published account of Rudi's work.

I had an ambivalent reaction to the invitation, not because I objected to a free trip to California, but because of Rudi's attitude toward Da Free John himself. Rudi made it a point of honor never to say anything negative about another teacher in a public gathering. His attitude was that each teacher was good for different students.

Rudi might make sarcastic or negative comments about teachers when talking informally and in private, but never in public. It was therefore noteworthy and somewhat shocking when in the early 1970's, in a public lecture he spoke of his ex-student turned guru in scathing terms. He went so far as to call him "a paranoid schizophrenic".

Naturally I never forgot what Rudi had said, and subsequently wanted nothing to do with Da Free John or his students. Over the years they had approached me about the possibility of Da Free John visiting Rudi's shrine at Big Indian. I agreed because as far as I was concerned, the Shrine was open to all who approached it with respect. But the visit never materialized.

Going to California was a different matter. However I finally decided I had nothing to lose, and was happy to talk about Rudi if that was what they wanted. I didn't quite know how I would respond when they would inevitably ask me, "what kind of a student was Franklin Jones in the old days?"

I went to California thoroughly on my guard and returned two weeks later essentially having become a student of Free John. I have never been so completely turned around in so short a time.

I have written a manuscript about all that followed in the next three years of my life entitled *In Between* that has yet to see the light of day. Looking back on that period after more than twenty years have elapsed, I can only shake my head in wonder at my willingness to be guided by what I encountered on that fateful visit that necessitated my going beyond and against everything I had believed up until that point, and to confront the possibility that Rudi might have been wrong about Free John.

In a sense Da Free John (or Adi Da as he later called himself) was Rudi's most successful student, in spite of the fact that they parted abruptly and with bitterness. Free John produced a vast and profound spiritual literature. He spoke brilliantly, leaving a large collection of videos and audio recordings.

While all of this was true from my point of view, the actual

Capella and John Mann, Big Indian, NY, 2013

experience of becoming a student in the Daist community was difficult. I was considered to be a beginner on the one hand; on the other, radical demands were made of me almost immediately. These included ceasing to teach Rudi's work and disposing of Big Indian as quickly as possible. Needless to say, this was not amusing.

As part of the future disposition of Big Indian, a notable Buddhist developer appeared and helped to prepare a fairly remarkable proposal. A short version is presented in Appendix B. Big Indian might have become a Tanglewood in the Catskills. That project didn't materialize.

As time passed I gradually came to the conclusion that Da Free John didn't quite know what to do with me. He had never had a qualified spiritual teacher sign on as a student. A further complication was that I gradually realized that he was projecting his unresolved issues with Rudi onto me.

I began to look for an exit. The problem was that the fundamental principal of his teaching was surrender to the guru. I couldn't run away; that would represent a failure which I would choose only in desperation. I finally realized that there was only one honorable exit — surrender everything, including the guru, to a higher power. This I did for several weeks until I finally felt that I could leave with honor.

✳ ✳ ✳

A New Life

During my whole life I have never known what a given experience is preparing me for until the answer unexpectedly appears. Then I am faced with the choice of opening to the new possibility or letting it pass by. Thus, several years later after leaving Free John and resuming the teaching of Rudi's work, I totally, unexpectedly, discovered that when I and one of my students simply surrendered in each other's presence an unknown spiritual force began to flow.

I want to be clear about this. Rudi's work always involved directed attention and conscious effort. He sometimes described it as similar to a salmon swimming upstream. And he always urged his students to "WORK HARDER!"

But what I had discovered was when I was in the immediate presence of Elizabeth, one of my students, a force began to spontaneously flow between us without the slightest effort. It was as if Rudi's work was happening all by itself.

The rest of the students in the class thought I was still teaching Rudi's work. I knew for sure that I wasn't. I wasn't breathing in a yogic manner; I wasn't circulating the spiritual force through the chakras. I basically wasn't doing anything at all, and yet the students didn't know the difference. BUT I DID!

What seemed to be an interesting experience proved to be a major crossroads in my own spiritual and personal development.

As you read these words you may wonder what was so remarkable. If that is your reaction, I can empathize. What I have described doesn't sound all that significant.

This new work for me constituted a moment out of time toward which I had been moving all my life. In fact it felt like discovering why it was that I had been born.

The first dilemma that confronted me was how I could pretend to be a teacher if I fundamentally wasn't doing anything. Considering all that I had gone through to become a spiritual teacher this was not a trivial question. I had the choice of ignoring what had happened and going back to teaching Rudi's work as I had known it, or stepping down from the teaching platform as a symbolic acknowledgment that, even though something spiritual was occurring, it had nothing to do with any conscious effort on my part.

I decided on the latter. I assumed that I could always change my mind if it proved to be a dead end. What occurred is recorded in my book *Divine Androgyny: The Path of Mutual Surrender* which describes the first five years of the development of this approach. As I now read the book thirteen years after it was published, I would hardly change a word.

The essence of *Divine Androgyny* can be summarized in the phrase "doing nothing together." That is what "mutual surrender" involves. In the format that has evolved, a couple commits to pursuing this path together as a form of spiritual marriage, when they meet to do nothing together. They create an oasis in which the masculine and feminine is harmonized, and within which a higher power can freely manifest for the benefit of the couple, and more particularly for all those who are present when the couple sit together.

* * *

In this final section I would like to briefly consider those aspects of my future that most directly relate to Rudi's continuing influence on my existence.

At this writing I am eighty-five years old. I had type 2 and 3 non-Hodgkin's lymphoma seven years ago which continues to be in remission. I have always felt that I would live for a long time, but as Rudi's history proves, everyone's future is uncertain.

Whatever time remains before the body undergoes its inevitable dissolution, the two most relevant concerns for me are the future of Big Indian, and the continuing vertical and horizontal evolution of Divine Androgyny. (See Appendix C for a divination conducted in relation to these issues.)

Big Indian has for all practical purposes ceased to function as a spiritual retreat center. The last event that involved more than a handful of people occurred almost five years ago. While such activity might revive, it is time for a change.

My vision is that Big Indian becomes transformed into a sacred site, a pilgrimage center open to all who seek to be revitalized by contact with its rich and powerful spiritual energy.

The property should be owned by a religious not-for-profit corporation that could financially ensure its care, support and continuity. There is nothing unrealistic about this vision if those who were directly and indirectly influenced by Rudi's teaching can come together and make it happen. I am completely open to working toward such a goal. Without question it must be a cooperative endeavor.

A New Life

And quite honestly if there is no such effort, I am not going to allow that to drive me crazy. I will have done my part to perpetuate the heritage.

However, I am not so sanguine in regard to Divine Androgyny. This is my life's work, though I didn't know it until I was in my mid-sixties. And I might never have discovered it then without Rudi's endless energy and guidance and the seeds that he placed in me that took so long to germinate.

Looking at the world today it is all too easy to see it as a set of competing problems any one of which is capable of overwhelming the world order. At the same time there has never been a time throughout recorded history when there has been as many choices and possibilities and competing influences available to each individual. It is hard to tell whether this richness of alternatives makes matters better or worse.

But from the viewpoint of the development of Divine Androgyny, it is inevitably competing with a vast number of attractive alternatives in the religious and spiritual marketplace. The odds are not in its favor. It has only one truly unique attribute. Unlike virtually every other alternative, it does not tell you what to do. In that respect it is like the number zero. No matter what you multiply it by, it stays the same.

When you examine the self-improvement literature — whether it tells you how to improve your bowling score, make friends or improve your mental, physical and spiritual well-being — it is always telling you what to do and how to do it.

Divine Androgyny suggests that none of that is really necessary. In this respect it is truly revolutionary. At the same time it does not threaten the existing order. How could it, if you are encouraged to do nothing or at least as little as possible?

And yet, as 2014 begins to unfold for me I must acknowledge that my life is undergoing yet another transformation. It is even carrying me beyond Divine Androgyny, opening a doorway to possibilities that I did not know existed. The new vistas opening for me was at the essence of what Rudi taught — the reward for work is more work.

***

In conclusion I have done the best that I can to give the reader a taste of what it might have been like to have met Rudi, but it is not false modesty to say that the best that I could do is pitiful compared to the reality of having met him in this life. There is no substitute for having been Before the Sun.

RUDI'S WORK 40 YEARS LATER

It is my contention that Rudi was a spiritual genius. Having read this book you have a basis for forming your own opinion. Any truly creative person is best judged by the work they leave behind, rather than the life that they have lived, though the one informs the other. Rudi's work was the spiritual growth he achieved within himself and fostered in his students. The former he took with him. The latter he left behind.

I have sketched out in the previous chapter how that played out in my case over the years. But each person who was deeply touched by him in the fourteen years that he taught could write their own chapter, or in some cases their own book, and they would all be equally valid and each equally necessary in assessing the enduring impact of Rudi's work.

And that would also include the endless parade of customers and friends who were affected by their contact with him. And even of more relevance it would include the second and third generation of teachers and students of his work who had no direct contact with him during his lifetime.

All of these considerations are rendered more poignant, at least for me, since I am actually writing these words on January 24th 2014, which what would have been Rudi's 86th birthday.

While I personally have no doubt that Rudi's death marked the end of what might very well have become a worldwide spiritual movement, the events that have occurred since that fatal moment have ensured that his mode of teaching endures. An incomplete listing of the Teachers and Centers where it can be found is given on the internet web site: *rudranandalineage.com*. It is fair to say that the interested student can certainly find a living form of the Teaching that Rudi created if he wishes to make contact with it.

Beyond that conclusion it is hard to make a simple statement. Like the blind men feeling the elephant — depending on whom you talk to, you would get a different answer. They would all be true and each incomplete. Listening to what I might have to say is equally restricted.

However the process of teaching that Rudi manifested in his lifetime is not limited by time and circumstance. As with the lifetime of any Genius, it is not so much a question of how others reacted to them that is important, as it is the reality of their existence which blazed briefly and moved on.

And with a great spiritual instructor, it is the interaction between teacher and student that constitutes the heart and essence of what he or she has to give. And it is this process that transcends any particular form or tradition within which it is given. It is this essence that I have done my best to present to you. If I have only partially succeeded I will be more than grateful.

Thank you for having come so far with me and sharing in the experience.

John Mann

APPENDIX A
RUDI'S BIG INDIAN CENTER SUMMER 1988 CATALOG

Appendix A

History

Rudi's Big Indian Center is located in a magical valley in the Catskill Mountains of New York. It is believed that the valley was used by Native American Indians as a site for their sacred ceremonies. Early in the twentieth century a summer family resort was built on the land. In 1969, Swami Rudrananda (Rudi) purchased the land and buildings and established a community for spiritual work. Rudi was killed in a plane crash in 1973, but the community continued until 1978. In the spring of 1979, Dr. John Mann, a long time friend and student of Rudi's and a teacher of his spiritual practices, purchased the property and initiated its eventual rebirth as Rudi's Big Indian Center (RBIC).

Qualities

Beyond the natural empowerments of the valley, RBIC is further enriched by the presence of Eastern Religious art and a number of sacred structures. Among the latter are Swami Rudrananda's Samadhi Shrine, the embodiment of the three levels of spiritual work developed by him — a Stupa of Transformation, receiver and transmitter of higher creative energies — and a Meditation Hall, the focus of the sacred energies flowing in the valley and a space in which is a statue of Bhagawan Nityananda, Rudi's teacher. Also, there are ceremonial sweat lodges built by Native Americans of today and a Medicine Wheel rediscovered and reactivated from the past.

In addition, RBIC contains the living presence of Rudi's extraordinary energies and those of the teachers whom he trained. It also includes the living presences of master teachers, past and present, who have taught or given their blessings within the valley. Such teachers include Swami Muktananda, Dr. Rammurti Mishra, Ram Dass, his Holiness Dyengo Kyentse Rinpoche, Namki Norbu Rinpoche, Master Mantak Chia and many others. Every year the diversity of teachers and students participating in the various programs further enhances the environment.

Purpose

The purpose of Rudi's Big Indian Center is two-fold. First, it constitutes an embodiment of Rudi's presence and his teachings. Second, it is a not-for-profit spiritual growth center devoted to the presentation of quality programs to help participants transform their lives through the cultivation of their physical-emotional, subtle, and spiritual bodies. This dual purpose is accomplished through year-round meditation classes given in the Rudi tradition and through one day or residential weekend and longer workshops guided by various noted teachers scheduled from May through October. These workshops are rooted in a number of traditions and practices. Among them are Tibetan Buddhism, Hinduism, Taoism, Native American Indian, Rudi Work, and varying forms of transformational psychology, body work, and creative expression.

Three Body Institute

The presentation and often times integration of these various traditions and practices at RBIC has led to the conception of the Three Body Institute. Its purpose is to provide individuals with a cross-traditional approach to transformational growth on all three levels of development — the physical-emotional, subtle, and spiritual. The form of the institute is currently under development.

Basic Transmission Class

Meditation classes as developed by Rudi are given throughout the year. The basis of this form is an eyes-opened meditation class during which higher creative energy is channeled through the teacher and absorbed by the student. This is accomplished through an inner system of Chakras and channels which he called the psychic digestive system. The schedule of classes varies with the season. Newcomers are welcomed and advised to schedule an introductory session before entering their first class.

Astral Flight and Transcending Time and Space

Rudi's advanced work begins with Astral Flight, a method that allows the spiritual practitioner to leave the physical plane and move vertically into higher realms of existence. In doing so an individual can grow many times faster than by performing only the basic work.

Transcending Time and Space, the final flowering of Rudi's spiritual development gives the practitioner a means for working on the spiritual horizontal. To do either, the practitioner must have established the psychic digestive system, the micro-cosmic orbit, or a similar practice.

These advanced methods will be taught this summer by Dr. John Mann, Director of RBIC, during the 4th of July weekend and immediately preceding the Labor Day weekend.

A Rudi Celebration
Fourth of July Weekend
July 1 to July 4

Rudi described himself as a spiritual engineer. A practical man, he developed methods for releasing surface tension, purifying negative

Appendix A

emotions, opening energy centers to receive inner nourishment, and practices for reaching into the higher realms.

This weekend will be a time of gathering and sharing this treasury of exercises. An introductory class in the basic work will be given for newcomers and practitioners of this work who wish to review it. Other classes will be given on various exercises for purification and opening the chakras. as well as some more unique, specialized practices. For advanced practitioners there will be classes in Astral Flight and Transcending Time and Space.

All teachers and students of the Rudi Work are invited to share their knowledge and experience during this weekend of celebration and exchange.

Individual Retreats

Individuals who wish to be in residence and participate in the Rudi Work classes for a week or more should contact RBIC for further information.

Calendar

May 20–June 3	Universe of the Heart, Mary Thunder
June 4-5	Nada Yoga, Roop Verma
June 10-12	Group Retreat, Murray Edelman (not public)
June 12-19	Soulspeak, Anna Ivara
June 20-23	Liberated Rainbow Energy, Ngakpa Chog-yam
June 25-July 2	Heart of Compassion, Lar Short
July 2-4	Rudi Celebration, A Shared Experience
July 5-9	Instructors Training, Lar Short
July 5-7	Being Whole, Barbara Benson
July 10–Sept. 1	Healing Tao Retreats, Mantak Chia
Sept. 3-5	Tantric Equation, John Mann
Sept. 10-11	Sacred Sexuality, Gunther Weil and Rylin Malone
Sept. 17-30	Workshop/Vision Quest, Mary Thunder
Oct. 8-10	Integration, Chris Brady
Oct. 11-23	Mandala of the Five Dakinis, Tsultrim Allione

The Vision Quest–A Native American Way
Mary Thunder
May 20–May 30

The Ojibway people say that it is Spring when the thunder comes. So it is with Big Indian. Each year Mary Thunder shares her time with us in the spring. From May 20 to 30 she will be in residence, teaching and sharing.

In her workshop, Saturday, May 21, she will talk about our connection to the Heart of the Universe through our own hearts. In her special, tender and loving way, Thunder guides each one to the places in their past where the life energy is blocked and emotions are locked in. She enables each person to release and bring healing to the emotions and reminds them of their freedom to make new choices.

In the philosophy of self-love and self-acceptance which she teaches, each person experiences peace and joy and comes to a fuller understanding of the beauty dwelling within. With this understanding begins the balancing of the physical, mental, emotional, and spiritual bodies, helping us acknowledge and connect with our planetary purpose in this life.

The time has come for humankind to make the shift from "learning and finding the path" to "living and walking the path". The opportunity for completing old Karmic patterns has been with us for a time, and the seeds of the "New Consciousness" have been planted. The roles of student-teacher-master blend to create a perfect dance of rhythmic balance, as each individual takes responsibility for his/her own expression of divinity. A "New Sun" has been born, and the memory of the power of the feminine side of consciousness has returned to the planet. It is time to energize and renew. During the full-day experience, Thunder will share her thoughts and feelings concerning this shift. Her goal is to enhance what each participant already knows. Please come prepared to share and be touched by each human experience that occurs, in the kind of safe and magical space which only Thunder can create.

While in residence, Thunder will be preparing people for Vision Quest, the Native American experience of facing yourself in direct and immediate connection with the Universe — alone, on a blanket, under the sky, sacred is one who has cried for a vision.

Every night while she is in residence, Thunder or one of her students will teach lessons of original instructions for the Pipe, sweat lodge, medicine wheel, etc. A love donation for these teachings is customary and expected. You must have Thunder's permission to Quest.

Mary Thunder is part Cheyenne, adopted Lakota, and Irish. She spent part of her working life as an administrator and counselor for various service organizations, including being assistant to the Mayor of Indianapolis. In 1981, Thunder suffered a heart attack and had an after-life experience. In response to this trauma and at the bidding of her Elders, Wallace Black Elk, Grace Spotted Eagle, Leonard Crow Dog and Rolling Thunder, she left her job at the Dallas Intertribal Center to begin a life on the road as a teacher. She follows the Sacred Pipe across the country, responding to the needs of the people. She has been blessed by the Dalai Lama and many Eastern masters for her work. She is a Sun Dancer who has spent some 25 years learning the ways of her Elders.

Nada Yoga Intensive–Silent Retreat
Roop Verma
June 4–5

A retreat is designated as a time to set apart or step away from one's daily routine; it is a time to enter a period of reflection, quiet, and inner direction.

Nada Yoga is the ancient yogic science of sound vibrations. In this system, musical frequency patterns are used to purify and transform the gross and subtle bodies. Continuous communion with the specific sounds produces a deep state of relaxation, stimulates the chakras and releases energy through every nerve fiber in the body. Through meditative communion with the outer and inner sounds, one comes to understand the language of the universe, beyond dynamic and resonating golden silence where the listener and the listened — to become one.

Roop Verma will present the carefully guided program on Saturday and Sunday to help the participants to become more aware of their own multi-dimensional selves and, thereby, attain deeper insight into the science of life. Participants will experience the healing property of music and its relationship to the awareness of inner sounds. The intensive is not a repetition of previous intensives but rather the next phase of working with sacred sounds as a means of spiritual unfoldment. Each time one goes through the process, one goes into deeper and more progressive states of awareness.

The Retreat is not in the nature of an Encounter Group. Instead, individuals will observe silence and will be carefully guided into "letting go", relaxation, meditations, sensitivity awareness, healing, and sharing of spiritual insights and experiences.

Roop Verma is an internationally respected musician, an accomplished composer and teacher of Indian Classical and Mystical Music. His training has been under the famous masters of our time — Sri J. P. Kaushik, Ustad Alt Akbar Khan, and Pandit Ravi Shankar. Roop Verma is a master of Nada Yoga. He studied under Swami Shyam of the Himalayas for many years.

Soulspeak
Anna Ivara
June 12 -19

This week of exploration and discovery for both men and women is taken from the perspective that personalities are the masks and costumes of the soul. It will be a journey to discover what one's individual soul longs to express.

The intention of the workshop will be to facilitate the emergence of new life experience and healing through a process which includes meditation, music, film, movement, dreams, voice dialogue, body energy fields, and personal and group rituals.

Anna Ivara is a psycho-spiritual therapist. She comes to teaching transformational process from a rich background of theater and dance. As an actress, director and therapist her life experience has included raising children and travelling the world extensively studying cultural energetics and behavior. She has trained and worked with Dr. Brugh Joy as well as other transformational metaphysicians, which has moved her to inspire and lead people into deeper, fuller experiences of life.

Rainbow of Liberated Energy
Emotions and the Path of Inner Tantra
Venerable Ngakpa Chogyam

June 20–23

During the workshop we will delve into the nature of our emotions and familiarize ourselves with what we actually are. We will touch the feelings we all have in common: insecurity and rigidity; fear and aggression; isolation and compulsion; vulnerability and suspicion; bewilderment and depression. We will discover a more open way of relating with the spectrum of emotion. We will set foot on the path of discovering our emotions as a rainbow of liberated energy utilizing the method of Zap-lam, a powerful and dynamic means of liberating the vast store of energy that is the basic 'stuff' or 'ground' of our emotional being.

Ven. Ngakpa Chogyam presents a radical and direct meditation technique for working with our emotions. With humor and vividness he will introduce the variety of personality types that emerge from the colour and element symbolism of Tibetan Tantra. The accent will be on the acute personal relevance of this unique system and its integration with everyday life.

The **Venerable Ngakpa Chogyam Ogyen Togden** *is an unusual and highly individual teacher. An English-born lama of Tibet's Ancient Tradition, his Spiritual Father is H. E. Khordong Terchen Tulku Chhimed Rigdzin Rinpoche — a Dzogchen Yogi and Grand Terma Master (Discoverer of mystic treasure teachings.). But he also studied under Tantric Masters of all Tibetan Schools. He is the author of The Tibetan Mystic Path Series for Element Books, which sets out to make available teachings that have hitherto been obscured by cultural and academic barriers. The first two books published in this series are: Rainbow of Liberated Energy and Journey into Vastness. He is the Spiritual Director of "San-ngak-cho-dzong" in Cardiff Wales and increasingly works with psychologists and those in the caring professions.*

Heart of Compassion Retreat
Lar Short
June 25–July 2

The Heart of Compassion Retreat is for those people who have already worked with Lar either through the Correspondence Course lessons or have previously taken Metas. Included in the retreat will be tantric techniques, NLP, and Five Family Power Exercises to transform the heart and to prepare it for the Mantra of Compassion OM MANI PADME HUM HRI among many other practices.

Instructors Training
Lar Short
July 5–9

To do this training it is recommended that individuals: have done the Way of Radiance Work consistently for a period of at least two years; have established a regular, daily meditation practice; have taken all the Correspondence Course lessons; have enrolled in a Meta study group or have done a Meta retreat; have participated in at least a Level I TPF training, and who view Lar as their teacher.

Lar Short, founder and director of Grace Essence Fellowship, has received teachings from martial arts instructors, American, Japanese, Tibetan, and Chinese spiritual teachers, and bodywork and psychology teachers. His root guru, Rudi, taught him how to absorb the essence of whatever teaching he was given. This proved itself to be an important gift as Lar went on to study with his Holiness Dyengo Kyentze Rinpoche and other teachers of this and other traditions. Lar's own gift is an ability to synthesize a multitude of teachings and to present them in a form readily accepted by Americans.

Being Whole: An Empowerment Workshop for Women
Barbara Benson
July 5-7

Opposites must be brought together, not kept apart. For their separation is only in your mind, and they are reconciled by union, as you are. —A Course in Miracles

This three-day empowerment workshop for women is about choosing wholeness over separation and eliminating fear in all of our relationships. We will explore opposites and conflicts in our lives and learn to bring them into unity and balance. Day one of the workshop focuses on the emotional body and healing the heart. We will deal with specific fears and face them with intuition and courage. We will also focus on balancing our inner female and healing the inner child. Day two looks at the mental body and reprogramming our mind by releasing judgment and reclaiming personal power. We will be balancing our inner male and working through such limiting beliefs as the Rescuer/Victim scenario. Day Three deals with integrating our male/female energies into wholeness as spiritual beings and receiving guidance from the God within. We will look at the doubts that block our spiritual certainty and learn to trust and accept our Higher Self.

The schedule of each day will involve morning meditation, morning workshop and then several hours of unstructured afternoon time so that participants can empower each other through networking and trading skills and services if desired. After dinner we will have some type of evening program.

For women of the Rudi Work tradition this three-day workshop is a unique opportunity to feel the sense of empowerment that comes from being together in such a dynamic setting as Rudi's Big Indian Center. Spiritual events and classes will be structured to help the participants feel the powerful role of women in our spiritual practice.

Please bring to the workshop a current photograph of yourself along with one of you as a small child, no older than five. Photos will be returned to you.

Barbara Benson, a teacher of the Rudi Work for over fifteen years, is also a Rebirther, Certified Life Pattern Counselor, Counseling Psychologist, and seminar leader. With the birth of her now two-year old son, she altered her life as partner in a law firm in Bloomington, Indiana to one of devoting her time and energies to her family, seminars, retreats, rebirthing, counseling, and yoga.

International Healing Tao Retreats
Master Mantak Chia
July 10–September 1

The Healing Tao is a practical system of self-development which enables one to complete harmonious evolution on the physical, emotional, and spiritual planes. Increased physical energy, release of tension, and improvements in health and self-defense ability result from the teaching of simple meditations, internal exercises, and Tai Chi Chuan methods of increasing sexual energy and of healing oneself and others. At higher levels, natural energies from the sun, moon, and earth are transformed into powerful spiritual energy by a process of internal alchemy kept secret until now. The ultimate goal is the development of a crystal or solid spiritual body with total freedom in time and space, beyond death.

Healing Tao Retreat Schedule

Teacher Training: July 10- 15
General Summer Retreat: July 16-23
Fusion: July 24-30
Tai Chi and Iron Shirt: July 31–Aug. 6
Chi Organ Transformation: Aug. 7- 13
Kan and Li Retreats:
Lesser Enlightenment: Aug. 14–20
Greater Enlightenment: Aug. 21-27
Greatest Enlightenment: Aug. 27-Sept. 1

Mantak Chia was born in Thailand of Chinese parentage in 1944. At the age of six he was taught meditation by Buddhist monks. His formal education took him to Hong Kong where he was introduced to Tai Chi Chuan, Aikido, and Kundalini Yoga. In the nearby mountains, he met Taoist Master White Cloud Hermit, originally from the mountains of Central China, who was nearly 90 years old at the time Over the next five years White Cloud transmitted to Mantak Chia the most sacred Taoist teachings: the seven secret formulas of internal alchemy that lead to the Reunion of Immortal Man with Heaven. Integrating these teachings, the results of two years study of scientific anatomy, Master Chia succeeded in creating a workable subtle energy system for Westerners that is a marriage of the best of East and West. Chia has a wife, Maneewan, and son, Max.

Maneewan Chia was born in China, spent her early years in Hong Kong, subsequently moving to Thailand where she grew up and attended the University, earning a B.S. Degree in Medical Technology. As a child, Maneewan became interested in nutrition by assisting her mother in Chinese health food cooking. Since her marriage to Mantak Chia, she has studied the Healing Tao System and presently assists him in teaching and running the Healing Tao Center.

Advanced Forms of the Tantric Equation
A Labor Day Weekend Intensive
Dr. John Mann PhD
September 3–5

During the 1987 Labor Day Program, the three levels of spiritual work developed by Swami Rudrananda (Rudi), were presented together for the first time. These included the basic energy transmission experience between teacher and student on the physical horizontal; Astral Flight on the spiritual vertical; and Transcending Time and Space on the spiritual horizontal.

Most spiritual practices are usually performed alone. This experience can be described by the simple equation $A \times C = D$: A is the individual; C is the form of spiritual practice; and D is the result. During the previous Labor Day program C represented the physical horizontal, spiritual vertical, and spiritual horizontal teachings.

If one or more additional persons are introduced into the situation, we are dealing with what can be called a Tantric Equation: $(A + B) C = D$. In this case the relation between A and B in the context of the method C produces the result D.

The present intensive will explore what occurs within such a Tantric Equation when C represents the practice of either Astral Flight or Transcending Time and Space. Utilizing such an approach constitutes an extension of Rudi's advanced work by presenting it within a tantric context. Expanding the basic situation in this manner enhances the power and effectiveness of these practices.

Participants should be familiar with the three levels of the Rudi Work. Relevant teachings of this work will be available during the July 4th weekend program and immediately preceding the Labor Day weekend.

Dr. John Mann has been studying advanced forms of the Tantric Equation for the last 16 years. This is the first time that these teachings have

Appendix A

been presented in an open program. He is the Director of RBIC, Professor of Sociology at the State University College of New York at Geneseo, and author and editor of 14 books, including the recently published Rudi: 14 Years With My Teacher.

Sacred Sexuality
Gunther Weil and Rylin Malone
September 10-11

Can we continue to evolve as sexual and spiritual beings, finding ever greater pleasure, joy and intimacy in our sexuality? The ancient, oriental tradition holds that sexual energy is a powerful key to physical, emotional, and spiritual transformation. Unfortunately, most efforts to explain these principles to Westerners are too vague or too technical and do not take into account contemporary psychological and cultural pressures that affect us, such as the changing relationship between the sexes.

In this weekend we will learn methods for realizing this knowledge through a unique synthesis of ancient oriental sexual wisdom and contemporary Western psychological and communication tools such as neurolinguistic programing (NLP) and relationship psychology.

This workshop has been created to open the way towards a new sexuality for individuals and couples who wish to integrate their sexuality and spirituality.

In a direct and simple way, Gunther and Rylin present a new model of sexual intimacy including practical techniques for revitalizing sexuality, improving communication, and creating a conscious, loving relationship.

Gunther Weil, who holds a PhD from Harvard, is a practicing psychologist with over 20 years experience in various Eastern and Western mind/body disciplines. He is editor of The Psychedelic Reader and co-author with Mantak Chia of the forthcoming book Transforming Negative Emotion: The Fusion of the Five Elements Meditation.

Rylin Malone has an active practice in psychotherapy and hypnotherapy. She specializes in women's issues, sex therapy, and couples work. Her broad experience includes yoga, aikido, and many years of performing and teaching dance. Gunther and Rylin are senior instructors of the Healing Tao system, which they teach internationally. They also study and teach Chi Kung and Tai Chi and are certified Master Practitioners and Trainers of NLP.

Integration: A Columbus Day Weekend Workshop

Chris Brady
October 8-10

Columbus Day weekend is a time to integrate the multitude of energies that have come together at RBIC during the summer season. Through a series of classes and meditations guided by Chris Brady, participants have the opportunity to inwardly accomplish this synthesis.

Chris Brady is a teacher of inner work in the Rudi tradition. His specialty is in the use of Tantric instruments, or spiritual tools, which help manifest and direct higher creative energies for inner growth. He is a practicing attorney in New York City and lives in New Brunswick with his wife, Mary.

Mandela of the Five Dakinis
Working with Emotions: A Women's Retreat
Tsultrin Ailione
October 11–23

The dakinis are playful, wild, undomesticated feminine forces. They represent the ever changing flow of energy with which the spiritual practitioner must work in order to realize wisdom. In Tantra, one of the primary ways of meeting the dakini is in the form of the five dakinis — the five colors, the five directions, and the transformation of the five gross passions or neurosis into wisdom. The process of transforming these five forms of energy into creative and expressive wisdom, completing the inner mandala, is the essence of the Tibetan Tantric path. — Tsultrin Ailione

The Dakini Retreat for women will begin by working with the emotions using Gestalt and other Western therapies, as well as meditative awareness and creative expression. After having experienced the texture, temperature and message of the emotions, each individual will work with the transitions into wisdom play of each of the five dakinis in each element and each direction, with creation of her mask and sacred psychic dance. This will bring about the experiential relationship with the wise and wild dakini which lies within us and bring this released wisdom energy into our lives.

Tsultrirn Ailione is the author of Women of Wisdom, the first major book on women teachers and the feminine in Tibetan Buddhism. She has been practicing Tibetan Buddhism for 20 years and in 1969 was one of the first Westerners to be ordained as a Buddhist nun. Since that time she has been married, is a mother, and now lives in New York when she is not traveling nationally or internationally teaching and conducting workshops on the feminine in a spiritual tradition.

Facilities

Appendix A

The main building is a renovated former resort hotel which includes a large dining room, commons area, bedrooms, shared bathrooms, and a popular, open-air front porch. A huge lawn area gives space for exercise and sitting and 300 acres of mostly wooded land provides an area for hiking and reflection.

What to Bring

Soap and other toilet articles, alarm clock, flashlight, insect repellent, casual summer clothing, with additional layers for cool evenings and variable temperatures, rain gear, and bathing suit (no nude swimming). We do not have laundry facilities.

What not to Bring

Personal hot plates, coffee pots, travel irons, or any appliances with heating elements will overburden the electrical system. Lighting candies and burning incense are not permitted in the main building. Pets, drugs, and alcohol are not allowed on the property and smoking is only permitted away from the buildings.

Children

Parents who plan to bring children should make prior arrangements.

Locating Rudi's Big Indian Center

RBSC is situated on the outer edges of the tiny town of Big Indian, about 140 miles north of NYC, a two and a half to three hour drive. It is a few miles from the Belleayre Ski Resort and approximately thirty miles Northwest of Woodstock.

Automobile: From the north and South of Big Indian: Take the New York State Thruway (I-87) to Kingston, NY. There you will take Exit 19 onto Route 28W heading towards Pine Hill and travel about 33 miles. You will see a small green marker on the right saying Big Indian. Continue on for about 1 mile. On your left you will see Rudi's Big Indian Restaurant. Turn left on the far side of the building and continue over a bridge and down the road which will wind for about a mile. You will come to a crossroads at which you will turn right onto Lost Clove Road. Continue for another 1/2 mile and turn right at the Rudi's Big Indian Center sign.

From the West of Big Indian: Take Exit 90 off Route 17 (55 miles East of Binghamton, NY). Go north on Route 30. This joins Route 28 after about 30 miles. Continue on Route 28 after you reach Margaretville for about 13 miles. Look for Rudi's Big Indian Restaurant on the right. Turn right, immediately before the building and continue over a bridge and down the road which will wind for about a mile. You will come to a crossroad at which you will turn right onto Lost Clove Road. Continue for another 1/2 mile and turn right at the Rudi's Big Indian Center sign.

Plane: Long distance travelers can fly into one of the New York City area airports (JFK, Newark, LaGuardia). Buses leave these airports every twenty minutes to an hour for the New York City Port Authority Bus Terminal, where connections can be made directly to Big Indian.

Bus: Adirondack Trailways has a bus to Big Indian from the Port Authority Bus Terminal. Telephone for times and reservations. When you arrive at the Big Indian stop, phone us from the phone booth at the gas station or from the corner store and someone will come to pick you up.

Appendix A

APPENDIX B

THE CENTER AT BIG INDIAN CONCEPTUALIZATION

This document was excerpted from an August, 1992 proposal as an elaborate conceptualization of Big Indian becoming a high profile self-supporting center for culture and the performing arts:

Executive Summary

The Center at Big Indian will be dedicated to culture and the arts with two theaters, a school of the performing arts, a gallery, an educational facility and residences and studios for artists of all disciplines in an environment of peace and natural beauty on the top of an outlying ridge of Belleayre Mountain approximately 30 miles west of Kingston NY in the heart of the Catskill Mountains.

The Center will be a not-for profit Corporation. It will own the land and operate the theaters, the educational and arts activities. It will be supported by a ground lease and other revenues from a hotel and conference center occupying part of the same ridge and by its own activities in the arts.

The hotel and conference center will be built and operated on the Center's land by an appropriate and carefully selected operating company and will pay its proper share of taxes for the portion of the land it occupies.

Performing arts facilities will consist of an 1800-seat opera/concert theater and a 500-seat "black-box" theater. These and the hotel and conference facility will be designed and constructed to harmonize with, and to have the least possible negative impact upon, the natural wild beauty of the site.

Activities will focus on a resident symphony orchestra, a dance company and a multi-discipline theater/opera company. Concerts, live productions and conferences will be coordinated as far as possible and

Appendix B

actively publicized and promoted by the marketing departments of the Center and of the hotel who will work closely together to attract not only regional but also national and international audiences all twelve months of the year.

The conservatory of theater will be developed from within the professional theater company, beginning as an apprentice program affiliated with an accredited school of Theater in New York City. It will get its own classroom and practice building in a second phase of construction at which time it will become the main campus of that school.

During that second phase there will be also a gallery for resident and affiliated artists, and an educational theater and museum for children dedicated to the history and natural environment of the Catskills and the Hudson River valley.

The Center's ongoing financial stability depends on attracting a steady level of audience, which in turn demands a critical mass of activities: conferences will tend to fill the theaters during the week, and the presence of the performing arts and educational center will tend to enhance the marketing of conferences. The excellence of these arts and of the hotel and conference center, focused on a select market, will tend to build a high level clientele which will grow steadily over the long term. Recordings, publications and touring companies will not only supply additional revenues but will also increase the effectiveness of the marketing effort and broaden its base.

The graduate school of theater, the orchestra and the ballet company will send out professional touring companies and will sponsor regional educational events. All the performing organizations will also, in the course of time, make audio and video broadcasts and recordings for the Center. The gallery and the educational center will produce materials for publication. These will all help build and international reputation for the Center and add to its revenues.

The Center is intended to become a national treasury of the traditions and practice of performance and related arts and a meeting place for business conferees, scholars, educators and others concerned with the preservation and advancement of culture and civilization.

General Description

Visitors will arrive at the Center via automobile on Route 28, or via a modern light-rail shuttle which has been proposed to be established along the existing right of way of the not-for-profit Catskill Mountain

Before The Sun

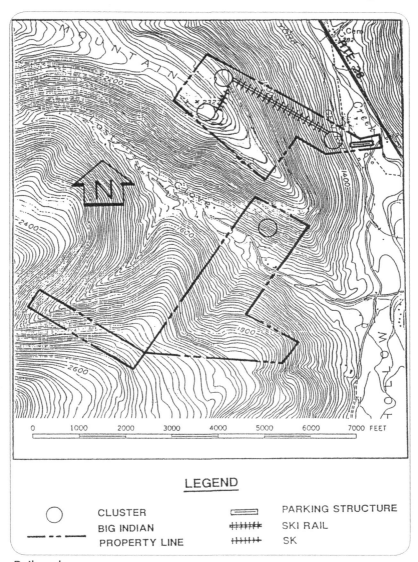

LEGEND

○	CLUSTER	⊂⊃	PARKING STRUCTURE
	BIG INDIAN	╫╫╫	SKI RAIL
— — —	PROPERTY LINE	╫╫╫	SK

Railroad.

    Automobiles will go into a parking facility at the base of the ridge. Their passengers, and those who arrive via the CMRR, will transfer to a silent, enclosed funicular system which will take them up through the forest to the crest of the ridge. No automobiles, except emergency and supply vehicles, will be permitted on the ridge itself.

Appendix B

On the crest there will be an 1800-seat opera house/concert hall, a smaller 500-seat theater, and a conservatory of theater arts, all built around an enclosed atrium. The Atrium, providing lobby and restaurant for both theaters, will be designed for spaciousness, quietness and comfort, with a panoramic view of the surrounding mountains. The names of those who have contributed to the creation of the Center will be carved into its stone walls.

All these buildings will be designed for perfect, natural acoustics and have unobtrusive provision for video recording and/or broadcast. The control room, which will serve both theaters, will also eventually house a state-of-the art high-definition video editing facility.

Conference participants and hotel guests will be taken across the ridge by an enclosed, silent and swift people-mover system to a low-profile hotel with a state-of-the-art conference center, health and recreation facilities.

The performing arts facilities will be the base for several resident organizations including The Brooklyn Philharmonic Orchestra, a ballet company and a new professional theater company. They will perform in all seasons. Other orchestras and companies will also appear for shorter stays. The graduate level Conservatory, closely associated with the theater company, will be accredited as a professional school and will be the basis for touring companies.

In the Valley South of the ridge, along Lost Clove Road, there will be two study centers, a residence area and a Commons. One study center will be fully equipped for smaller conferences of a scholarly or philosophical nature, including teleconferences. The other will complement an existing studies building and be owned by, and dedicated to continue the work of, Rudi's Big Indian Center, a separate not-for-profit philosophical organization, established on this site in the 1980s. The residence area will provide housing for students of the Conservatory of Theater, visiting performers and visiting scholars. The Commons will provide meeting rooms, gallery space, dining, medical, postal and other common faculties for students and artists in a later phase of building, artists of every discipline who are willing to enter into management contracts with Big Indian will be invited for long or short-term residencies in studios planned for them in a more secluded area on the slopes above the study centers on Lost Clove Road.

Several companies, separate from the Center but related to it through joint ventures or long-term contracts, will handle commercial activities. A gallery of art will mount appropriate traveling exhibits and shows by Big Indian's affiliated visual artists and will represent them. A video recording company will produce and market programs for broadcast and other purposes. A publishing company will produce and market materials (including video and audio recordings) particularly related to the performing arts, resident artists, and "the studies which may come from the educational facility. Another company will produce and market a magazine devoted to these fields. Royalties from all these activities will help support the Center.

The Center may also set up a joint venture to provide business services such as publicity, printing, cataloging and mailing list maintenance for its own marketing department, and those and other services for its joint-venture partners. A central administrative group will perform management and booking functions for the performance units of the Center and for affiliated artists.

Big Indian intends to enter into business agreements which will provide it with shares of any revenues that derive from the activities, products or services of any organizations and businesses that are permitted to make appropriate use of the Center's name, whether commercially or in the arts.

To recapitulate, the Center will include in its first phase of building:
At the entrance off Route 28:
- An environmentally protective parking facility
- A station for the light-rail system (Soulé) of the CMRR.
- A medium-priced hotel.
- Access to a service road for emergency and supply vehicles.
- An all-weather funicular system leading to the top of the ridge

On the ridge:
- An 1800-seat opera house/concert theater
- A 500-seat "black box" theater
- An "upscale" hotel with health and recreation facilities
- A state-of-the art conference center
- An administrative center
- An all-weather people-mover system.

Along Lost Clove Road:
- Housing for students, performers and visiting scholars.
- A study center for visiting scholars

In the second phase:
On the ridge:

Appendix B

- A classroom and practice building for the Conservatory of Theater
- An educational facility for children, dedicated to the Hudson River Valley
- A day-care center

Along Lost Clove Rood:
- A study center for Rudi's Big Indian Center
- Artists live-in studios

At a site to be chosen (either on or off campus):
A business service center, if required.

Environmental Protection

The site lies within the watershed of the New York City Water Supply. A plan has been worked out and discussed informally with engineers who work with the City on such matters, to upgrade an existing treatment plant a short distance up Route 28 from the site. This would eliminate any problem with effluent and has the advantage of being the responsibility of the City's engineers in design and operation.

We shall also explore the feasibility and desirability of establishing a co-generation facility in connection with the treatment process.

The Big Indian site already has a copious spring-fed water supply, which will be increased by new wells. We expect to specify a gray-water system for the re-use of water, as a means to reduce both the demand for new water (though the supply is ample) and the need for treatment.

The Center will have its own fire-fighting capability based upon fully equipped half-track vehicles stationed within each of the building clusters. They will be capable of instant response anywhere on the site, and will be able to inhibit the spread of dangerous situations until additional help can arrive.

If environmental protection requires that parking facilities are to be enclosed, a garage has already been engineered by the Mulach Corporation so that there will be no run-off or seepage of contaminants into the ground.

The architects have recommended that all buildings be designed in accordance with the principles of "Green Architecture" so that they will have minimal negative effect, including aesthetic effect, on the environment. The buildings on the ridge, including the theaters, will have very low profiles, so that the appearance of the ridge will remain as close to its natural state as possible. The funicular system will be essentially invisible from Route 28 because it will be built in an already existing logging road which is surrounded by high trees.

The Continental Insurance Company, having reviewed our preliminary plans and inspecting the site, has affirmed the insurability of the project.

History of the Project

This land was formerly the site of an ashram established by the American-born spiritual teacher Rudi. When Rudi died in a plane crash, his followers continued his work for five years until financial pressures became acute. One of them, John Mann, did not want the site to become the base for a wholly commercial enterprise. He bought the land to preserve its tradition. Eventually it became necessary for Dr. Mann to divest himself of this property and Andrew Merlo, a developer, became interested. With the firm idea of preserving its character, they came to an understanding which Mann describes as follows:

> *The Big Indian Center is devoted to conducting activities that promote positive human functioning. It can be described as a spiritual-cultural-growth center.*
>
> *It is located on a site that has been utilized historically for the cultivation of higher energies and which has the remarkable property of enhancing the effectiveness of any activity that is conducted there. This is due partly to the setting itself. The atmosphere has been intensified by the spiritual work of Rudi, an American spiritual leader, and his followers, who utilized the setting for over ten years. In the last decade (1979-1989) the Center has expanded its focus to include leading teachers of major eastern and western spiritual traditions, each of whom has enriched the atmosphere.*
>
> *In its present formulation the Center includes (or will include) not only spiritual but also cultural and growth centered activities that may be conducted by independent organizations.*
>
> *Any program that is offered at the Center must fulfill two conditions: First it must harmonize with the energy of the setting. Second it must complement other programs currently being offered.*

Appendix B

The Center will be organized in such manner as to ensure its financial stability and will be committed from the start to the maintenance and upgrading of the physical facilities. Further, it will undertake the obligation of caring for the spiritual spaces which are the enduring treasure of the property.

To put these principles into practice, Andrew Merlo proposed setting up a self-supporting center for the arts and culture on the site. His idea has been developed into this plan.

Proposed Start-up Organization
Architecture
Sanders & Tilly Associates
Childs Bertman Tseckares & Casendino Inc.
James Stewart Polshek and Partners
Real Estate Analysis
REsearch Inc.
Site and Highway Engineering
Raymond Keyes Associates, Inc.
Environmental Services
Blasland and Bouck, Enqineers, P.C.
Transportation Systems
Soulé Corporation (People Mover and Light-Rail System)
Skirail (Funicular System)
Garage Engineering
Mulach Parking Structure Corp.
Market Potential
Guideline Research Corporation
Promotion and Public Relations
Carole Sorell Inc.

Proposed Board of Trustees
Maurice Edwards, Artistic Director of the Brooklyn Philharmonic. Co-founder and Director of The Classic Theater (NYC). Mr. Edwards was the driving force behind the development of the Brooklyn Philharmonic Orchestra from a local, community symphony to one of the major orchestras in the United States with Lukas Foss, then Dennis Russell Davies as Conductors. He was also instrumental in establishing the first CETA Orchestra of New York, with Paul Dunkel as Music Director. He was in the original Broadway companies of Fiddler

on the Roof, and The Golden Apple, and the Three Penny Opera off Broadway. Mr Edwards staged the premiere of Eaton's The Cry of Clytemnestra and many other works both for the "Meet the Moderns" Series in Brooklyn, and independently in Manhattan. He developed The Cubiculo, an experimental center for music, drama, dance, mixed media and poetry in 1969 and ran it through 1974. He has also published a number of translations from German, and introduced the playwright Dario Fo to this country when his translations of three of Fo's one-act plays were presented in New York.

Donelson Hoopes, an Art Historian, has been Director of the Thomas Cole Foundation in Catskill NY since 1983. Previous to that, he was Director of the Portland (ME) Museum of Art, Curator of the Corcoran Gallery of Art, Washington DC, Curator of Paintings and Sculpture at the Brooklyn Museum (NY), Curator of American Art at the Los Angeles Museum, and a member of the Advisory Committee, Archives of America in Art. From 1977 through 1982 he was a member of the Committee for the Preservation of The White House. He is the author of many books and articles on art.

John Mann is a Professor of Sociology Emeritus of the State University College of New York at Genesee. He has been the Director and Member of the Board of Rudi's Big Indian Center since its inception in 1984. He is the current owner of the land on which the Big Indian Art and Culture Center will be built. Dr. Mann is the author, co-author and editor of over 14 books for professional and general audiences on scientific, educational and spiritual subject matter. He is currently writing a book about his experience with the development of the Big Indian Art and Culture Center. Dr. Mann has also been a teacher of advanced aspects of Kundalini Yoga for twenty years.

Frank Ledlie Moore attended Rutgers University, studied music with Ernst Levy at the New England Conservatory of Music, with Paul Boepple at the Dalcroze School of Music and held a fellowship in drama with Francis Fergusson at Bennington College. During the Korean conflict he was an administrative engineer in rocketry for the U S Navy, then originator and supervisory designer of the summary building of the United States Science Exhibit at the Seattle Worlds' Fair of 1962. He was co-designer, scenarist and composer of the Triumph of Man at the New York Worlds' Fair of 1964. He has composed and conducted music for concert, dance, legitimate theater, for two worlds fairs and for about forty documentary motion pictures, and is the author of both music and words for seven theatrical works. Mr. Moore was executive producer and/or director of approximately 360 educational and documentary films for the Walden Film Corporation and for NET (now PBS). He was vice president and general manager in North America for Novello & Company, and vice president for international business for G. Schirmer, Inc.; both large international music publishers. He has published four books, two on opera and two on video production.

Carole Sorell, a leading New York public relations consultant on arts-related events in both the public and private sectors. In May, 1992, she was appointed Assistant Commissioner for Cultural Affairs, City of New York. She has been a member of the Big Indian advisory team since its inception.

Joel Thome, Founder and conductor of Orchestra of Our Time (in New York) and the Philadelphia Composers Forum. Mr. Thome has conducted major symphony orchestras around the world. Mr. Thome is also a composer of many symphonic and ballet works including a continuing series of works, the Savitri Series, based on the classic Hindu legend Savitri from the Mahabharata. He was US Coordinator for the 1990/91 major festival of Mexican music entitled Mexico, a Work of Art, and is active in establishing a new series of concerts in Latin America.

Paul G.Y. Tscharskyj is a consultant in real estate with special expertise in transportation systems, infrastructure and the like. He has been involved in many large projects in the United States and is developing others in Europe.

Norbert F. Wall is a recognized expert in real estate evaluation. His book, "Real Estate Investment by Objective", is published by McGraw Hill. He holds the MAI and SREA designations and is a founding member of NACORE (National Association of Corporate Real Estate Executives). He has appraised such properties as the John Hancock Center in Chicago, the Watergate Complex in Washington, the entire city of Pinehurst, N.C., and the Waldorf Astoria in New York. Some of Mr. Wall's more prominent market analysis assignments include Hilton Head in South Carolina, the World Trade Center in New York, the Lake Airport in Chicago and the Essex House in New York. He has also developed, acted as an adviser to or been a general partner in numerous other large scale developments in the U.S., Europe, the Middle East and Africa.

APPENDIX C
DIVINATION

I had requested help and clarity concerning the future of Big Indian and my spiritual work with Divine Androgyny by requesting a divination from Dr. Mumford in Australia. These were our correspondences:

Dear Dr. Mumford,

I have two areas of interest and concern.

The first is the future of the Center at Big Indian which was originally Rudi's country ashram. It has been active as a spiritual retreat center for a variety of teachings since I acquired the property in 1979. In the last few years it has been hibernating. I have recently subdivided the property with the sacred portion containing Rudi's Shrine, Stupa and Meditation Hall in one parcel, and the Main House with 32 bedrooms in the other. I am putting the latter up for sale.

My major question is how to proceed with that sale process so that it has an appropriate and successful outcome.

My hope for the sacred parcel is that it becomes a permanent pilgrimage site.

The second question concerns the future development of the spiritual work which I have called "Divine Androgyny". What it involves is a man and a woman sitting in each other's presence in a state of effortless awareness. This allows a condition of mutual harmony to arise into which a higher power can flow for the benefit of the couple and all those who are present at the time.

I have written a book about this work that was published in 1999.

My basic question is how I can best approach the continued evolution of Divine Androgyny so that it can fulfill its inherent possibility beyond the limits of my own lifetime. It is what I fundamentally feel I am here to accomplish.

Appendix C

Is the preceding enough for you to be able to move ahead? Would a Skype conversation between us be helpful?

In either case I would like to express my gratitude for your willingness to undertake this Divination and await hearing from you about what comes next.

This was Dr. Mumford's reply:
Dr. Mann;

I am concerned only with how I can serve you, and the more I delve into what you are asking the more I wonder if another approach is needed.

I am not ready to yet do a divination for you, and what I have cross-checked so far is practically a no-brainer that one could intuit except I have actually done your individual cycle pattern.

Last year (2011), probably about the middle you really began to concern yourself about how to dispose of the properties and your lineage with "Divine Androgyny" surviving. Last year was a cycle influence under *Mangala* which gives people the urge to finalize and wrap up loose ends – 2012 is the start of a new 9-year cycle, and an excellent time to renew your lineage plans and reappraise everything.

What bothers me is that I do not know what normal measures you have undertaken to solve the problem.

1: As I understand it the land is divided into two parcels and the special one is "Rudi's shrine"? Surely there are disciples of this great man's legacy that would be willing to purchase the Shrine to keep his memory in perpetuity?

2: In regard to your legacy concerning your wonderful work on "Divine Androgyny" do you have disciples who will carry this work on?

I am very impressed, from browsing your site, with this refreshing and dynamic approach and the fact that you have written and published about it bodes well for "some" continuation of this valuable treasure.

I can only speak of perpetuation from my personal viewpoint in regard to my own work. I do have several officially designated students who certainly will carry some of my work on past my own transition and I have published two classic books which may well outlive me for a while – beyond that one can guarantee nothing in regard to perpetuation, and my job is to not be attached to expectations of an outcome.

The world is shifting so rapidly that no one can guarantee anything except if humans survive they will always, some at least, seek out the exploration of inner worlds and strive to find out about those systems that have been left as guides to inner space.

So dealing with your dilemma has many unknowns from my perspective.

Recapitulating your queries:

1: *The first question concerns how to proceed with that sale process so that it has an appropriate and successful outcome:* Surely this involves Real Estate agents with specific instructions to them regarding the division of the 32 room property. From the "Sacred Parcel" do you have Students who could handle this for you?

2: *The second question concerns your hope for the sacred parcel is that it becomes a permanent pilgrimage site:* This seems to me to be a matter of networking to find someone who honors Rudi's work and would be happy to take this over.

3: *The third question concerns the future development of the spiritual work called "Divine Androgyny":* Again this is up to your closest disciples or students: such valuable work will not be lost – indeed this is a special contribution

I am impressed and I do not become impressed easily.

Please accept my apologies as in asking these questions I am not insulting your obvious intelligence but only wishing to clarify how much I can be of assistance to your endeavors.

Finally, I don't wish you to incur expense however, it might help if you rang me and we talked. When it is daytime in the states it is nighttime here, and I am up all night to handle international correspondence.

After further correspondence the following Divination was reported:
22 ETHER – SEEDS OF EARTH: GESTATION

The Egg is well fertilized and has survived a prior testing phase. Soon the chick will break free and lay its own golden eggs, each a miniature Alembic. The current stress is actually a foreshadowing of successful futures.

Despite any present problematic situation, this is the natural cycle for rapid growth in your personal and business life. He who can navigate through one "Gale" can navigate through all storms, and certainly hold the rudder steady in a "squall"!

You need more space; this is the season to get 'elbow room'. The womb has become crowded as full term approaches.

Appendix C

The birth, in the next cycle phase (budding) will involve decisions with your "Family." Prepare the immediate near future NOW!

The degree, to which you help "Family" even if only by listening empathically, is the degree to which you will be assisted in the forthcoming harvest.

For now, and in the near future, favor your "Ears" over your mouth.

OTHER BOOKS BY JOHN MANN

Mann, J. , *Frontiers of Psychology*, New York: Macmillan, 1963.

— , *Sigmund Freud*, New York: Macmillan, 1964.

— , *Louise Pasteur: Father Of Bacteriology*, New York: Scribners, 1964.

— , *Changing Human Behavior*, New York: Scribners, 1965.

— , "Human Possibilities," *In Human Possibilities: The Challenge And The Promise*, H. Otto, ed, Mississippi: Warren Green, 1967.

— , and H. Otto, eds. *Ways Of Growth*, New York: Grossman, 1968.

— , *Encounter: A Weekend With Intimate Strangers*, New York: Grossman, 1970.

— , *Learning To Be*, New York: The Free Press, 1972 (paper, 1974)

— , *Students Of The Light*, New York: Grossman, 1973.

— , and M. Richard, *Exploring Social Space*, New York: The Free Press, 1973.

— , ed. *Behind The Cosmic Curtain: The Further Writings of Swami Rudranando*, Neolog Publishing, 1984.

— , *Rudi: 14 Years With My Teacher*, Rudra Press, 1987.

— , and Lar Short, *The Body of Light*, New York: Globe Press, 1990.

— , *Divine Androgyny*, Portal Press, 1996 @ Xlibris Publishing, 2012.

— , *Exploring Open Secrets*, Xlibris Publishing, 2012.

— , *The Invisible Child*, Xlibris Publishing, 2012.

— , *Viewing Sacred Art*, Xlibris Publishing, 2012.

— , *Experiments On Myself*, Xlibris Publishing, 2014.

— , *In Search of the Goddess & The Frozen Year* , Xlibris Publishing, 2014.

— , *Transformation*, Xlibris Publishing, 2014.

Made in United States
North Haven, CT
24 May 2024